Gamification for Resilience

Gamification for Resilience

Resilient Informed Decision-Making

Adrian V. Gheorghe
Department of Engineering Management and Systems Engineering
Old Dominion University
Norfolk, Virginia

Polinpapilinho F. Katina
Department of Informatics and Engineering Systems
University of South Carolina Upstate
Spartanburg, South Carolina

Library of Congress Cataloging-in-Publication Data

Names: Gheorghe, Adrian V., 1945 - author. | Katina, Polinpapilinho F., 1982 - author.
Title: Gamification for resilience : informed resilience decision-making / Adrian V. Gheorghe, Polinpapilinho F. Katina.
Description: Hoboken, New Jersey : John Wiley & Sons, Inc., [2023] | Includes bibliographical references and index.
Identifiers: LCCN 2023007846 (print) | LCCN 2023007847 (ebook) | ISBN 9781394157747 (hardback) | ISBN 9781394157754 (pdf) | ISBN 9781394157761 (epub) | ISBN 9781394157778 (ebook)
Subjects: LCSH: City planning--Decision making. | Gamification. | Resilience (Ecology) | Systems engineering.
Classification: LCC HT166 .G487 2023 (print) | LCC HT166 (ebook) | DDC 307.1/216--dc23/eng/20230330
LC record available at https://lccn.loc.gov/2023007846
LC ebook record available at https://lccn.loc.gov/2023007847

Cover Image: © issaro prakalung/Shutterstock
Cover design by Wiley

Set in 9.5/12.5pt STIXTwoText by Integra Software Services Pvt. Ltd, Pondicherry, India

To my children, Anastasia, Alexandra, and Paul
–Adrian V. Gheorghe

To my young brothers, Gavin and Ryan, to whom the term "gamification" is dedicated
– Polinpapilinho F. Katina

Contents

Contents

Foreword

In the twenty-first century, the well-being of the public is intrinsically intertwined with certain infrastructures and key asset provisions. The destruction of key assets can cause large-scale property damages, human injury, and/ or death. Furthermore, the destruction of key assets can profoundly damage national prestige and confidence. As the demand for provisions (products, goods, and services) has increased, so have inside and outside influences that disrupt normal operations of the infrastructure system activities and processes rendering such systems inoperable. The inoperability of infrastructure systems is linked to several societal changes that occurred in the late twentieth and twenty-first centuries. For example, technological advancement, rapid institutional changes, increasing complexity, transboundary dependencies, and increasing demand for quality services coupled with increasing natural threats present a grave challenge for policymakers, engineers, and scientists in sustaining societal operations. Even so, the intricate interdependencies among infrastructures have already illustrated a need for a shift in infrastructure management. For example, a single blackout in Germany on November 4, 2006, caused a loss of power for millions in France, Italy, Spain, and Austria. Cascading unintended electric failure resulted in transport systems (i.e. trains, traffic signals) delays and disruptions of other interconnected operations.

It is from this perspective that understanding the relationship among elements, components, and infrastructure systems is an essential step in improving infrastructure designs, protection, and security measures. In one form, many have gravitated toward different strategies. For example, those in system safety will call for a risk management strategy based on the identification, analysis of hazards, and application of remedial controls. The concept of system safety is useful in demonstrating the adequacy of technologies when difficulties are faced with probabilistic risk analysis. On the other hand, it might not be possible to rely only on probabilistic risk analysis. Thus, there is a need to go beyond the "obvious." To illustrate, let's consider the concept of dependability. A dependable infrastructure performs normally, especially when its services are needed. However, given the nature of infrastructure systems, one has to consider the relationship that exists between infrastructure and larger issues in public health, economy, and security. A destruction of a dependable infrastructure can have a severe impact on public health/safety, the economy, or any combination of those matters. Consider the events that shocked the world on September 11, 2001. Four planes were hijacked from a dependable aviation sector leading to over 2,500 deaths, over 6000 injured, loss of power and water, and closure of the New York Stock Exchange – *all of which affected the local as well as the international economy and security.* Therefore, the dependability of the aviation sector is linked to public health, the economy, and security.

The public's increasing dependency on certain systems (e.g. agriculture and food, water systems, public health and safety, emergency services, electricity, etc.) along with rapid institutional changes (i.e. shifting from public to private, deregulation, privatization, market-driven economies, etc.) and increasing technological changes have changed the landscape of traditional infrastructure systems. For example, more than half of the world's population resides in cities. The rapid growth in urbanization has made cities more and more exposed and vulnerable to a broad spectrum of threats and hazards: *natural and anthropogenic.* To respond to such difficulties, we cannot proceed using the traditional and tested approaches. In the present research, the authors suggest gamification.

The term "gamification" first appeared online in the context of computer software and did not gain popularity until 2010. However, even before the term came into use, other fields borrowing elements from video games was common, such as learning disabilities and scientific visualization. Usage of the term increased around 2010 and it began to refer to incorporating social and reward aspects of games into the software. Research reported in the present book provides a chronology of the topic and how present research adds to the current body of knowledge.

The authors have gone to great lengths to use several well-tested concepts including project management and risk as well as emerging ideas, including Vulnerability Assessment (VA), and show how these concepts can be used to enable the Resilient Informed Decision-Making Process (ReIDMP). The authors bring convincing case applications, providing a consistent theoretical framework and adequate applications challenging researchers and public policy-makers interested in using gamification to create credible scenarios for further investigations and decisions.

The paradigm of using games to create more resilient cities is not only timely but necessary. Timely, because it is novel. Necessary because as the global human population surpasses eight billion, much of the population will be clustered around cities that serve as centers of human culture and economic activity. And yet, these cities, unfortunately, come with urban risks and vulnerabilities. Perhaps, the ideas in this book provide insights into how we might create better cities while relying on concepts of critical infrastructure systems, safety, risk, vulnerability, and resilience within gamification to enable informed decision-making.

Milan, Italy
January 2023

Enrico E. Zio, PhD
Professor and Director, Department of Energy,
Politecnico di Milano, Milan, Italy
Professor, École Nationale Supérieure des Mines de Paris,
Paris, France

Preface

Humans are living in a moment when, perhaps due to technological innovation, we praise ourselves with the belief of being well-informed, intelligent, wiser, and capable of making even better judgments. Yet people are still unable to address much of the root causes of dysfunctional society and economy: armed conflicts, epidemics, natural disasters, poverty, prejudice, and violent crime.

First and foremost, this book will not solve these problems, and it should not be taken as such. However, when dysfunctionality strikes, many experience disbelief and hopelessness, leading to emotional flatness – an emotional blunting where a person has difficulty feeling emotions and indifference, even to activities/causes they once found necessary. At the junction of dysfunctionality leading to emotional flatness, we suggest resilience and gamification might prove essential in dealing with the volatility, uncertainty, complexity, and ambiguity in the twenty-first century.

Over half of the population of the world resides in cities. Rapid urbanization has made cities more exposed and vulnerable to a broad spectrum of threats and hazards. To respond to such difficulties, "resilience" has emerged as a significant component of cities' long-term planning and sustainable development. In fact, emerging paradigms (e.g. "resilient city") implicitly challenge the ideological principle of stability and resistance to change in sustainable development and long-term success. Moreover, "gamification" is the strategic attempt to enhance systems, services, organizations, and activities by creating similar experiences to those experienced playing games to motivate and engage users in a non-game context. Therefore "resilience-enabled gamification" can be used against "emotional flatness" by encouraging strategic design for resilient people and organizations.

The term "gamification" first appeared online in the context of computer software in 2008 (Walz and Deterding 2015). Gamification did not gain popularity until 2010 (GoogleTrends 2021). However, even before the term came into wide usage, borrowing elements from video games was common, such as learning disabilities (Adelman et al. 1989) and scientific visualization (Rhyne et al. 2000). The term gained wide usage around 2010, and many began to refer to it when incorporating social/reward aspects of games into software development (Mangalindan 2012). This approach captured the attention of venture capitalists, who suggested "many aspects of life could become a game of sorts [and that these games] ... would be the best investments to make in the game industry" (Sinanian 2010). Another observed that half of all companies seeking funding for consumer software applications mentioned game design in their presentations (O'Brien 2010).

Soon after, several researchers suggested that they considered gamification closely related to earlier work of adapting game-design elements and techniques to non-game contexts. For example, Deterding et al. surveyed human–computer interaction research that uses game-derived elements for motivation and interface design (Deterding et al. 2011). Meanwhile, Nelson (2012) suggests a connection between the Soviet concept of socialist competition and the American management trend of "fun at work." Moreover, Fuchs (2012) points out that gamification might be driven by new forms of ludic interfaces such as Wii Remote, Move, and Kinect. Gamification conferences have also retroactively incorporated simulation with Will Wright, designer of the 1989 video game "SimCity 2013®," serving as a keynote speaker at the gamification conference, G-Summit 2013.

Organizations have also seen the value of gamification and are enhancing this concept with different platforms. For example, in October 2007, Bunchball (http://www.bunchball.com), backed by Adobe Systems Incorporated, was the first company to provide game mechanics as a service (Taylor 2011). Another example of a gamification services provider is Badgeville. Badgeville launched in late 2010 and raised $15 million in venture-capital funding in its first year of operation (Arrington 2011). Attempts to use games for learning hit the traditional landscape in 2012 when the US Department of Energy co-funded multiple research trials (Rai and Beck 2016), including those addressing consumer behavior (Beck et al. 2017), adapting the format of "programmed learning" into mobile microlearning to experiment with the impacts of gamification in energy usage reduction (Feeney 2017). Moreover, Mazur-Stommen and Farley (2016) suggest that gamification can be used to address climate change and sustainability with surprising results. For example, note that their research "broadened the scope of the kinds of activities we were looking at, beyond utilities and into market-based and education games, which took many forms including card-games (Cool Choices), videogames (Ludwig), and games for mobile devices such as smartphones (Ringorang) … gamification, such as that used in the Opower/Facebook application, whereby the incorporation of game mechanics heightens the experience and/or performance of everyday, real-world activities" (Mazur-Stommen and Farley 2016, p. 9).

Finally, there is a Gamification Research Network (GRN), a communication hub for researchers and students interested in studying the use of game design in non-game contexts. It was launched in November 2010 alongside the call for participation in the 2011, 2013, and 2015 CHI workshops on gamification (http://gamification-research.org/about). It is import to recall that a key fundamental aspect of games is education as well as behavior modification – which is related to resilience. In conclusion, gamification as a concept for solving real-life problems is in the beginning stages, and its future looks bright!

However, building a resilient organization, including a city, requires a holistic approach and the appropriate adoption of knowledge and application of tools during the planning and management process. Several studies aspire to enhance the capacity of city resiliency (https://resilientcitiesnetwork.org). However, few explicitly focus on developing a roadmap (i.e. practical sequential steps) to build a resilient city. Therefore, this book attempts to close this knowledge gap by developing a methodological framework, which involves procedural steps in assisting the planning and management processes for developing a resilient city. The platform proposed in this research is grounded on a theoretical approach called "Resilient Informed Decision-Making Process." The efficacy of the developed framework and the research is demonstrated through a case applied to two US cities as well as space systems.

Rasmussen and Batstone (1989) suggested that "management and organization … had not kept pace with the sophistication of technology and its complexity. As a result, the frequency and magnitude of organizational failures and the subsequent economic and environmental impacts are increasing at an alarming rate" (p. ii). With this in mind, the authors hope this book can catalyze those in management to promote resilience through gamification to enable informed decision-making. Armed conflicts, epidemics, natural disasters, poverty, prejudice, and violent crime and impacts are increasing at an alarming rate. And while humanity expresses the desire to stop them outright, it appears we don't have that capability. Perhaps the next best thing is to develop resilient people, organizations, and cities – and in the case of this book, through gamification, we can reduce emotional blunting.

This research should attract policy-makers since they are ultimately responsible for society's resilience. However, researchers (as well as students and laypersons) should "pay close attention" to how gamification can be used to enhance resilience. With this audience in mind, fourteen chapters have been developed. **Chapter 1** sets the stage for the remainder of the book by exploring aspects of general systems theory (i.e. systems science, systems technology, and systems philosophy) as a basis for bridging the gap between systems science and engineering systems to deal more effectively with the increasing volatility, uncertainty, complexity, and ambiguity of the twenty-first century.

Chapter 2 articulates the many facets of infrastructure systems and the need for resilient critical infrastructure systems for public well-being. The role of cities as centers of human culture and economic activity, as well as the catastrophic and unforeseen events they face (e.g. climate change, disease pandemics, economic fluctuations, and terrorist attacks), are discussed in the context of the need for resilient cities. The notion of resilient critical infrastructure is then explained regarding risks and vulnerabilities faced by cities in the twenty-first century.

Chapter 3 sets the stage for research on creating resilient cities and people through gaming. Resilience is defined in the context of the ability to withstand stress in infrastructure systems as well as "positive adaptation" after a stressful or adverse situation. The general qualities of resilience are then established. The chapter delves into gaming as a powerful tool for creating resilient people, emphasizing the positive impact of gaming on the quality of life.

Chapter 4 introduces the concept of gamification (and serious gaming) and its value and utility, which are explored through cognitive, emotional, and social lenses and issues revolving around critical infrastructure systems design. Gaming cycles (i.e. pre-gaming, gaming, and post-gaming) and the role of expert opinions are discussed to establish foundations for understanding infrastructure systems through gaming, data analysis, and game validation.

Chapter 5 presents the concept of mix game to increase energy system resilience. First, the chapter proposes looking at systems in the context of parts – coupled together; the parts can form systems and these systems can respond to stresses. A mix game is then proposed as an awareness-raising appendix mainly addressing layperson energy stakeholders. The model is simplified for the objective of oriented design for optimal primary energy mixes deliberately designed to avoid the arcane of the nonlinear programming technology. The chapter also discusses serious gaming as means for good energy governance amplified by emerging concepts in complex system governance.

Chapter 6 describes the vital components of the simulation computer game "SimCity 2013." In this game, a player assumes the role of the mayor of the city, with the central aspect being construction and zoning, which comprises a wide range of responsibilities (e.g. providing the essential facilities, maximizing the service capacities, and otherwise balancing between demand and supply of resources). A player works with an interface containing several buttons corresponding to different features and options. The chapter includes insights regarding the limitations/opportunities of SimCity 2013.

Chapter 7 discusses a proposed platform (i.e. ReIDMP: Resilient Informed Decision-Making Process) for developing resilient cities. An overview of the platform is provided involving the simulation computer game (SimCity 2013) and the means for analysis and assessment of risk and vulnerability as well as evaluation using the guidelines of the International Atomic Energy Agency (IAEA) and Science Applications International Corporation (SAIC). A four-phase approach (i.e. project planning and management, learning by doing through gaming strategy, multi-criteria decision analysis, and object-oriented programming) is then articulated as a means for analyzing technical process and actions required for the realization of resilient critical infrastructure systems.

Chapter 8 discusses three key risk and vulnerability assessment approaches in engineered systems: Rapid Risk Assessment (RRA) as a method for classifying and prioritizing risks in major accidents in processes and related industries, Vulnerability Assessment (VA) as a means for identifying cost-effective countermeasures to deter vulnerabilities and potential threats, and Integrated Regional Risk Assessment (IRRA), a method focused on assessing the risk due to continuous emissions instead of the risk due to major accidents. Each method is viewed as key to contributing to the ReIDMP platform for developing resilient cities.

Chapter 9 focuses on applying multiple-criteria decision analysis (MCDA) through a decision support system (DSS) to support determinations, judgments, and courses of action in an organization or a business. Following a brief introduction to MCDA and DSS in the context of the ReIDMP platform, three primary areas of interest for creating a resilient city are described, along with the proposed actions. Logical Decision® for Windows (LDW) is then used to model each area of interest (i.e. environment, economy, and society) to explore a ranking of proposed actions (alternatives) regarding their associated strategies and targeted objectives. The analysis is then repeated using Intelligent Decision System (IDS) and its enhanced capability to address probability uncertainty, subjective judgments, belief function, and the evidential reasoning approach for attribute aggregation.

Chapter 10 illustrates how a regional network of complex systems can be a representation using object-oriented programming. First, object-oriented programming (OOP) is described as a programming paradigm that uses "objects" to design applications. Then TopEase® is introduced as software that allows the user to manage critical information of focused systems and holistically visualize those entities. The described approach is then applied to a region in the eastern part of the United States (i.e. Hampton Roads) as a case application. TopEase® is used to structure data regarding critical infrastructure systems, components, people, roles, responsibilities, and interdependencies. The research suggests that the TopEase® OOP approach is viable for performing disaster risk analysis for different infrastructure systems, including cyberattacks, industrial accidents, meltdowns, and earthquakes.

Chapter 11 discusses how transforming cities into "resilient cities" is significant. Yet, it remains achievable. The case of a US city (i.e. Norfolk, VA) along with its strategic goals (i.e. Norfolk Resilient Strategy) is used as an example. Norfolk Resilient Strategy goals: (i) designing a coastal community of the future, (ii) creating economic opportunity by advancing efforts to grow existing and new industry sectors, and (iii) advancing initiatives to connect communities, deconcentrate poverty, and strengthen neighborhoods set the foundations. The chapter then discusses how the mentioned goals aided in the development of the ReIDMP platform along with implications, limitations, and potential future research directions.

Chapter 12 attempts to demonstrate the applicability of the ReIDMP platform in assessing risks and vulnerabilities. The City of Portland, Oregon (USA) is used as a case application. Three manuals are used: (i) *Manual for the Classification of Prioritization of Risks Due to Major Accidents in Process and Related Industries*, (ii) *Guide to Highway Vulnerability Assessment for Critical Asset Identification and Protection*, and (iii) *Guidelines for Integrated Risk Assessment and Management* *in Large Industrial Areas*. Electromagnetic Pulse (EMP) Assessment is also used to evaluate the possible effects of an EMP blast. Analyses and visualization include probabilities, consequences, prioritization, and pollution classification, further validating the adaptability and utility of the ReIDMP platform to transforming cities.

Chapter 13 examines the relationship between smart cities and critical space infrastructure systems. Critical space infrastructure systems encompass several systems (e.g. satellites) whose loss or disruption would significantly impact virtually any nation. This chapter depicts the multidirectional interactions between smart cities and critical space infrastructure. Threat analysis is used to explore possible relationships between smart cities and critical space infrastructure through actions and their possible impact on cities. Several risk scenarios are presented, along with a general risk multimodel that could be used to address risks and their possible impacts on smart cities. The chapter concludes with a call for a "system of systems" approach to the governance of space and smart cities.

Finally, **Chapter 14** provides an initial research agenda on gamification for a city's resilience. The proposed research agenda goes beyond the present research's limitations to include critical knowledge issues involving ontology, epistemology, methodology, and the nature of human beings. A framework for the purposeful and balanced development of gamification for resilience is provided with several interrelated lines of inquiry along the philosophical, theoretical, axiological, methodological, axiomatic, and applications underpinnings.

The book also includes a glossary of terms often used in gamification and their definitions. In general, explanations of concepts are relevant to the current research. However, the reader might also reference the listed concepts and their meaning elsewhere.

Adrian V. Gheorghe
Norfolk, Virginia, USA

Polinpapilinho F. Katina
Spartanburg, South Carolina, USA

References

Adelman, H.S., Lauber, B.A., Nelson, P., & Smith, D.C. (1989). Toward a procedure for minimizing and detecting false positive diagnoses of learning disability. *Journal of Learning Disabilities*, 22(4), 234–244. https://doi.org/10.1177/002221948902200407

Arrington, M. (2011, July 13). Badgeville raises $12 million, celebrates with an infographic. *TechCrunch*. https://social.techcrunch.com/2011/07/12/badgeville-raises-12-million-celebrates-with-an-infographic/.

Beck, A. L., Lakkaraju, K., & Rai, V. (2017). Small is big: Interactive trumps passive information in breaking information barriers and impacting behavioral antecedents. *PLOS ONE* 12 (1): e0169326. https://doi.org/10.1371/journal.pone.0169326.

Deterding, S., Dixon, D., Khaled, R. et al. (2011). From game design elements to gamefulness: Defining "gamification." IN: *Proceedings of the 15th International Academic MindTrek Conference: Envisioning Future Media Environments*, pp. 9–15. Association for Computing Machinery. https://doi.org/10.1145/2181037.2181040.

Feeney, R. (2017). Old tricks are the best tricks: Repurposing programmed instruction in the mobile, digital age. *Performance Improvement* 56 (5): 6–17. https://doi.org/10.1002/pfi.21694.

Fuchs, M. (2012). Ludic interfaces: Driver and product of gamification. *G|A|M|E Games as Art, Media, Entertainment*, 1 (1): 19–26. https://www.gamejournal.it/ludic-interfaces-driver-and-product-of-gamification/.

GoogleTrends. (2021). Gamification. *Google Trends*. https://trends.google.com/trends/explore?date=all &q=gamification.

Mangalindan, J. (2012, November 12). Play to win: The game-based economy. *Fortune Tech*.https://fortune.com/2010/09/03/play-to-win-the-game-based-economy/.

Mazur-Stommen, S. and Farley, K. (2016). *Games for grownups: The role of gamification in climate change and sustainability*. Indicia Consulting. http://indiciaconsulting.com/downloads/Games-for-Grownups-Climate-Change-Edition.pdf.

Nelson, M.J. (2012). Soviet and American precursors to the gamification of work. In: *Proceedings of the 16th International Academic MindTrek Conference on – MindTrek '12*, p. 23. AMC Press. https://doi.org/10.1145/2393132.2393138.

Rasmussen, J. and Batstone, R. (1989). Why do complex organisational systems fail? World Bank Environmental Working Paper, No. 20. https://documents1.worldbank.org/curated/en/535511468766200820/pdf/multi0page.pdf.

Rhyne, T.-M., Doenges, P., Hibbard, B. et al. (2000). The impact of computer games on scientific and information visualization (panel session): "If you can't beat them, join them." In: *Proceedings of the Conference on Visualization '00*, 519–521. IEEE.

Sinanian, M. (2010, April 12). The ultimate healthcare reform could be fun and games. *VentureBeat*. https://venturebeat.com/2010/04/12/healthcare-reform-social-games-gamification/.

Taylor, C. (2011). For startups, timing is everything – Just ask Bunchball. *The New York Times*. https://archive.nytimes.com/www.nytimes.com/external/gigaom/2011/05/02/02gigaom-for-startups-timing-is-everything-just-ask-bunchb-88664.html?ref=technology%20.

Walz, S.P. and Deterding, S. (2015). *The Gameful World: Approaches, Issues, Applications*. MIT Press.

Acknowledgments

The academic citation apparatus acknowledges the relevance of the works of others to the topic of discussion, which we have done throughout this textbook. However, this mechanism can fail to capture the influences of many of the research endeavors involved. With this in mind, the authors wish to acknowledge the different organizations and people instrumental in helping shape the present research.

First, the authors are appreciative of graduate students and young researchers in the Department of Engineering Management and Systems Engineering (Old Dominion University, USA), Department of Informatics and Engineering Systems (University of South Carolina Upstate, USA), European Institute for Risk, Security and Communication Management (EURISC, Romania), and Faculty of Entrepreneurship, Business Engineering, and Management (POLITEHNICA University of Bucharest, Romania).

Also, beyond the authors' hustling, this book is a measurable expression of their intense intellectual interaction and cross-fertilization of ideas with several distinguished colleagues and partners in mind from academia and industry. Most significantly, our gratitude goes to the following:

Adolf J. Dörig (Dörig + Partner AG, Salzburg, Austria), Cornel Vintila (AuraChain, Bucharest, Romania), Dr. Alexandru Georgescu (National Institute for Research and Development in Informatics, Bucharest, Romania), Dr. Clif Flynn (University of South Carolina Upstate, Spartanburg, SC, USA), Dr. Dan V. Vamanu (Horia Hulubei National Institute for R&D in Physics and Nuclear Engineering, Bucharest, Romania), Dr. Frank Stumpe (KBC Group, Brussels, Belgium), Dr. Griffin Fernandez (Educe Group, Bethesda, MD, USA), Dr. Jeannie M. Chapman (University of South Carolina Upstate, Spartanburg, SC, USA), Dr. Liviu Muresan (EURISC, Bucharest, Romania), Dr. Paul Niculescu-Mizil Gheorghe (National Institute for Research and Development in Informatics, Bucharest, Romania), Dr. Ricardo S. Santos (University of Aveiro, Aveiro, Portugal), Dr. Roland Pulfer (Action4Value, Kirchseelte, Germany), James J. Katina (Charlottesville City Schools, Charlottesville, VA, USA), Jürg Birchmeier (Zürich Insurance Company Ltd., Zürich, Switzerland), Laura Manciu (AuraChain, Bucharest, Romania), Marcelo Masera (Joint Research Centre, Petten, The Netherlands), Prof. Dr. Andreas Tolk (MITRE Corporation, Charlottesville, VA, USA), Prof. Dr. Cesar A. Pinto (Old Dominion University, Norfolk, VA, USA), Prof. Dr. Enrico Zio (CentraleSupélec, Paris, France), Prof. Dr. Len Troncale (Cal Poly Pomona, Pomona, CA, USA), Prof. Dr. Radu Cornel (University Politehnica of Bucharest, Bucharest, Romania), Prof. Dr. Resit Unal (Old Dominion University, Norfolk, VA, USA), Prof. Dr. Unal Tatar (University at Albany -State University of New York, Albany, NY, USA), Prof. Dr. Winx Lawrence (University of Virginia, Charlottesville, VA, USA), Prof. Dr. Wolfgang Kröger (ETH Zürich, Zürich, Switzerland), and Prof. Olga Bucovetchi (Politehnica University of Bucharest, Bucharest, Romania).

Also, we wish to acknowledge several students, many of whom we proudly now call colleagues, in classes where we tested teaching/research materials: Anouar Hallioui, Farinaz Sabz AliPour, Jarutpong Vasuthanasub, Max Siangchokyoo, Nima Shahriari, Omer Keskin, Omer Poyraz, Sujatha Alla, Ulpia-Elena Botezatu, and Ying Thaviphoke.

For help with preparing the manuscript, we are thankful to our managing editor, Sarah Lemore, for working tirelessly to ensure we produced the highest quality textbook.

We want to thank our editor at Wiley, Brett Kurzman, for his encouragement throughout the project. We also want to thank the anonymous reviewers for their insightful comments that helped to improve the presentation of the material in the book.

Our sincere apologies to everyone else with whom we've had stimulating discussions and interchanges and that ought to have been remembered here. Thank you for helping shape this research and what will emerge from these thoughts.

Adrian V. Gheorghe
Norfolk, Virginia, USA

Polinpapilinho F. Katina
Spartanburg, South Carolina, USA

About the Authors

 **Adrian V. Gheorghe** is a professor and the Batten Endowed Chair on System of Systems Engineering in the Department of Engineering Management and Systems Engineering at Old Dominion University (Norfolk, Virginia, USA). Prof. Dr. Gheorghe holds MSc in Electrical Engineering (Bucharest Polytechnic Institute, Bucharest, Romania), PhD in Systems Science/Systems Engineering (City University, London, UK), MBA from the Academy of Economic Studies (Bucharest, Romania), and MSc Engineering Economics (Bucharest Polytechnic Institute, Bucharest, Romania).

Dr. Gheorghe is a senior scientist with the European Institute for Risk and Communication Management (Bucharest, Romania) and Vice President World Security Forum (Langenthal, Switzerland). He has worked with different organizations, including Battelle Memorial Institute (Columbus, Ohio), Beijing Normal University (Beijing, China), International Atomic Energy Agency (Vienna, Austria), International Institute for Applied Systems Analysis (Laxenburg, Austria), Joint Research Centre of the European Commission (Ispra, Italy), Riso National Laboratory (Roskilde, Denmark), Stanford University (Stanford, California), Swiss Federal Institute of Technology (Zürich, Switzerland), and United Nations University (Tokyo, Japan).

His profile includes nearly 400 scholarly outputs of peer-reviewed journal articles, conference papers, book chapters, and technical reports. He has published several books, including: *Blockchain-Enabled Resilience: An Integrated Approach for Disaster Supply Chain and Logistics Management* (CRC Press, 2023), *Critical Infrastructures at Risk: Securing the European Electric Power System* (Springer International Publishing, 2006), *Critical Infrastructures: Risk and Vulnerability Assessment in Transportation of Dangerous Goods — Transportation by Road and Rail* (Springer International Publishing, 2016), *Critical Space Infrastructures: Risk, Resilience, and Complexity* (Springer International Publishing, 2019), *Emergency Planning Knowledge* (VdF Verlag, 1996), and *Integrated Risk and Vulnerability Management Assisted by Decision Support Systems: Relevance and Impact on Governance* (Springer International Publishing, 2005).

Dr. Gheorghe is an editor of several journals, including the *International Journal of Critical Infrastructures* and the *International Journal of System of Systems Engineering*. He is a reviewer for several journals, including the *International Journal of Technology Management*. He has served as a guest editor for several journals, including the *International Journal of Environment and Pollution*, the *International Journal of Global Energy Issues*, and the *International Journal of Technology Management*.

Polinpapilinho F. Katina is an assistant professor in the Department of Informatics and Engineering Systems at the University of South Carolina Upstate (Spartanburg, South Carolina, USA). He has served in various capacities in industry and academia, including the National Centers for System of Systems Engineering (Norfolk, Virginia, USA), Old Dominion University (Norfolk, Virginia, USA), Politecnico di Milano (Milan, Italy), Syracuse University (Syracuse, New York, USA), and the University of Alabama in Huntsville (Huntsville, Alabama, USA).

Dr. Katina holds BSc in Engineering Technology, MEng in Systems Engineering, and PhD in Engineering Management and Systems Engineering (Old Dominion University, Norfolk, Virginia, USA). He received additional training at the Politecnico di Milano (Milan, Italy).

He focuses on teaching and research in the areas of Complex System Governance, Critical Infrastructure Systems, Decision Making and Analysis, Emerging Technologies (e.g. IoT), Energy Systems (Smart Grids), Engineering Management, Infranomics, Manufacturing Systems, System of Systems, Systems Engineering, Systems Pathology, Systems Theory, and Systems Thinking. He has experience leading large-scale research projects and has achieved many established research outcomes.

His profile includes nearly 200 scholarly outputs of peer-reviewed journal articles, conference papers, book chapters, and technical reports. He has also co-authored several books, including: *Blockchain-Enabled Resilience: An Integrated Approach for Disaster Supply Chain and Logistics Management* (CRC Press, 2023), *Complex System Governance: Theory and Practice* (Springer Nature, 2022), *Critical Infrastructures, Key Resources and Key Assets* (Springer International Publishing, 2018), *Critical Infrastructures: Risk and Vulnerability Assessment in Transportation of Dangerous Goods: Transportation by Road and Rail* (Springer International Publishing, 2016), *Critical Space Infrastructures: Risk, Resilience, and Complexity* (Springer International Publishing, 2019), and *Infranomics: Sustainability, Engineering Design, and Governance* (Springer International Publishing, 2014). Dr. Katina is a reviewer for several journals and serves on the editorial board for MDPI. He is an editor for John Wiley & Sons/Hindawi and Inderscience. He is a senior member of the Institute of Electrical and Electronics Engineers (IEEE) and the American Society for Engineering Management (ASEM). He is a recipient of several awards, including Excellence in Teaching and Advising (University of South Carolina Upstate), top 1% for the 2018 Publons Global Peer Review Awards, and 2020 IAA Social Sciences Book Award (IAA: International Academy of Astronautics).

Part I

Fundamental Issues for the Twenty-first Century

1

Systems Theory as the Basis for Bridging Science and Practice of Engineering Systems

1.1 Introduction

The International Council on Systems Engineering (INCOSE) has suggested that the conceptual and theoretical basis of Systems Theory and Systems Science might offer a vital grounding to advance the discipline of systems engineering. There is a concerted effort under the Future of Systems Engineering (FuSE) initiative to explore the potential contributions that Systems Science might make to the evolution of systems engineering. The INCOSE Vision 2025 states an imperative as "Expanding the theoretical foundation for systems engineering" (Beihoff et al. 2014, p. iv). The vision continues by suggesting that the current state of systems engineering is only weakly connected to underlying theoretical foundations, suggesting that "Systems engineering's theoretical foundations will advance to better deal with complexity and the global demands of the discipline, forming the basis for systems education as well as the methods and tools used by practicing systems engineers for system architecting, system design and system understanding" (Beihoff et al. 2014, p. 24). In response, several INCOSE-supported activities are targeted to enhance the Systems Science and theoretical foundations for systems engineering (Rousseau and Calvo-Amodio 2019; Watson 2019).

Arguably, INCOSE's call for a more robust theoretical grounding of systems engineering is driven by the realization of an increasingly changing world for systems engineering practitioners. The increasingly changing world for systems engineering practitioners is recited in the literature (Keating 2014; Keating and Katina 2012, 2019a; Keating et al. 2015). The following is a concise summary of the challenging world for systems engineering practitioners:

- *The increasing complexity of systems and their problems:* the present and future world of the systems engineering practitioner will be marked by more highly interconnected systems, emergence in their behavior/structure/performance, higher levels of uncertainty, incomplete/shifting/fallible knowledge, and exponentially increasing information.
- *The contextual influences impacting system design, execution, and development:* every system is influenced by unique circumstances, factors, patterns, stakeholders, and conditions that enable (and constrain) the structure, behavior, and performance of a system.
- *The ambiguity in system definition, understanding, and predictability:* lack of clarity in systems and their context creates conditions where historically stable approaches and expectations are questionable for continued relevance in producing successful outcomes.
- *The holistic nature of complex systems:* in addition to technical (or technological) aspects of a system, there is an increasing need to consider the human/social, organizational/managerial,

Gamification for Resilience: Resilient Informed Decision-Making, First Edition.
Adrian V. Gheorghe and Polinpapilinho F. Katina.
© 2023 John Wiley & Sons, Inc. Published 2023 by John Wiley & Sons, Inc.

policy, political, and information aspects of systems – this results in the "joint optimization" of the technical and social subsystems that constitute the totality of our systems and is critical for complete system development.

This landscape amplifies the criticality of looking to new and untapped sources of strength for systems engineering discipline sustainability and evolution into the future. A more explicit grounding of systems engineering in the theoretical and conceptual foundations of Systems Science/Theory can enhance sustainability and evolve the systems engineering discipline more effectively – a point amplified by the INCOSE 2025 vision (Beihoff et al. 2014). However, the literature is replete with extolling the virtues and noble intentions of bringing a more theoretical and conceptual grounding to systems engineering (e.g. Foundations for Systems Engineering [F4SE]). And although there is a recognition that Systems Science/Systems Theory is essential to systems engineering's future, this foundation seems challenging for practitioners to grasp. In essence, there is a lack of decent articulation of the link between theory and practice for practitioners. The divide between a pragmatic practice worldview for systems engineering and advancing the theoretical foundations of systems engineering may create a range that is, at first glance, intractable. From the practitioner's viewpoint, there may even seem to be little patience for theoretical formulations that offer ambiguous, irrelevant, and academic formulations that are not readily translatable to systems engineering practice.

On the other hand, from the science/theory viewpoint, systems engineering may seem too entrenched in tools, processes, and technologies incapable of providing rigorous explanatory and predictive power sought by robust theoretical formulations from underlying science. We believe this is a false separation limiting systems engineering discipline enhancement and Systems Science/Theory advancement. To bring clarity and examine this "false" divide between science (theory) and practice, we have focused on Systems Theory as a potential bridge between the theoretical and practice worlds of systems engineering. Our development suggests that both worlds benefit from closer examination, appreciation, and coupling for future growth. Figure 1.1 shows how Systems Theory can bridge Systems Science and systems engineering

The remainder of this chapter focuses on the detailed examination of Systems Theory as a potential bridge between Systems Science and systems engineering. This chapter also sets the stage for resilience and gamification in dealing with the volatility, uncertainty, complexity, and ambiguity

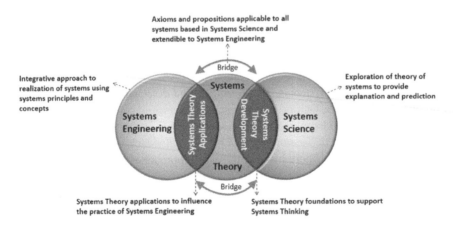

Figure 1.1 Systems Theory as a bridge between systems engineering and Systems Science. *Source:* adapted from Keating et al. (2020).

in the twenty-first century. First, we provide an overview of the developments of Systems Theory. Second, we focus on the methodologies supporting Systems Theory tenets. Third, axioms and propositions that seek to explain systems' nature, behavior, structure, and performance are articulated. Practical implications for engineering systems are developed for thinking, decision-making, actions, and interpretations. The chapter concludes with the need for resilience through gamification to support informed decision-making.

1.2 An Overview of Systems Theory

Systems Theory provides a robust conceptual foundation that can influence complex systems' design, execution, and development. Following works on Systems Theory (Adams et al. 2014; Keating et al. 2016; Whitney et al. 2015), at a basic level, Systems Theory can be described as a set of *axioms* (taken for granted truths about systems) and *propositions* (principles, concepts, and laws serving to explain system phenomena). Systems Theory suggests several central tenets concerning the capacity to deal with environments marked by increasing volatility, uncertainty, complexity, and ambiguity (VUCA), as suggested by Bennis (2001). The central tenets suggest that (i) all systems are subject to the propositions of Systems Theory that define behavior and performance, (ii) all systems perform a set of Systems Theory-based system functions that, subject to propositions, determine system performance, (iii) the violations of system propositions (in the design, execution, or development of systems) have dire consequences. They can degrade system performance and lead to system failure and collapse (Katina 2016a). In fact, it has been suggested that the evaluation of systems to identify Systems Theory-based proposition violations can provide novel insights into the practice of systems engineering (Katina 2020).

Further examination of Systems Theory inevitably leads one to General Systems Theory (GST). GST does not have a single commonly accepted definition. However, GST emerged in the 1940s as an attempt to provide an alternative to *reductionism*. *Reductionism* (focus on the successive "breaking apart" to produce understanding) is closely aligned with the "scientific method, which holds that a complex organism is understood as the sum of its parts, and can, therefore, be reduced to constituent elements (Hammond 2002; von Bertalanffy 1968). In contrast to reductionism (Laszlo 1969), GST is related to ideas of "wholes," "having irreducible properties," "environment," "centralization," "self-organization," and "holarchy of nature." Fundamentally, these ideas are meant to grasp the concepts of organization, relationships, and interrelations among all systems (von Bertalanffy 1972). Additionally, these ideas attempted to link different and diverse systems; they also suggest a commonality among other disciplines, which could be found in GST, and this commonality should be leveraged when attempting to understand problems in our current world.

The foundation of the Society for General Systems Research (SGSR; since renamed International Society for the Systems Sciences, or ISSS) in 1954 provides further clarification on the need for Systems Theory. The original bylaws state that the aims of GST are:

- To investigate the isomorphy of concepts, laws, and models from various fields and to help in useful transfers from one domain to another.
- To encourage the development of adequate theoretical models in the fields that lack them.
- To minimize the duplication of theoretical efforts in different fields
- To promote the unity of science through improving communications among specialists. (Adams et al. 2014; Hammond 2002; von Bertalanffy 1972).

The prospects and research associated with the founding of the ISSS and the precursor SGSR continue to be critical to the twenty-first century (Rousseau 2015). However, the three main aspects of GST (von Bertalanffy 1972) remain: (i) Systems Science, (ii) systems technology, and (iii) systems philosophy.

- *Systems science:* dealing with "scientific exploration and theory of 'systems' in various sciences (e.g. physics, biology, psychology, social sciences), and general Systems Theory as the doctrine of principles applying to all (or defined subclasses of) systems" (von Bertalanffy 1972, p. 414). In essence, the laws and principles associated with Systems Theory reside within Systems Science.
- *Systems technology:* dealing with "problems arising in modern technology and society, including both 'hardware' (control technology, automation, computerization, etc.) and 'software' (application of systems concepts and theory in social, ecological, economical, etc., problems)" (von Bertalanffy 1972, p. 420). In essence, this is where methods (e.g. operational research) reside.
- *Systems philosophy:* dealing with philosophical issues related to paradigm change within which systems supposedly operate. Three elements epitomize this aspect of Systems Theory: (i) systems ontology, (ii) systems epistemology, and (iii) nature of man. Systems ontology deals with how an observer views reality. Reality is addressed on the opposite extremes of realism and nominalism. Systems epistemology deals with how one obtains and communicates knowledge. Knowledge is addressed on the opposite extremes of positivism and anti-positivism. The nature of man deals with how human beings should be seen. The nature of human beings is addressed along with opposite extremes of determinism and voluntarism.

Extended discussions regarding systems philosophy, ontology, and the nature of man are discussed elsewhere (Burrell and Morgan 1979; Flood and Carson 1993; Katina et al. 2014). However, the preceding discussion is meant to highlight two points: First, our systems and their operating environment are increasingly volatile, uncertain, complex, and ambiguous. Second, complex systems and systems of systems must be addressed at a different logical level, and ideas grounded in Systems Theory can be used to offer alternative insights into our systems and their operating environment. Much of this depends on looking at systems and their environment along systems philosophy dimensions of ontology, epistemology, and human nature.

Beyond ontology, epistemology, and human nature is a matter of methodology. It is generally agreed that there is a need for robust methodologies capable of holistically and systemically analyzing behaviors of systems under the current conditions within which they must function. Again, these conditions are marked by increasing volatility, uncertainty, complexity, and ambiguity (Conrad and Gheorghe 2011; Jackson 1991, 2003, 2019; Keating 2014; Keating et al. 2014). In such cases, a methodology includes theoretical underpinnings and is used to "refer to methods for exploring and gaining knowledge about systems" (Jackson 1991, p. 3). Consistent with Checkland's (1993) perspective on a methodology, Jackson (1991) suggests that a methodology is "procedures for gaining knowledge about systems and structured processes involved in intervening in and changing systems" (p. 134). Hence, methodologies might be used to investigate and obtain knowledge about our twenty-first-century world systems. Furthermore, it is essential to establish that methodological approaches might be categorized into two opposing extremes of idiographic and nomothetic (Burrell and Morgan 1979; Flood and Carson 1993; Katina et al. 2014). An idiographic view of a methodology supports subjectivity in the research of complex systems. In fact, Flood and Carson (1993, p. 248) posit:

> the principal concern is to understand the way an individual creates, modifies, and interprets the world. The experiences are seen as unique and particular to the individual rather than general and universal. External reality is questioned. An emphasis is placed on the relativistic nature of the world to such an extent that it may be perceived as not amenable to study using the ground rules of the natural sciences. Understanding can be obtained only by acquiring firsthand knowledge of the subject under investigation.

The opposing view of nomothetic methodology supports the traditional scientific method and its reductionist approach to addressing problematic issues (Churchman 1968, 1971). A nomothetic view of methodology (Flood and Carson 1993, pp. 247–248)
claims to:

> analyze relationships and regularities between the elements of which the world is composed ... identification of the elements and the way relationships can be expressed. The methodological issues are concepts themselves, their measurement, and the identification of underlying themes. In essence, there is a search for universal laws that govern the reality that is being observed. Methodologies are based on systematic processes and techniques.

Thus, one can argue that systems-based methodologies are idiographic in nature since they adhere to the notions put forward by Flood and Carson (1993). Moreover, this is supported by Systems Theory ideas of complementarity (Bohr 1928; Mehra 1987) and complexity (Gharajedaghi 1999; Sousa-Poza et al. 2008) in which understanding and bringing about change in complex systems and systems of systems requires subjectivity. Furthermore, a review of systems literature indicates that there is no shortage of systems-based methodologies that might be used to gain knowledge and intervene in the behaviors of systems. Table 1.1 is drawn from systems literature suggesting two significant categories of systems-based methodologies.

Table 1.1 A classification and listing of system-based methodologies along "hard" and "soft" systems thinking.

Classification	Systems-based methodology	Primary proponents
Hard systems thinking	Systems analysis	Atthill (1975); Digby (1989); Gibson et al. (2006)
	Systems engineering	INCOSE (2011); Blanchard and Fabrycky (2006)
	Operational research	Churchman et al. (1957)
Soft systems thinking	Systems dynamics	Forrester (1961); Sterman (2000)
	Organizational cybernetics	Beer (1979, 1981, 1985)
	Strategic assumption surfacing and testing	Mason and Mitroff (1981); Mitroff and Emshoff (1979)
	Interactive planning	Ackoff (1974, 1981a, 1981b, 1999)
	Soft systems methodology	Checkland (1990); Wilson (1984)
	Systems of systems engineering methodology	Adams and Keating (2009; 2011); Keating et al. (2003)
	Critical systems heuristics	Ulrich (1983, 1987)
	Organizational learning	Argyris and Schön (1978, 1996)
	Sociotechnical systems	Trist and Bamforth (1951); Cherns (1976, 1987)
	Total systems intervention	Flood and Jackson (1991); Flood (1995); Jackson (1991)
	Complex system governance	Keating et al. (2014); Keating and Katina (2016)

The hard systems approach (Jackson 1991, p. 30):

> assume[s] that problems are set in mechanical-unitary contexts. Hard methodologies take it as a given that it is relatively easy to establish clear objectives for the system in which the problem resides – so context must be unitary. They then try to represent that system in a quantitative model that simulates its performance under different operational conditions – something only possible if the system is simple and the context mechanical.

Exemplars of hard systems approaches include systems analysis, systems engineering, and operations research (Checkland 1978; Jackson 1991, 2019). These methodologies share "the assumption that the problem task they tackle is to select an efficient means of achieving a known and defined end" (Checkland 1978, p. 73). However, since "it is often difficult to define precise objectives on which all stakeholders can agree," especially in complex systems (Jackson 2003, p. 20), soft systems thinking approaches emerged to accommodate multiple and sometimes conflicting values, beliefs, and worldviews that are prevalent in complex systems. To support a needed change, "the solution was to make subjectivity central, working with a variety of world views during the methodological process" (Jackson 2003, p. 22). This is the logic that underlies the second category of systems-based approaches. While a "hard" systems approach aims to optimize the system based on a known goal, the "soft" systems approach recognizes that "the vast numbers of relevant variables and the myriads of interactions make this [optimization] an impossible requirement. The solution ... [is] to identify those key mechanisms or structures that govern the behavior of the elements or subsystems ... aspects that lie behind system viability and performance" (Jackson 2003, p. 21). As an exemplar of the "soft" systems approach, we can add systems of systems engineering methodology insofar as it embraces systems ideas (Adams and Keating 2011) and yet rejects the notion of optimization (Hester 2012).

1.3 Systems Theory: An Overview of Methodologies

Suppose a methodology is a source of "guidance given to practitioners about how to translate [systems] philosophy and [systems] theory of an approach into practical application" (Jackson 2003, p. 51), Systems Theory could then be used to confront "problems confronting humanity at this stage in our history (poverty, violence, crime, environmental degradation and nuclear weapons ... terrorism) [since these problems] are systemic and cannot be understood or resolved in isolation" (Hammond 2002, p. 430). Moreover, as such problems do not occur in isolation, systems-based methodologies could be used since they embrace ideas such as participatory decision-making processes, self-organization, free will, creativity, and holism – concepts synonymous with Systems Theory – to address the interdisciplinary and multidisciplinary nature of world issues (Strijbos 2010; von Bertalanffy 1972; Warfield 1976).

Ultimately, learning and bringing about positive change are the hallmarks of any methodological approach. The nature of human beings and systems and their environment make it challenging to select an efficient means to achieve a known objective and a defined end (Jackson 2000, 2003). Warfield (1976) notes that man has faced highly intensified and interlocked shortages in necessities (e.g. energy, food, knowledge) and yet experiences excessive pollution, crime, and wars. Thus, it is evident that a methodology must be multifaceted and should enable the exploration and promotion of diversity, ensure fairness, contribute to understanding, and increase the performance and viability of systems holistically (Jackson 2003; Laszlo and Krippner 1998). In this case, a systems-based methodology must support "grappling with complexity [and] has to be a methodology for human learning" (Warfield 1976, p. 2). Table 1.2 is drawn from various literature on systems-based methodologies suggesting applicability and specific phases of the methodologies.

Table 1.2 An overview of the systems-based methodologies and their phases.

Systems-based methodology	Description and phases of the methodology
Systems analysis	Attributed to the RAND Corporation and used extensively in the US military, this methodology emerged out of operations research after World War II (Jackson 2003). Intrinsically related to systems engineering and mechanistic in nature, this methodology is largely dependent on feedback loops and black boxes of cybernetic management to optimize sociotechnical systems based on fixed parameters such as cost and benefits (Atthill 1975; Checkland 1993; Digby 1989; Ryan 2008). Miser and Quade (1988) suggest that this methodology has three stages. Gibson et al. (2006) expand these stages into six phases: • Determine goals of the system • Establish criteria for ranking alternative candidates • Develop alternative solutions • Rank alternative candidates • Iteration • Taking action to improve the system
Systems engineering	Traced to Bell Telephone Laboratories in the 1940s, systems engineering is an interdisciplinary field of engineering and a methodology for enabling the realization of successful systems out of many interacting systems (INCOSE 2011; Schlager 1956). It focuses on defining technical and business customer needs with the goal of producing quality products that meet user needs (INCOSE 2011). A generic life-cycle model associated with this approach includes five high-level stages (Blanchard and Fabrycky 2006): • Need identification (conceptual design) • Preliminary design • Detail design and system development • Production/construction of system components • Operational use and system support
Operations research	Initially developed in the United Kingdom before and during World War II, operational research is defined as "the application of the methods of science to complex problems arising in the direction and management of large systems of men, machines, materials and money in the industry, business, government, and defense. The distinctive approach is to develop a scientific model of the system, incorporating measurements of factors such as chance and risk, with which to predict and compare the outcomes of alternative decisions, strategies, or controls. The purpose is to help management determine its policy and actions scientifically" (Jackson 2000, p. 128) by the British Operational Research Society. Commonly associated with determining a maximum or minimum variable (e.g. profit, performance, yield, loss, risk) inventory, resource allocation, waiting time, replacement, competition, and combined processes, operations research was developed to deal with complex organizations that are under management control (Churchman et al. 1957; Jackson 2000). A generic model associated with this approach includes six high-level phases (Churchman et al. 1957; Jackson 2000): • Formulating the problem • Constructing a mathematical model representing a system under study • Deriving a solution from the developed model • Testing the model and the derived solution • Establishing controls over the solution • Implementing the solution to real system problems

(Continued)

Table 1.2 (Continued)

Systems-based methodology	Description and phases of the methodology
Systems dynamics	Developed by Jay Wright Forrester at the Massachusetts Institute of Technology, this methodology is concerned with limits of growth and understanding of the system structure using feedback loops as the main determinants of system behavior (Forrester 1961; Senge 1990; Sterman 2000). Four major variables associated with this methodology include (i) system boundary, (ii) network of feedback loops, (iii) variables of "rates" or "flows" and "levels" or "stocks," and (iv) leverage points. Mathematical in nature, this methodology is comprised of five phases (Maani and Cavana 2000): ● Problem structuring ● Causal loop modeling ● System dynamic modeling ● Scenario planning and modeling ● Implementation and organizational learning
Organizational cybernetics	Developed by Stafford Beer, this cybernetic methodology embodies the idea that organizations are black boxes characterized by complexity, self-regulation, and probabilistic behaviors (Jackson 2003). Using the human body as the most complex known viable system, Beer set out to create a model that can be used to explore complex system behavior without breaking it into parts (Espejo and Reyes 2011). The output was the Viable System Model (VSM) which is based on a neurocybernetic model consisting of five essential subsystems that are aligned with major viable organizational functions: ● System 1 – elements concerned with performing the key transformations of the organization ● System 2 – information channels that enable System 1 elements to communicate between each other and allow System 3 to monitor and coordinate System 1 activities ● System 3 – consists of structures and control mechanisms that establish rules, resources, rights, and responsibilities for System 1 and provides an interface with Systems 4 and 5 ● System 4 – elements that look outward to the environment for issues that might affect the viability of the organization ● System 5 – creates policy decisions within the organization as a whole to balance demands from different organizations and provides direction for the organization as a whole (Beer 1979; Beer 1981; Beer 1985). It is important to note that the VSM is more "a model rather than a methodology and can be used for purposes other than those prescribed by Beer" (Jackson 2003, p. 88). Being a model, it does not have a clear set of prescribed phases for deployment. Nonetheless, Jackson (2003) suggests two general stages: ● System identification – arriving at an identity for the system and working out appropriate levels of recursion ● System diagnosis – reflecting on the cybernetic principles that should be obeyed at each level of recursion (Jackson 1991)
Strategic assumption surfacing and testing	Attributed to Ian Mitroff and Richard Mason, this methodology is concerned with policy and planning aimed at organized complexity of "wicked problems" characterized by interconnectedness, complicatedness, uncertainty, ambiguity, conflict, and societal constraints (Mason and Mitroff 1981). The methodology is based on the premise that formulation of the right solutions to the right problem requires uncovering critical assumptions underlying policy, plan, and strategy. This enables management to compare, contrast, and gain new insights into their assumptions and "wicked" problems (Mitroff and Emshoff 1979). There are five phases associated with this methodology (Mason and Mitroff 1981; Mitroff and Emshoff 1979): ● Group formation ● Assumption surfacing and rating (regarding the problem) ● Dialectic ● Assumption integration ● Composite strategy creation

Table 1.2 (Continued)

Systems-based methodology	Description and phases of the methodology
Interactive planning	Russell L. Ackoff's methodology focuses on creating a desired future by designing present desirable conditions. It is made up of two parts: idealization and realization. These parts are divisible into six interrelated phases (Ackoff 1974, 1981a, 1981b,1999): <ul><li>Formulating the mess</li><li>Ends planning</li><li>Means planning</li><li>Resource planning</li><li>Design of implementation</li><li>Design of controls</li></ul>
Soft systems methodology	Attributed to Peter Checkland and his colleagues at Lancaster University, this methodology emerged as a response to the need for methods that can be used to intervene in "ill-structured" problem situations where it is important to learn about systems while still focusing on "goal-seeking" endeavors that answer "what" should be done and "how" it should be done (Jackson 2003). Checkland's (1990) work suggested that understanding issues such as context, largely ignored in systems engineering, provided a more rigorous attempt to tackle problematic situations coherently. This methodology is comprised of seven stages (Checkland 1990; Checkland and Poulter 2006; Wilson 1984): <ul><li>Situation considered problematical</li><li>Problem situation expressed</li><li>Root definitions of relevant purposeful activity systems</li><li>Conceptual models of relevant systems named in the root definitions</li><li>Comparison of models and the real-world situation</li><li>Define changes that are desirable and feasible</li><li>Take actions to improve the problem situation</li></ul>
Systems of systems engineering methodology (SoSEM)	Attributed to researchers at the National Centers for Systems of Systems Engineering (see Adams and Keating 2009; Adams and Keating 2011; Keating et al. 2003), this methodology is intended to provide a high-level analytical structure to explore complex system problems (Adams and Keating 2011). In order to enhance our understanding of complex systems, SoSEM is taken as a "rigorous engineering analysis that invests heavily in the understanding and framing of the problem under study" (Adams and Keating 2011, p. 113). In DeLaurentis et al. (2006) research, a three-phase approach (i.e. defining SoS problem, abstracting the system, modeling and analyzing the system for behavioral patterns) is suggested. In Adams and Keating (2009; 2011) and Keating (2011), a seven (7) stage process that consists of twenty-three (23) constituent elements is suggested: <ul><li>Framing the system under study</li><li>Designing the unique methodology</li><li>Designing the SoSE team</li><li>SoSE exploration and analysis</li><li>Transforming the analysis into action</li><li>Reporting the results of SoSE study</li><li>Assessing the impact of the SoSE study</li></ul>
Critical system heuristics	Developed by Werner Ulrich, this methodology is concerned with "unfairness in society" (Jackson 2003). It promotes emancipatory systems thinking for planners and citizens alike. Synonymous with this methodology are three phases (Ulrich 1983; Ulrich 1987): <ul><li>Identify system of interest in terms of time, space, and human intentionality (i.e. system purposefulness)</li><li>Reveal human understanding of the whole using "system," "moral," and "guarantor" concepts</li><li>Make system transparent to system designers and stakeholders using twelve boundary questions. The methodology uses four levels of categorization of stakeholders – clients, decision-makers, designers, and witnesses</li></ul>

(Continued)

Table 1.2 (Continued)

Systems-based methodology	Description and phases of the methodology
Organizational learning	Developed by Chris Argyris and Donald Schön, this methodology is concerned with single-loop and double-loop learning, where the management of the organization is able to contrast "expected outcomes" with the "obtained outcomes." Contrasting these outcomes involves learning based on errors discovered during single-loop learning and provides the basis for modifying organizational norms, policies, and objectives (Fiol and Lyles 1985). A key premise of this methodology is that learning and adapting new knowledge must be generated at both the individual and organizational level (Argyris and Schön 1978; Argyris and Schön 1996; Argyris 1985). This is done through (Argyris and Schön 1996): • Shared ideas regarding problem system • Shared understanding of possible actions • Developing a common meaning of problem system, including solutions
Sociotechnical systems	Attributed to Eric Trist, Ken Bamforth, and Fred Emery and their work at the Tavistock Institute in London, this methodology is concerned with joint optimization of both social (i.e. soft) systems, including human and technical (i.e. hard) aspects of organizations (Pasmore 1988). This methodology involves seven phases, or nine major steps as postulated by Pasmore (1988), for redesigning sociotechnical systems (Taylor and Felten 1993): • Discovery (recognizing a need for change) • Open system scan • Technical system analysis • Social system analysis • Joint optimization designing • Provisional design • Implementation
Total systems intervention	Developed in the early 1990s by Robert Flood and Michael Jackson, this meta-methodology emerged out of the recognition of strengths of capabilities of individual systems approaches, the need for pluralism in systems thinning, and calls for emancipatory ideas in systems thinking – in reference to critical systems thinking (Jackson 2003). This methodology is based on the premise that contemporary systems-based methodologies are not complementary. Laszlo and Krippner (1998) thus suggested that a successful complex organizational intervention might require a "combination" of any set of systems-based approaches. This methodology is underpinned by principles of complex situations and consists of three phases (Flood and Jackson 1991; Flood 1995; Jackson 1991): • Creativity – highlighting dominant concerns, issues, and problems in a problem context • Choice – selection of suitable systemic strategy • Implementation – employing the selected systems methodology to impose change on reality
Complex system governance	Complex System Governance (CSG) is an emerging field representing an approach to improving system performance through purposeful design, execution, and evolution of nine essential metasystem functions that provide control, communication, coordination, and integration (C3I) of a complex system. CSG was developed at the National Centers for System of Systems Engineering and is anchored in GST and Management Cybernetics, emphasizing the effective performance of metasystem functions necessary to maintain system viability (see, e.g. Keating et al. 2014; Walters et al. 2014). CSG consists of three phases (Keating and Katina 2016): • Initialization – directed to providing an initial understanding of the situation, including problem formulation involving framing and context • Readiness level assessment – establishing the feasibility of success for engaging activities to improve system governance • Governance development – continuous system development through establishing, executing, and evaluating readiness levels

A critical unifying theme among these methodologies is problem formulation. Regardless of different descriptors, there is a wide acknowledgment of the importance of problem formulation – ranging from ideas of defining problems to developing practical solutions. Moreover, the problem formulation is intrinsically linked to how human beings view the world. For example, Quade's (1980) work suggests that a major element of problem formulation relates to being "dissatisfied with current or projected state of affairs" (Quade 1980, p. 23). Additionally, problem formulation is not simply "a descriptive definition [of situations], for it does not merely describe but also chooses certain aspects of reality as being relevant for action in order to achieve certain goals" (Dery 1984, p. 35). As supported by Vennix's (1996) work that suggests "people [may] hold different views on (a) whether there is a problem and if they agree there is, (b) what the problem is" (Vennix 1996, p. 13) and the fact that problems "arise from a problem area or nexus of problems rather than a well-defined problem" (Quade and Miser 1985, p. 17) coupled with Dery's (1984) supposition that "problems are not objective entities in their own right" (Dery 1984, p. 65), problem formulation must address a plurality of objectives held by involved stakeholders (Rittel and Webber 1973). It would thus appear that problem formulation includes the identification of issues, aids in directing solutions, and accounts for the human element. Consequently, the problem formulation phase, irrespective of what it is named, "has subsequently been considered the most critical stage in policy analysis" (Dery 1984, p. 2) and is "probably the single most important routine, since it determines in large part ... the subsequent course of action" (Mintzberg et al. 1976, p. 274).

Even so, society is still grappling with armed conflicts, epidemics, natural disasters, poverty, prejudice, and violent crime and cannot address many of the root causes of dysfunctional societies. Several tenets of Systems Theory (along with problem formulation) have implications for the engineering of systems, including: (i) all systems are subject to the axioms/propositions of Systems Theory that define behavior and performance, (ii) all systems perform functions that can be examined, understood, and interpreted through the theoretical lenses of Systems Theory, (iii) inconsistencies (violations) of Systems Theory propositions in design, execution, or development of systems have consequences that can degrade performance or produce system failures, and (iv) holistic Systems Theory-based evaluation of systems and systems engineering practitioners. However, there remains a need for development of impactful methods and tools for the sake of humanity's well-being.

Again, the contributions of Systems Theory to practice are substantial. For the systems engineering practice, Keating et al. (2020) suggest:

- *Grounded philosophical and theoretical foundations are essential to sustainable and balanced systems engineering discipline development.* Systems Theory is grounded philosophically and conceptually in the concepts of *holism* (behavior of the system exists beyond the behavior of constituent elements) and *emergence* (behavior evolving in unpredictable ways as a complex system operates). The theoretical roots of Systems Theory (the set of axioms and propositions that govern the structure, behavior, and performance of all complex systems) offer a solid foundation upon which the systems engineering discipline, methodologies, and methods can be grounded and more effectively evolve.
- *Strong multidisciplinary appreciation of the holistic nature of complex systems and their problem domain.* A primary strength of Systems Theory is the consideration of problem domains across the totality of their essence, including the technical aspects of the domain and the human, social, organizational, managerial, policy, and political dimensions. This holistic and multidisciplinary focus offered by Systems Theory resists the domination of a "technology-centric" guide. It includes the complete spectrum of "hard" (e.g. technology, structure, process, policy, function) and "soft" (e.g. human, social, political) aspects of system design, execution, and development – explained by Systems Theory axioms and propositions.

- *A broad-based conceptual foundation that has withstood the test of time.* Possibly the most substantial contribution of Systems Theory to advance the systems engineering discipline and practice development is the reliance on a set of *axioms* and *propositions* that have been demonstrated as conceptually sound over time. This offers a significant conceptual foundation for further development of the systems engineering discipline and practice.
- *Incorporation of new and novel concepts, language, and grounding paradigm.* The concepts and language of Systems Theory can drive different thinking, decision, action, and interpretation. This exists across the boundaries of the individual, system, and societal problem development. The rigorous theoretical grounding offered by Systems Theory provides a stable foundation and consistent reference point against which system development can be advanced. Systems Theory offers development that engages a *holistic paradigm* to influence development to more effectively address increasingly complex systems, problems, and situations.

Ultimately, Systems Theory suggests that complex systems' behavior/performance/structure stems from "compliance to" or "violation of" system laws, principles, and theorems. In this case, a *systems law* is a generalization based upon empirical evidence; it is well established, widely accepted, and has a considerable history behind it. A *systems principle* is also a generalization based upon empirical evidence, but it is not widely accepted and thus doesn't enjoy the status of a systems law. A *systems theorem* is a generalization proven formally or logically (Clemson 1984). In domains such as systems engineering, observable surface manifestations (e.g. cost overruns, schedule delays, missed program performance targets) indicate the underlying violations of Systems Theory system laws, principles, and theorems (Katina 2015a, 2015b; Keating and Katina 2012). From a systems engineering practitioner's perspective, understanding system laws, principles, and theorems and their implications for engineering systems should hold a more significant promise for advancing the state of practice.

At this point, we have suggested Systems Theory as a basis for widening the range of "different" thinking available to a practitioner. Therefore, the corresponding range of decisions, actions, and possible interpretations is also widened. Table 1.3 amplifies the significance of Systems Theory for systems engineering practitioners. And while this listing is not exhaustive, it should provoke a central challenge to notions of the often "false" separation of theory from practical contribution.

Table 1.3 Possible Systems Theory contributions to the practice of engineering systems.

Area	Systems Theory contribution to the practice of engineering systems
Alternative framing of systems and problems	• Provides a paradigm based on a systems worldview focused on holism • Provides a basis for different methodologies, methods, tools, and techniques that can enhance practice • Appreciates complexity and multiple perspectives in the formulation of systems
Challenging dominant thinking patterns	• Provides a different "language" (axioms and propositions) to support different levels of thinking • Commences a greater range of considerations and thinking about complex situations • Engages multiple stakeholders with different worldviews, objectives, and thinking patterns
Enhancing decision space	• Creates a different range of potential decisions based on systemic formulation • Provides an alternative (and more robust) decision space for dealing with complex situations

Table 1.3 (Continued)

Area	Systems Theory contribution to the practice of engineering systems
Realization of wider array of available actions	• Provides an opportunity for actions that implement decisions across a more holistic view of complex situations • Emphasizes actions across the spectrum of "hard" (technical, process, strategy, structure) and "soft" (context, human, social, policy, political) aspects of the system problem domain
Expanded range of interpretation	• Provides a more robust range of possible interpretations of outputs, outcomes, and consequences experienced in dealing with complex situations • Explains convergence/divergence in perspectives concerning all aspects of complex situations and efforts aimed at design, execution, and development

1.4 Systems Theory and Support for Engineering Systems Practice

Axioms and propositions are introduced in this section to establish means for enhancing practice. First, we need to elucidate the philosophical questions that are consistent with several current struggles related to issues in the engineering of systems, including worldview (Rousseau and Billingham 2018; Sillitto et al. 2018). This depiction of the historical genesis and aims of systems theory suggests an obvious connection and contributions to the FuSE. As noted earlier, Systems Theory provides a solid conceptual foundation that can influence complex systems' design, execution, and development. Lacking a widely accepted definition of Systems Theory and following the work of Keating et al. (2016), at a bare stage, Systems Theory can be described as a set of *axioms* as taken for granted truths about systems and *propositions* as system laws, principles, and theorems serving to explain system phenomena. Again, while a single and universally accepted GST has yet to emerge, the aspect of GST describing isomorphic concepts, laws, principles, and theorems applicable to different systems is evident in the literature (Adams et al. 2014; Clemson 1984; Flood and Carson 1993; Katina 2015a, 2015b, 2016a, 2016b; Mobus and Kalton 2015). For example, in the work of Adams et al. (2014) and Whitney et al. (2015), thirty propositions – inclusive of laws, principles, and theorems – are proposed as means to investigate situations from a systems viewpoint along with seven axioms (i.e. centrality, context, design, goal, information, operational, and viability).

Furthermore, over eighty principles can be attributed to GST (Katina 2015b). Thus, while far from complete, Systems Theory provides an excellent science-based foundation for the further development of disciplines, including systems engineering. Table 1.4 is organized from the works of Adams et al. (2014) and Whitney et al. (2015) to provide the axioms, the associated propositions, and the applicability to the practice of engineering systems.

The implications for practice vary based on the stipulated axiom for a domain such as systems engineering. For the centrality axiom, we suggest that:

- All systems engineering endeavors rely on communications – within designed systems, between systems and their environment, within the systems engineering team, and with stakeholders. A more rigorous understanding of communications can enhance systems engineering practice.
- Control means the establishment of constraints and regulatory capacity in systems and their development processes.
- Emergence results in system patterns, behavior, or performance that cannot be predicted in advance. However, systems engineering practitioners can use emergence concepts to more effectively design, execute, and develop systems more adept at dealing with emergent conditions.

Table 1.4 Systems Theory axioms and propositions.

Axiom	Proposition	Explanation
Centrality (central to all systems are two pairs of propositions: emergence and hierarchy, and communication and control)	**Communication** (Shannon 1948a, Shannon 1948b; Skyttner 2005)	Communication is a transaction between the information source terminal and the destination terminal, with the sole aim of generation and reproduction of symbols. Information is transmitted as a selection along with possible alternative states
	Control (Checkland 1993)	The process by which a whole entity retains its identity and/or performance under changing circumstances
	Emergence (Aristotle 2002; Checkland 1993; Katina and Keating 2022; Keating and Katina 2019b)	Whole entities exhibit properties and patterns that are meaningful only when they are attributed to the whole, not its parts
	Hierarchy (Pattee 1973; Checkland 1993)	Entities meaningfully treated as wholes are built up of smaller entities, which are themselves wholes. In a hierarchy, emergent properties denote the levels
Contextual axiom (system meaning is informed by the circumstances and factors that surround the system)	**Complementarity** (Bohr, 1928)	Two different perspectives or models of a system will reveal truths regarding the system that are neither entirely independent nor entirely compatible
	Incompressibility (Cilliers, 1998; Richardson, 2004)	Each element in the system is ignorant of the behavior of the system as a whole and only responds to information that is available to it locally. As such, the best representation of a complex system is the system itself, and that any representation other than the system itself will necessarily misrepresent certain aspects of the original system
	Holism (Smuts 1926)	A system must be considered as a whole, rather than a sum of its parts
	Boundary (Von Bertalanffy 1968; Skyttner 2005)	The abstract, semipermeable perimeter of the system defines the components that make up the system, segregating them from environmental factors and possibly preventing or permitting entry of matter, energy, and information
Design axiom (system design is a purposeful imbalance of resources and relationships)	**Minimal critical specification** (Cherns 1976, Cherns 1987)	This principle has two aspects: negative and positive. The negative implies that no more should be specified than is absolutely essential; the positive requires that we identify what is essential
	Power law (Newman 2005)	The probability of measuring a particular value of some quantity varies inversely as a power of that number
	Requisite Parsimony (Miller 1956; Simon 1974)	The capacity of human short-term recall is no greater than seven plus or minus two items
	Requisite saliency (Boulding 1966)	The factors that will be considered in a system design are seldom of equal importance. Instead, there is an underlying logic awaiting discovery in each system design that will reveal the significance of these factors

Table 1.4 (Continued)

Axiom	Proposition	Explanation
Goal axiom (systems achieve specific goals through purposeful behavior using pathways and means)	**Equifinality** (Von Bertalanffy 1950)	If a steady-state is reached in an open system, it is independent of the initial conditions and determined by the system parameters, e.g. rates of reaction and transport
	Multifinality (Buckley 1967)	Radically different end states are possible from the same initial conditions
	Purposive behavior (Rosenblueth et al. 1943)	Purposeful behavior is meant to denote that the act or behavior may be interpreted as directed to the attainment of a goal (i.e. to a final condition in which the behaving object reaches a definite correlation in time or space with respect to another object or event)
	Satisficing (Simon 1955, 1956)	The decision-making process whereby one chooses an option that is, while perhaps not the best, good enough
Information axiom (systems create, possess, transfer, and modify information)	**Information redundancy** (Shannon and Weaver 1949)	The number of bits used to transmit a message, minus the number of bits of actual information in the message
	Redundancy of Potential command (McCulloch 1965)	Effective action is achieved by an adequate concatenation of information
Operational axiom (systems must be addressed in situ, where the system is exhibiting purposeful behavior)	**Dynamic equilibrium** (J.G. Miller 1978; Von Bertalanffy 1968)	An entity exists as expressions of a pattern of processes of an ordered system of forces, undergoing fluxes and continuing flows of matter, energy, and information in an equilibrium that is not static
	Homeorhesis (Waddington 1957, 1968)	The concept encompassing dynamical systems that return to an acceptable trajectory through adjustments in dynamic equilibrium controlled by interrelated regulation mechanisms
	Homeostasis (Cannon 1929)	The property of an open system to regulate its internal environment to maintain a stable condition, utilizing multiple dynamic equilibrium adjustments controlled by interrelated regulation mechanisms
	Redundancy (Pahl et al. 2011)	Means of increasing both the safety and reliability of systems by providing superfluous or excess resources
	Relaxation time (Clemson 1984; Holling 1996)	Systems need adequate time to recover from disorders that disturb their equilibrium, at which point characteristic behavior resumes
	Self-organization (Ashby 1947)	The spontaneous emergence of order out of the local interactions between initially independent components
	Suboptimization (Hitch 1953)	If each subsystem, regarded separately, is made to operate with maximum efficiency, the system as a whole will not operate with utmost efficiency

(Continued)

Table 1.4 (Continued)

Axiom	Proposition	Explanation
Viability axiom (key parameters in a system must be controlled to ensure continued existence)	**Circular causality** (Korzybski 1994)	An effect becomes a causative factor for future "effects," influencing them in a manner particularly subtle, variable, flexible, and of an endless number of possibilities
	Feedback (Wiener 1948)	All purposeful behavior may be considered to require negative feedback. If a goal is to be attained, some signals from the goal are necessary at some time to direct the behavior
	Recursion (Beer 1979)	The fundamental laws governing the processes at one level are also present at the next higher level
	Requisite hierarchy (Aulin-Ahmavaara 1979)	The weaker, on average, the regulatory abilities and the larger the uncertainties of available regulators, the more hierarchy is needed in the organization of regulation and control to attain the same result, if possible at all
	Requisite variety (Ashby 1956)	Control can be obtained only if the variety of the controller is at least as great as the variety of the situation to be controlled

- Appreciation of hierarchy means that systems engineering practice should organize large sets (e.g. data, requirements) into meaningful "categorizations" that permit greater organization and actionable understanding.

For the contextual axiom, we suggest that:

- Considering multiple viewpoints and perspectives strengthens systems engineering practice (complementarity). Accepting that there is logic and assumptions that make alternative viewpoints correct, challenging logic/assumptions can enhance systems engineering dialogs and reduce unnecessary conflict.
- Incompressibility means that all representations (models) are abstractions of a complex system and are inevitably subject to abstraction error. Thus, systems engineering practice is enhanced by accepting incomplete and fallible knowledge and continually questioning appropriateness, and evolving formulations based on new knowledge.
- Holism means that the systems engineering practice must be deployed across technology, social, human, organizational, managerial, policy, and political dimensions. System failure can occur across this holistic spectrum, not just in technology.
- Boundary means determining what is included/excluded for systems engineering efforts and should be made explicit through criteria for inclusion/exclusion. Compensation should be made for their change over time and for shifts in conditions and understanding.

For the design axiom, we suggest that:

- Minimal critical specification means that excessive constraint to regulate systems reduces autonomy and wastes scarce system resources. Care must be made to only constrain a system to the degree necessary to preserve outputs and outcomes desired.
- Power law means that the systems engineering practice must anticipate nonlinear (exponential) relationships in complex systems. System performance tradeoffs are not directly related to either resource invested or effort expended.

- Requisite parsimony means that systems engineering practitioners should note human limitations to simultaneously focus on multiple factors. This suggests striving for the greatest simplicity possible in systems that are designed, operated, and evolved by people.
- Requisite saliency means that all characteristics (e.g. design parameters) are not of equivalent importance. Systems engineering practice should clarify criticality and priorities for making effective tradeoff decisions throughout the system life cycle.

For the goal axiom, we suggest that:

- Equifinality means that systems engineering practice must accept that alternative approaches can produce equivalent results in systems engineering efforts. Execution of systems engineering is not achieved by one "optimal" approach.
- Multifinality means that there are invariably different results that can occur in the execution of systems engineering design, for systems engineering must anticipate that circumstances and conditions can influence initial designs.
- Purposive behavior means that designs in systems engineering should be clear in the desired purpose related to fulfilling a need or addressing a problem. Irrespective of intent, system purpose is a function of utility (what a system provides).
- Satisficing means that systems engineering practices should accept that, for complex systems, "optimal" is not achievable (multiple possibilities can achieve desirable outputs/outcomes) nor desirable (unreasonable resources can be expended in pursuit of "perfection").

For the information axiom, we suggest that:

- Information redundancy information means that systems engineering processes should be designed with the multiple pathways/mechanisms (redundancy) necessary to ensure both "receipt" and intended "interpretation" are met.
- Redundancy of potential command means that decision authority in systems engineering should reside, to the greatest degree possible, at the point in closest proximity to where decision execution actions will be implemented.

For the operational axiom, we suggest that:

- Dynamic equilibrium means that systems engineering designs, processes, and activities are in constant flux, experience changing circumstances, and should be adjusted "on the fly" to maintain stability in the face of change.
- Homeorhesis means that the key to systems engineering achievement is the constant adjustment of the path toward a goal. Changes in external circumstances will require adjustment of trajectory – better by purposeful adjustment of regulatory mechanisms than by chance/crisis encounters.
- Homeostasis means that systems engineering practice must provide adjustments to assure that key (internal) parameters maintain balance in response to the inevitable internal flux that might impact the ability to achieve systems engineering objectives.
- Redundancy means that sufficient mechanisms and resources should be allocated in a systems engineering effort to ensure that achievement of objectives can be attained – given inevitable variabilities whose specific form cannot be known in advance.
- Relaxation time means that significant changes in systems engineering processes, design, or execution should be taken with clear understanding of the intent and determinants of success for the effort. Engaging multiple "changes" can result in indeterminate sources of system oscillation (positive or negative).

- Self-organization means that self-organization in systems engineering is an effective (least energy-consuming) approach to design and execution. Patterns are permitted to emerge without interference (constraint) being invoked.
- Suboptimization means that integrating system elements requires surrendering autonomy in favor of system integration. Systems engineering practice should, by design, achieve a balance between subsystem autonomy and system integration.

For the viability axiom, we suggest that:

- Circular causality means that systems engineering practice must appreciate that some tightly coupled relationships cannot be broken into simple cause–effect understanding. Instead, these relationships can only be understood as a whole, not by breaking them down.
- Feedback reminds us that there is no perfect human-engineered system. Variabilities in the deployment context require initiation of feedback to make corrections to account for variability impacting system outputs.
- Recursion means that the same system functions must be performed, irrespective of a particular system. If these functions are understood for one system, they are understood for all systems a systems engineering practitioner will encounter.
- Requisite hierarchy means that systems engineering practitioners should "flatten" the hierarchy through the design of regulatory capacity to ensure consistent performance (outputs/outcomes) and diminish uncertainty through design.
- Requisite variety means that the environment within which systems engineering is performed will generate disturbances (e.g. stakeholder requirement changes). Systems engineering practitioners must provide a design that matches the types and quantities of disturbances that can be experienced.

This section was deliberately developed to serve two objectives: First, there is a matter of bringing systems theory closer to the practice of practice; in this case, we see how the discipline of systems engineering is affected by Systems Theory. This provides a bridge from Systems Science to systems engineering through Systems Theory, as suggested in Figure 1.2. If a level of thinking can be shifted, this creates an opportunity for "different" corresponding actions, decisions, and interpretations. Second, the work of Adams et al. (2014) and Whitney et al. (2015) provides a robust means for a science-based foundation for further development of disciplines, including systems

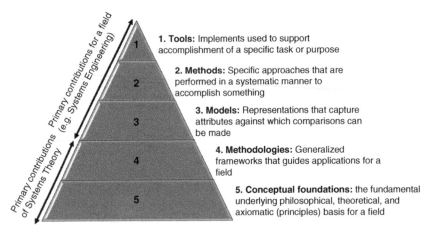

Figure 1.2 The relationship of Systems Theory to means to enhance practice.

engineering. However, much research is still needed to enable informed decision-making, especially for those that must operate in volatile, uncertain, complex, and ambiguous situations. Furthermore, research suggests that over eighty principles can be attributed to GST (Katina 2015a). In this research, a deliberate effort is undertaken to use one of those concepts (i.e. resilience) and a new kid-on-the-block (i.e. gamification) to develop resilient people, organizations, and cities.

1.5 Toward Gamification for Resilience

Resilience is the ability to prepare for and adapt to changing conditions and withstand and recover rapidly from disruptions (Gheorghe and Katina 2014). It includes withstanding and recovering from deliberate attacks, accidents, or naturally occurring threats or incidents – and these threats could take the form of armed conflicts, epidemics, natural disasters, poverty, prejudice, and violent crime. The term "gamification" first appeared online in the context of computer software in 2008 (Walz and Deterding 2015). However, gamification did not gain recognition until 2010 (GoogleTrends 2021), when many began to refer to it when incorporating social/reward aspects of games into software development (Mangalindan 2012). This approach captured the attention of venture capitalists, who suggested that "many aspects of life could become a game of sorts [and that these games] ... would be the best investments to make in the game industry" (Sinanian 2010). Another observed that half of all companies seeking funding for consumer software applications mentioned game design in their presentations (O'Brien 2010). Soon after, gamification began to be related to earlier work of adapting game-design elements and techniques to non-game contexts. For example, Deterding et al. surveyed human–computer interaction research that uses game-derived elements for motivation and interface design (Deterding et al. 2011).

Meanwhile, Nelson (2012) noted a connection between the Soviet concept of "socialist competition" and the American management trend of "fun at work." Moreover, Fuchs (2012) posited that gamification might be driven by new forms of ludic interfaces such as Wii Remote, Move, and Kinect. Gamification conferences have also retroactively incorporated simulation with Will Wright, the designer of the 1989 video game "SimCity 2013®," serving as a keynote speaker at the gamification conference, G-Summit 2013.

Organizations have also seen the value of gamification and are enhancing this concept with different platforms. For example, in October 2007, Bunchball (http://www.bunchball.com), backed by Adobe Systems Incorporated, was the first company to provide game mechanics as a service (Taylor 2011). Badgeville, which launched in late 2010 and raised $15 million in venture-capital funding in its first year of operation (Arrington, 2011), is another example of a gamification services provider. Attempts to use games for learning hit the traditional landscape in 2012 when the US Department of Energy co-funded multiple research trials (Rai and Beck 2016), including those addressing consumer behavior (Beck et al. 2017), adapting the format of "programmed learning" into mobile microlearning to experiment with the impacts of gamification in energy usage reduction (Feeney 2017). Moreover, Mazur-Stommen and Farley (2016) suggest that gamification can be used to address climate change and sustainability with surprising results. For example, note that their research "broadened the scope of the kinds of activities we were looking at, beyond utilities and into market-based and education games, which took many forms including card-games (Cool Choices), videogames (Ludwig), and games for mobile devices such as smartphones (Ringorang)... gamification, such as that used in the Opower/Facebook application, whereby the incorporation of game mechanics heightens the experience and/or performance of everyday, real-world activities" (Mazur-Stommen and Farley 2016, p. 9).

Finally, there is the Gamification Research Network (GRN), a communication hub for researchers and students interested in studying the use of game design in non-game contexts. It was launched in November 2010 alongside the call for participation in 2011, 2013, and 2015 CHI workshops on gamification (http://gamification-research.org/about). It is import to recall that a key fundamental aspect of games is education as well as behavior modification – which is related to resilience.

However, building a resilient organization, including a city, requires a holistic approach and the appropriate adoption of knowledge and application of tools during the planning and management process. Several studies aspire to enhance the capacity of city resiliency (see, for example, the Organisation for Economic Co-operation and Development's Resilient Cities: https://www.oecd.org/cfe/resilient-cities.htm). However, few studies explicitly link Systems Theory to creating resilient cities while also providing roadmaps (i.e. practical sequential steps) that can be followed in building a resilient city. Thus, we have attempted the prior and it vibrates throughout the remainder of this book. In the case of the latter, we try to close this body of knowledge gap by developing a methodological framework, which involves procedural steps in assisting the planning and management processes for developing a resilient city. The platform proposed in this research is grounded on a theoretical approach called "Resilient Informed Decision-Making Process." The efficacy of the developed framework and the research is demonstrated through a case applied to two US cities and as well as space systems.

The articulated worldview of systems theory makes a case for actionable axioms/propositions in the sense that practitioners are required to question the implications of the axioms/propositions for their unique effort – incorporating appropriate design, execution, and development strategies/actions. This section, however, has suggested that axioms/propositions are not limited to any one stage in any field and that, instead, there remains an opportunity to extend Systems Theory across all aspects of systems and scenarios. And in this case, using gamification to enhance resilience. However, this approach should not be taken to suggest that the application of systems theory is quick, easy, routine, and resource-free. On the contrary, applying systems theory is not without substantial investment (resources, conceptual energy) in pursuit of substantially leveraged returns across design, execution, and development practices.

1.6 Concluding Remarks

In this introductory chapter, we have shown the potential contributions of Systems Theory as a potential conduit between systems science and practice through an examination of systems engineering. We further elaborate on the development of systems theory to advance the gamification for resilience. First, *Systems Theory can support the grounding and development of gamification for resilience.* INCOSE has identified Systems Science/Theory as a theoretical basis to advance the systems engineering discipline. However, Systems Theory is not discipline specific. It brings a theoretical grounding to gamification for resilience through the language (axioms/propositions) that can more rigorously inform development. A primary contribution of Systems Theory is provided at the base of the pyramid, where Systems Theory serves as the conceptual foundation (i.e. Systems Science, systems technology, and systems philosophy) for understanding phenomena of resilience through gamification. Second, a primary strength of Systems Theory is the consideration of increasing volatility, uncertainty, complexity, and ambiguity. The reflection of volatility, uncertainty, complexity, and ambiguity includes the technical aspects of complex systems and the human, social, organizational, managerial, policy, and political dimensions that act according to the dictates of Systems Theory axioms/propositions. The holistic and multidisciplinary focus that

Systems Theory offers resists the domination of a "technology-centric" focus and includes the complete spectrum of both "hard" (e.g. technology, structure, process, policy, function) and "soft" (e.g. human, social, political) aspects of system design, execution, and development – all of which are necessary elements for creating a resilience society. Third, gamification for resilience can support the development of actionable Systems Theory. Systems Theory is often criticized (arguably unfairly) for not offering "actionable" support for practical deployment. Therefore, gamification for resilience offers strength in the development of technologies (tools, methods, models) that are deployable for practitioners.

Finally, let's provide a synopsis of this textbook. The global human population will reach eight billion by the end of 2022. Much of the population is clustered around cities that have been the centers of human culture and economic activity. Unfortunately, the promise of the prosperity of these cities comes with urban risks and vulnerabilities that tend to increase with the number of people living in them. The concept of resilience is considered a significant component of the cities' long-term planning and sustainable development. Informed decision-making is a fundamental part of long-term planning and sustainable development for cities and their residents.

A starting point might as well be resilience through gamification. The development, application implications, and research agenda for gamification for resilience are the basis for the remainder of this book.

1.7 Exercises

1 Discuss the need for Systems Theory.
2 List and discuss the applicability of Systems Theory-based methodologies.
3 How can Systems Theory enhance the field of systems engineering?
4 Explain the relevance of gamification in dealing with complex situations.
5 How can gamification enhance the resilience of people, organizations, and cities?

References

Ackoff, R.L. (1974). *Redesigning the Future: A Systems Approach to Societal Problems*. Wiley.

Ackoff, R.L. (1981a). *Creating the Corporate Future*. Wiley.

Ackoff, R.L. (1981b). The art and science of mess management. *Interfaces* 11(1), 20–26. https://www.jstor.org/stable/25060027.

Ackoff, R.L. (1999). *Re-creating the Corporation: A Design of Organizations for the 21st Century*. Oxford University Press.

Adams, K.M., Hester, P.T., Bradley, J.M. et al. (2014). Systems theory as the foundation for understanding systems. *Systems Engineering* 17(1): 112–123. https://doi.org/10.1002/sys.21255.

Adams, K.M. and Keating, C.B. (2009). *SoSE Methodology Rev 0.2* (NCSoSE technical report 009-2009). National Centers for System of Systems Engineering.

Adams, K.M. and Keating, C.B. (2011). Overview of the system of systems engineering methodology. *International Journal of System of Systems Engineering* 2 (2/3): 112–119. https://doi.org/10.1504/IJSSE.2011.040549.

Argyris, C. (1985). *Strategy, Change, and Defensive Routines*. Pitman.

Argyris, C. and Schön, D. (1978). *Organizational Learning: A Theory of Action Perspective*. Addison-Wesley.

Argyris, C. and Schön, D. (1996). *Organizational Learning II: Theory, Method, and Practice*. Addison-Wesley.

Aristotle. (2002). *Metaphysics: Book H – Form and Being at Work* (trans. J. Sachs, 2nd ed.). Green Lion Press.

Arrington, M. (2011, July 13). Badgeville raises $12 million, celebrates with an infographic. *TechCrunch*. https://social.techcrunch.com/2011/07/12/badgeville-raises-12-million-celebrates-with-an-infographic.

Ashby, W.R. (1947). Principles of the self-organizing dynamic system. *The Journal of General Psychology* 37(2): 125–128. https://doi.org/10.1080/00221309.1947.9918144.

Ashby, W.R. (1956). *An Introduction to Cybernetics*. Chapman and Hall.

Atthill, C. (1975). *Decisions: West Oil Distribution*. P.B. Educational Services.

Aulin-Ahmavaara, A.Y. (1979). The law of requisite hierarchy. *Kybernetes* 8(4): 259–266. https://doi.org/10.1108/eb005528.

Beck, A.L., Lakkaraju, K., and Rai, V. (2017). Small is big: Interactive trumps passive information in breaking information barriers and impacting behavioral antecedents. *Plos One* 12(1): e0169326. https://doi.org/10.1371/journal.pone.0169326.

Beer, S. (1979). *The Heart of the Enterprise*. Wiley.

Beer, S. (1981). *The Brain of the Firm: The Managerial Cybernetics of Organization*. Wiley.

Beer, S. (1985). *Diagnosing the System for Organizations*. Oxford University Press.

Beihoff, B., Oster, C., Friedenthal, S. et al. (2014). A world in motion: Systems engineering vision 2025. *INCOSE-SE Leading Indicators Guide* (Vol. 2014). INCOSE. https://www.incose.org/docs/default-source/aboutse/se-vision-2025.pdf.

Bennis, W. (2001). Leading in unnerving times. *MIT Sloan Management Review* 42(2): 97–102.

Blanchard, B.S. and Fabrycky, W.J. (2006). *Systems Engineering and Analysis* (4th ed.). Pearson/Prentice Hall.

Bohr, N. (1928). The quantum postulate and the recent development of atomic theory. *Nature* 121(3050): 580–590.

Boulding, K.E. (1966). *The Impact of Social Sciences*. Rutgers University Press.

Buckley, W. (1967). *Sociology and Modern Systems Theory*. Prentice Hall.

Burrell, G. and Morgan, G. (1979). *Sociological Paradigms and Organisational Analysis*. Ashgate Publishing.

Cannon, W.B. (1929). Organization for physiological homeostasis. *Physiological Reviews* 9(3): 399–431.

Checkland, P.B. (1978). The origins and nature of "hard" systems thinking. *Journal of Applied Systems Analysis* 5(2): 99–110.

Checkland, P.B. (1990). Soft systems methodology: A thirty year retrospective. In P.B. Checkland and J. Scholes (eds.), *Soft Systems Methodology in Action* (pp. A1–A66). Wiley.

Checkland, P.B. (1993). *Systems Thinking, Systems Practice*. Wiley.

Checkland, P.B. and Poulter, J. (2006). *Learning for Action: A Short Definitive Account of Soft Systems Methodology and Its Use for Practitioner, Teachers, and Students*. Wiley.

Cherns, A. (1976). The principles of sociotechnical design. *Human Relations* 29(8): 783–792. https://doi.org/10.1177/001872677602900806.

Cherns, A. (1987). Principles of sociotechnical design revisited. *Human Relations* 40(3): 153–161.

Churchman, C.W. (1968). *Challenge to Reason*. McGraw Hill.

Churchman, C.W. (1971). *The Design of Inquiring Systems*. Basic Books.

Churchman, C.W., Ackoff, R.L., and Arnoff, E.L. (1957). *Introduction to Operations Research*. Wiley.

Cilliers, P. (1998). *Complexity and Postmodernism: Understand Complex Systems*. Routledge.

Clemson, B. (1984). *Cybernetics: A New Management Tool*. Abacus Press.

Conrad, T.P. and Gheorghe, A.V. (2011). Editorial: System of systems engineering in naval application. *International Journal of System of Systems Engineering* 2(2/3): 89–90.

DeLaurentis, D.A., Sindiy, O.V., and Stein, W.B. (2006). Developing sustainable space exploration via a system-of-systems approach. The American Institute of Aeronautics and Astronautics. http://arc.aiaa.org/doi/pdfplus/10.2514/6.2006-7248.

Dery, D. (1984). *Problem Definition in Policy Analysis*. University Press of Kansas.

Deterding, S., Dixon, D., Khaled, R. et al.(2011). From game design elements to gamefulness: Defining "gamification." In: *Proceedings of the 15th International Academic MindTrek Conference: Envisioning Future Media Environments* (eds. A. Lugmayr, H. Franssila, C. Safran et al.), pp. 9–15. Association for Computing Machinery. https://doi.org/10.1145/2181037.2181040.

Digby, J. (1989). *Operations research and systems analysis at RAND, 1948–1967* (RAND/N-2936-RC; p. 4). RAND.

Espejo, R. and Reyes, A. (2011). *Organizational Systems: Managing Complexity with the Viable System Model*. Springer Berlin / Heidelberg.

Feeney, R. (2017). Old tricks are the best tricks: Repurposing programmed instruction in the mobile, digital age. *Performance Improvement* 56(5): 6–17. https://doi.org/10.1002/pfi.21694.

Flood, R.L. (1995). Total systems intervention (TSI): A reconstitution. *Journal of the Operational Research Society* 46(2): 174–191.

Flood, R.L. and Carson, E.R. (1993). *Dealing with Complexity: An Introduction to the Theory and Application of Systems Science*. Plenum Press.

Flood, R.L. and Jackson, M.C. (1991). *Creative Problem Solving: Total Systems Intervention*. Wiley.

Fiol, C.M., and Lyles, M.A. (1985). Organizational learning. *The Academy of Management Review* 10 (4): 803–813. https://doi.org/10.2307/258048.

Forrester, J.W. (1961). *Industrial Dynamics*. MIT Press.

Fuchs, M. (2012). Ludic interfaces: Driver and product of gamification. *G|A|M|E Games as Art, Media, Entertainment* 1(1). https://www.gamejournal.it/ludic-interfaces-driver-and-product-of-gamification.

Gharajedaghi, J. (1999). *Systems Thinking: Managing Chaos and Complexity: A Platform for Designing Business Architecture*. Butterworth-Heinemann.

Gheorghe, A.V. and Katina, P.F. (2014). Editorial: Resiliency and engineering systems—research trends and challenges. *International Journal of Critical Infrastructures* 10(3/4): 193–199.

Gibson, J.E., Scherer, W.T., and Gibson, W.F. (2006). *How to Do Systems Analysis*. Wiley-Interscience.

GoogleTrends. (2021). Gamification. GoogleTrends. https://trends.google.com/trends/explore?date=all&q=gamification.

Hammond, D. (2002). Exploring the genealogy of systems thinking. *Systems Research and Behavioral Science* 19(5): 429–439. https://doi.org/10.1002/sres.499.

Hester, P.T. (2012). Why optimisation of a system of systems is both unattainable and unnecessary. *International Journal of System of Systems Engineering* 3(3/4): 268–276. https://doi.org/10.1504/IJSSE.2012.052691.

Hitch, C. (1953). Sub-optimization in operations problems. *Operations Research* 1(3): 87–99. https://doi.org/10.1287/opre.1.3.87.

Holling, C. S. (1996). Engineering resilience versus ecological resilience. In: *Engineering Within Ecological Constraints* (ed. P. Schulze), 31–43. National Academies Press.

INCOSE. (2011). *Systems Engineering Handbook: A Guide for System Life Cycle Processes and Activities* (H. Cecilia). 3.2.

Jackson, M.C. (1991). *Systems Methodology for the Management Sciences*. Plenum Press.

Jackson, M.C. (2000). *Systems Approaches to Management*. Springer.

Jackson, M.C. (2003). *Systems Thinking: Creative Holism for Managers*. Wiley.

Jackson, M.C. (2019). *Critical Systems Thinking and the Management of Complexity* (1st ed.). Wiley.

Katina, P.F. (2015a). Emerging systems theory-based pathologies for governance of complex systems. *International Journal of System of Systems Engineering* 6(1/2): 144–159. https://doi.org/10.1504/IJSSE.2015.068806.

Katina, P.F. (2015b). *Systems Theory-based Construct for Identifying Metasystem Pathologies for Complex System Governance*. PhD, Old Dominion University. http://search.proquest.com.proxy.lib.odu.edu/docview/1717329758/abstract/29A520C8C0A744A2PQ/2.

Katina, P.F. (2016a). Systems theory as a foundation for discovery of pathologies for complex system problem formulation. In: *Applications of Systems Thinking and Soft Operations Research in Managing Complexity* (ed. A.J. Masys), 227–267. Springer International Publishing. http://link.springer.com/chapter/10.1007/978-3-319-21106-0_11.

Katina, P.F. (2016b). Metasystem pathologies (M-Path) method: Phases and procedures. *Journal of Management Development* 35 (10): 1287–1301. https://doi.org/10.1108/JMD-02-2016-0024.

Katina, P.F. (2020). System acquisition pathology: A comprehensive characterisation of system failure modes and effects. *International Journal of Critical Infrastructures* 16(3): 255–292. https://doi.org/10.1504/IJCIS.2020.108499.

Katina, P.F. and Keating, C.B. (2022). Deepwater horizon: Emergent behavior in a system of systems disaster. In: *Emergent Behavior in System of Systems Engineering: Real-World Applications* (eds. L.B. Rainey and O.T. Holland), 193–230. CRC Press. https://doi.org/10.1201/9781003160816-11.

Katina, P.F., Keating, C.B., and Jaradat, R.M. (2014). System requirements engineering in complex situations. *Requirements Engineering* 19(1): 45–62. https://doi.org/10.1007/s00766-012-0157-0.

Keating, C.B. (2011). Perspective 2 of the SoSE methodology: Designing the unique methodology. *International Journal of System of Systems Engineering* 2(2): 208–225.

Keating, C.B. (2014). Governance implications for meeting challenges in the system of systems engineering field. In *2014 9th International Conference on System of Systems Engineering (SOSE)*, (IEEE, pp. 154–159). https://doi.org/10.1109/SYSOSE.

Keating, C.B. and Katina, P.F. (2012). Prevalence of pathologies in systems of systems. *International Journal of System of Systems Engineering* 3(3/4): 243–267. https://doi.org/10.1504/IJSSE.2012.052688.

Keating, C.B. and Katina, P.F. (2016). Complex system governance development: A first generation methodology. *International Journal of System of Systems Engineering* 7(1/2/3): 43–74. https://doi.org/10.1504/IJSSE.2016.076127.

Keating, C.B. and Katina, P.F. (2019a). Complex system governance: Concept, utility, and challenges. *Systems Research and Behavioral Science* 36(5): 687–705. https://doi.org/10.1002/sres.2621.

Keating, C.B. and Katina, P.F. (2019b). Emergence in the context of system-of-systems. In: *Engineering Emergence: A Modeling and Simulation Approach* (eds. L.B. Rainey and M. Jamshidi), 1, pp. 491–523. CRC Press. https://www.crcpress.com/Engineering-Emergence-A-Modeling-and-Simulation-Approach/Rainey-Jamshidi/p/book/9781138046160.

Keating, C.B., Katina, P.F., and Bradley, J.M. (2014). Complex system governance: Concept, challenges, and emerging research. *International Journal of System of Systems Engineering* 5(3): 263–288. https://doi.org/10.1504/IJSSE.2014.065756.

Keating, C.B., Katina, P.F., and Bradley, J.M. (2015). Challenges for developing complex system governance. In: Proceedings of the 2015 Industrial and Systems Engineering Research Conference. (Sila Çetinkaya and J. K. Ryan). https://www.xcdsystem.com/iie2015/abstract/finalpapers/I1401.pdf.

Keating, C.B., Katina, P.F., Bradley, J.M. et al. (2016). Systems theory as a conceptual foundation for system of systems engineering. *INSIGHT* 19(3): 47–50. https://doi.org/10.1002/inst.12108.

Keating, C.B., Katina, P.F., Hodge, R., and Bradley, J.M. (2020). Systems theory: Bridging the gap between science and practice for systems engineering. *INCOSE International Symposium*, 30(1): 1017–1031. https://doi.org/10.1002/j.2334-5837.2020.00769.x.

Keating, C.B., Rogers, R., Unal, R. et al. (2003). System of systems engineering. *Engineering Management Journal* 15(3): 35–44.

Korzybski, A. (1994). *Science and Sanity: An Introduction to Non-Aristotelian Systems and General Semantics*. Wiley.

Laszlo, E. (1969). *System, Structure, and Experience: Toward a Scientific Theory of Mind*. Gordon and Breach Science.

Laszlo, A. and Krippner, S. (1998). Systems theories: Their origins, foundations, and development. In: *Systems Theories and a priori Aspects of Perception* (ed. J.S. Jordan), pp. 47–74. Elsevier Science. http://www.academia.edu/713345/Systems_Theories_Their_origins_foundations_and_development.

Maani, K.E. and Cavana, R.Y. (2000). *Systems Thinking and Modelling*. Pearson Education.

Mangalindan, J. (2012, November 12). Play to win: The game-based economy. *Fortune Tech*. https://web.archive.org/web/20121112074424/http://tech.fortune.cnn.com/2010/09/03/the-game-based-economy.

Mason, R.O. and Mitroff, I.I. (1981). *Challenging Strategic Planning Assumptions: Theory, Cases, and Techniques*. Wiley-Interscience.

Mazur-Stommen, S. and Farley, K. (2016). *Games for grownups: The role of gamification in climate change and sustainability*. Indicia Consulting. http://indiciaconsulting.com/downloads/Games-for-Grownups-Climate-Change-Edition.pdf.

McCulloch, W.S. (1965). *Embodiments of Mind*. MIT Press.

Mehra, J. (1987). Niels Bohr's discussions with Albert Einstein, Werner Heisenberg, and Erwin Schrödinger: The origins of the principles of uncertainty and complementarity. *Foundations of Physics* 17(5): 461–506. https://doi.org/10.1007/BF01559698.

Miller, G.A. (1956). The magical number seven, plus or minus two: Some limits on our capacity for processing information. *Psychological Review* 63(2): 81–97. https://doi.org/10.1037/h0043158.

Miller, J.G. (1978). *Living Systems*. McGraw Hill.

Mintzberg, H., Raisinghani, D., and Théorêt, A. (1976). The structure of the "unstructured" decision processes. *Administrative Science Quarterly* 21(2): 246–275.

Miser, H.J. and Quade, E.S. (1988). *Handbook of Systems Analysis: Craft Issues and Procedural Choices* 2. North-Holland.

Mitroff, I.I. and Emshoff, J.R. (1979). On strategic assumption-making: A dialectical approach to policy and planning. *The Academy of Management Review* 4(1): 1–12. https://doi.org/10.2307/257398.

Mobus, G.E. and Kalton, M.C. (2015). *Principles of Systems Science*. Springer-Verlag. www.springer.com/us/book/9781493919192.

Nelson, M. J. (2012). Soviet and American precursors to the gamification of work. In: *Proceeding of the 16th International Academic MindTrek Conference on MindTrek '12* (ACM Press), p. 23. Retrieved from https://dl.acm.org/doi/10.1145/2393132.2393138.

Newman, M.E.J. (2005). Power laws, Pareto distributions and Zipf's law. *Contemporary Physics* 46(5): 323–351. https://doi.org/10.1080/00107510500052444.

O'Brien, C. (2010, October 21). Get ready for the decade of gamification. *The Mercury News*. https://www.mercurynews.com/2010/10/21/obrien-get-ready-for-the-decade-of-gamification.

Pahl, G., Beitz, W., Feldhusen, J.et al. (2011). *Engineering Design: A Systematic Approach* (eds. and trans. K. Wallace and L.T.M. Blessing; 3rd ed.). Springer.

Pasmore, W.A. (1988). *Designing Effective Organizations: The Sociotechnical Systems Perspective*. Wiley.

Pattee, H.H. (1973). *Hierarchy Theory: The Challenge of Complex Systems*. Braziller.

Quade, E.S. (1980). Pitfalls in formulation and modeling. In: *Pitfalls of Analysis* (eds. G. Majone and E.S. Quade), Vol. 8, pp. 23–43. Wiley-Interscience.

Quade, E.S. and Miser, H.J. (1985). The context, nature, and use of systems analysis. In: *Handbook of Systems Analysis: Overview of Uses, Procedures, Applications, and Practice* (eds. H.S. Misser and E.S. Quade), pp. 1–32. Elsevier Science Publishing Co., Inc.

Rai, V. and Beck, A. (2016). *Serious Games in Breaking Informational Barriers in Solar Energy* (SSRN scholarly paper ID 2816852). Social Science Research Network. https://doi.org/10.2139/ssrn.2816852.

Richardson, K.A. (2004). Systems theory and complexity: Part 2. *E:Co* 6(4): 77–82.

Rittel, H.W.J. and Webber, M.M. (1973). Dilemmas in a general theory of planning. *Policy Sciences* 4(2): 155–169. https://doi.org/10.1007/BF01405730.

Rosenblueth, A., Wiener, N., and Bigelow, J. (1943). Behavior, purpose and teleology. *Philosophy of Science* 10(1): 18–24.

Rousseau, D. (2015). General systems theory: Its present and potential. *Systems Research and Behavioral Science* 32(5): 522–533. https://doi.org/10.1002/sres.2354.

Rousseau, D. and Billingham, J. (2018). A systematic framework for exploring worldviews and its generalization as a multi-purpose inquiry framework. *Systems* 6(3): 27. https://doi.org/10.3390/systems6030027.

Rousseau, D. and Calvo-Amodio, J. (2019). Systems principles, systems science, and the future of systems engineering. *INSIGHT* 22(1): 13–15. https://doi.org/10.1002/inst.12232.

Ryan, A.J. (2008). *What is a Systems Approach?* (ArXiv E-Print 0809.1698). Cornell University Library. http://arxiv.org/abs/0809.1698.

Schlager, K.J. (1956). Systems engineering: A key to modern development. *IRE Transactions on Engineering Management EM-3* 3: 64–66. https://doi.org/10.1109/IRET-EM.1956.5007383.

Senge, P.M. (1990). *The Fifth Discipline: The Art and Practice of the Learning Organization*. Doubleday/Currency. http://edrev.asu.edu/reviews/rev92.htmhttp://www.loc.gov/catdir/description/random041/90002991.htmlhttp://www.loc.gov/catdir/enhancements/fy0703/90002991-s.html.

Shannon, C.E. (1948a). A mathematical theory of communication: Part 1. *Bell System Technical Journal* 27(3): 379–423.

Shannon, C.E. (1948b). A mathematical theory of communication: Part 2. *Bell System Technical Journal* 27(4): 623–656.

Shannon, C.E. and Weaver, W. (1949). *The Mathematical Theory of Communication*. University of Illinois Press.

Sillitto, H., Griego, R., Arnold, E. et al. (2018). What do we mean by "system"? – System beliefs and worldviews in the INCOSE community. *INCOSE International Symposium* 28(1): 1190–1206. https://doi.org/10.1002/j.2334-5837.2018.00542.x.

Simon, H.A. (1955). A behavioral model of rational choice. *The Quarterly Journal of Economics* 69(1): 99–118. https://doi.org/10.2307/1884852.

Simon, H.A. (1956). Rational choice and the structure of the environment. *Psychological Review* 63(2): 129–138.

Simon, H.A. (1974). How big is a chunk? *Science* 183(4124): 482–488.

Sinanian, M. (2010, April 12). The ultimate healthcare reform could be fun and games. *VentureBeat*. https://venturebeat.com/2010/04/12/healthcare-reform-social-games-gamification.

Skyttner, L. (2005). *General Systems Theory: Problems, Perspectives, Practice* (2nd ed.). World Scientific Publishing Co. Pte. Ltd.

Smuts, J. (1926). *Holism and Evolution*. Greenwood Press.

Sousa-Poza, A.A., Kovacic, S., and Keating, C.B. (2008). System of systems engineering: An emerging multidiscipline. *International Journal of System of Systems Engineering* 1(1/2): 1–17. https://doi.org/10.1504/IJSSE.2008.018129.

Sterman, J.D. (2000). *Business Dynamics: Systems Thinking and Modeling for a Complex World*. McGraw Hill.

Strijbos, S. (2010). Systems thinking. In: *The Oxford Handbook of Interdisciplinarity* (eds. R. Frodeman, J.T. Klein, and C. Mitcham), pp. 453–470. Oxford University Press.

Taylor, C. (2011). For startups, timing is everything – Just ask Bunchball. *The New York Times*. http://cms-service/article_delivery.php.

Taylor, J.C. and Felten, D.F. (1993). *Performance by Design: Sociotechnical Systems in North America*. Prentice Hall.

Trist, E.L. and Bamforth, K.W. (1951). Some social and psychological consequences of the longwall method of coal-getting: An examination of the psychological situation and defences of a work group in relation to the social structure and technological content of the work system. *Human Relations* 4(1): 3–38. https://doi.org/10.1177/001872675100400101.

Ulrich, W. (1983). *Critical Heuristics of Social Planning: A New Approach to Practical Philosophy*. Paul Haupt.

Ulrich, W. (1987). Critical heuristics of social systems design. *European Journal of Operational Research* 31(3): 276–283. https://doi.org/10.1016/0377-2217(87)90036-1.

Vennix, J. (1996). *Group Model Building: Facilitating Team Learning Using System Dynamics* (1st ed.). Wiley.

von Bertalanffy, L. (1950). An outline of general system theory. *The British Journal for the Philosophy of Science* 1(2): 134–165. https://doi.org/10.1093/bjps/I.2.134.

von Bertalanffy, L. (1968). *General System Theory: Foundations, Developments, Applications*. George Braziller.

von Bertalanffy, L. (1972). The history and status of general systems theory. *Academy of Management Journal* 15(4): 407–426. https://doi.org/10.2307/255139.

Waddington, C.H. (1957). *The Strategy of Genes: A Discussion of Some Aspects of Theoretical Biology*. Allen and Unwin.

Waddington, C.H. (1968). Towards a theoretical biology. *Nature* 218(5141): 525–527.

Walters, D., Moorthy, S., and Carter, B. (2014). System of systems engineering and enterprise architecture: Implications for governance of complex systems. *International Journal of System of Systems Engineering* 5(3): 248–262. https://doi.org/10.1504/IJSSE.2014.065755.

Walz, S.P. and Deterding, S. (2015). *The Gameful World: Approaches, Issues, Applications*. MIT Press.

Warfield, J.N. (1976). *Societal Systems: Planning, Policy and Complexity*. Wiley-Interscience.

Watson, M.D. (2019). Future of systems engineering. *INSIGHT* 22(1): 8–12. https://doi.org/10.1002/inst.12231.

Whitney, K., Bradley, J.M., Baugh, D.E. et al. (2015). Systems theory as a foundation for governance of complex systems. *International Journal of System of Systems Engineering* 6(1–2): 15–32. https://doi.org/10.1504/IJSSE.2015.068805.

Wiener, N. (1948). *Cybernetics: Or Control and Communication in the Animal and the Machine*. MIT Press.

Wilson, B. (1984). *Systems: Concepts, Methodologies, and Applications*. Wiley.

2

Critical Infrastructure Systems at Risk

2.1   Introduction

The global human population had reached eight billion by the end of 2022. And the number is projected to escalate steadily to 8.5 billion in 2030, 9.7 billion in 2050, and 11.2 billion in 2100. India is expected to outnumber China four to six years from now (United Nations 2015, 2017). Cities have been the centers of human culture and economic activity for centuries, attracting skilled workers and productive businesses worldwide. In the upcoming years, most major cities' populations will continually increase (Rockefeller Foundation 2014). Many more people from remote and rural areas will flow into the cities to seek opportunities for a better lifestyle and quality of life.

Regarding this information, Dobbs et al. (2012) projected that between 2010 and 2025, an estimated 600 million inhabitants would populate only around 440 cities, which are expected to generate roughly half of global GDP growth. These people are drawn to cities by job opportunities, economic activities, and modern productivity. Moreover, more than half of the projected increase in global population up to 2050 will be concentrated in just eight countries: the Democratic Republic of the Congo, Egypt, Ethiopia, India, Nigeria, Pakistan, the Philippines, and the United Republic of Tanzania. Disparate growth rates among the world's largest countries will reorder their ranking by size (United Nations 2022). In Africa, the extreme population growth is driven by East Africa, Middle Africa, and West Africa, in which regions are projected to more than quintuple their populations over the twenty-first century. The most extreme of these is Middle Africa, with an estimated population increase of 681%, from less than 100 million in 2000 to more than 750 million in 2100 (almost half of this figure is driven by the Democratic Republic of the Congo, projected to increase from 47 million in 2000 to 362 million in 2100 (UN 2022)). For this reason, infrastructure systems will play primary roles in city system mechanisms to support and ease human well-being.

As the twenty-first century unfolds, the occurrences of catastrophic and unforeseen events, such as climate change, disease pandemics, economic fluctuations, and terrorist attacks, have played out on a global scale. Moreover, the International Council of Local Environmental Initiatives (Mitroliou and Kavanaugh 2015) suggests that urban risk and vulnerability levels tend to keep increasing due to the number of people living in the cities. They are also exceedingly unpredictable due to the complexity of city systems, exacerbated by the uncertainty of external variables (Rockefeller Foundation 2014). Resilience is a significant component of the cities' long-term planning and sustainable development (Mitroliou and Kavanaugh 2015). As cities all over the world are facing numerous risks and vulnerabilities posed in particular by climate change, natural disasters, and economic recession, the terms "resilient city" and "city resilience" have emerged

Gamification for Resilience: Resilient Informed Decision-Making, First Edition.
Adrian V. Gheorghe and Polinpapilinho F. Katina.
© 2023 John Wiley & Sons, Inc. Published 2023 by John Wiley & Sons, Inc.

over recent years in response to the need for more security and protection (ARUP 2012). These terms refer to cities that can withstand and recover from any disturbance or disruption of unexpected events while maintaining their essential functions, structures, and identity.

However, the current efforts on the subject are more likely to be practical or feasible in the short term, as they only seek to improve existing technological and infrastructural systems by evidence from past experiences (Yanez and Kernaghan 2014). In other words, climate change, disease pandemics, economic fluctuations, and terrorist attacks are not a set of threatening events in which simplistic implementation or remediation plans can provide the city with sustainable and resilient solutions. And yet ARUP (2012) suggest that applying the concept of resilience to cities requires different sets of professional and practical entry points, especially different scales of multiple collaborations. These approaches would create a severe challenge in clearly defining city resilience in a way that can be succinctly communicated and cautiously implemented.

Under these circumstances, the analysis and assessment of risks and vulnerabilities will continue to play essential roles in planning and developing existing and next-generation critical infrastructure (CI) systems. Additionally, stakeholders, including governments, donors, investors, and policy-makers, must also ensure that their investments, strategies, regulation, and decisions will reduce or even eliminate the potential risks and vulnerabilities and enhance the city's resilience. Thus, it is a crucial moment that a concept of resilience is not only needed to enlighten the development direction of cities, but a resilience-based action is also required to ensure the performability and capability of city systems in the future (Yanez and Kernaghan 2014).

2.2 Critical Infrastructures at Risk

CIs represent systems and services, whether physical or virtual, so vital and ubiquitous to the nation that their destruction or incapacitation would cause a debilitating effect on national security, economy, safety, healthcare, or any combination of those matters (US Department of Homeland Security 2013). The high level of development and functionality in human society assumes a longer list of CI systems and a more severe dependence on them and interdependence among them. According to the US Department of Homeland Security (US Department of Homeland Security 2009, 2013), the most notable CI systems include chemicals, commercial facilities, communications, critical manufacturing, dams, defense industrial bases, emergency services, energy, financial services, food and agriculture, government facilities, healthcare and public health, information technology, nuclear reactors – materials – waste, transportation systems, and water supply and wastewater systems.

Over the last decades, the advancements in CI systems, such as current information, cloud technology, clean energy, intelligent transportation systems, and better healthcare systems, have significantly changed human and societal well-being (Moteff 2005). Many new inventions and technologies have aided the world with comfort and convenience available daily; society has become dependent upon them to survive. CI systems, however, can have service interruptions for many reasons. A service interruption to any infrastructure system would have a more or less negative impact on the typical functionality of society. The Internet, for instance, is now an integral part of human life and business activities. An unexpected interruption with its service would result in disruption to everyday routines or operations. CI systems in the digital era are indispensable. They support various national activities, from food and agricultural production to electricity and power generation. Table 2.1 provides a collection of more or less formal definitions for CIs.

CIs are essential to modern society and provide goods and services that enable the maintenance and sustainment of public well-being, including public safety, economic vitality, and security.

Table 2.1 Defining features for CIs.

Author(s)	Perspectives on infrastructures
US Congress 2001, p. 115 Stat. 401	... systems and assets, whether physical or virtual, so vital to the United States that the incapacity or destruction of such systems and assets would have a debilitating impact on security, national economic security, national public health or safety, or any combination of those matters
European Council 2004, p. 3	... consist of those physical and information technology facilities, networks, services and assets which, if disrupted or destroyed, would have a serious impact on the health, safety, security or economic well-being of citizens or the effective functioning of governments in the Member States
Germany Federal Ministry of the Interior, FRG 2009, p. 4	... organizational and physical structures and facilities of such vital importance to a nation's society and economy that their failure or degradation would result in sustained supply shortages, significant disruption of public safety and security, or other dramatic consequences
Clinton 1996, p. 37347	... are so vital that their incapacity or destruction would have a debilitating impact on the defense or economic security of the United States
Zio 2016, p. 99	... large scale, man-made systems that function interdependently to produce and distribute essential goods (such as energy, water and data) and services (such as transportation, banking and healthcare). An infrastructure is termed critical if its incapacity or destruction has a significant impact on health, safety, security, economics and social well-being
Gheorghe et al. 2006, p. 5	Infrastructures are critical because they provide services that are vital to one or more broad governmental or societal functions or attributes. This can be related to survivability of citizens as far as the safety of their life is concerned, or to their quality of life
Gheorghe and Katina 2014, p. 195	The domain of critical infrastructures deals with engineering systems which are characterized by a high degree of technical complexity, social intricacy, and elaborate processes, aimed at fulfilling important functions in the society
Calida and Katina 2012, p. 87	... current approach to CI protection and mitigation primarily focuses on large malicious and cataclysmic events of terrorism, cyber-attacks, and natural events... [there is] ... need to understand the slow, evolving, and inane events that could accumulate into significant events over-time

Discussions concerning the deterioration of public works have always dominated infrastructure. Additionally, Vaughan and Pollard (1984) postulated that public well-being depended on services provided by roads, bridges, water and sewer systems, airports, ports, public buildings, schools, health facilities, jails, recreation facilities, electric power production, fire safety, solid waste disposal, and telecommunications infrastructures. However, the increasing occurrences of man-made events (e.g. acts of terrorism) have resulted in widening concerns in the infrastructure field.

The increasing focus on natural events (i.e. hurricanes, floods, tornados, earthquakes, heat waves, and pandemics), as well as man-made events (i.e. theft and vandalism, acts of terrorism, and sabotage), has led to multiple legislative actions (e.g. President's Commision of Critical Infrastructure Protection (PCCIP) of 1996, Presidential Decision Directive No. 63 of 1998, and the European Programme for Critical Infrastructure Protection of 2004). These legislative actions have protected CIs and the beneficiaries of their continued operation, including owners, operators, and consumers. At the most fundamental level, an effective paradigm for infrastructures must establish the conceptual underpinnings and provide the foundation for the future coherent development of the field. In effect, this foundation must offer a reference base from which coherence and identity for the field can reside. However, we presently question whether this foundation can be definitively identified for the CI field. This suggestion stems from our analysis of the current state of the CI field, summarized with the following assertions:

- CIs encompass *physical (hard) systems* such as roads and highways, hospitals, electrical systems, and water systems (Moteff et al. 2003; The White House 2003) and *soft systems* such as supervisory control and data acquisition (SCADA) and information and telecommunication systems (GAO 2004; Masera et al. 2006).
- Threats to the sustained performance of CIs stem from natural events such as earthquakes, hurricanes, and heat waves, as well as man-made acts such as human error, accidents, terrorism, and sabotage (Kröger and Zio 2011).
- CIs operate primarily in the *open* and therefore are exposed in ways that make them vulnerable and susceptible to attacks (Wolf et al. 2011).
- Ubiquitous computing and the increasing use of information technologies create *interdependencies* among infrastructures (Anderson 2002; Katina et al. 2014; Kröger and Zio 2011). These interdependencies increase the probability that the seemingly isolated and inane events can cause cascading failures away from the point of origin (Calida and Katina 2012).
- As modern society evolves, creating new *social changes* (e.g. demand for quality products, goods, and services, globalization, and private–public governance policies), traditional concepts of protection, management, and controlling of infrastructures are also evolving (Klaver et al. 2008; Masera et al. 2006).
- Infrastructure systems are critical because daily societal activities revolve around their *continued operations*. The distinction between critical and non-critical infrastructures can be difficult to pinpoint, especially since the goods and services they provide are always restored as quickly as possible to support public well-being (Macaulay 2009).

However, societal changes continue to shape the field and the meaning of the term *CIs*. For example, infrastructures identified as critical in the 1996 PCCIP include "telecommunications, electrical power systems, gas and oil storage and transportation, banking and finance, transportation, water supply systems, emergency services (including medical, police, fire, and rescue), and continuity of government" (Clinton 1996, p. 37347). Subsequently, the Homeland Security Presidential Directive (HSPD-7), which was issued in 2003, identified *terrorism* as its area of focus and introduced the notions of *key resources*, *public morale*, and *confidence* as significant elements that can have a debilitating impact on society's well-being (The White House 2003). Moreover, previously unidentified elements (sectors) such as chemical and hazardous, and postal and shipping industries are now characterized as *critical* (The White House 2003). These shifts are not surprising considering the still early stages of an emerging CI field.

Most recently, national monuments, icons, dams, and critical manufacturing have been identified as *critical* under an annex to the National Infrastructure Protection Plan (Obama 2013; Thorsen and Keil 2013). The broadening of the term *CIs* is also evident in the Patriot Act of 2001 when compared to the 1996 PCCIP. The Patriot Act is concerned with "security, national economic security, national public health or safety, or any combination of those matters" (US Congress 2001, p. 115 Stat. 401), although conversely, PCCIP was mainly concerned with "defense or economic security" (Clinton 1996, p. 37347) of the United States. Again, the palpable shifting landscape of CI can be seen through the expanding boundaries of evolving perspectives as well as legislative actions.

Furthermore, the CI field encompasses the notion of *soft* targets within infrastructures brought about by computing and information technologies. Ubiquitous computing and omnipresent information technologies connect infrastructures and transform them into interdependent systems (Cavelty 2007a, 2007b; Rinaldi et al. 2001). This has created a new landscape for cyber-battles with potentially faceless agents and organizations seeking to exploit vulnerabilities in susceptible cyber and physical infrastructures. Access to cheap computing power, use of software-based control systems, and applying commercial off-the-shelf technologies are essential in maintaining and serving CIs. However, Cavelty (2007b) suggests that this also represents a source of threat to the availability of goods and services of infrastructures due to lack of security. A challenge for modern society is ensuring that computing and information systems such as SCADA do not become an Achilles' heel as exploiting vulnerabilities in information systems continues to become a preferred mode of attack against well-fortified CIs. The expansion of CI to include information represents another major evolution of the field, further expanding both the boundaries and interconnectedness of the CI field.

In the abovementioned discussion, we introduced *situation-based CIs*. Situation-based CIs encompass taken-for-granted systems that become critical due to increased need after an adverse event (e.g. a pandemic) – planned or otherwise. An example is technology platforms such as Zoom. That was demonstrated dramatically on Monday, August 24, 2020, when a widespread outage blocked many users from accessing Zoom. Just before 6 a.m. Pacific time, the company acknowledged the problem in a statement: "We are currently investigating and will provide updates as we have them." An hour later, Zoom said that it had "identified the issue" and was "working on a fix." Finally, over three hours after it first acknowledged the problem, Zoom announced, "We have resolved the issue." A single California-based company, Zoom, is now the foundation for education access from elementary school to graduate school. It has also become a critical tool for many businesses. When Zoom goes down, teachers can't teach, students can't learn, and business meetings, conferences, and webinars grind to a halt (Villasenor 2020).

Zoom, one of many social platforms, is not unique in being classified within the situation-based CIs – this conclusion is supported by other recent events as well as their implications on public well-being, including public safety, economic vitality, and security (Clancy and Frye 2020). Consider the Twitter hacks of July 15, 2020, targeting accounts of well-known national figures, including Joe Biden, Elon Musk, and leaders at Twitter, Uber, Apple, and other companies are simply part of a long history of security breaches and scandals targeting social media platforms. With millions of people being forced to stay home to help stop the spread of COVID-19, many have found creative ways to keep social through happy hours virtually, trivia nights, and birthday parties. And Zoom, one of the dozens of video conferencing services, has risen to the top, thanks to extreme separation measures and a profound resonance within this new social distancing culture.

Daily downloads of the Zoom app have increased by thirty times year-over-year, and the app has been the top free app for iPhones in the United States since March 18, 2020 according to Bernstein Research and Apptopia. Zoom said daily users spiked to 200 million in March 2020, up from 10 million in December of the previous year. But it hasn't been without scrutiny. Privacy concerns have been rising around Zoom, including "Zoombombing," where a malicious user will join a Zoom meeting and show explicit or disturbing images. CEO Eric Yuan apologized for the security lapses and outlined what the company is doing to fix those problems. From the inception of the CI field, we can draw three essential points:

- The boundaries of what is considered to be CI will continue to evolve, encompassing an ever-increasing array of elements, actors, and events.
- The interconnectedness of different elements, actors, and events continues to escalate in importance.
- The incompleteness of singular perspectives (e.g. legislative) for framing and responding to CI issues might continue to limit the development of the field.

Therefore, where the inception of the CI field provides a vital grounding insight into the context from which the field's current state has evolved, there remains a need for continued research into methods, tools, and approaches for assessing, evaluating, protecting, and mitigating consequences in this evolving domain.

Moreover, the interconnection and interdependence between CI systems allow participants greater control, faster response times, and more information access than traditional (simple) system models. However, with such a high level of interconnection and interdependence, it is hard to determine where exactly one system ends and another begins (Gheorghe et al. 2006). The overlapping characterizations of CIs have developed to the level of risk and vulnerability inherent in any system, which requires a comprehensive and elaborate study on the subject to determine their long-term ramifications. Every possible risk and vulnerability to CI systems needs to be individually considered, measured, and addressed to prepare the implementation plan (Gheorghe 2005). The complexity of CI systems means that complete analysis and assessment for their typical operating scenarios is required, for example, how they are supposed to function daily and especially how they are expected to perform in specific circumstances or events. Systems are also needed for extensive evaluation on how vulnerable they are to interruption due to failure from risk or perhaps due to malice from terrorists or those with malicious intent (Gheorghe et al. 2006).

Currently, CI systems are exposed to multiple threats or catastrophic events, including climate change, natural disasters, institutional or regulatory changes, and terrorist attacks, which pose risks and vulnerabilities. They are highly interconnected, interdependent, and embedded in a socio-technical system of systems; therefore, it is even more challenging to predict how a crisis might evolve or what systems would be affected (Gheorghe et al. 2006). As Rinaldi (2004) stated that "CIs have become increasingly interdependent," in the meantime, human life quality and economic prosperity have also become more dependent on their functioning (Gheorghe 2005; Moteff 2005). Indeed, their reliability and safety level should come as the top priority. Table 2.2 is adapted from Katina et al. (2014) and summarizes infrastructure interdependencies describing system relationships.

Table 2.2 Types of CI interdependencies.

Interdependency type	Relevant themes	Implications for infrastructure development
Physical interdependency	This is a relationship that "arises from the physical linkage between the inputs and outputs of two agents [where the] commodity produced or modified by one infrastructure (an output) is required by another infrastructure for it to operate (an input)" (Rinaldi et al. 2001, p. 15) such as drinking water and electricity.	A consideration of external systems' direct and physical influence, including outputs, products, goods, and services to a system of interest. For example, an operator of a water system should be concerned with risks in the electrical grid since the availability of clean drinking water is physically dependent on the electricity used in water treatment.
Cyber interdependency	A relationship based on the ubiquitous and pervasive use of information and communications technologies (ICT). Many critical systems provide essential goods and services with the help of control systems such as supervisory control and data acquisition (SCADA) systems that remotely monitor, and control operations using coded signals over ICT communication channels (Katina et al. 2016; Rinaldi et al. 2001).	A consideration of cyber interdependency could enable one to examine the nature of reliance on ICT within a given scenario. This analysis might include an overview of cyber aspects of a system including an articulation of relation between internal and extern systems, processes monitored and controlled, types of SCADA architectures deployed (i.e. 1st generation, 2nd generation, 3rd generation, 4th generation), and cyber-related risks as well as countermeasures.

Table 2.2 (Continued)

Interdependency type	Relevant themes	Implications for infrastructure development
Geographical interdependency	This is a relationship that exists when different infrastructure systems share the same environment such as electrical power lines that share the same corridor with a bridge (DiSera and Brooks 2009; Katina et al. 2014).	This involves a consideration of geographical interdependencies associated with the need for a common environment that typically enables coupling of infrastructure systems. Coupling creates a situation in which an attack on one is an attack to all. For example, a destruction of a bridge affects electricity transmission, if there is a shared corridor.
Logical interdependency	A logical interdependency exists between infrastructures if the state of each infrastructure depends on the state of the other via some mechanism that is neither physical, cyber, nor geographical (Rinaldi 2004) such as power deregulation policy.	An exploration into "other mechanisms" beyond physical, cyber, and geography. Other mechanisms could involve the role of time, space, perception, and geo-politics.
Policy and/or procedural interdependency	This is a "hidden" and not-so-obvious relationship that only becomes apparent after a change, in the form of a policy and/procedure that takes effect in one part of the system. For example, several regulations that were issued in the wake of the 9/11 attacks affected all air transport systems, changing the flying experience (Mendonca and Wallace 2006).	Attempts to feedforward and the development of scenarios that might offer insights into how quality of goods and services could be influenced by changes in policy at national, state, regional, and local level. The intent of such efforts is the discovery of possible direct effects of changes as well as "unintended" consequences on critical infrastructures.
Societal interdependency	Societal interdependency is a situation in which infrastructure operations are affected by public opinion. For example, after the 9/11 attacks, air traffic was reduced due to the public's evaluation of travel safety, resulting in job cuts and bankruptcies (Dudenhoeffer et al. 2006; Katina et al. 2014).	This analysis involves examination of public opinion on critical topics as they relate to infrastructure goods, services, and operations. The intent of such efforts is an attempt to understand the impact of infrastructure operations. This might include, for example, understanding public perception of emerging concepts, for example, Smart Grids.

Safeguards against single-point failures generally depend on the proper functioning of the rest of the national infrastructure, a plausible assumption for high-reliability infrastructure systems when they experience random, uncorrelated single-point failures (Georgescu et al. 2019). Single-point losses can be anticipated in the design of infrastructure systems. The planning for multiple failures, particularly when they are closely correlated in time, is much less common, yet this is where CI systems operate – *a scenario with the loss of hundreds or even thousands of nodes across all the critical national infrastructures, all simultaneously.* Particularly difficult to anticipate are situations in which simultaneous failures can bring dormant and previously hidden interaction pathways, in which a destructively synergistic amplification of failure, normally locally contained, may be propagated through the network at large (Foster et al. 2008). In particular, Charles Perrow has drawn attention to these types of failures, which he has termed *normal accidents*, and which are posited as an inherent property of any tightly coupled system once a threshold of complexity has been passed (Perrow 1999).

The multitude and variety of nodes and links in these networks, the operations and services deployed, and the hosts of owners, operators, suppliers, and users involved have created enormously convoluted constructs. The intricacy of infrastructures limits understanding of their behavior and, consequently, the options to control and steer the processes involved effectively. There is an urgent need to generate more systematic knowledge of these complex systems if one is to handle the many threats and vulnerabilities adequately. In this case, one might argue in support of Arbesman (Arbesman 2016, p. 2):

> Our technologies – from websites and trading systems to urban infrastructures, scientific models, and even the supply chains and logistics that power large businesses – have become hopelessly interconnected and overcomplicated, such that in many cases even those who build and maintain then [sic] on a daily basis can't fully understand them any longer.

The aforementioned statement should not come as a surprise, given the increasing number of failures associated with such systems. Critical infrastructure protection (CIP) has emerged as a means to provide a comprehensive framework for managing such systems. CIP needs to involve stakeholder models, agent-principal models, decision-making models, public-private partnerships with attendant legislation, lines of communication and feedback, security standards, technical systems, security culture, modeling, and simulation capabilities. It is thus, not a surprise that CI work with several closed-related concepts, the most important of which are (Georgescu et al. 2019; Hokstad et al. 2012; Johnson and Gheorghe 2013; Katina and Hester 2013):

- *Antifragility:* a system's ability to withstand stressors is, to a certain degree, a function of previous exposures to manageable stresses. A clear example can be found in the area of terrestrial and space infrastructure systems, where the various damages caused by recurring high levels of "space weather" activity have served to highlight the need for robustness and redundancy. The incremental improvement in their systemic resilience will be invaluable in the face of expected peak events that would otherwise be guaranteed to have devastating consequences.
- *Fragility:* fragility and vulnerability are similar but have critical differences, the first being endogenous and the second exogenous. Vulnerable systems fail because of their degree of exposure to the stress of a specific nature, while fragile systems fail because they are easily broken regardless of the nature of stress they are exposed to.
- *Rapidity:* another closely linked concept to resilience, it is a system's ability to recover from an undesired event as measured by the speed of recovery.
- *Reliability:* reliability points to a system or a component's ability to perform the predefined required functions. Reliability is measured in terms of the probability that a system or a component is able to perform its required function at a given point in time or over a given period of time for a given set of conditions which may be at the extreme end of specified limits.
- *Resilience:* the ability of a system to react and recover from unanticipated disturbances and events. The concept has gained in popularity in recent years and is now viewed as the ultimate goal of CIP processes, implying the minimization of damages and the rapid restoration of normal functions.
- *Risk analysis:* a process of identifying potential hazards based on the severity of consequence and likelihood of occurrence. The intent is to sort potential hazards and prioritize them for action based on objective criteria. One method is to grade likelihood and consequence on various scales.
- *Robustness:* closely linked to resilience, it is a system's ability to withstand a certain amount of stress with respect to the loss of function of the system.

- *Vulnerability:* a vulnerable system is open to losing its design functions. Vulnerability can then be taken as the degree to which a system, subsystem, or component is in situations where it is exposed to those specific hazards that would be harmful or damaging to the system. The focus in a vulnerability analysis moves away from the possibility that adverse events occur to system properties determining how easy it is to eliminate major system functions.
- *Governance:* there is not just one definition of "governance." Many of the various perspectives are driven by the nature of the systems and interest and system operations, or rather in-operability in such systems. Following Calida (2013) and the subsequent works (Calida and Keating 2014; Keating et al. 2014), Table 2.3 depicts the multitude of perspectives on governance; showing that there is a large spectrum of views on this topic. For CI, governance implies direction, oversight, and accountability (Katina and Keating 2015).

Table 2.3 Different perspectives on governance.

Governance type	Description	Proponents
Process-centric	A governing arrangement where one or more public agencies directly engage non-state stakeholders in a collective decision-making process that is formal, consensus-oriented, and deliberative and that aims to make or implement public policy or manage public programs or assets	Ansell and Gash 2008, p. 544
	... social turbulence kept within bounds, and change steered in desired directions ... preserves order and continuity, but not necessarily the maintenance of the status quo	Dunsire 1990, p. 18
Structure-centric	... the totality of conceptual ideas about these Interactions ... (these in relation to the act of governing)	Kooiman 2003, p. 79
	... the activity of coordinating communications in order to achieve collective goals through collaboration	Willke 2007, p. 10
State-centric	... the process through which state and nonstate actors interact to design and implement policies within a given set of formal and informal rules that shape and are shaped by power ...	The World Bank 2017, p. 3
Hybrid	... the reflexive self-organization of independent actors involved in complex relations of reciprocal interdependence, with such self-organization being based on continuing dialogue and resource-sharing to develop mutually beneficial joint projects and to manage the contradictions and dilemmas inevitably involved in such situations	Jessop 2003, p.142
	... interdependence between organizations ... continuing interactions between network members, caused by the need to exchange resources and negotiate shared purposes ... game-like interactions, rooted in trust and regulated by rules of the game negotiated and agreed by network participants ... a significant degree of autonomy; they are self-organizing	Rhodes 2007, p. 1246
Corporate governance	... the system of checks and balances, both internal and external to companies, which ensures that companies discharge their accountability to all their stakeholders and act in a socially responsible way in all areas of their business activity	Solomon and Brennan 2008, p. 890
New public management	... the means for achieving direction, control, and coordination of wholly or partially autonomous individuals or organizations on behalf of interests to which they jointly contribute	Lynn et al. 2000, p. 235
Public policy	... the ways in which stakeholders interact with each other in order to influence the outcomes of public policies	Bovaird 2005, p. 220
	... the processes and institutions, both formal and informal, that guide and restrain the collective activities of a group	Nye et al. 2000

(Continued)

Table 2.3 (Continued)

Governance type	Description	Proponents
International security	... the emergence and recognition of principles, norms, rules and behavior that both provide standards of acceptable public behavior and that are followed sufficiently to produce behavioral regularities	Keohane and Nye 1977
Social and political	Governance denotes the structures and processes which enable a set of public and private actors to coordinate their interdependent needs and interests through the making and implementation of binding policy decisions in the absence of a central political authority	Krahmann 2003, p. 11
	... arrangements in which public as well as private actors aim at solving societal problems or create societal opportunities, and aim at the care for the societal institutions within which these governing activities take place	Kooiman 2000, p. 139
Earth	... the interrelated and increasingly integrated system of formal and informal rules, rule-making systems, and actor-networks at all levels of human society (from local to global) that are set up to steer societies towards preventing, mitigating, and adapting to global and local environmental change and, in particular, earth system transformation, within the normative context of sustainable development	Biermann et al. 2009

Any of the above can (and should) generate a robust discussion in the context of CI systems. The present volume, however, emphasizes the development of resilient cities through gamification.

2.3 Critical Infrastructure Resiliency

Again, CI systems are networks of complex systems that provide essential services to a population or nation. The systems are complex by nature because they are widely distributed across large geographical regions and are becoming increasingly interconnected and interdependent as they evolve, boosting the potential for risk and vulnerability. And yet, there is a scarcity of practical approaches to quantify vulnerability in CIs. In previous research (see Gheorghe et al. 2018), the proposed model offered: (i) a two-parameter description of the vulnerability and the respective equation of the state of the system: "operable" and "inoperable;" (ii) a division of the two-parameter phase space of the system into "vulnerability basins;" and (iii) a scale of 0–100 "vulnerability" and the means to measure the respective "vulnerability index." In essence, the proposed method can offer the ability to diagnose current system vulnerability. The technique uses an extensive set of indicators involving internal and external elements with the capability to monitor the time-evolvement of the vulnerability as change occurs dynamically.

Risks and vulnerability may seem separate, but they are fundamentally interrelated concepts that have broad implications for CI systems. Risk, technically, refers to a measure of the probability and severity of undesirable outcomes (adverse effects) resulting from a threat, incident, event, or occurrence to the system. More specifically, it is a combination of the likelihood of an event occurring and the consequences of the event. Probability is a measure of the uncertainty of occurrence of the event or scenario that initiates the event, while a consequence is represented as levels of severity (Aven 2010). Risk quantification in this manner is intentionally used both as an analysis and design tool. For an analysis tool, risk assessment can begin with presumed scenarios that are considered threats against continued operation or system performance to discover the system's weaknesses. As a design tool, reliability values can be applied to system functions based on their malfunctioning or failure state where misleading data is generated from the system's purposes without detection (Gheorghe and Yuchnovicz 2015). So much so that by developing risk analysis to set reliability design goals, the attempts would deliberately lead to better design of resilient systems, which respectively make CI systems less susceptible to threats.

On the other hand, vulnerability is "a fault or weakness that reduces or limits a system's ability to withstand a threat or to resume a new stable condition" (Aven 2007). Based on this definition, a threat is an event or scenario with an associated uncertainty (probability of occurrence) and corresponding consequence (level of severity). CI systems are becoming so complex that they can be vulnerable to various events based on their system characteristics and intended functions. Vulnerability analysis and assessment can unveil the events that can be harmful to a system, and must be conducted in all phases of operation and system configurations. Risk analysis and assessment of these events will allow further quantification of the events regarding uncertainty and the consequence of occurrence regarding severity. Overall knowledge of risk and vulnerability assessments will help to prioritize risk mitigation efforts.

For more than a decade, CI systems protection and resilience have received serious attention from public and private sectors, including government, academic institutions, and profit and non-profit research foundations. It has also become a national top priority mission in most developed countries (US Department of Homeland Security 2013). Nevertheless, the sheer complexity of CI systems has shifted the degree of investigation to a level where much more comprehensive research on the subject is significantly imperative. The basic study of essential systems of infrastructure resilience framework is now moving toward the discipline of modeling and simulation to determine system sustainment and future development direction. For instance, Kröger (2008) strongly asserts that to successfully develop the vulnerability reduction model for CI systems, the risk management, and risk governance strategies must be clearly defined. Second, advanced object-oriented programming and simulation tools are needed to analyze and assess.

2.4 Concluding Remarks

Decision-making is a fundamental part of human life. Decisions can be made quickly and efficiently when the objectives are clear, the information necessary to evaluate alternatives is available, and the outcomes of decisions can be accurately predicted. However, as the complexity of the decision increases, the decision-making process becomes more difficult because of the number of factors that must be considered for the analysis. In other words, the decision is directly related to the value assigned to its consequences or results, especially when it involves large-scale complex systems and can significantly impact the population or a nation. In this case, Risk-Informed Decision-Making Process (RIDMP) is a method that was designed to fulfill this gap. This technique intends that whenever there is a significant decision between design alternatives, the process can inform decision-makers about the risk involved in each alternative (Zio and Pedroni 2012).

According to the National Aeronautics and Space Administration (NASA, 2010), RIDMP is a fundamentally deliberative process that uses diverse performance measures and other considerations to inform decision-making. This approach combines the input of stakeholders as well as cost and feasibility and then focuses on informing the decision makers (NASA 2010; Zio and Pedroni 2012). With this applicability, a decision can be made with considerations beyond just technical information. Unfortunately, one issue with RIDMP is that it is impossible to include or evaluate every risk for each alternative in all decision-making situations. There are insufficient resources to assess all risks, especially for decisions involving complexly interconnected and interdependent systems. Also, even if enough resources were available, there would always be unforeseen or unknown risks constantly emerging due to the operation and evolution of the systems and their environment. In recent years, resilient governance has rapidly received more attention and popularity in academic and industrial societies. This paradigm is now shifting from the risk and vulnerability perspective to the view of resilience (Mitchell 2013). For this reason, resilience should also be included as part of the decision-making process in what would be called the "Resilience-Informed Decision-Making Process (ReIDMP)."

ReIDMP could simply be taken as an extended version of RIDMP. However, the concept of resilience is considered instead of looking at risk. This idea seems partially correct because, in reality, there are apparent differences. To be more specific, RIDMP focuses on identifying and understanding every risk and vulnerability in all possible aspects and then selecting the best alternative to prevent those potential risks and vulnerabilities. ReIDMP should focus on a comprehensive study of the effectiveness of selected alternatives based on the ability to recover. So much so that an informed decision can be made concerning striving for a resilient solution. A step further would be to analyze and assess the ability of the system to anticipate, absorb, restore, and adapt to the effects of catastrophic and threatening events in a timely and efficient manner (Mitchell and Harris 2012). ReIDMP has required a completed analysis of all the alternatives evaluated during the decision-making process.

We suggest that when policy-makers are armed with resilience-based action approaches, they can select the most effective and viable solution to resilient issues. Meantime, the ReIDMP may also provide other benefits since it can enhance the analysis and deliberation results of alternatives. For instance, there may be some situations where an option can be selected if additional required actions are done to improve infrastructure resilience. Furthermore, as the population of the world continues to grow, the demand for essential services and facilities will continue to increase. It's no surprise that the trend is expected to be on sustainable and resilient development to address present issues without compromising the need of the next generations. CI systems are at the heart of this discussion. To enable making decisions on how to increase the resilience of CI systems and drive down risk and vulnerability, an in-depth analysis needs to be performed to define the primary areas of investment. The essential resources are limited; therefore, the selection of knowledge to focus on should be carefully made to prevent expending the resources in a way that minimizes CIs. In particular, education and experience are keys to ensuring CI systems resilience. The true meaning of resilience is that engineering managers and systems engineers are correctly educated about the risks, vulnerabilities, and hazards that essential systems of infrastructure may face and what to do in catastrophic events. CI systems that are better prepared to deal with events like natural disasters and terrorist attacks will have a better chance of quicker recovery. The remainder of this book expounds on the means to develop a *resilience quantification platform based on an informed decision-making process* resulting in better understanding and guidance on sustainable and resilient development of CI systems. Simultaneously, gamification, as part of "serious gaming," and "SimCity 2013*" are introduced as means for teaching and learning concepts of risks and vulnerability.

2.5 Exercises

1 Discuss the relevance of CI systems.
2 Discuss emerging risks and their possible impacts on the functionality of CI systems.
3 Why is resilience a relevant aspect of managing infrastructure systems?
4 Discuss the critical attributes of resilience in CI systems.
5 How can governance be related to risk and vulnerability in infrastructure systems?

References

Anderson, P.S. (2002). Critical infrastructure protection in the information age. In : *Networking Knowledge for Information Societies: Institutions & Intervention* (ed. R. Mansell, R. Samarajiva, and A. Mahan), pp. 188–194. DUP Science, Delft University Press.

Ansell, C. and Gash, A. (2008). Collaborative governance in theory and practice. *Journal of Public Administration Research and Theory* 18(4): 543–571. https://doi.org/10.1093/jopart/mum032.

Arbesman, S. (2016). *Overcomplicated: Technology at the Limits of Comprehension*. Current.

ARUP. (2012). *Visions of a Resilient City*. Engineers Without Borders-UK. https://www.arup.com/en/perspectives/publications/research/section/visions-of-a-resilient-city.

Aven, T. (2007). A unified framework for risk and vulnerability analysis covering both safety and security. *Reliability Engineering and System Safety* 92(6): 745–754.

Aven, T. (2010). On how to define, understand and describe risk. *Reliability Engineering & System Safety* 95(6): 623–631. https://doi.org/10.1016/j.ress.2010.01.011.

Biermann, F., Betsill, M.M., Gupta, J. et al. (2009). *Earth System Governance: People, Places and the Planet. Science and Implementation Plan of the Earth System Governance Project* (Earth system governance report 1, IHDP report 20). IHDP: The Earth System Governance Project. http://www.earthsystemgovernance.org/sites/default/files/publications/files/Earth-System-Governance_Science-Plan.pdf.

Bovaird, T. (2005). Public governance: Balancing stakeholder power in a network society. *International Review of Administrative Sciences* 71(2): 217–228. https://doi.org/10.1177/0020852305053881.

Calida, B.Y. (2013). *System Governance Analysis of Complex Systems* PhD., Old Dominion University. http://search.proquest.com.proxy.lib.odu.edu/pqdtlocal1005724/docview/1508276628/abstract/FDE683C1495948B1PQ/1?accountid=12967.

Calida, B.Y. and Katina, P.F. (2012). Regional industries as critical infrastructures: A tale of two modern cities. *International Journal of Critical Infrastructures* 8(1): 74–90. https://doi.org/10.1504/IJCIS.2012.046555.

Calida, B.Y. and Keating, C.B. (2014). System governance: Emergence of practical perspectives across the disciplines. In: *Infranomics* (ed. A.V. Gheorghe, M. Masera, and P.F. Katina.), pp. 269–296. Springer International Publishing. http://link.springer.com/chapter/10.1007/978-3-319-02493-6_18.

Cavelty, M. (2007a). *Cyber-security and Threat Politics: US Efforts to Secure the Information Age*. Routledge. http://www.loc.gov/catdir/toc/ecip0719/2007022679.html.

Cavelty, M.D. (2007b). Critical information infrastructure: Vulnerabilities, threats and responses. In: *Disarmament Forum* (ed. K. Vignard), Vol. 3, pp. 15–22. United Nations Institute for Disarmament Research.

Clancy, C. and Frye, E. (27 July 2020). *Is it time to designate social media as "critical infrastructure"?* [Text]. *The Hill*. Nexstar Media Inc. https://thehill.com/opinion/cybersecurity/509154-is-it-time-to-designate-social-media-as-critical-infrastructure.

Clinton, W.J. (1996). Executive order 13010: Critical infrastructure protection. *Federal Register* 61(138): 37345–37350.

European Council. (2004). Communication from the commission to the council and the European parliament: Critical infrastructure protection in the fight against terrorism. (pp. 1–11). Commission of the European Communities. EUR-Lex - 52004DC0702 - EN - EUR-Lex (europa.eu).

DiSera, D. and Brooks, T. (2009). The geospatial dimensions of critical infrastructure and emergency response. *Pipeline and Gas Journal* 236(9): 1–4. https://pgjonline.com/magazine/2009/september-2009-vol-236-no-9/features/the-geospatial-dimensions-of-critical-infrastructure-and-emergency-response.

Dobbs, R., Remes, J., Manyika, J. et al., (2012). Urban world: Cities and the rise of the consuming class. McKinsey and Company. https://www.mckinsey.com/featured-insights/urbanization/urban-world-cities-and-the-rise-of-the-consuming-class.

Dudenhoeffer, D., Permann, M.R., and Manic, M. (2006). CIMS: A framework for infrastructure interdependency modeling and analysis. In: *Proceedings of the 38th Conference on Winter Simulation*, 478–485. IEEE. https://doi.org/10.1109/WSC.2006.323119.

Dunsire, A. (1990). Holistic governance. *Public Policy and Administration* 5(1): 4–19. https://doi.org/10.1177/095207679000500102.

Foster, J.S., Gjelde, E., Graham, W.R. et al. (2008). Report of the commission to assess the threat to the United States from electromagnetic pulse (EMP) attack (No. A2473-EMP). EMP Commission. http://www.empcommission.org/docs/A2473-EMP_Commission-7MB.pdf.

FRG. (2009). National strategy for critical infrastructure protection (pp. 1–18). Federal Ministry of the Interior. http://www.bmi.bund.de/cae/servlet/contentblob/598732/publicationFile/34423/kritis_englisch.pdf.

GAO. (2004). Critical infrastructure protection: Challenges and efforts to secure control systems. (pp. 1–47). US Government Accountability Office.

Georgescu, A., Gheorghe, A.V., Piso, M.-I. et al. (2019). *Critical Space Infrastructures: Risk, Resilience and Complexity*. Springer International Publishing. https://www.springer.com/us/book/9783030126032.

Gheorghe, A., Vamanu, D.V., Katina, P. et al. (2018). *Critical Infrastructures, Key Resources, Key Assets: Risk, Vulnerability, Resilience, Fragility, and Perception Governance* (Vol. 34). Springer International Publishing. https://www.springer.com/us/book/9783319692234.

Gheorghe, A.V. (ed.). (2005). *Integrated Risk and Vulnerability Management Assisted by Decision Support Systems: Relevance and Impact on Governance* (Vol. 8). Springer.

Gheorghe, A.V. and Katina, P.F. (2014). Editorial: Resiliency and engineering systems – research trends and challenges. *International Journal of Critical Infrastructures* 10(3/4): 193–199.

Gheorghe, A.V., Masera, M., Weijnen, M.P.C. et al. (eds.). (2006). *Critical Infrastructures at Risk: Securing the European Electric Power System* (Vol. 9). Springer.

Gheorghe, A.V. and Yuchnovicz, D. (2015). The space infrastructure vulnerability cadastre: Orbital debris critical loads. *International Journal of Disaster Risk Science* 6(4): 359–371. https://doi.org/10.1007/s13753-015-0073-2.

Hokstad, P., Utne, I.B., and Vatn, J. (eds.). (2012). *Risk and Interdependencies in Critical Infrastructures: A Guideline for Analysis*. Springer-Verlag.

Jessop, B. (2003). Governance and metagovernance: On reflexivity, requisite variety, and requisite irony. In: *Governance, as Social and Political Communication* (ed. H.P. Bange), pp. 142–172. Manchester University Press.

Johnson, J. and Gheorghe, A.V. (2013). Antifragility analysis and measurement framework for systems of systems. *International Journal of Disaster Risk Science* 4(4): 159–168. https://doi.org/10.1007/s13753-013-0017-7.

Katina, P.F. and Hester, P.T. (2013). Systemic determination of infrastructure criticality. *International Journal of Critical Infrastructures* 9(3): 211–225. https://doi.org/10.1504/IJCIS.2013.054980.

Katina, P.F. and Keating, C.B. (2015). Critical infrastructures: A perspective from systems of systems. *International Journal of Critical Infrastructures* 11(4): 316–344. https://doi.org/10.1504/IJCIS.2015.073840.

Katina, P.F., Keating, C.B., Zio, E. et al. (2016). A criticality-based approach for the analysis of smart grids. *Technology and Economics of Smart Grids and Sustainable Energy* 1(1): 14. https://doi.org/10.1007/s40866-016-0013-2.

Katina, P.F., Pinto, C.A., Bradley, J.M. et al. (2014). Interdependency-induced risk with applications to healthcare. *International Journal of Critical Infrastructure Protection* 7(1): 12–26. https://doi.org/10.1016/j.ijcip.2014.01.005.

Keating, C.B., Katina, P.F., and Bradley, J.M. (2014). Complex system governance: Concept, challenges, and emerging research. *International Journal of System of Systems Engineering* 5(3): 263–288. https://doi.org/10.1504/IJSSE.2014.065756.

Keohane, R.O. and Nye, J.S. (1977). *Power and Interdependence: World Politics in Transition* (1977 ed.). TBS The Book Service Ltd.

Klaver, M.H.A., Luiijf, H.A.M., Nieuwenhuijs, A.H. et al. (2008). European risk assessment methodology for critical infrastructures. *2008 First International Conference on Infrastructure Systems and Services: Building Networks for a Brighter Future (INFRA)*, 1–5. IEEE. https://doi.org/10.1109/INFRA.2008.5439614.

Kooiman, J. (2000). Societal governance: Levels, models and orders of social-political interaction. In: *Debating Governance* (ed. J. Pierre), pp. 138–166. Oxford University Press.

Kooiman, J. (2003). *Governing as Governance.* SAGE Publications Ltd. https://doi.org/10.4135/9781446215012.

Krahmann, E. (2003). Conceptualizing security governance. *Cooperation and Conflict* 38(1): 5–26. https://doi.org/10.1177/0010836703038001001.

Kröger, W. (2008). Critical infrastructures at risk: A need for a new conceptual approach and extended analytical tools. *Reliability Engineering & System Safety* 93(12): 1781–1787.

Kröger, W. and Zio, E. (2011). *Vulnerable Systems.* Springer-Verlag.

Lynn, L.E., Heinrich, C.J., and Hill, C.J. (2000). Studying governance and public management: Challenges and prospects. *Journal of Public Administration Research and Theory* 10(2): 233–262. https://doi.org/10.1093/oxfordjournals.jpart.a024269.

Macaulay, T. (2009). *Critical Infrastructure: Understanding its Component Parts, Vulnerabilities, Operating Risks, and Interdependencies.* CRC Press.

Masera, M., Stefanini, A., and Dondossola, G. (2006). The security information and communication systems and the E+I paradigm. In: *Critical Infrastructures at Risk: Securing the European Electric Power System* (ed. A.V. Gheorghe, M. Masera, M.P.C. Weijnen et al.), pp. 85–116. Springer.

Mendonca, D. and Wallace, W.A. (2006). Impacts of the 2001 World Trade Center attack on New York city critical infrastructures. *Journal of Infrastructure Systems* 12(4): 260–270. https://doi.org/10.1061/(ASCE)1076-0342(2006)12:4(260).

Mitchell, A. (2013). Risk and resilience: From good idea to good practice. In *OECD Development Co-operation Working Papers* (No. 13; OECD Development Co-Operation Working Papers). OECD Publishing. https://ideas.repec.org/p/oec/dcdaaa/13-en.html.

Mitchell, T. and Harris, K. (2012). *Resilience: A Risk Management Approach – Background Note.* Overseas Development Institute.

Mitroliou, E. and Kavanaugh, L. (2015). Resilient cities report 2015: Global developments in urban adaptation and resilience. *Resilient Cities.* //efaidnbmnnnibpcajpcglclefindmkaj/https://www.cakex.org/sites/default/files/documents/RC2015__Congress_Report__Final.pdf.

Moteff, J. (2005). *Risk Management and Critical Infrastructure Protection: Assessing, Integrating, and Managing Threats, Vulnerabilities and Consequences.* (pp. 1–28). Congressional Research Service . CRS.

Moteff, J.D., Copeland, C., and Fischer, J. (2003). *Critical Infrastructures: What Makes an Infrastructure Critical?* (pp. 1–17). The Library of Congress.

NASA. (2010). *Risk-informed Decision-making Handbook.* NASA Headquarters. https://ntrs.nasa.gov/archive/nasa/casi.ntrs.nasa.gov/20100021361.pdf.

Nye, J.S.J., Nye, J.S., and Donahue, J. D. (2000). *Governance in a Globalizing World* (1st ed.). Brookings Institution Press.

Obama, B.H. (2013). *Critical Infrastructure Security and Resilience.* The White House. http://www.fas.org/irp/offdocs/ppd/ppd-21.pdf.

Perrow, C. (1999). *Normal Accidents: Living with High Risk Technologies.* Princeton University Press.

Rhodes, R.A.W. (2007). Understanding governance: Ten years on. *Organization Studies* 28(8): 1243–1264. https://doi.org/10.1177/0170840607076586.

Rinaldi, S.M. (2004). Modeling and simulating critical infrastructures and their interdependencies. In: *Proceedings of The 37th Annual Hawaii International Conference on System Sciences, 2004,* 1–8. IEEE. https://doi.org/10.1109/HICSS.2004.1265180.

Rinaldi, S.M., Peerenboom, J., and Kelly, T.K. (2001). Identifying, understanding, and analyzing critical infrastructure interdependencies. *IEEE Control Systems* 21(6): 11–25. https://doi.org/10.1109/37.969131.

Rockefeller Foundation. (2014). *City Resilience Framework.* Rockefeller Foundation/ARUP. https://www.rockefellerfoundation.org/wp-content/uploads/City-Resilience-Framework-2015.pdf.

Solomon, J. and Brennan, N.M. (2008). Corporate governance, accountability and mechanisms of accountability: An overview. *Accounting, Auditing & Accountability Journal* 21(7): 885–906. https://doi.org/10.1108/09513570810907401.

Thorsen, K.A. and Keil, T.M. (2013). *National Monuments and Icons Sector-specific Plan: An Annex to the National Infrastructure Protection Plan.* The White House. http://www.dhs.gov/xlibrary/assets/nipp-ssp-national-monuments-icons.pdf.

US Department of Homeland Security. (2013). NIPP 2013: Partnering for Critical Infrastructure Security and Resilience. US Department of Homeland Security. https://www.dhs.gov/publication/nipp-2013-partnering-critical-infrastructure-security-and-resilience?topics=all.

United Nations. (2015). The world population prospects: 2015 revision [report]. UN Department of Economic and Social Affairs. https://www.un.org/en/development/desa/publications/world-population-prospects-2015-revision.html.

United Nations. (2017). The world population prospects: The 2017 revision, key findings and advance tables [report]. UN Department of Economic and Social Affairs. https://www.un.org/development/desa/publications/world-population-prospects-the-2017-revision.html.

United Nations. (2022). The world population prospects 2022: Summary of results (UN DESA/POP/2021/TR/NO. 3). UN Department of Economic and Social Affairs.

US Congress. (2001). Uniting and strengthening America by providing appropriate tools required to intercept and obstruct terrorism (USA PATRIOT ACT) Act of 2001 (No. 147; p. 115 Stat. 271–402). 107th Congress. http://www.gpo.gov/fdsys/pkg/PLAW-107publ56/content-detail.html.

US Department of Homeland Security. (2009). *NIPP 2009: Partnering for critical infrastructure security and resilience.* Retrieved from https://www.cisa.gov/publication/nipp-2009-partnering-enhance-protection-resiliency?topics=all.

Vaughan, R. and Pollard, R. (1984). *Rebuilding America's Infrastructure: An Agenda for the 1980s* (Vol. 1). Council of State Planning Agencies.

Villasenor, J. (27 August 2020). Zoom is now critical infrastructure. *That's a concern.* Brookings. https://www.brookings.edu/blog/techtank/2020/08/27/zoom-is-now-critical-infrastructure-thats-a-concern.

The White House. (2003). *The National Strategy for the Physical Protection of Critical Infrastructures and Key Assets.* The White House. https://www.dhs.gov/xlibrary/assets/Physical_Strategy.pdf.

Willke, H. (2007). *Smart Governance: Governing the Global Knowledge Society.* Campus Verlag GmbH.

Wolf, T., Tessier, R., and Prabhu, G. (2011). Securing the data path of next-generation router systems. *Computer Communications* 34(4): 598–606. http://dx.doi.org/10.1016/j.comcom.2010.03.019.

The World Bank. (2017). World Development Report 2017: Governance and the Law. https://doi.org/10.1596/978-1-4648-0950-7.

Yanez, K. and Kernaghan, S. (2014). Briefing: Visions of a resilient city. In: *Proceedings of the Institution of Civil Engineers – Urban Design and Planning* 167(3): 95–101. Institution of Civil Engineers. https://doi.org/10.1680/udap.13.00013.

Zio, E. (2016). Critical infrastructures vulnerability and risk analysis. *European Journal for Security Research* 1(2): 97–114. https://doi.org/10.1007/s41125-016-0004-2.

Zio, E. and Pedroni, N. (2012). *Overview of Risk-informed Decision-making Processes*. Foundation for an Industrial Safety Culture. https://www.foncsi.org/en/publications/collections/industrial-safety-cahiers/risk-informed-decision-making-processes/CSI-RIDM.pdf.

3

The Need for Systems Resilience

3.1 Introduction

Again, as the world's population continues to grow, so too shall the demand for essential services and facilities. The future trend will focus more and more on an ever-increasing need for sustainable development and resilience frameworks for present and next-generation critical infrastructure (CI) systems. An in-depth analysis needs to be performed to define the primary areas to invest resources. Moreover, this approach can inform means for increasing CI systems' resilience and driving down risk and vulnerability. The essential resources are limited; therefore, the selection of knowledge to focus on should be carefully made to prevent expending the resources in a way that minimizes CI systems. In particular, education and experience are keys to ensuring the resilience of CI systems. In this case, we suggest that the true meaning of resilience is one where engineering managers and systems engineers are correctly educated about the risks, vulnerability, and hazards that CI systems may face and what to do in the occurrence of catastrophic events. CI systems that are better prepared to deal with events like natural disasters and terrorist attacks will have a better chance of quicker recovery. From this perspective, the primary objective of this research is to develop a resilience quantification platform based on an informed decision-making process. The result of the effort is expected to provide a better understanding and guidance on sustainable development and resilience framework for existing and next-generation CI systems. The secondary objective is to introduce an idea of a serious gaming concept as a teaching application at the graduate level and the use of the simulation computer game "SimCity 2013®" as a teaching tool in a way that effectively enhances students' learning experience on risks and vulnerability concepts. Figure 3.1 provides a graphical summary of this research.

3.2 Multiple Facts of Resilience

In a general sense, resilience is thought of as an ability to withstand stress in infrastructure systems. However, resilience is also seen as a "positive adaptation" after a stressful or adverse situation (Hetherington and Elmore 2003). There is even research that suggests that routine stressors of daily life can have positive impacts which promote resilience. Some psychologists believe that it is not the stress that promotes resilience but rather the individual's perception of their stress and

Gamification for Resilience: Resilient Informed Decision-Making, First Edition.
Adrian V. Gheorghe and Polinpapilinho F. Katina.

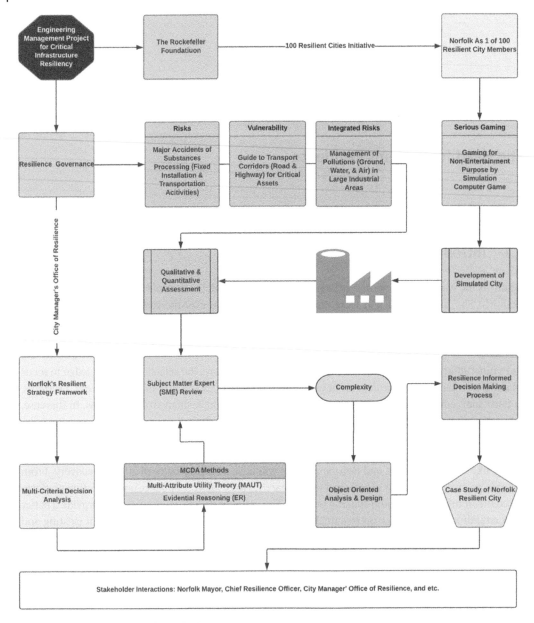

Figure 3.1 Elements of research necessary for developing resilient cities.

their perceived personal level of control (McGonigal 2016). And while the "dosage" of necessary stress to enable resilience is still unknown, what is known is that resilience can take many forms depending on context. The essential context for the present research is articulated.

3.2.1 Definitions of Resilience

According to the Definitions of Community Resilience: An Analysis by Community and Regional Resilience Institute (2013), it verifies that "resilience" is a term that was originally derived from the Latin "resalire" and means "to spring back." It has been becoming a popular term in many fields of study and discipline and is considered one of the most important aspects in the context of achieving sustainable development in the last fifteen years (Folke 2006; Robert et al. 2005; Walker et al. 2004; Westrum 2006). The term resilience was initially introduced and formally used by an ecologist in the 1970s and a psychologist in the 1980s to develop somewhat distinct phenomena (Community and Regional Resilience Institute 2013; Rockefeller Foundation 2014). In an ecological community, the term was applied to describe the capability of an ecosystem to maintain and recover its functionality from the disruption or disturbance of catastrophic events (Folke et al. 2010; Gunderson 2000; Holling 1973). For a psychological society, the term was used to identify a group of test subjects with consistent behaviors in adversity or distress situations (Folke 2006). Even though the conceptualization of resilience has noticeably gained widespread attention from various sectors, including government, academia, and industry, and seriously applies to many areas of past, current, and possible future research and projects, unfortunately, there is no agreement or approval on a universally accepted definition that is used across all fields of study (Vasuthanasub 2019). For this reason, subject reviews present the diversity of developed definitions based on a core concept of resilience.

After the 9/11 attacks in 2001, the term resilience began being earnestly adopted by the government in developed countries to re-examine and re-evaluate their national security, especially in the United States, and also systematically employed by the engineering community to design the protection plans and security frameworks for CI systems. Since then, the core concept has been mostly related to the ability to absorb, recover from, and adapt to hazards (Community and Regional Resilience Institute 2013). Nowadays, resilience has numerous definitions based on its applicability and suitability in the different domains of research communities. Table 3.1 provides a sample of widely recognized definitions of resilience (Community and Regional Resilience Institute 2013).

The above table is meant to highlight the core of the concept of resilience: *How the community should respond to an adverse event.* The debate for the definition is left to others. However, we suggest that the spirit of the definition should follow the core concept's themes and the appropriate context of the discussion/research. Moreover, the Community and Regional Resilience Institute (2013) research suggest that resilience can be metaphorical, as in "resistibility and adaptability." Many ontological definitions begin with "The ability" or "The capability" of entities, organizations, or societies and then reflect the idea of "resistance vs. adaptation" to cope with shocks and stresses (Walker et al. 2004). That is to say, a system resists the threat to avoid change, and its resilience is determined by how much difficulty it can withstand and endure without collapsing. In contrast, a system can adapt to great danger by altering its functionality or spending resources in preservative ways (Anderies et al. 2004).

Another way to classify resilience is through the notion of "predictability." Because some of the developed definitions partially borrow from different fields of a research community, therefore, the definitions in this environment often can be referred to as a prediction on how long and how well a system will be able to regain its intended functions compared to the others (Holling 1996). While this classification may be useful (and appropriate) for making predictions, it lends resilience to an issue that can only be applicable after an occurrence of an event (Butler et al. 2007).

Resilience can also be viewed in the context of "trajectory." As has been noted, since ecologists firstly utilized the terminology, most of the derived definitions in an ecological domain are typically focused on whether or not a system evolves in difficult circumstances and do not try to evaluate whether the change is an innovation or deterioration (Folke et al. 2010). This definition offers a more straightforward view of resilience: If the system can survive stressful situations, it is resilient; the system is not resilient if it does not survive (Vasuthanasub 2019).

All in all, it seems difficult to choose one as the best from the above, exemplified, definitions. While some depict resilience as an emergent property that appears only in the wake of a crisis (Butler et al. 2007), others view resilience as a process of dealing with adversity (Community and Regional Resilience Institute 2013). Therefore, since each perspective offers relevant insights, the selection of the definition is less relevant than the context of the application of the definition. In the context of CI systems, suffice to say resilience is the capability of a system – systems as a whole – to withstand, absorb, recover from, or adapt to a change in environment or conditions (Moteff 2012).

Table 3.1 Common perspectives on community resilience.

Resilience domain	Resilience definition	Proponents
Ecology	The persistence of relationships within a system; a measure of the ability of systems to absorb changes in state variables, driving variables, and parameters, and still persist.	(Holding 1973)
Ecology	Buffer capacity or the ability of a system to absorb perturbation or the magnitude of disturbance that can be absorbed before a system changes its structure.	Holling et al. (1995)
Ecology	Positive adaptation in response to adversity; it is not the absence of vulnerability, not an inherent characteristic, and not static.	Waller (2001)
Ecology	The transition probability between states is a function of decision makers' consumption and production activities.	Brock et al. (2002)
Ecology	The ability of a system that has undergone stress to recover and return to its original state; more precisely (1) the amount of disturbance a system can absorb and still remain within the same state or domain of attraction and (2) the degree to which the system is capable of self-organization.	Klein et al. (2003)
Ecology	The amount of change or disruption required to transform a system's maintenance from one set of mutually reinforcing processes and structures to a different set of processes and structures.	Anderies et al. (2004)
Ecology	Maintenance of natural capital (as the basis for social systems' functioning) in the long run.	Ott and Döring (2011)
Ecology	The capacity of a system to absorb disturbance and re-organize while undergoing change so as to still retain essentially the same function, structure, identity, and feedback.	Walker et al. (2004)
Ecology	The ability of an individual, group, or organization to continue its existence (or remain more or less stable) in the face of some sort of surprise. Resilience is found in systems that are highly adaptable (not locked into specific strategies) and have diverse resources.	Longstaff (2005)
Ecology and society	The ability of communities to withstand external shocks to their social infrastructure systems.	Adger (2000)
Ecology and society	The ability to persist (i.e. to absorb shocks and stresses and still maintain the functioning of society and the integrity of ecological systems) and the ability to adapt to change, unforeseen circumstances, and risks.	Adger (2003)
Society	A system's capacity to absorb and recover from the occurrence of a hazardous event; reflective of a society's ability to cope and to continue to cope in the future.	Timmerman (1981)
Society	The capacity to cope with unanticipated dangers after they have become manifest, learning to bounce back.	Wildavsky (1988)
Society	The ability to recover from or adjust easily to misfortune or sustained life stress.	(Brown and Kulig 1996)
Society	The process through which mediating structures (schools, peer groups, family) and activity settings moderate the impact of oppressive systems.	(Sonn and Fisher 1998)
Society	The capacity to adapt existing resources and skills to new systems and operating conditions.	Comfort (1999)
Society	The ability to withstand an extreme event without suffering devastating losses, damage, diminished productivity, or quality of life without a large amount of assistance from outside the community.	(Mileti, 1999)

Table 3.1 (Continued)

Resilience domain	Resilience definition	Proponents
Society	The ability to respond to crises in ways that strengthen community bonds, resources, and the community's capacity to cope.	Chenoweth and Stehlik (2001)
Society	The capability to bounce back and to use physical and economic resources effectively to aid recovery following exposure to hazards.	Paton and Johnston (2001)
Society	A sustainable network of physical systems and human communities, capable of managing extreme events; during disaster, both must be able to survive and function under extreme stress.	Godschalk (2003)
Society	The ability of individuals and communities to deal with a state of continuous long-term stress; the ability to find unknown inner strengths and resources in order to cope effectively; the measure of adaptation and flexibility.	Ganor and Ben-Lavy (2003)
Society	Two types of social resilience: (1) a social system's capacity to facilitate human efforts to deduce the trends of change, reduce vulnerabilities, and facilitate adaptation; and (2) the capacity of a [social-ecological system] to sustain preferred modes of economic activity.	Kofinas (2003)
Society	Resilience consists of (1) the amount of change a system can undergo and still retain essentially the same structure, function, identity, and feedback on function and structure, (2) the degree to which a system is capable of self-organization (and re-organize after disturbance), and (3) the degree to which a system expresses capacity for learning and adaptation.	Quinlan (2003)
Society	A community's capacities, skills, and knowledge allow it to participate fully in recovery from disasters.	Coles and Buckle (2004)
Society	The capability of a system to maintain its function and structure in the face of internal and external change and to degrade gracefully when it must.	(Allenby and Fink 2005)
Society	The return or recovery time of a social-ecological system, is determined by (1) that system's capacity for renewal in a dynamic environment and (2) people's ability to learn and change (which, in turn, is partially determined by the institutional context for knowledge sharing, learning, and management, and partially by the social capital among people).	Gunderson (2000)
Society	The capacity of a system, community or society potentially exposed to hazards to adapt, by resisting or changing in order to reach and maintain an acceptable level of functioning and structure.	United Nations (2004)
Society	The ability to anticipate risk, limit impact, and bounce back rapidly through survival, adaptability, evolution, and growth in the face of turbulent change.	(Community and Regional Resilience Institute, CARRI, 2013)

3.2.2 Norfolk: A Resilient City?

In 2014 the Rockefeller Foundation started the 100 Resilient Cities (i.e. 100RC) project. At that time, many cities, including Bangkok, Barcelona, Glasgow, Lisbon, London, Melbourne, Milan, Montreal, Paris, Rio de Janeiro, Rome, Sydney, and San Francisco, were selected to join the program. The foundation also selected the City of Norfolk (Virginia, United States) as among the first group of members of 100RC. 100RC is committed to supporting cities all over the globe to become more resilient under the challenging situations of physical sustainability, social complexity, and economic difficulty (City of Norfolk 2015). Physical sustainability, social complexity, and economic difficulty are key concerns for the twenty-first century, which need addressing by direct partnerships and close collaborations between member cities to understand resilience challenges and seek viable solutions. A program promotes the adoption and incorporation given resilience that includes the shocks caused by natural disasters and the stresses resulting from global situations or human errors. The vision of 100RC is not just helping individual member cities to strive for resilient development but it also aims to facilitate the global creative practices of urban resilience planning among governments, private organizations, non-profit associations, and citizen groups (City of Norfolk 2015).

Norfolk, Virginia, was established in August 1682 based on the British Act of 1680. The Elizabeth River surrounded the lower part of the county on the east, west, and south. For more than 300 years, this historic city on water has been a key part of American history, military, commerce, and innovation (City of Norfolk 2015). Nowadays, Norfolk is the home of Naval Station Norfolk, the largest naval base in the world, and Port of Virginia's Norfolk International Terminals, one of the essential economic assets on the East Coast of the United States (Jeffers et al. 2016). It acts as an international city that drives global trading activities and the main hub of the Hampton Roads region that links national logistic nodes. According to these notable privileges, water access is the greatest advantage of Norfolk. The shoreline and waterways are always and will be the most critical assets of a city, as they render the opportunities and additionalities to strengthen a foundation of transportation infrastructure. However, locating next to the water also presents a city with a huge drawback. Norfolk has experienced several floods throughout its history, but the frequency and severity of occurrences have steadily increased in recent decades. In recent times, the city was forced to look into several sustainable solutions due to accelerating water risks and hazards, including:

- **Sea level rise**: With the subsidence of local lands and coastal areas around Norfolk's coastline, the city is now facing the highest relative sea level rise rate on the East Coast (Jeffers et al. 2016). While the average global sea level rise has been between 5–8 inches over the last century, the sea level at Norfolk has risen over 14 inches since 1930 (City of Norfolk 2015).
- **Storm incidences**: Regarding statistical data on water level elevations of major storms at Sewells Point tide gauge that have affected Norfolk since 1933, by the National Oceanic and Atmospheric Administration (NOAA), six out of the eleven storms occurred during the last twelve years (City of Norfolk 2015). As a matter of fact, the percentage of tidal flooding areas around the city has increased by 3.25 times since 1960, and the sea level at the Norfolk location is projected to rise between 1.5–7.5 feet in the next 85–100 years (City of Norfolk 2015; Jeffers et al. 2016). Therefore, in order to help Norfolk withstand this unavoidable circumstance, the direction is clear that the city will definitely need to plan ahead or even do something better for the near future.
- **Flood risk**: While more frequent and more intense storms, as well as repeatedly routine flooding, keep threatening Norfolk's residents, some of the city's most commercially and industrially at-risk zones are openly vulnerable to floods and storms (City of Norfolk 2015).

At this juncture, we can make three points: First, risks of geographic conditions around the city continue to shift. The city faces tough times now, and yet it must prepare for the future. Moreover, the city's economy will continue to rely on access to the waters and thus must adapt to the changing environment in practical ways. Second, to build a resilient city (as well as forming solid communities and societies), several stakeholders – city leaders, the private sector, neighbor groups, and residents – must collaborate to develop solutions that lead to the flourishing of business and living quality. Finally, this resilience involves infrastructure, people, and governance mechanisms.

3.2.3 Qualities of Resilient Systems

In the context of CI systems, resilience becomes conceptually pertinent when either an extensive range of sudden shocks and chronic stresses or the collapses of physical and social systems threaten national security. Considering this experience, the Rockefeller Foundation (2014) clarifies that resilience has filled the gap between disaster risk reduction and natural hazards adaptation by moving away from traditional disaster risk management, usually recognized in conventional risk assessments related to specific events. In other words: "Instead of accepting the possibility that a wide range of threatening incidents – both tensions and collapses – may occur but are not necessarily predictable. Resilience focuses on enhancing the performance of a system in the face of multiple hazards, rather than preventing or mitigating the loss of assets due to specific events" (Rockefeller Foundation 2014). Nevertheless, one conceptual limitation of this evidence is that resilience does not account for the power dynamics integrated with how CI systems function and cope with disruptions and disturbances.

Assigning the qualities listed below to infrastructure systems can enhance the overall performance of resilience of CI systems. In this manner, extensive research and studies have indicated that there are at least seven distinctive qualities that truly resilient systems should demonstrate (Vasuthanasub 2019):

- **Flexibility** – This characteristic refers to the ability or capability of systems to react, adjust, evolve, and adapt by using allocated alternative strategies corresponding to the needs of changing circumstances or sudden crises (Rockefeller Foundation 2014). It is directly related to the decentralized and modular approaches to infrastructure management. Rockefeller Foundation (2015) suggested that the successful development of flexible systems can be achieved through introducing new knowledge and innovative technologies, as well as the additional combination of local experiences and management in new ways.
- **Inclusion** – A inclusion strategy underlines completeness of communication, including comprehensive consultation, commitment, and especially the engagement of all decision-makers and stakeholders. Addressing and monitoring the potential risks, hazards, and events related to one sector or set of CI systems in isolation from the others is an obstruction to reaching the core concept of resilience (Foundation 2015; Rockefeller Foundation 2014). Hence, an inclusive approach is needed to create a sense of shared ownership or joint vision and produce effective leadership or attentive governance on systems resilience.
- **Integration** – This attribute emphasizes an integrated process and alignment between the interrelated or interconnected set of CI systems to maintain and promote consistency in decision-making among decision-makers and stakeholders. Integration must be evident within systems and across different scales of their operation. It helps to ensure that investments and actions mutually and appropriately address the common needs or outcomes. Exchanging the data and information between systems and sub-systems allows them to function collectively and respond rapidly in shorter periods or loops throughout the whole system (Rockefeller Foundation 2014).
- **Redundancy** – This feature refers to a spare capacity or secondary alternative within systems purposely designated to accommodate disruption due to extreme pressures or external

interferences (Rockefeller Foundation 2014). The intent of redundant systems must be diversified so that there are multiple selections to obtain a given objective or to fulfill a particular function. An example of existing systems in the real world incorporating redundancy is power distribution networks and multiple delivery pathways of energy infrastructures (Rockefeller Foundation 2015). Redundancies should be well-considered, cost-effective, and prioritized at a large-scale implementation.

- **Reflectiveness** – Reflective systems signify an acceptance of inherent uncertainties and necessary changes in the real world. Rather than seeking permanent solutions based on theoretical beliefs, individuals and institutions must continuously evolve, modify their norms, and adjust their behaviors based on emerging evidence (Rockefeller Foundation 2014). Thus, reflective or thoughtful people are always enthusiastic to systematically look, listen, and learn from past experiences and then leverage this learning and understanding to inform future decision-making (Rockefeller Foundation 2015).

- **Resourcefulness** – This qualification implies that individuals, groups, and organizations are the key to success in finding and discovering different ways to accomplish their goals or satisfy their needs during difficult times or challenging moments (Rockefeller Foundation 2014). It is more like a personal trait of persons rather than a qualification of systems. A resourceful workforce may include decision-makers, stakeholders, and other associated persons responsible for or involved in the investment and development processes, such as future state forecasts, set priorities ranking, and financial and physical resources allocation and management (Rockefeller Foundation 2014). Resourcefulness is considered an essential instrument of CI systems' ability to maintain and restore their functionality under critical conditions or severe constraints at times of crisis.

- **Robustness** – Robust systems are a reflection of robust design. They represent how well systems are conceived, constructed, and are mainly managed physical assets (Rockefeller Foundation 2015). As a result, the systems can resist the outcomes or impacts of catastrophic events without significant damage or loss of functionality. The robust design of CI systems should focus on scanning potential internal failures and making precautions to ensure failure is predictable, safe, and not deviant from the root causes (Rockefeller Foundation 2014). That is to say, when the design thresholds of robustness are exceeded, the protective systems will not quickly or suddenly fail.

3.3 Applicability of Gaming in Education

Arguably, games are developed entertainment. Moreover, people are attracted to games since they can be used to generate fun and excitement. For this reason, game developers have tried very hard to invent and introduce new ways of enjoyment. Thanks to the rapid advancement and extensive expansion in computer hardware and visualization technologies, each and every time, the graphical detail and definition of games have become more realistic and accurate to the player. With the ability to mimic or simulate reality, some game designers started to adopt a purpose of playfulness to develop another kind of game, a more serious one. Those applications can be used for research, education, and training if they are seen fit or compatible with the study and finding objectives (Squire and Jenkins 2003). When discussing the concept of gaming in education, there are at least four categories of games in the literature (Susi et al. 2007):

- **Serious gaming** – This term represents using games for specific purposes or other benefits, such as learning, researching, and training, instead of entertainment value only. It may look just like playing digital games, but its objective is to achieve something extraordinary.

- *Simulations:* simulation technologies are quite similar to serious games unless they have the ability to replicate and visualize real-world objects or environments for real-life training.
- *Game-based learning:* this concept refers to using games in the traditional classroom to strengthen the course objectives and enhance the learning and teaching experience. Game-based learning is considered a serious gaming branch designed to deal with designated learning outcomes (Corti 2006).
- *Gamification:* the use of game design elements in non-game contexts to motivate or influence desired behaviors. Those attributes include features including leaderboards, badges, levels, trophies, or any other rewards. Moreover, gamification can be considered new to scholarly society and yet old in the business world – additional details on gamification are provided in Chapter 4.

During the past 20 years, numerous research studies have been conducted on the effectiveness and productiveness of using serious games as a learning tool or gaming concepts as a teaching technique. For example, Griffiths (2002) quotes that one investigation from a psychological association dating back to the early 1980s has logically revealed that playing digital games, both video-based and computer-based, reduces response times and improves hand-eye coordination and encouragement in players' self-esteem and self-respect. Considering this found evidence, Griffiths (2002) also concludes that video games or computer games have great benefits and positive potentials not only for their entertainment value but also for non-entertainment purposes. The future success of this initiative can be achieved when appropriate game selection and playing requirements are designed to address a particular problem clearly or to teach a specific skill. With this in mind, a literature review in the following sub-section will focus on a conceptual framework of a particular technique, notably serious gaming, regarding educational benefits.

More recently, research suggests that gaming is a powerful tool for creating resilient people and can positively impact the quality of life. For example, Lokhorst (2020) states that gaming can be used for several reasons:

- *Better decision-making:* action video games train the brain's neurons to make faster and more accurate decisions.
- *Dream control:* gamers are far more likely to have dreams that they can consciously control than those who don't play. It is also used therapeutically to analyze and battle nightmares, phobias, and fears.
- *Trauma management:* an Oxford study suggests that playing Tetris after a traumatic incident reduces the chance of developing traumatic memories by keeping the mind occupied from reliving the incident.
- *Effective and alternative therapy:* video games used as therapy for fighting depression and other psychological problems in teenagers have proven more effective than counseling. Depression is a psychological problem seen in teenagers and adults that affects their quality of life and increases their psychological stress. In a study conducted with 168 teenagers, half were assigned to play SPARX, and the other half were assigned to attend traditional therapy. The first half was able to battle depression much faster, with 44% even completely cured, compared to the other half. The excitement of the game can help people fight self-consciousness and feelings of inadequacy.

In Shadow's Edge, a study shows that young people playing the game only three times a week for six weeks have more optimism and a more positive self-identity. Thus, young people are able to handle emotions better – making them more resilient. Players felt more natural, encouraged to reach out and connect, and more validated in their feelings (Lokhorst, 2020).

3.3.1 Serious Gaming

Digital games always have outstanding motivational potential. They manipulate a set of design elements to encourage players to interact with them willingly without any rewards, but just for the satisfaction of playing and the opportunity to win, so much so that playing video games or computer games undoubtedly consumes the attention of players. By watching students or participants play video or computer games, it becomes apparent that they prefer this way of learning rather than traditional approaches (Griffiths 1996, 1997, 2002). However, it is unquestionably relevant to investigate the extent to which serious game technologies positively impact education.

As serious games can require concentration and stimulate players' motivation in learning experiences and outcomes, they have led to the emergence of gaming terminologies in education, such as edutainment, serious gaming, and gamification. Serious gaming can be viewed as a redefined version of the first fundamental gaming concept in education called "edutainment," which was considerably popular during the 1990s. At that time, edutainment – educating through entertainment – became well known due to the booming growth of the personal computer market (Michael and Chen 2005). The term was usually used to describe any types of education that are concurrently knowledgeable and enjoyable. The primary target group was young children in elementary and junior high school, focusing on reading, mathematics, and science.

Unfortunately, due to a growing interest in the Internet and the poor quality of the games themselves, edutainment has finally failed to mark itself as the first milestone in the history of gaming in the academic world (Michael and Chen 2005; Eck 2006). Yet, the development of digital games for non-entertainment purposes began and evolved long before a flourishing era of edutainment. As edutainment failed to prove its applicability and practicality, the concept of serious gaming was subsequently re-examined during the late 1990s. In 2002 with a campaign video game (America's Army) released by the United States Army and the institution of the Serious Games Initiative founded by the Wilson Center in Washington, DC, a journey of serious gaming had started (Susi et al. 2007).

In general terms, serious gaming usually refers to video and computer games for informing, educating, and training all genders and ages. The concept itself inherits the same primary goals as edutainment but extends far beyond teaching facts and routine memorization (Michael and Chen 2005). By way of example, Corti (2006, p. 1) simplifies the term: "Serious gaming is all about leveraging the power of computer games to captivate and engage end-users for a specific purpose, such as to develop new knowledge and skills." Today's "serious games" are serious business, as stated by Ben Sawyer, co-founder of the Serious Games Initiative (Susi et al. 2007). In 2006 the digital gaming sector industry was estimated to have a value of $10 billion per year, and the market of serious games only was roughly worth $20 million. However, it is expected to grow continuously over the next decade (van Eck 2006).

During the last decade, serious gaming has been applied to a broad spectrum of applications areas and research domains, including military, government, education, corporate, and healthcare, and also earning widespread recognition of distinctive features and intrinsic capability from both public and private organizations. Nowadays, the concept of serious gaming is becoming even more and more popular in the global education and training market. The term itself is already established, but there is still no universally accepted definition (Susi et al. 2007). Many sources or references either describe the concept vaguely or do not define it clearly. As of October 2022, a Google search on "serious games" resulted in over 700 million hits. "Serious gaming" resulted in over 160 million hits. These results suggest that serious gaming is indeed a serious business and that digital games are interested in achieving something greater than entertainment alone.

Serious gaming involves using concepts and technologies derived from (computer) entertainment games for non-entertainment purposes such as research, policy and decision-making, training, and learning. Serious gaming often combines analog techniques (pen and paper) and social interaction with state-of-the-art game and simulation technology (immersive 3D virtual game worlds) Cidota et al. (2016). This view of serious gaming suggests that, for example, CI systems can be characterized as complex systems; their behaviors, functions, activities, relationships, and interactions can be modeled and simulated in different ways for decision-making, research, and learning experiences. Furthermore, much research and experimentation also suggest that some critical or unique skills may be developed or strengthened by playing serious games (Griffiths 2002; Michael and Chen 2005; Squire and Jenkins 2003; Susi et al. 2007; van Eck 2006). For instance, spatial planning and visualization abilities, such as creative and critical thinking, data allocation and management, and three-dimensional object rotation and manipulation, can gradually evolve along with gaming experiences (Mitchell and Savill-Smith 2004; Subrahmanyam and Greenfield 1994). Given that serious games may seem to be more effective and advantageous for young people, like children and teenagers who started with relatively beginner skills (Griffiths 1996, 1997), consequently, researchers, educators, and corporates are now using video games and computer games as an application or a tool for studying individuals, teaching students, and training personnel and staff.

Regarding the studies and results from various literature conducted by Griffiths (2002), many reasons have provided insights as to why serious gaming may be useful for educational purposes (Griffiths 2002; Vasuthanasub 2019):

- Serious games can be used as measurement tools or applications for research; as investigation and study tools, their potentials are diverse.
- Serious games attract participation across different demographic boundaries, including age, gender, ethnicity, and educational level.
- Serious games can aid students in establishing objectives, ensuring goal rehearsal, providing feedback and support, and maintaining records of behavioral change.
- Serious games are productive instruments since they help researchers measure performance on various tasks and can be easily applied, standardized, and perceived.
- Serious games can be utilized to examine individual characteristics, like self-esteem, self-dignity, and self-respect.
- Serious games can be playful, fanciful, and purposeful to participators simultaneously. Consequently, it seems simpler to receive and maintain participants' attention for more extended periods of time (Donchin 1995). Also, because they are amusing and exciting, they may promote a learning experience in innovative ways.
- Serious games can create an element of interactive thinking, which may stimulate learning.
- Serious games allow players to encounter novelty, curiosity, and difficulty, which may also motivate learning.
- Serious games interact with players through state-of-the-art technology. This implicit interaction may help participants overcome the fear of advanced technology or complex devices (Technophobia), notably computers (Griffiths 2002).
- Serious games can be computer-based simulations. This innovation enables participants and players to engage in extraordinary events or unusual activities in the form of complex computer models and to interact with each other without real consequences.

However, using serious games as applications or educational tools also has some disadvantages. For example, Vasuthanasub (2019) suggests that:

- Serious games may cause young participants, especially children, to become excessively excited. Under this condition, those players can produce unpleasant emotions or inappropriate behavior, such as competitiveness or aggressiveness.
- Serious game technologies have unceasingly developed over time. As a result, they are frequently being upgraded, making it even harder for researchers or educators to test and evaluate the impacts across studies in an academic environment.
- Serious game exercises may enhance certain skills and experiences of some participants, which can lead to inconsistent or incompatible evaluation results. Put another way, serious games are always good for all learning experiences and outcomes (van Eck 2006).

Notwithstanding the drawbacks, it would be clear that employing serious gaming in an academic context would influence positive educational purposes in any case. Inevitably, researchers and educators must examine and evaluate serious games' benefits and positive potentials while remaining aware of possible unintended adverse effects. Given all these points, most people would probably support the use of serious gaming if they were confident that those digital games were appropriately selected to help them learn about difficult topics or complicated problems.

3.4 Urban Planning Simulation Computer Game "SimCity 2013®"

SimCity 2013® is an opened-ended simulation computer game for city building and urban planning, which was initially designed and formally introduced by US video game designer named "Will Wright," a co-founder of the game development company "Maxis." Regarding the massive and ongoing success of all five previous editions during the past two decades, a whole new redesign of SimCity 2013® edition was officially introduced and released again in early March 2013. The game was first published in 1989 as SimCity Classic®, and then continually spawned its first original version to several different editions later, including SimCity 2000® in 1994, SimCity 3000® in 1999, SimCity 4® in 2003, and SimCity Society® in 2007 (Bereitschaft 2016; Bos 2001). This latest version is a successor that proposes to continue the story of the legendary simulation game from its predecessors and to succeed at the next level of achievement of the all-time best city building and urban planning simulation computer game.

SimCity 2013® is considered to be a reboot with reprogramming of game functionality and advanced features from all previous SimCity® series. In the 2013 version, players can construct a settlement that can consistently grow into a city by zoning land, including residential, commercial, and industrial development, as well as essential service facilities, as shown in Figure 3.2, Figure 3.3, and Figure 3.4. Cities in a region will be interconnected and interdependent with each other via predefined regional networks, such as highways, railways, and waterways. The major infrastructures, like economic, energy, transportation, and pollution management systems – part of CI systems – will visibly flow between cities. Moreover, cities can trade resources or share public services with their neighbors, like garbage collection or healthcare services. Cities can pool their collective wealth and help to build a more excellent and more extensive system network and to provide benefits for the entire region, such as a massive solar power plant or an international airport as in the concept: "The larger the size of the region, the higher the number of cities and great works that can be built."

Figure 3.2 Simulated city using SimCity 2013® – residential zone. *Source:* Electronic Arts Inc.

Figure 3.3 Simulated city using SimCity 2013® – commercial zone. *Source:* Electronic Arts Inc.

Figure 3.4 Simulated city using SimCity 2013® – industrial zone. *Source:* Electronic Arts Inc.

In terms of game planning, operation, and management strategies, players must specialize their cities into particular industries, such as manufacturing, education, tourism, gambling, and others. Each will require distinctive urban planning, simulation behavior, and economic strategies. Players can either heavily specialize in a single industry in each city or assign multiple specializations in any given city for diversification. The game also features a simulated global currency and economy. For instance, prices of essential resources, including coal, ore, and crude oil, will fluctuate depending on the game's worldwide supply and demand. In other words, if players worldwide are predominantly selling specific resources on the global market (in the game) during the same period, this will drive the price for that resource down. Conversely, a resource that experiences very little exposure in the world market will be considered a scarce resource, driving the price up.

Consequently, besides the fact that SimCity® has been a surprising commercial success based on the advancement of complex simulation, it is still remarkable and peculiar because of what it does not have. To be more specific, SimCity® is missing a couple of standard elements which is considered most counter-productive by motivational theorists. First, there is no competitive element: playing SimCity® against another person or the computer is not possible. Second, there is no external imposition of goal structure. It is impossible to win at SimCity®, unless by fulfilling self-chosen and self-defined goals. According to SimCity®'s designer, Will Wright exclaims: "as a matter of fact that SimCity's lack of goals, it makes SimCity® not a game, but just a toy" (Bos 2001; Minnery and Searle 2014). Whatever goal players have chosen, they have turned it into a game. Bos (2001) also noted that self-defined goals are potentially superior from a motivational theorist's point of view since they avoid or, in some cases, replace the intrinsic motivation with the extrinsic motivation of self-defined goals, which is most likely the same as inspiring players to develop their habits of goal setting and goal monitoring. For a classroom environment, for example, teachers may need to assign specific goals for students using the simulation or at least help them define their self-chosen goals. But in any case, those goals must not be set against the imposed external goals of the game.

Last but not least, SimCity 2013® also offers a unique style of the learning experience by increasing its challenge level. In the early stages of building a new city, players can ignore some minor rules, policies, or constraints, and their city will still grow (Bos 2001). However, players must progressively learn how to manage tax rates, land values, crime rate, air and ground pollution, waste disposal, mass transit, and other factors as they expand the city to become a metropolis. These conditions are not required to be dealt with within a given period, but all of them must be considered for a city's continuous growth (Bereitschaft 2016). This is a natural but remarkable way to introduce the complexity of a large-scale system. Comparing this primary characteristic of a learning experience, "organic scaffolding" from SimCity 2013® to arcade-style games, it would not only provide players the ability to control how fast they approach and react to new challenges but also generate an actively responsive system to keep them engaged (Bos 2001)

3.5 Concluding Remarks

At a fundamental level, the domain of CIs addresses elements of assessment, remediation, indications and warnings, mitigation, response, reconstruction about hazards, risks, and threats from natural and artificial events affecting public well-being, as well as public safety, economic vitality, and security. The frequency of occurrences and increasing loss of lives and property associated with natural and artificial events leads us to question the effectiveness and applicability of traditional scientific methods. This chapter highlights the need for resilience as a critical concept in dealing with current threats and a means to prepare for future threats. Resilience is seen as the ability to withstand stress in infrastructure systems and yet also relevant to humans as "positive adaptation" after a stressful or adverse situation. In this case, resilience is applied to systems and people. Moreover, resilience can also be applied to cities, especially as suggested by the so-called 100 Resilient Cities.

Moreover, CI systems can enhance their overall resilience through several means. Seven distinctive qualities that can improve the resilience of CI systems include flexibility, inclusion, integration, redundancy, reflectiveness, resourcefulness, and robustness. However, there is a need for deliberate efforts to enhance resilience – one of which is gaming. And although all gaming is not always good for all learning experiences and outcomes, the positive impacts of serious gaming in an academic context cannot be dismissed – an in-depth discussion on gaming proceeds in the following chapter.

3.6 Exercises

1 Discuss how the different aspects of resiliency can be used to support city development.
2 Apply the qualities of resilient systems to your selected city.
3 Discuss the need for serious gaming in city development.
4 How can serious gaming be used to address risks and vulnerabilities in a city?
5 Discuss at least five games (including their advantages and disadvantages) that can be used for urban planning.

References

Adger, W.N. (2000). Social and ecological resilience: Are they related? *Progress in Human Geography* 24(3): 347–364. https://doi.org/10.1191/030913200701540465.

Adger, W.N. (2003). Social capital, collective action, and adaptation to climate change. *Economic Geography* 79(4): 387–404. https://www.jstor.org/stable/30032945.

Allenby, B. and Fink, J. (2005). Toward inherently secure and resilient societies. *Science (New York, N.Y.)* 309(5737): 1034–1036. https://doi.org/10.1126/science.1111534.

Anderies, J., Janssen, M., and Ostrom, E. (2004). A framework to analyze the robustness of social-ecological systems from an institutional perspective. *Ecology and Society* 9(1): 1–28. https://doi.org/10.5751/ES-00610-090118.

Bereitschaft, B. (2016). Gods of the city? Reflecting on city building games as an early introduction to urban systems. *Journal of Geography* 115(2): 51–60. https://doi.org/10.1080/00221341.2015.1070366.

Bos, N.D. (2001). *What do Game Designers Know About Scaffolding? Borrowing SimCity Design Principles for Education, Technical Report for the CILT PlaySpace Working Group.* University of Michigan, and Center for Innovative Learning Technologies.http://playspace.concord.org/Documents/Learning%20from%20SIMCITY.pdf.

Brock, W.A., Mäler, K.G., and Perrings, C. (2002). Resilience and sustainability: The economic analysis of nonlinear systems. In: *In Panarchy: Understanding Transformations in Systems of Humans and Nature* (ed. L.H. Gunderson and C.S. Holling), pp. 261–289. Island Press.

Brown, D.D. and Kulig, J.C. (1996). The concepts of resiliency: Theoretical lessons from community research. *Health and Canadian Society*, 4 (1): 29–52. https://hdl.handle.net/10133/1275.

Butler, L.D., Morland, L.A., and Leskin, G.A. (2007). Psychological resilience in the face of terrorism. In: *Psychology of Terrorism* (ed. B. Bongar, L.M. Brown, L.E. Beutler, J.N. Breckenridge, and P.G. Zimbardo), pp. 400–417. Oxford University Press.

Chenoweth, L. and Stehlik, D. (2001). Building resilient communities: Social work practice and rural Queensland. *Australian Social Work* 54(2): 47–54. https://doi.org/10.1080/03124070108414323.

Cidota, M.A., Lukosch, S.G., Dezentje, P. et al. (2016). Serious gaming in augmented reality using HMDs for assessment of upper extremity motor dysfunctions: User studies for engagement and usability. *I-Com* 15(2): 155–169. https://doi.org/10.1515/icom-2016-0020.

City of Norfolk. (2015). *Norfolk Resilience Strategy. The Norfolk City Manager's Office of Resilience.* https://www.norfolk.gov/3612/Office-of-Resilience.

Coles, E. and Buckle, P. (2004). Developing community resilience as a foundation for effective disaster recovery. *The Australian Journal of Emergency Management* 19(4): 6–15. https://search.informit.org/doi/pdf/10.3316/ielapa.375435145094637.

Comfort, L.K. (1999). *Shared Risk: Complex Systems in Seismic Response* (ed. K.C.L.K. Comfort). Emerald Publishing.

Community and Regional Resilience Institute, CARRI. (2013). *Building Resilience in America's Communities: Observations and Implications of the CRS Pilots Report – Restore your Economy.* https://restoreyoureconomy.org/blog/2013/06/03/community-resilience/building-resilience-in-america-s-communities-observations-and-implications-of-the-crs-pilots-report.

Corti, K. (2006). *Games-based Learning; a Serious Business Application.* PIXELearning Limited. https://www.cs.auckland.ac.nz/courses/compsci777s2c/lectures/Ian/serious%20games%20business%20applications.pdf.

Donchin, E. (1995). Video games as research tools: The space fortress game. *Behavior Research Methods, Instruments, & Computer*, 27(2): 217–223. https://doi.org/10.3758/BF03204735.

Folke, C. (2006). Resilience: The emergence of a perspective for social–ecological systems analyses. *Global Environmental Change* 16(3): 253–267. https://doi.org/10.1016/j.gloenvcha.2006.04.002.

Folke, C., Carpenter, S., Walker, B. et al. (2010). Resilience thinking: Integrating resilience, adaptability and transformability. *Ecology and Society* 15(4). https://doi.org/10.5751/ES-03610-150420.

Ganor, M. and Ben-Lavy, Y. (2003). Community resilience: Lessons derived from gilo under fire. *Jewish Communal Service Association of North America (JCSA)* 79, 105–108. https://archive.jpr.org.uk/object-bjpa1223.

Godschalk, D.R. (2003). Urban hazard mitigation: Creating resilient cities. *Natural Hazards Review* 4(3): 136–143. https://doi.org/10.1061/(ASCE)1527-6988(2003)4:3(136).

Griffiths, M.D. (1996). *Computer Game Playing in Children and Adolescents: A Review of the Literature* T. Gill (ed.), National Children's Bureau. 41–58. http://irep.ntu.ac.uk/id/eprint/20063.

Griffiths, M.D. (1997). Computer game playing in early adolescence. *Youth & Society* 29(2): 223–237.

Griffiths, M.D. (2002). The educational benefits of videogames. *Education and Health* 20(3): Article 3. https://sheu.org.uk/sheux/EH/eh203mg.pdf.

Gunderson, L.H. (2000). Ecological resilience – In theory and application. *Annual Review of Ecology and Systematics* 31(1): 425–439. https://doi.org/10.1146/annurev.ecolsys.31.1.425.

Hetherington, E.M. and Elmore, A.M. (2003). Risk and resilience in children coping with their parents' divorce and remarriage. In: *Resilience and Vulnerability: Adaptation in the Context of Childhood Adversities* (ed. S.S. Luthar), pp. 182–212. Cambridge University Press. https://doi.org/10.1017/CBO9780511615788.010.

Holling, C.S. (1973). Resilience and stability of ecological systems. *Annual Review of Ecology and Systematics* 4(1): 1–23. https://doi.org/10.1146/annurev.es.04.110173.000245.

Holling, C.S. (1996). Engineering resilience versus ecological resilience. In: *Engineering within Ecological Constraints* (ed. P. Schulze), pp. 31–43. National Academies Press.

Holling, C.S., Schindler, D.W., Walker, B.W. et al. (1995). Biodiversity in the functioning of ecosystems: An ecological synthesis. In: *Biodiversity Loss: Economic and Ecological Issues* (ed. B.-O. Jansson, C.S. Holling,C. Folke et al.), pp. 44–83. Cambridge University Press. https://doi.org/10.1017/CBO9781139174329.005.

Jeffers, R., Fogleman, W., Shaneyfelt, C. et al. (2016). *Development of an Urban Resilience Analysis Framework with Application to Norfolk, VA*. (SAND–2016-2161, 1600107, 683825; p. SAND–2016-2161, 1600107, 683825). Sandia National Laboratories. https://doi.org/10.2172/1600107.

Klein, R.J.T., Nicholls, R.J., and Thomalla, F. (2003). Resilience to natural hazards: How useful is this concept? *Global Environmental Change Part B: Environmental Hazards* 5(1): 35–45. https://doi.org/10.1016/j.hazards.2004.02.001.

Kofinas, G. (2003). *Resilience of Human-rangifer Systems: Frames Of Resilience Help to Inform Studies of Human Dimensions of Change and Regional Sustainability*. (IHDP Update 2; pp. 6–7).IHDP: The Earth System Governance Project.

Lokhorst, R. (2020). *The Power of Gaming to Build Resilience*. XPRIZE Foundation. https://ai.xprize.org/articles/the-power-of-gaming-to-build-resilience.

Longstaff, P. (2005). *Security, Resilience, and Communication in Unpredictable Environments such as Terrorism, Natural Disasters, and Complex Technology*. Harvard University Press.

McGonigal, K. (2016). *The Upside of Stress: Why Stress is Good for You, and How to Get Good at It*. (Reprint ed.). Avery.

Michael, D. and Chen, S. (2005). *Serious Games: Games that Educate, Train, and Inform* (1st ed.). Cengage Learning PTR.

Mileti, D. (1999). *Disasters by Design: A Reassessment of Natural Hazards in the United States*. Joseph Henry Press. https://doi.org/10.17226/5782.

Minnery, J. and Searle, G. (2014). Toying with the city? Using the computer game SimCity4 in planning education. *Planning Practice & Research* 29(1): 41–55. https://doi.org/10.1080/02697459.2013.829335.

Mitchell, A. and Savill-Smith, C. (2004). *The Use of Computer and Video Games for Learning: A Review of the Literature*. Learning and Skills Development Agency. http://www.lsda.org.uk/files/PDF/1529.pdf.

Moteff, J.D. (2012). *Critical infrastructure resilience: The evolution of policy and programs and issues for congress* (United States) [Report]. Congressional Research Service. https://digital.library.unt.edu/ark:/67531/metadc122245.

Ott, K. and Döring, R. (2011). *Theorie und praxis starker nachhaltigkeit* (2., überarbeitete und erweiterte Auflage). Metropolis Verlag.

Paton, D. and Johnston, D. (2001). Disasters and communities: Vulnerability, resilience and preparedness. *Disaster Prevention and Management: An International Journal* 10(4): 270–277. https://doi.org/10.1108/EUM0000000005930.

Quinlan, A. (2003). *Resilience and Adaptive Capacity: Key Components of Sustainable Social-ecological Systems*. (IHDP Update 2; pp. 4–5). IHDP: The Earth System Governance Project.

Robert, K.W., Parris, T.M., and Leiserowitz, A.A. (2005). What is sustainable development? Goals, indicators, values, and practice. *Environment: Science and Policy for Sustainable Development* 47(3): 8–21. https://doi.org/10.1080/00139157.2005.10524444.

Rockefeller Foundation. (2014). *City Resilience Framework*. Rockefeller Foundation/ARUP. https://www.rockefellerfoundation.org/wp-content/uploads/City-Resilience-Framework-2015.pdf.

Rockefeller Foundation. (2015). *City Resilience and the City Resilience Framework*.

Sonn, C.C. and Fisher, A.T. (1998). Sense of community: Community resilient responses to oppression and change. *Journal of Community Psychology* 26(5): 457–472. https://psycnet.apa.org/record/1998-10784-005.

Squire, K. and Jenkins, H. (2003). Harnessing the power of games in education. *Insight* 3(1): 5–33. https://d1wqtxts1xzle7.cloudfront.net/68325707/digital_20gaming_20education-libre.pdf?1627332230=&response-content-disposition=inline%3B+filename%3DHarnessing_the_Power_of_Games_in_Educati.pdf&Expires=1679353272&Signature=aaR445EQjR8MsKxFGE0tNsVtkf~CBFpv.

Subrahmanyam, K. and Greenfield, P.M. (1994). Effect of video game practice on spatial skills in girls and boys. *Journal of Applied Developmental Psychology* 15: 13–32. https://doi.org/10.1016/0193-3973(94)90004-3.

Susi, T., Johannesson, M., and Backlund, P. (2007). *Serious Games: An Overview*. (HS-IKI-TR-07-001; pp. 1–28). University of Skövde.

Timmerman, P. (1981). *Vulnerability, Resilience and the Collapse of Society: A Review of Models and Possible Climatic Applications*. Institute for Environmental Studies, University of Toronto. http://www.utoronto.ca/env/mono1.pdf.

United Nations. (2004). *Living with Risk: A Global Review of Disaster Reduction Initiatives*. United Nations Office for Disaster Risk Reduction. https://www.undrr.org/publication/living-risk-global-review-disaster-reduction-initiatives.

van Eck, R. (2006). Digital game-based learning: It's not just the digital natives who are restless. *Educause Review* 41(2): 16–30. https://er.educause.edu/articles/2006/3/digital-gamebased-learning-its-not-just-the-digital-natives-who-are-restless.

Vasuthanasub, J. (2019). The resilient city: A platform for informed decision-making process. Dissertation. Old Dominion University. https://digitalcommons.odu.edu/emse_etds/151.

Walker, B., Holling, C.S., Carpenter, S.R. et al., (2004). Resilience, adaptability and transformability in social–ecological systems. *Ecology and Society* 9(2): 5–5. https://doi.org/10.5751/ES-00650-090205.

Waller, M.A. (2001). Resilience in ecosystemic context: Evolution of the concept. *American Journal of Orthopsychiatry* 71(3): 290–297. https://doi.org/10.1037/0002-9432.71.3.290.

Westrum, R. (2006). A typology of resilience situations. In: *Resilience Engineering* (ed. E. Hollnagel, D.D. Woods, and N. Leveson), pp. 49–60. CRC Press.

Wildavsky, A. (1988). *Searching for Safety*. Transaction Publishers.

Part II

Gamification and Resilience

4

Introduction to Gamification

4.1 Introduction

It is a well-known fact that students often complain about traditional lecturing methods of teaching, suggesting that they can be boring and ineffective (Vasuthanasub 2019). While instructors continuously seek to innovate in the ways of teaching and motivating students, they still admit that existing educational lessons and instructional strategies lack incentive and engagement powers (Lee and Hammer 2011). Serious games as a learning tool are one of the most promising approaches. Games can deliver knowledge and strengthen skills such as communication, collaboration, and problem-solving (Dicheva et al. 2015). However, creating and utilizing such a highly engaging classroom atmosphere with serious games is complicated, expensive, and time-consuming. This class implementation requires an integration of appropriate pedagogical contents and certain technical infrastructures (Kapp 2012). Under these situations, another approach many lecturers are now pursuing is gamification.

In recent years, gamification has firmly positioned itself in the commercial sector. Various companies and firms have rapidly adopted it to encourage employee performance, improve corporate management, and thus far promote marketing strategies and customer engagement. For instance, customers can earn stars, points, tiers, discount coupons, and any other forms of reward for visiting retail shops or shopping through the online store via the mobile phone application (Lee and Hammer 2011). This result is driven by its capability to shape and influence consumers' behavior in a desirable direction. Loyalty programs, such as credit card rewards and frequent-flyer mileage rewards, are often provided as clear case studies of successful gamified mass-market products.

Nonetheless, while the term is gaining ground in the business world, the potential uses of its application in an academic discipline are quite a relatively emerging trend (Dicheva et al. 2015). Traditional schoolings already have several similarities in in-game elements. Students must complete and submit the assignment to get points, and then these points would transform later to letter grades. Students may also receive rewards for desirable behaviors or punishments for improper actions. With these grading and rewarding systems, if students perform well, they will earn an equivalent grade point average and be promoted to a higher level at the end of every academic year. Given all these points, school is already the ultimate gamified experience. However, something about this environment of game-like elements fails to fascinate not all but many students. The typical classroom atmosphere often leads to schooling misconduct and undesirable

Gamification for Resilience: Resilient Informed Decision-Making, First Edition.
Adrian V. Gheorghe and Polinpapilinho F. Katina.
© 2023 John Wiley & Sons, Inc. Published 2023 by John Wiley & Sons, Inc.

outcomes, including absence, cheating, withdrawal, incomplete grades, and dropping out. Those students, at any rate, would not describe classroom-based activities in school as playful experiences. Thus, the existing game-like elements do not satisfactorily generate the power of engagement and encouragement.

Today, gamification is becoming more prevalent in the educational system because of its persuasive ability to inspire students and reinforce the learning process and experience (Vasuthanasub 2019). Speaking about this technique in scholastic terms, gamification, defined by Deterding et al. (2011), refers to the use of game design elements, including mechanics, dynamics, and frameworks in non-gaming environments. According to this definition, it is important to be aware that the fundamental concept of gamification is different from serious gaming. While serious gaming is annotated as the use of full context or the end product of games for non-entertainment purposes, the gamified application is emphasized on the employment of merely game elements (Lee and Hammer 2011). Educational gamification focuses on using or adapting game-like culture roles, player experiences, and rule systems to influence students' behavior. To maximize the potential of gamification, it is significant to understand how this technique can be best deployed in practice. In this case, there are three primary domains of development in which gamification can serve as an intervention, including:

- *Cognitive:* games provide a complex set of rules for players to explore and discover through active experimentation. They guide players through unconsciously skillful processes and keep evolving with potentially challenging missions or complex assignments (Koster 2004). Games also provide multiple routes to fulfill main and sub-objectives and allow players to choose their goals to succeed in complex tasks. These are benefits of games with regards to motivation and engagement (Locke and Latham 1990). Therefore, gamification most likely, when applied to teaching, will transform students' perspectives on schooling. It can help students to perform with an understanding of a clear purpose and true value of the tasks or works. In the case of the best-designed games, the reward for accomplishing a mission or solving a problem is more complex and more complicated (Gee 2008). Gamification hopes to replace the same aspect in schools as well.
- *Emotional:* games usually stimulate powerful emotions, ranging from curiosity to frustration to enjoyment (Lazzaro 2004). They can invoke many positive emotional experiences, such as dignity, integrity, respect, and sympathy (McGonigal 2011). Likewise, they can help players persist through negative sentimental encounters, like aggressiveness, egoism, and impatience, and even convert these into optimistic ones. Comparing these advantages to existing game-like environments in school where the stakes of failure are high and the cycles of feedback are extended, on the other hand, students frequently feel hesitant to risk their stakes with few opportunities. No wonder many students experience anxiety instead of anticipation because if they try but fail, it will cost them high stakes (Pope 2003). Gamification is a promising strategy that offers resilient opportunities for students to face failures by reframing those failures as an essential part of schooling. It can also shorten feedback cycles, render low-stakes options to determine learners' performances, and create an ambiance in which effort can be rewarded. With these intentions, students will perceive failures as learning opportunities instead of feeling fearful, hopeless, and overwhelmed.
- *Social:* games allow players to experience new identities and roles and direct them to make decisions based on their in-game positions and perspectives (Gee 2008; Squire 2006). Players can select less explicitly fictional characters to explore their new sides or predominant skills in a safer learning environment. For instance, a shy adolescent may become a governor who leads a dozen

mayors (other players) in regional urban planning and city development. Having a solid foundation of school-based identity helps students with schooling in the long term (Nasir and Saxe 2003). Even if they feel like "they cannot do school" (Pope 2003), gamified environments allow these helpless students to try on unfamiliar identities, roles, and tasks. Gamification also helps students to openly identify and confidently present themselves as scholars through gaming sessions. In other words, games can provide social credibility for outstanding performance and public recognition for academic achievement. In addition to recognition, which is usually provided by educators only, gamification can induce students to reward each other with in-game currency. Overall, a well-structured gamification environment would influence students to explore meaningful roles, which are fruitful for learning. By ensuring a playfulness of new identity development and the appropriateness of a rewarding system, educators can convince students to think differently about schooling purposes and not underestimate their potential in school.

The integration of game-like components and conventional education can be complementary but are not always necessary (Lee and Hammer 2011). Indeed, gamification can provide educators with powerful instruments to guide and reward students, drive students to participate in classroom activities, and especially allow them to perform at their peak performance in academic pursuits. It can reveal to students the trends that education in the modern era can be an enjoyable experience. A gamified environment design and implementation design procedure might adsorb instructors' endeavors, consume extensive resources, or even mislead students, so they should only try and learn when rewarded (Lee and Hammer 2011). Therefore, there are significant risks that gamification and schools could either damage one another or make each other worse. The results of combining gamification and school, at any event, could be a downfall.

4.2 Serious Gaming and Policy Making

Over the last few decades, practitioners and management scholars have increasingly criticized conventional strategy-making methods, arguing that rapidly changing environments require emerging and creative approaches. Serious gaming discipline is increasingly useful within mainstream strategy literature involved with former strategy-making approaches (Geurts et al. 2007). A definition of gaming simulation is given as a representation of a set of key relationships and structural elements of a particular issue or a problem environment, where the behavior of actors and the effects of their decision are a direct result of the rules guiding the interaction between these actors (Wenzler et al. 2005).

Serious gaming is an activity where two or more independent decision-makers are seeking to achieve their objectives within a limited context (Greenblat and Duke 1975). Again, these games are labeled "serious" because their primary objective is educational and/or informative as opposed to pure entertainment – they allow researchers to model problems with societal aspects, which include the management of critical infrastructure systems. The advantage of simulation gaming over traditional computer simulation models is that the stakeholders do not have to be represented by mathematical formulations; instead, they are played by the participants themselves (Bekebrede 2010). Conveying complex systems with serious gaming models saves the model builders the need to build in the psychological assumptions since the stakeholders represent them.

Simulation games have many forms and aim to provide insights for various goals. The common point of each simulation game is that reality is simulated through the interaction of role players using non-formal symbols and formal, computerized sub-models when necessary. This approach allows the participants to create and analyze future worlds they are willing to explore. Lately, large organizations have reported serious gaming simulation uses for their organizational change management efforts (Wenzler 2008).

Duke (1974) argues that formal complexity communication methods are inadequate for future problems due to their exponentially increasing complexity. He believes that "the citizen, policy researcher or other decision-maker must first comprehend the whole – the entirety, the system, the gestalt – before the particulars can be dealt with" (Duke 1974, p. 10). Gaming simulation techniques can handle "many variables" and are distinguished from other techniques by being relatively uncalibrated and intuitive (Duke 1974, p. xv). Each serious game is situation-specific; consequently, they should only be performed within the intended and designed context. Failure to do so will result in poor results.

Moreover, there remains a debate over whether simulation (and gaming) is a standalone academic field of study or a helpful tool that other disciplines can use. The source of the ongoing debates is stemmed from the interdisciplinary nature of these games. Simulation (and gaming) is certainly an advanced tool in various areas like education, business, urban studies, environmental issues, etc., yet, to date, gaming researchers are still working towards a common theory and an established field of academic study (Shiratori et al. 2005).

4.2.1 Gamification: A Brief History

The earliest and the most common uses of simulation gaming are so-called war games dating back to the nineteenth century and involve exploration, planning, testing, and training of military strategies, tactics, and operations in a simulated interactive and sociotechnical environment (Mayer 2009). With the emergence of decision sciences like operations research, systems analysis, and policy analysis, early serious gaming efforts initially received considerable skepticism. However, simulation and gaming methods (or soft systems thinking) became an alternative to formal complexity modeling techniques like systems analysis, systems dynamics, and operational research. These techniques were successfully applied to well-structured problems; yet, when considering the ambiguous and often ill-structured and complex systems, their contribution was limited since adequate theory and empirical data were absent. Serious gaming methods can provide decision-makers with an environment in which the totality of the system and its dynamics are present. With a holistic approach that includes a wide range of perspectives, skills, information, and mental models of the involved parties, the quality of the decision-making environment increases dramatically (CLP 2021; Geurts et al. 2007).

In the late 1940s, the RAND Corporation (Research and Development) created systems and policy analysis methods to improve government decision-making. Although gaming alone was still not considered a scientific approach within the policy analysis toolbox, the decision-making society saw gaming as the "language of complexity," a beneficial approach to designing computer models. Several European nations, especially the Netherlands, practiced various gaming exercises and gaming styles like spatial planning of the country on a national scale (participants played the roles of private and public investors, governmental licensers, stakeholders, and citizens). In the late 1990s, many scientists leaned into computer-based simulations, given the developments on that platform. They adopted the concepts and technology derived from games for entertainment purposes and developed games like SimHealth (US healthcare simulation), SPLASH (water resource management), and NitroGenius (multiplayer, multi-stakeholder game aiming to solve nitrogen problems). By 2000, games started to be employed for purposes like healthcare, policy making, education, etc., with the adoption of the term "serious games" as an oxymoron (Mayer 2009).

4.2.2 Uses of Serious Gaming

Serious games are developed to serve several different purposes. However, the most crucial contribution of gaming methods is their ability to enhance communication among various actors. This led researchers to utilize gaming methods intensively in complex system exposition where complex systems with social aspects are examined (Duke 1974; Geertje et al. 2005). Policy gaming exercises include understanding system complexity, improving communication, promoting individual and collective learning, creating consensus among players, and motivating participants to enhance their creativity or collaboration (Geurts et al. 2007). Policy games are often used to understand the performance of complex infrastructure systems.

Again, serious gaming methods are often used as an educational technique to train players, from high school students to professional emergency responders (Greenblat and Duke 1975; Shiratori et al. 2003). Additionally, gaming methods are often employed in various fields (e.g. war gaming, business gaming, policy gaming, and urban gaming). Policy gaming exercises assist organizations in exploring policy options, developing decision-making, and strategic change support. Such policy exercises can be used in a variety of problems; from deregulating public utility sectors to reorganizing the Office of the Secretary of Defense, to restructuring cities with urban planning games, to investigating various policy options for global climate change, to restructuring the UK's National Healthcare System, and crisis management at national levels (Brewer 2007; Crookall and Arai 1995; Geurts et al. 2007; Mayer 2009; Wenzler et al. 2005). Games that are designed for individual learning can be categorized under three main objectives: training participants for a situation/scenario, changing participants' mental models with increased awareness, and attaining participants' support. In games where the collective learning is aimed, three categories of objectives are observed: discovering (i.e. understanding a situation and exchanging ideas), testing (i.e. carrying out experiments to check the value or effectiveness of the options), and implementing (i.e. realizing the organizational change for training purposes) (Greenblat and Duke 1975; Joldersma and Geurts 1998).

4.2.3 Serious Gaming in Infrastructure Design Gaming

Arguably, there is the complexity associated with governing large, complex, and interdependent critical infrastructure systems (Ancel 2011). The discrepancies associated with such infrastructure transitions are related to the lack of understanding of the societal aspects of these systems. For that reason, several severe gaming exercises are developed to assist decision-makers, experience system complexity, and train stakeholders. Serious games can represent the multi-level system architecture by proprietary rules at the player level, interaction of the players, and the system levels. The complexity associated with infrastructures (both the technical/physical and social-political levels) is integrated within the gaming platform for stakeholders to experience an abstract representation of the system and make informed decisions (Mayer 2009). Several infrastructure systems are represented using serious games.

Unlike hard-system methods, the gaming and simulation approach is quite flexible and easily adaptable to other quantitative methods, scenarios, and computer models (Mayer 2009). Policy gaming methods can help participants and modelers understand the big picture and identify critical elements of the complex problem. Because of the iterative and experimental nature of these gaming and simulation environments, participants can test different approaches within both a safe environment and a condensed timeframe (CLP 2021). INFRASTRATEGO is an example of a serious gaming-based decision-making tool that encapsulates the Dutch electricity market. Game developers used the game to examine strategic behavior in a liberalizing electricity market while examining the effectiveness of two main types of regulatory regimes. Strategic behavior is using administrative and regulatory processes such as stalling, delaying, or appealing interconnection negotiations, engaging in anti-competitive pricing, or other methods that can be encountered within the liberalization of utility industries. Empirical research indicates that strategic behavior may affect the level playing field and public values negatively. Overall, the game could identify undesirable, unintended, and unforeseen effects of strategic behavior phenomena. Serious gaming enabled monitoring and measurement of strategic behavior as it occurred since participants did not have any fear of litigation and were able to report the development of the strategic behavior, which cannot be observed in real-world situations (Kuit et al. 2005; Wilson et al. 2009).

Similar to INFRASTRATEGO, games like THE UTILITY COMPANY and UTILITIES 21, along with other market, policy, or performance simulation models, are related to the deregulation of utility companies (Wenzler et al. 2005). One example of a fully-computer-based simulation game is SimPort, involving infrastructure planning and land designation for the extension of the Port of Rotterdam. SimPort is used to support the actual decision-making process characterized by a high level of uncertainty, path dependence, and strategic stakeholder behavior, coupled with technical, political, and external factors such as the national and global economies (Geertje et al. 2005; Warmerdam et al. 2006). Furthermore, games like Rescue Team and The King of Fishermen are examples of games geared towards teaching and training business ethics, which were the causes of two major corporate accidents in Japan's nuclear industry (Wenzler et al. 2005).

4.3 Dealing with Uncertainty and Expert Elicitation

4.3.1 Uncertainty

Uncertainty is one of the core elements that must be considered when analyzing and designing critical infrastructure systems. Moreover, sound risk decision strategy formulations require prior identification and quantification of uncertainties (Chytka 2003). Uncertainty is the inability to determine the actual state of a system and is caused by incomplete knowledge or stochastic variability (Chytka 2003). There are two types of uncertainty in engineering, classified as internal and external. Internal uncertainty is caused by (i) limited information in estimating the characteristics of model parameters for a given, fixed model structure; and (ii) limited information regarding the model structure itself. External uncertainties come from variability in model prediction caused by plausible alternatives, also referred to as input parameter uncertainty (Ayyub 2001; Chytka 2003).

The design and implementation process of sociotechnical systems does not contain specifications, regulations, or codes as in the case of designing traditional engineering systems. Instead, designing for uncertainty requires that policy-makers make decisions in situations where scenarios of competitive forces, shifts in customer preferences, and changing technological environments are largely unpredictable (Cooke and Goossens 2004; Roos et al. 2004). The uncertainty emerges from two sources: knowledge of the system and understanding the social response. As previously suggested, large, complex, and interdependent critical infrastructure systems are often considered wicked (or ill-structured) problems. Therefore, infrastructure planners and designers need to obtain data regarding the future phases of the system transition. And while the required data for developing the sociotechnical transition model and governing risks can be provided by expert judgment and elicitation (Ancel 2011), other approaches exist, including gamification.

4.3.2 Expert Elicitation and Aggregation Methods

Expert judgment can be defined as data given by an expert in response to a technical problem. Experts are people who have a background in the subject area and are recognized by their peers or those conducting the study as qualified to answer questions (Meyer and Booker 1987). Expert judgment is used when information from other sources like observations, experimentation, or simulation is not available. Subject matter expert opinions are often employed in the estimation of new, rare, complex, or otherwise inadequately understood cases, future forecasting efforts, or integrating/interpreting existing qualitative/quantitative data (Meyer and Booker 1987). Multiple methods exist regarding the different elicitation techniques, such as group interaction, independent assessment, questionnaires, qualitatively obtained data, calibrating expert judgment data, knowledge acquisition dynamics, and learning process studies (Chytka et al. 2006; Cooke and Goossens 2004; Gustafson et al. 1973; Keeney and von Winterfeldt 1989). Large-scale sociotechnical systems are composed of multiple components involving various stakeholders, technologies, policies, and social factors (Frantzeskaki and Loorbach 2008). The multi-dimensional aspect of the next-generation infrastructure systems requires decision-makers to consider all the complexity and uncertainty associated with such systems (Roos et al. 2004). Decision- and policy- makers often require expert opinions to comprehend and manage the complexity within such systems. The data regarding various subsystems within the meta-system needs to be obtained from a group of experts and combined (or aggregated) in order to assist the decision-making process (Cooke and Goossens 2004). Individual expert assessments are elicited and aggregated by mathematical and behavioral approaches (Chytka 2003; Cooke and Goossens 2004; Singuran 2008). Aggregation algorithms such as the Bayesian method, Logarithmic Opinion Pool, and Linear Opinion Pool are used to combine expert opinions regarding a system with known results. However, behavioral methods and a linear opinion pool were found to be more adequate for future events with unknown results (Ancel 2011).

Bayesian approaches are used for a subjective type of information where knowledge (i.e. probabilities) is a combination of objective (prior) and subjective (obtained from the experts) knowledge. Although subjective expert opinion is integrated into the knowledge, the Bayesian method still requires prior knowledge regarding parameters which doesn't exist for future events with unknown results (Ayyub 2001; Bedford and Cooke 2001). The opinion pool methods combine the elicited distribution via linear or logarithmic weighted averages. The opinion pools have been used in fields like meteorology, banking, marketing, etc., where the expert's weighting factors are validated with either historical data or the observance of the event.

The behavioral approaches seek to reach a consensus among the participants through different forms of interaction, including brainstorming, the Delphi method, the Nominal Group Technique (NGT), and Decision conferencing (Ayyub 2001; Cooke and Goossens 2004; French et al. 1992). The Delphi method was heavily used in the 1960s and 1970s on long-range technological innovation forecasting studies and policy analysis. The process involves an initial estimation session, followed by discussions and revision of the initial assessments. Typically the opinions converge to a high degree of consensus following two or three iterations (Meyer and Booker 1987).

The Delphi method is no longer used extensively since it does not carry uncertainty indicators and falls short on complex system forecasts with multiple factors (Cooke and Goossens 2004). The NGT allows expert interaction by presenting and discussing their assessments in front of the group. Following the discussions, each expert ranks the portrayed opinions silently, where the aggregated ranking of these opinions represents the consensus among stakeholders. Scenario analysis revolves around two questions (i) how a certain hypothetical condition can be realized; and (ii) what are the alternatives for preventing, diverting, or facilitating the process? Decision and event trees, along with respective scenario probabilities, are used to predict a future state (Ayyub 2001). Decision conferencing is used to establish context and explore the issues at hand. It is used to facilitate making decisions and reaching consensus on complex issues such as planning the events following the Chornobyl disaster. Decision conferencing is often based upon multi-criteria decision analysis

(MCDA) and helps stimulate discussions and elicit issues. Events are often short, two-day conferences where interested parties and experts gather to formulate and implement policy actions to offer the best way forward (French et al. 1992). However, behavioral approaches tend to suffer from different expert personalities leading to the dominance of certain individuals or group polarization.

The mathematical approaches covered earlier are often used to determine the technical parameters of systems, including the performance or safety values of newly developed systems. However, uncertainties resulting from the interdependency of stakeholder groups also have to be considered when modeling critical infrastructure systems. Similarly, behavioral approaches received considerable criticism since participants of these methods had the urge to over-simplify their assumptions. Because complex systems often exhibit strongly counter-intuitive behavior, researchers simply cannot rely on intuition, judgment, and arguments from experts when eliciting behavioral data regarding complex systems. In fact, Linstone and Turoff (1975) suggest: "everything interacts with everything and the tools of the classical hard sciences are usually inadequate. And certainly most of us cannot deal mentally with such a magnitude of interactions" (p. 579). Also, when it comes to employing experts to elicit data, researchers often realized that specialists usually focus on the subsystem and mostly ignore the larger system characteristics (Ancel 2011).

4.3.3   Data Generation for Serious Gaming

A literature review revealed a limited number of studies regarding the use of serious games as a data generation method. A survey by Rosendale (1989) employed role-playing as a data generation method about the use of language in speech act situations. The study was designed to reveal basic characteristics of how invitations within platonic and romantic situations occur. The gaming method was the only adequate method to gather data in these situations because authentic interactions cannot be observed without violating participants' privacy. Although Rosendale states that the role-play method is a valid and reliable method, the limitations of using this method brought up questions about its validity and ability to represent real-world interactions between humans (Rosendale 1989).

Like Rosendale, Demeter (2007) also suggested using role-play as a data collection method related to apology speech acts by analyzing how apologies occur in different situations. Participants, chosen from English majors at a university in Romania, were engaged in a role-playing environment and asked to apologize within the scenarios presented. The naturally occurring discussions were collected and compared against another method called discourse completion tests (DCT). The author concluded that in some instances, role-playing produced more realistic data since it allowed participants to speak instead of writing their responses. They were more authentic since the scenarios created a natural setting (Demeter 2007). Another qualitative study using role-playing to generate data was conducted by Halleck (2007). The gaming method was used to evaluate a non-native speaker's oral efficiency using simulated dialogues. The biggest advantage of using role-playing is given as its ability to simulate a real conversation environment without violating participants' privacy.

Besides generating data for speech act studies, the only study related to data elicitation was the REEFGAME, simulating the marine ecosystems in order to learn from different management strategies, livelihood options, and ecological degradation (Cleland et al. 2012). The data generation ability of the game was limited to the decision-making processes of the stakeholders (fishers), which can be categorized under collective learning regarding complexity, and it was not elaborated on any further.

4.4 Cycles in Gaming

Given the complexity associated with governing complex and interdependent infrastructure systems, a gaming methodology is necessary. Ancel (2011) suggests a three-phase method consisting of pre-gaming, gaming, and post-gaming. Each phase is supported by "add-ons," including formal expert elicitation methods and ranking tools. With the help of these tools and techniques, data (both quantitative and qualitative) are gathered regarding the problem at hand (Ancel et al. 2010):

- During the *pre-gaming cycle*, it is necessary to collect all the gaming variables depending on the modeled system. Such variables include scenarios, stakeholders and their interactions, historical data regarding the system, and information on the parameter(s) upon which the success of the transition process will be measured. The computer-based simulation mechanism keeps track of the process throughout the gaming exercise. Depending on the application, the computer-based simulation can evaluate the risk or reliability of an infrastructure system or keep track of the generation capacity or throughput of a particular utility. Once the adequate numerical simulation mechanism and all the supporting data are collected, the game is developed. Developing the game is an iterative process where versions are often tested by playing with several groups and then fine-tuning.
- The *gaming cycle* includes the execution of the gaming exercise with the participation of experts. The game usually starts with the presentation of the scenario to the participants. Participants are asked to perform according to their predetermined roles. Considering the new information they have presented, participants are asked to make collective decisions about the investigated parameters. The decisions are taken as the input variables for the computer-assisted simulation mechanism, where initial conditions for the next step are calculated. The iterative process enables participants to experience and shape the future phases of the transition process. The presence of participants (preferably experts or real stakeholders), social values, norms, and beliefs provide realistic input for social interaction and decision-making.
- The *post-gaming cycle* involves data collection and analysis, which surfaced during the gaming cycle. At this level, the elicited data are arranged and presented back to the participants for further analysis and feedback. Although not performed, depending on the type of data elicited, it is possible to use several other types of Commercial-Off-The-Shelf Software (COTS) to organize and analyze the data. The high-level gaming architecture of the expert elicitation methodology within the problem domain context is given in Section 4.4.1.

4.4.1 Serious Gaming: A Foundation for Understanding Infrastructures

Luna-Reyes et al. (2005) state that social and organizational factors can cause up to 90% of information system project failures, resulting in not delivering the expected benefits. For that reason, it is crucial to integrate such societal factors into large-scale infrastructure design processes. As previously mentioned, simulation gaming methods have recently shown promise in large-scale sociotechnical system planning efforts. Their ability to integrate infrastructure development's social and technical aspects delineates these methods as the most appropriate approach for creating a venue combining computer-assisted stakeholder interaction. In this way, serious games provide insights into how to address issues arising from the interaction of players, roles, rules, and scenarios. Mayer describes serious gaming derived applications as "a hard core of whatever the computer model incorporated in a soft shell of gaming (usually through some form of role-play)" (Mayer 2009, p. 835). To support the case study, the Rapid Risk Assessment Model (RRAM) described below is used as the hardcore computer model to measure throughout the exercise; the more detailed demonstration of gaming methodology. Besides the RRAM, the commercially available decision support software, Logical Decisions® for Windows (LDW) v.6.2, can be used to support decision-making. The software assists the gaming process by helping participants evaluate and prioritize among the available decisions they have throughout the game (Logical Decisions: http://www.logicaldecisionsshop.com/catalog). LDW's dynamic ranking capability of various alternatives provides real-time support in selecting alternatives according to their parameters (e.g. cost/benefit values, environmental impact, implementation risks, timelines, etc.). The RRAM estimates and quantifies risk values, comprised of separately calculated accident probabilities and their respective consequences. The probabilities within the model are estimated via the Probability Number Method (PNM), and the consequences are approximated via numerical manipulations. The RRAM is supported by historical and expert-elicited data as well as the gaming to generate the risk values throughout the methodology numerically. The RRAM was used as the risk simulation mechanism selected for the case study. However, depending on the problem at hand, this model can be replaced with any adequate software, method, or existing research measuring issues related to network capacity, throughput, financial status, etc. The adaptability of the gaming method allows developers to switch and/or combine different approaches, which will provide a systemic view of the problem.

The RRAM was created through the joint effort of the International Atomic Energy Agency (IAEA), the United Nations Environment Programme (UNEP), the United Nations Industrial Development Organization (UNIDO), and the World Health Organization (WHO) under the United Nations umbrella. The model and the associated method were developed as an affordable solution for a quick turnaround needed to determine risks associated with the handling, storage, processing, and transportation of hazardous materials. The risk assessment methodology (including the PNM approach) was supported by an extensive database containing various types of substances, including flammable, toxic, safety precaution measures, population densities, and environmental factors (IAEA 1996). However, as opposed to answering questions such as the maximum number of fatalities or the effect of distance, the PNM induced risk assessment methodology was more focused on the prioritization of actions in the field of emergency preparedness.

In this case, the risk is defined as the product of the probability of an accident and its respective consequences (Bedford and Cooke 2001). The IAEA study estimates probabilities and consequences separately. The consequences of an accident (e.g. an event caused by storage or transportation of certain hazardous materials) are calculated via simple numerical manipulations, taking into consideration the characteristics of the substance and correcting factors regarding the area, population density, accident geometry, etc. The required data to form the components of the equation are obtained through previous modeling efforts and expert opinions. On the other hand, the probabilities are estimated via PNM, where the likelihood of a particular accident happening is calculated via a dimensionless "probability number," N, which is transformed into actual probabilities. The probability number is adjusted/updated according to the various correcting factors. The relationship between the probability and N is given via $N = |log_{10}P|$. Risk is defined as the product of the consequences and the probabilities of unwanted outcomes (hazardous events).

Section 4.3 provided calculations of human casualties (fatalities) associated with an accident and the probabilities of such accidents occurring. The risk to the public from these activities is estimated by combining these two values. The consequences are categorized with respect to the fatalities, and the probability classes are categorized by order of magnitude of the number of accidents per year (e.g. societal risk operational instrument). The consequence-frequency (x-y) diagram is created. The main goal is to obtain a list of activities whose risks must be further analyzed before others. The risk matrix representation is one of the primary outcomes of the method.

4.4.2 Post Gaming: Analysis of Data

Throughout the gaming effort, the discussions and possible negotiations between the opposing parties are significant findings that can lead to different problem-solving approaches. The results of a game run are analyzed to examine if the gaming exercise influenced participants' beliefs, intentions, attitudes, and behavior, yielding a better understanding of complexity (Joldersma and Geurts 1998). The serious gaming exercise serves as an individual and collaborative learning platform for the stakeholders, leading to an elevated level of knowledge of the system (Wilson et al. 2009). Individual learning occurs during the decision-making process, where each stakeholder group represents its respective point of view. The reflective conversations between the participants enable feedback and help participants build informed judgments. Therefore, realistic interactions among players help the future testing and evaluation of NextGen-related technologies (Ancel 2011; Joldersma and Geurts 1998). Also, like individual learning, collective or organizational education provides insight into the system at hand, such as the resilience of critical infrastructure systems.

Besides collective and individual learning, another main contribution of the gaming methodology is generated data. Considering the nature of predicting future states of complex infrastructure systems, fusing simulation mechanisms with the soft gaming method creates the best possible venue for expert elicitation for cases when the game is played with real stakeholders and subject matter experts. An intuitive mechanism may need to be developed based on the scenario under consideration to collect, sort, and visualize the data. However, since the validity of the extracted data cannot be revealed until the system's future states are attained, the sole way to check the generated methodology's internal validity again is by using expert opinions.

Expert feedback is a leading contributor in all phases of the methodology. Experts from all stakeholder groups help shape possible scenarios, provide numerical data regarding future technological enablers, and evaluate the developed methodology in different categories. Expert participation in all three phases of the gaming-based elicitation methodology is prominent since it allows game developers to modify the gaming components constantly by considering participant comments and recommendations. Due to the large level of the system, no one expert is sufficient to gather all the data needed to develop gaming based on the given methodology.

It is crucial to seek seamless integration between the components of this methodology in order to create an efficient representation of the reference system. For example, this chapter suggests gaming cycles (pre-gaming, gaming, and post-gaming) coupled with the use of several models (RRAM, PNM), methods (serious gaming, expert elicitation), COTS solutions (LDW, TopRank®), and data sources to understand and perhaps make a better decision. However, these efforts require seamless integration of the elements discussed. Besides the methodology components, the adequate capturing of the system's characteristics (e.g. motivation for change, constraints, system context, as well as the societal, technical, and economic aspects) carries vital importance for the validity of the generated data. Because system characteristics vary with the context, the modeler's steps change from problem to problem. For this reason, adapting this methodology to other infrastructure system transitions most likely requires modifying the contents of the tools and approaches, yet it is important to develop a thorough balance in the methodology integration to capture both societal and technical aspects of large infrastructure transition problems.

4.4.3 Validation in Gaming

The early adopters of gaming were quite skeptical of its ability to test strategies or forecast developments confidently. They concluded the major benefit of the game was to suggest research priorities and identify major problems related to policy and action requirements (Mayer 2009). The main criticism of the field was caused by gaming's eclectic, diverse, and interdisciplinary nature along with the lack of defining terms and concepts (Gosen and Washbush 2004). However, the failure to implement a sustainable infrastructure model indicated that the multi-dimensional complexity of modern systems required different approaches and design principles (Roos et al. 2004). As an alternative answer, research studies employing gaming methods increased exponentially after the 1970s (Duke 1974).

Although one can come across a vast amount of literature regarding the validity of experimental situations (internal and external validity), measurement instruments (content and construct validity), and the specific research method or its results, the concept of validity regarding simulation games is barely elaborated in the literature (Peters et al. 1998). The validity of gaming usage was mostly investigated regarding its ability to enhance education and training. Researchers studied the specific gaming attributes that contribute to learning outcomes and evaluation of gaming methods' training effectiveness (Feinstein and Cannon 2002; Gosen and Washbush 2004; Wilson et al. 2009). The simulation approach received several criticisms regarding its ability to serve as an educational tool where the main concerns focused on internal and external validities, for the cases where the changes in the classroom environment or generalizability of the learning effects to outside classroom situations were problematic (Gosen and Washbush 2004). Generally, the validity within the simulation games can be given as the correspondence between the model and the system itself (or the reference system). However, this definition is not very accurate since the level of correspondence between the model and the referent system is unknown; it could mean that the model has a one-to-one representation of the complex system or only a few components of the system are modeled. Additional criteria are necessary to distinguish the level of association between the model and the modeled system (Peters et al. 1998). The conclusions reached via a simulation game should be similar to those that can be experienced in the real-world system (Feinstein and Cannon 2002).

The literature review demonstrated three relevant validation definitions regarding the contents of this research. Peters et al. (1998) review the concept of validity under four criteria, as suggested by Raser (1969): psychological reality, structural validity, process validity, and predictive validity. Greenblat and Duke (1975) describe the types of validity related to gaming models with common sense or face validity, empirical validity, and theoretical validity. Chytka (2003) provides a validation triad containing performance, structural, and content validities to validate her methodology.

Embarking from the definitions of Greenblat and Duke (1975) complemented by Peters et al. (1998), face validity or psychological reality refers to the realistic gaming environment experienced by the participants. For a game to be valid, the environment must portray similar characteristics to the reference system. The empirical validity given by Greenblat designates the closeness of the game structure to the reference system. The definition given by Peters et al. separates empirical validity into two sections: structural validity (i.e. covering the game structure, theory, and assumptions) and process validity (i.e. concerning the information/resource flows, actor interactions, negotiations, etc.). For the simulation to be valid all the game elements (i.e. actors, information, data, laws, norms, etc.) should be isomorphic – *elements and relations do not necessarily have to be identical but should be able to demonstrate congruency between them.* Finally, the last feature covered by both definitions is related to theoretical validity: the models' ability to reproduce historical outcomes or predict the future and conform to existing logical principles.

At times the validation triad is necessary (Ancel 2011; Chytka 2003). A validation triad consists of performance, structural, and content validities. These components are elaborated within an unstructured interview process to obtain the validity of the methodology. The performance validity

Table 4.1 Gaming validation parameters.

Proponents	Validity parameters
Greenblat and Duke (1975)	Common sense (face validity)
	Empirical validity
	Theoretical validity
Peters et al. (1998)	Psychological reality
	Structural validity
	Process validity
	Predictive validity
Chytka (2003)	Performance validity
	Structural validity
	Content validity

includes the methodology's efficiency and the uncertainty representation's usefulness. Structural validity concerns the usability and added value of the method and its applicability beyond the test case. Finally, content validity is involved with the appropriateness of the aggregation method chosen for the study. Table 4.1 provides a summary of validation parameters.

4.5 Concluding Remarks

The term "gamification" first appeared online in the context of computer software in 2008 (Walz and Deterding 2015). Gamification did not gain popularity until 2010 (GoogleTrends 2021). However, even before the term came into wide usage, borrowing elements from video games was common, such as for learning disabilities (Adelman et al. 1989) and scientific visualization (Rhyne et al. 2000). The term gained wide usage around 2010, and many began to refer to it when incorporating social/reward aspects of games into software development (Mangalindan 2012). This approach captured the attention of venture capitalists, who suggested "many aspects of life could become a game of sorts [and that these games] ... would be the best investments to make in the game industry" (Sinanian 2010). However, there remains no universally accepted definition of gamification.

The debate for the definition of gamification is left to others; the history and the value are much more interesting. To this end, we suggest that the value of gamification is demonstrable at the cognitive, emotional, and social levels. Therefore, gaming can be used as a guide for "players" through unconsciously skillful processes and keep them evolving with potentially challenging missions or difficult assignments. Emotionally, gaming can be used to invoke many positive emotional experiences, such as dignity, integrity, respect, and sympathy. And finally, gaming can serve as a catalyst for "players" to select characters (and situations) that are less explicitly fictional in order to explore their new sides and develop new social skills in a safe-to-learn environment.

However, involvement in gaming requires a significant investment in understanding how gaming works and how it ought to work for practical deployment. At this stage, suffice to say that the examination of gaming through the lens of policy-making, design, expert systems, data generation, and gaming cycles and validation provides the necessary background for applications – discussed in the proceeding chapters. Moreover, it is essential to recall that the current research methodology relies heavily on subjective assessments obtained from experts at all levels (pre-gaming, gaming, and post-gaming phases). Subsequently, the validation parameters of the method require subject matter expert opinions. And yet, it is clear that the value of gaming, in its various names, is here to stay. For example, Gartner's Top 10 Strategic Technology Trends for 2023 emphasize gaming in IT systems for greater optimization to offer improved data-driven decision-making and maintain the value and integrity of artificial intelligence (AI) systems in production (Groombridge 2022)

Moreover, the metaverse allows people to replicate or enhance their physical activities. This could happen by transporting or extending physical activities to a virtual world or transforming the physical one. It is a combinatorial innovation made up of multiple technology themes and capabilities. In any case, this is an attempt to enable sustainable technologies to enable societal resiliency. In fact, Gartner suggests that investing in sustainable technology can create excellent operational resiliency and financial performance while providing new avenues for growth (Groombridge 2022).

4.6 Exercises

1 Discuss how gaming can be used to enhance decision-making in city development.
2 Discuss how gaming can be used to reduce uncertainty in city development.
3 Discuss the nature and role of validation in city development.
4 How can serious gaming serve as a foundation for understanding infrastructure design?
5 Discuss how gaming can affect policy for resilient city development.

References

Adelman, H.S., Lauber, B.A., Nelson, P. et al. (1989). Toward a procedure for minimizing and detecting false positive diagnoses of learning disability. *Journal of Learning Disabilities* 22(4): 234–244. https://doi.org/10.1177/002221948902200407.

Ancel, E. (2011). *A Systemic Approach to Next Generation Infrastructure Data Elicitation and Planning Using Serious Gaming Methods*. PhD., Old Dominion University. http://search.proquest.com.proxy.lib.odu.edu/docview/896960555/abstract/C4484A36FA444018PQ/5.

Ancel, E., Gheorghe, A., and Jones, S.M. (13 October 2010). NextGen future safety assessment game. *2010 MODSIM Conference and World Expo*, Hampton, VA. MODISIM World. https://ntrs.nasa.gov/citations/20100036351.

Ayyub, B.M. (2001). *Elicitation of Expert Opinions for Uncertainty and Risks* (1st ed.). CRC Press.

Bedford, T. and Cooke, R. (2001). *Probabilistic Risk Analysis: Foundations and Methods*. Cambridge University Press.

Bekebrede, G. (2010). *Experiencing Complexity: A Gaming Approach for Understanding Infrastructure Systems*. Delft University of Technology. http://resolver.tudelft.nl/uuid:dae75f36-4fb6-4a53-8711-8aab42378878.

Brewer, G.D. (2007). Inventing the future: Scenarios, imagination, mastery and control. *Sustainability Science* 2(2): 159–177. https://doi.org/10.1007/s11625-007-0028-7.

Chytka, T. (2003). *Development of an Aggregation Methodology for Risk Analysis in Aerospace Conceptual Vehicle Design*. Dissertation. Old Dominion University.

Chytka, T.M., Conway, B.A., and Unal, R. (2006). An expert judgment approach for addressing uncertainty in high technology system design. *2006 Technology Management for the Global Future – PICMET 2006 Conference*, 1, 444–449. IEEE. https://doi.org/10.1109/PICMET.2006.296590.

Cleland, D., Dray, A., Perez, P. et al. (2012). Simulating the dynamics of subsistence fishing communities: REEFGAME as a learning and data-gathering computer-assisted role-play game. *Simulation & Gaming* 43(1): 102–117. https://doi.org/10.1177/1046878110380890.

CLP. (February 22, 2021). The benefits of using a change management simulation game. *CLP*. https://www.change-leadership.net/the-benefits-of-using-a-change-management-simulation-game.

Cooke, R.M. and Goossens, L.H.J. (2004). Expert judgement elicitation for risk assessments of critical infrastructures. *Journal of Risk Research* 7(6): 643–656. https://doi.org/10.1080/1366987042000192237.

Crookall, D. and Arai, K. (eds.). (1995). *Simulations and Gaming Across Disciplines and Cultures: ISAGA at a Watershed* (1st ed.). SAGE Publications, Inc.

Demeter, G. (2007). Symposium article: Role-plays as a data collection method for research on apology speech acts. *Simulation & Gaming* 38(1): 83–90. https://doi.org/10.1177/1046878106297880.

Deterding, S., Dixon, D., Khaled, R. et al. (2011). From game design elements to gamefulness: Defining "gamification". *Proceedings of the 15th International Academic MindTrek Conference: Envisioning Future Media Environments*, 9–15. ACM. https://doi.org/10.1145/2181037.2181040.

Dicheva, D., Dichev, C., Agre, G. et al. (2015). Gamification in education: A systematic mapping study. *Journal of Educational Technology & Society* 18(3): 75–88. https://www.jstor.org/stable/jeductechsoci.18.3.75.

Duke, R.D. (1974). *Gaming: The Future's Language*. Sage Publications. https://trove.nla.gov.au/version/45243363.

Feinstein, A.H. and Cannon, H.M. (2002). Constructs of simulation evaluation. *Simulation & Gaming* 33(4): 425–440. https://doi.org/10.1177/1046878102238606.

Frantzeskaki, N. and Loorbach, D. (2008). Infrastructures in transition role and response of infrastructures in societal transitions. *2008 First International Conference on Infrastructure Systems and Services: Building Networks for a Brighter Future (INFRA)*, 1–8. IEEE. https://doi.org/10.1109/INFRA.2008.5439669.

French, S., Kelly, N., and Morrey, M. (1992). Decision conferencing and the international Chernobyl project. *Journal of Radiological Protection* 12(1): 17. https://doi.org/10.1088/0952-4746/12/1/003.

Gee, J.P. (2008). Learning and games. In: *The Ecology of Games: Connecting Youth, Games, and Learning* (ed. K. Salen) . MIT Press.

Geertje, B., Igor, M., Pieter, V.H.S. et al. (2005).How serious are serious games? Some lessons from infra-games.In: *Proceedings of Digital Games Research Association (DiGRA) Conference: Changing Views – Worlds in Play*, Vancouver, BC. Digital Games Research Association. http://www.digra.org/wp-content/uploads/digital-library/06278.53186.pdf.

Geurts, J.L.A., Duke, R., and Vermeulen, P.a.M. (2007). Policy gaming for strategy and change. 558. *Long Range Planning*, 40 (6): 535–558. https://doi.org/10.1016/j.lrp.2007.07.004

GoogleTrends. (2021). Gamification. *Google Trends*https://trends.google.com/trends/explore?date=all&q=gamification.

Gosen, J. and Washbush, J. (2004). A review of scholarship on assessing experiential learning effectiveness. *Simulation & Gaming* 35(2): 270–293. https://doi.org/10.1177/1046878104263544.

Greenblat, C.S. and Duke, R.D. (1975). *Gaming Simulation: Rationale, Design and Applications*. Wiley.

Groombridge, D. (2022). Gartner top 10 strategic technology trends for 2023. Gartner. https://www.gartner.com/en/articles/gartner-top-10-strategic-technology-trends-for-2023.

Gustafson, D.H., Shukla, R.K., Delbecq, A. et al. (1973). A comparative study of differences in subjective likelihood estimates made by individuals, interacting groups, Delphi groups, and nominal groups. *Organizational Behavior and Human Performance* 9(2): 280–291. https://doi.org/10.1016/0030-5073(73)90052-4.

Halleck, G. (2007). Symposium article: Data generation through role-play: Assessing oral proficiency. *Simulation & Gaming* 38(1): 91–106. https://doi.org/10.1177/1046878106298268.

IAEA. (1996). *Manual for the Classification and Prioritization of Risks Due to Major Accidents in Process and Related Industries*. International Atomic Energy Agency. http://www-pub.iaea.org/books/IAEABooks/5391/Manual-for-the-Classification-and-Prioritization-of-Risks-due-to-Major-Accidents-in-Process-and-Related-Industries.

Joldersma, C. and Geurts, J.L.A. (1998). Simulation/gaming for policy development and organizational change. *Simulation & Gaming* 29(4): 391–399. https://doi.org/10.1177/104687819802900402.

Kapp, K.M. (2012). Games, gamification, and the quest for learner engagement. *Talent Development* 66: 64–68. https://www.td.org/magazines/td-magazine/games-gamification-and-the-quest-for-learner-engagement.

Keeney, R.L. and von Winterfeldt, D. (1989). On the uses of expert judgment on complex technical problems. *IEEE Transactions on Engineering Management* 36(2): 83–86. https://doi.org/10.1109/17.18821.

Koster, R. (2004). *Theory of Fun for Game Design*. Paraglyph Press.

Kuit, M., Mayer, I.S., and de Jong, M. (2005). The INFRASTRATEGO game: An evaluation of strategic behavior and regulatory regimes in a liberalizing electricity market. *Simulation & Gaming* 36(1): 58–74. https://doi.org/10.1177/1046878104272666.

Lazzaro, N. (2004). *Why We Play Games: Four Keys to More Emotion without Story*. XEODesign, Inc.

Lee, J. and Hammer, J. (2011). Gamification in education: What, how, why bother? *Academic Exchange Quarterly* 15(2): 1–5. https://www.semanticscholar.org/paper/Gamification-in-Education%3A-What%2C-How%2C-Why-Bother-Lee-Hammer/dac4c0074b6d0d86977313664a7da98e577a898a.

Linstone, H.A. and Turoff, M. (eds.). (1975). *The Delphi Method: Techniques and Applications*. Addison Wesley Publishing Company.

Locke, E.A. and Latham, G.P. (1990). *A Theory of Goal Setting and Task Performance* (pp. xviii, 413). Prentice-Hall, Inc.

Luna-Reyes, L.F., Zhang, J., Ramón Gil-García, J. et al. (2005). Information systems development as emergent socio-technical change: A practice approach. *European Journal of Information Systems* 14(1): 93–105. https://doi.org/10.1057/palgrave.ejis.3000524.

Mangalindan, J. (November 12, 2012). Play to win: The game-based economy. Fortune Tech. https://web.archive.org/web/20121112074424/http://tech.fortune.cnn.com/2010/09/03/the-game-based-economy.

Mayer, I.S. (2009). The gaming of policy and the politics of gaming: A review. *Simulation & Gaming* 40(6): 825–862. https://doi.org/10.1177/1046878109346456.

McGonigal, J. (2011). *Reality is Broken: Why Games Make us Better and How they Can Change the World* (Reprint ed.). Penguin Books.

Meyer, M.A. and Booker, J.M. (1987). *Eliciting and Analyzing Expert Judgment: A Practical Guide*. Society for Industrial and Applied Mathematics.

Nasir, N.S. and Saxe, G.B. (2003). Ethnic and academic identities: A cultural practice perspective on emerging tensions and their management in the lives of minority students. *Educational Researcher* 32(5): 14–18. https://journals.sagepub.com/doi/10.3102/0013189X032005014.

Peters, V., Vissers, G., and Heijne, G. (1998). The validity of games. *Simulation & Gaming* 29(1): 20–30. https://doi.org/10.1177/1046878198291003.

Pope, D.C. (2003). *Doing School: How we are Creating a Generation of Stressed-out, Materialistic, and Miseducated Students* (unknown edition). Yale University Press.

Raser, J.C. (1969). *Simulations and Society: An Exploration of Scientific Gaming*. Allyn & Bacon.

Rhyne, T.-M., Doenges, P., Hibbard, B. et al. (2000). The impact of computer games on scientific and information visualization (panel session): "If you can't beat them, join them." In: *Proceedings of the Conference on Visualization '00*, 519–521. IEEE.

Roos, D., de Neufville, R., Moavenzadeh, F. et al. (2004). The design and development of next generation infrastructure systems. *2004 IEEE International Conference on Systems, Man and Cybernetics (IEEE Cat. No.04CH37583)*, 5, 4662–4666. https://doi.org/10.1109/ICSMC.2004.1401267.

Rosendale, D. (1989). Role-play as a data-generation method.*Simulation & Games* 20(4): 487–492. https://doi.org/10.1177/104687818902000410.

Shiratori, R., Arai, K., and Kato, F. (2005). *Gaming, Simulations and Society: Research Scope and Perspective*. Springer. https://doi.org/10.1007/b138103.

Sinanian, M. (April 12, 2010). The ultimate healthcare reform could be fun and games. VentureBeat. https://venturebeat.com/2010/04/12/healthcare-reform-social-games-gamification.

Singuran, G.F. (2008). *System Level Risk Analysis of New Merging and Spacing Protocols*. Thesis. Delft University of Technology. https://repository.tudelft.nl/islandora/object/uuid%3Adae75f36-4fb6-4a53-8711-8aab42378878.

Squire, K. (2006). From content to context: Videogames as designed experience. *Educational Researcher* 35(8): 19–29. https://doi.org/10.3102/0013189×035008019.

Vasuthanasub, J. (2019). *The Resilient City: A Platform for Informed Decision-making Process*. Dissertation. Old Dominion University. https://digitalcommons.odu.edu/emse_etds/151.

Walz, S.P. and Deterding, S. (2015). *The Gameful World: Approaches, Issues, Applications*. MIT Press.

Warmerdam, J., Knepfle, M., Bidarra, R. et al. (2006). *SimPort: A Multiplayer Management Game Framework* (eds. Q. Mehdi, F. Mtenzi, B. Duggan et al.), 219–224. University of Wolverhampton School of Computing.

Wenzler, I. (2008). The role of simulation games in transformational change. In: Planspiele für die Organisationentwicklung (ed. W.C. Kritz), pp. 63–74. WVB.

Wenzler, I., Kleinlugtenbelt, W.J., and Mayer, I. (2005). Deregulation of utility industries and roles of simulation. *Simulation and Gaming* 36(1): 30–44. https://doi.org/10.1177/1046878104273218.

Wilson, K.A., Bedwell, W.L., Lazzara, E.H. et al. (2009). Relationships between game attributes and learning outcomes: Review and research proposals. *Simulation & Gaming* 40(2): 217–266. https://doi.org/10.1177/1046878108321866.

5

Regional Mix Game for Renewable Energy Resources

5.1 Introduction

It is commonly understood that systems (e.g. energy systems) consist of parts. If one is to take these parts as $P_i = 1, 2, ..., M$, once defined, parts may be seen as individual, atomic (indivisible) components that (i) usually come in large numbers (M), (ii) are coupled with each other with a strength that may conveniently be expressed as a generic, coupling "energy," $\epsilon_{ij}, i = 1,2,3...M, j = 1,2,...M$, and (iii) respond to external stresses (i.e. fields of influences), H with each system part featuring an "energy," $u_i H$, of the coupling with the fields via a coupling strength, u_i (Gheorghe et al. 2018).

Interestingly, the notion of "part" embraces a virtually unlimited variety of representations. And as an example, for an energy system, parts may include anything such as mines, mills, wells, pipes, power stations, switchyards, transmission lines, distribution facilities, control rooms, dispatch centers, and IT assistance facilities. Moreover, parts can have subassemblies, including fuel cycles, workers, working units, enterprises, companies, regulators, and political pressure entities. At this point, it is necessary to remind the reader that CI systems can enhance their overall resilience through several means. The deliberate efforts to improve CI system resilience include flexibility, inclusion, integration, redundancy, reflectiveness, resourcefulness, and robustness. A fun and intentional way to enhance system resilience is gaming. And although all gaming is not always good positive, serious gaming can serve as a means to learn and increase resilience at a personal level as well as an organizational level. This chapter extends the basics of gamification through a *mix game* – the mix game model was developed as a means for promoting energy efficiency and renewable energy sources.

5.2 Mix Game Model

Given the vocation of the mix game – to stand for only a ludic, awareness-raising appendix mainly addressing layperson energy stakeholders – the model is simplified for the objective of oriented design for optimal primary energy mixes. It is set to deliberately avoid the arcane of the textbook linear and nonlinear programming technology while retaining its basic philosophy that, as these authors believe, can be summarized as "pursue your target while observing the given constraints."

Gamification for Resilience: Resilient Informed Decision-Making, First Edition.
Adrian V. Gheorghe and Polinpapilinho F. Katina.
© 2023 John Wiley & Sons, Inc. Published 2023 by John Wiley & Sons, Inc.

Instead of betting on consecrated mathematical techniques, the game draws on the implicit ability of fast, mechanical computation to sort out many thousand random throws. In this case, random throws are values assigned to hosts of variables by their degree of compliance with numerical and logical (Boolean) constraints. The master plan of the approach goes as described in Sections 5.2.1 and 5.2.2.

5.2.1 Organization of Variables

Let

$$Mix(i, j), i = 1, 2, \ldots, nMix \tag{5.1}$$

be an array of features of *nMix* energy sources. In this context, an energy source is a pair consisting of a primary energy species (e.g. natural gas, oil, coal) and conversion technology to an end-use form – electric power, or heat and work. However, a feature is a physical quantity attached to "energy sources" on both the input side (i.e. as variables feeding a multi-attribute source assessment) and the output side (i.e. as containers for assessment results, the aggregation of which would result in a *choice*) and in this case, a choice should be the best energy mix which is based on analyst criteria and preferences considered. In the present case, the energy sources and features have emerged as a compilation of data adopted in the EU communique reference (European Commission 2007). There are nineteen sources, as depicted in Tables 5.1, 5.2, and 5.3. Table 5.1 shows the energy sources along with the advantages and disadvantages of different sources of electrical energy based on current oil, gas, and coal prices.

Table 5.2 depicts the energy sources along with the advantages and disadvantages of different energy sources for heating.

Table 5.3 depicts the energy sources along with the advantages and disadvantages of different energy sources for road transport.

Where $i = 1, 2, \ldots, 19$ is the first array index in Equation (5.1), the features are grouped in the manner shown in Table 5.4, the index in the first column being the j-index in the mix(i,j) array, of Equation (5.1).

The mix assessment also requires additional data. Table 5.5 depicts the quantity and variables of the additional data: *energy demand data, reserve-driven consumption ceilings, and other related constraints*.

In fact, the composition of the data palette in Table 5.5 is reflective of an assessment philosophy that looks for a primary energy mix: (i) starting from the end-use demand, (ii) observing a discipline of not exceeding a certain annual rate of depletion of proven reserves, and (iii) compliant with national commitments. These commitments should include the politicking level concerning GHG emissions while also giving away an allowance to other, non-energy-related activities prone to increment the GHG environmental burden.

5.2.2 Design for an Algorithm Implementing the Mindset

The following steps describe the design for implementing the mindset described in Sections 5.2.1 and 5.2.2:

a) Initialize data

```
maxProfit=0          'maximum profit, of a game session
maxSales=0           'maximum sales, of a game session
```

Table 5.1 The advantages and disadvantages of different sources of electrical energy.

Energy sources	Technology considered for the cost estimate	2005 cost (€/MWh) Source IEA	Projected cost 2030 (€/MWh with €20–30/tCO₂) Source IEA	GHG emissions (kg CO2eq/MWh)	EU-27 import dependency 2005	2030	Efficiency	Fuel price sensitivity	Proven reserves / Annual production
Natural gas	Open cycle gas turbine	45–70	55–85	440	57%	84%	40%	Very high	64 years
	CCGT (combined cycle gas turbine)	35–45	40–55	400			50%	Very high	
Oil	Diesel engine	70–80	80–95	550	82%	93%	30%	Very high	42 years
Coal	PF (pulverized fuel with flue gas desulfurization)	30–40	45–60	800	39%	59%	40–45%	medium	155 years
	CFBC (circulating fluidized bed combustion)	35–45	50–65	800			40–45%	medium	
	IGCC (integrated gasification combined Cycle)	40–50	55–70	750			48%	medium	
Nuclear	Light water reactor	40–45	40–45	15	Almost 100% for uranium ore		33%	low	Reasonable reserves: 85 years
Biomass	Biomass generation plant	25–85	25–75	30	nil		30–60%	medium	Renewable
Wind	On shore	35–175 35–110	28–170 28–80	30			95–98%	nil	
	Off shore	50–170 60–150	50–150 40–120	10			95–98%		
Hydro	Large	25–95	25–90	20			95–98%		
	Small (<10MW)	45–90	40–80	5			95–98%		
Solar	Photovoltaic	140–430	55 –260	100			/		

Table 5.2 The advantages and disadvantages of different energy sources for heating.

Energy sources		EU-25 market share by energy source	Market price (€/toe)	Lifecycle cost (€/toe)	GHG emissions (t CO_2eq/toe)	EU-27 importdependence	
						2005	2030
Fossil fuels	Heating gas oil	20%	**525** (€0.45/l)	**300–1300**	**3.1**	82%	93%
	Natural gas	33%	**230–340** (€20–30/MWh)		**2.1**	57%	84%
	Coal	1.8%	**70** (€100/tce)		**4**	39%	59%
Biomass	Wood chips	5.7%	**280**	**545–1300**	**0.4**	0	?
	Pellets		**540**	**630–1300**	**0.4**	0	?
Electricity		31%	**550–660** (€50–60/MWh)	**550–660**	**0 to 12**	<1%	?
Solar		0.2%	/	**680– 2320**	Very low	0	0
Geothermal		0.4%	/	**230–1450**	Very low	0	0

Table 5.3 The advantages and disadvantages of different energy sources for road transport.

	Market price (€/toe)	CO_2 emissions (t CO_2/toe)[32]	Import dependence	
			2005	2030
Petrol and diesel	398–582[33]	3.6–3.7	82%	93%
Natural gas	230–340 (NB: requires a specially adapted vehicle and a dedicated distribution system)	3.0	57%	84%
Domestic biofuel	609–742	1.9–2.4	0%	0%
Tropical bio-ethanol	327–540	0.4	100%	100%
Second-generation biofuel	898–1 109	0.3–0.9	/	15%

Table 5.4 Energy features for the mix game.

Index	Feature
On the input side:	
0	source is (value = 1), or is not (value = 0), selected in the mix;
1	source addresses electric power as an end use (value = 0), or heat-and-work (value = 1);
2	the market price of energy delivered by source, in euro/toe (ton oil equivalent);
3	cost of energy delivered by source, in euro/toe;
4	the efficiency of energy conversion from primary to end use;

Table 5.4 (Continued)

Index	Feature
5	the specific greenhouse gas (GHG) emissions, in tCO_2eq/toe (ton of CO_2 equivalent emission per ton of oil equivalent energy generated);
On the output side:	
6	electric power supply secured by the "source," in toe/year;
7	heat-and-work supply secured by the "source," in toe/year;
8	energy sales secured by the source, in euro/year;
9	energy costs incurred by the source, in euro/year;
10	profit (raw) obtained (sales–costs) from the source, in euro/year;
11	pollution entailed by operating the source, in $tCO_2eq/year$.

Table 5.5 Additional mix games quantities and variables.

Quantity	Variable name
Energy demand data	
Population (persons)	Population (this variable – idle in the current model version)
Total demand (toe/year); of which:	Demand
• electric power (% of total)	Demand power
• heat and work (% of total)	Demand heat
• nonenergy uses (% of total)	Demand other
• demand satisfaction target (% covered by supply)	Demand target
Reserve-driven consumption ceilings (independent of conversion technology)	
Natural gas	Stress $(1)
Oil	Stress $(2)
Coal	Stress $(3)
Nuclear	Stress $(4)
Biomass	Stress $(5)
Wind	Stress $(6)
Hydro	Stress $(7)
Solar	Stress $(8)
Geothermal	Stress $(9)
OTHER CONSTRAINTS	
GHG national target ceiling (tCO_2eq/yr)	GHG target
Allowance for non-energy polluters (% of target)	Allowance

```
minCosts=val("1.0e30")        'minimum costs, of a game session
minPollution=val("1.0e30")    'minimum pollution, of a game
session
minImports=val("1.0e30")      'minimum imports, of a game session
```

b) Set a number of iterations, niter, for a game session; default is 10.

c) Loop throughout iterations:

```
for jiter=1 to niter          'tart with iteration #1 and end with iter-
ation #niter
gosub [plan]                  'the through-and-optimize routine
```

d) As the [plan] routine has delivered the current iteration's "best" findings – maximal or minimal, as appropriate, namely

```
'profit - maximum,
'sales - maximum,
'costs - minimum,
'totImportCost - minimum of the total costs of imports required to
complement the
'supply from domestic resources, and
'pollution - minimum
```

'proceed to retain the extremes that would enable a summary of options' by the end of the iteration:

```
if profit>maxProfit then
        maxProfit=profit
        profitIter=jiter
if sales>maxSales then
        maxSales=sales
        salesIter=jiter
if costs<minCosts then
        minCosts=costs
        costsIter=jiter
if totImportCost<minImports then
        minImports=totImportCost
        importIter=jiter
if pollution<minPollution then
        minPollution=pollution
        pollutionIter=jiter
```

e) Display the results of the current iteration.

f) Go for the next iteration:

```
next jiter
```

g) Summarize.

All iterations are designed to *maximize profit* while observing the constraints of the admitted limited capability to satisfy the demand. Moreover, the model accounts for physical and economic limitations based on the domestic reserves. There have to be commitment targets based on the energy import ceiling and the politically committed environmental (GHG) targets – not necessarily in this order. However, given the stochastic nature of the game, of any number of iterations, several may catch the attention of the designer by the end of a game session, apart from "the highest-profit mix choice," including:

- the high-profit-*highest-sales* mix choice
- the high-profit-*lowest-costs* mix choice
- the high-profit-*lowest pollution* mix choice
- the high-profit-*lowest-imports* mix choice

These are all deserving of the label "highest-profit mix choice" in this mix game, with none having priority over another. At this point, the priority might be driven by the gamer and the stakeholders.

5.3 Key of the Game

Key to the entire process is the [plan] throw-and-optimize routine. It works on a number of iterations ("throws") of its own. The respective variable is n, which is hard-coded in this version to n = 25000. And in this case, one has:

```
[plan]
n=25000      'Set the number of throws to 250000
Emax=0' Initialize a variable holding the highest profit, to 0

for jn=1 to n  'Start throwing …
for k=1 to 9   'Initialize the reserves depletion container
stress(k,1)=0
(see the stress$(k), k = 1, 2,  …,  9 vector in Table 3)
next

pSupply=0          'Initialize cumulative power supply, of mix
hSupply=0          'Initialize cumulative heat-and-work supply, of mix
sales=0            'Initialize cumulative sales, of mix
costs=0            'Initialize cumulative costs, of mix
profit=0           'Initialize cumulative profit, of mix
pollution=0        'Initialize cumulative pollution, of mix

E=0' Initialize trial profit variable to 0

'The natural steering factor in code's 'throws' (random, trial allo-
cations per mix) 'is the demand. Using the inputs one then computes,
first:
    pDemand=demand*demandpower*0.01
    hDemand=demand*demandheat*0.01
    oDemand=demand*demandother*0.01

for i=1 to nmix' Loop throughout the mix
if mix(i,0) then    'Assess only components that were user-selected
in the mix
if mix(i,1)=0 then      'In the sequel, all quantities are per
year:
```

```
mix(i,6)= rnd(1)*2.0*pDemand/nPower        'trial power supply, as a
fraction of demand
pSupply=pSupply+mix(i,6)                    'cumulate …
else
mix(i,7)= rnd(1)*2.0*hDemand/nHeat         'trial heat supply, as a
fraction of demand
hSupply=hSupply+mix(i,7)                    'cumulate …
end if
mix(i,8)=(mix(i,6)+mix(i,7))*mix(i,2)       'resulting trial sales
sales=sales+mix(i,8)                        'cumulate …
mix(i,9)=(mix(i,6)+mix(i,7))*mix(i,3)       'resulting trial
costs
costs=costs+mix(i,9)                        'cumulate
mix(i,10)=mix(i,8)-mix(i,9)                 'resulting profit
profit=profit+mix(i,10)                     'cumulate
mix(i,11)=(mix(i,6)+mix(i,7))*mix(i,5)      'resulting
pollution
pollution=pollution+mix(i,11)              'cumulate …

for k=1 to 9                               'compute cumulated stress
from
if instr(mix$(i),stress$(k))>0 then        'trial supply, on domes-
tic reserves

if mix(i,1)=0 then stress(k,1)=stress(k,1)+mix(i,6)
if mix(i,1)=1 then stress(k,1)=stress(k,1)+mix(i,7)
end if next k

end if

next i      'close the mix loop per throw

E=profit' set optimization variable to the profit/year

okstress=1' determine whether reserves
for k=1 to 9' constraints are observed
if stress(k,1)>stress(k,0) then okstress=0 next

okpollution=1' determine whether GHG
if pollution>GHGtarget*(1-allowance/100) then okpollution=0 'targets
are observed

pAvgPrice=0      'compute an average market price,
mm=0' over mix components ('sources')
for m=1 to 19
if mix(m,0) then mm=mm+1
pAvgPrice=pAvgPrice+mix(m,2)
```

```
end if next
pAvgPrice=pAvgPrice/mm              'the mix-averaged price

pImport=(pDemand-pSupply)           'power import needed, physical
hImport=(hDemand-hSupply)           'heat-and-work-oriented import
needed, physical
totImport=pImport+hImport           'total imports needed, physical
pImportCost=pImport*pAvgPrice       'power imports cost
hImportCost=sImport*pAvgPrice       'heat-and-work-oriented imports
cost
totImportCost=pImportCost+hImportCost'  total cost of annual
imports required to
demandCost=demand*pAvgPrice         'fully meet the demand
okdemand=1

'now test whether the costs of imports exceed the Demand
Satisfaction Target (v. Table 3) if totImportCost/
demandCost>demandTarget/100 then okdemand=0
'… And the moment of truth:
'- if the error in meeting the current Maximum Profit Target, Emax,
is larger than '1/100 of the current profit, E, then reset the
Maximum Profit' Target to the
'current profit value, and continue to throw, within the preset
limit of '25000'throws;
'- if, otherwise, the error falls below 0.01 of the current profit,
then exit the '250000-throws loop, and exit the routine, leaving to
the main code to print the 'current iteration results and go for the
next iteration. This reads:

if okstress=1 and okpollution=1 and okdemand=1 and E>=Emax then
if abs(E-Emax)>=0.01*E then(2)
Emax=E else
exit for end if
end if next jn

return
```

The inequality (2) was proved in numerical experiments to ensure an acceptable convergence of the process so that conclusive mix options could be obtained without open-loop incidents, despite the random nature of the initializing ("throwing") drill.

5.4 Serious Gaming for Good Energy Governance

Clearly, gaming can be used to simulate realities, including those involving energy usage, and can do so well within current parameters, given the potential for weaponizing energy resources (Center for Strategic and International Studies 2022; Depetris 2022; Royal 2019). Moreover, the interaction of role players using non-formal symbols and formal, computerized sub-models is not just a game; it is only the beginning of good energy governance. In good energy governance, there is the purposeful engagement of participants (i.e. private and government organizations) in a safe environment to (i) create and analyze potential "futures" involving critical systems (e.g. energy systems) they want to explore, (ii) pre-test strategic initiatives, and (iii) deal with the increasing organizational complexity by enhanced communication. In harmony with good energy governance, we suggest understanding the big picture, having a memory of the future, and having shared intelligence.

5.4.1 Understanding the Big Picture

Simulation games are successful in providing a mechanism for visualizing and identifying the critical elements of a complex problem relating these elements to the situation as a whole, and combining the analysis of this whole with appropriate attention to detail. Games also enable envisioning alternative futures within a condensed time frame and help us get a holistic view (big picture) of the change journey and its results. The totality of problems and opportunities awaiting us in the future (although at a higher level of abstraction) are comprehended.

5.4.2 Memories of the Future

Through their iterative and experiential nature, simulation games allow us to test different approaches within a safe setting, thus helping us learn how to perform in the future. By facilitating such rehearsals of the future and by helping us envision and explore a multitude of time paths (alternative futures) within a condensed time, simulation games effectively build our memories of the future. The results are critical insights into value-creating opportunities and an increased ability to manage uncertainty and adapt to the changing environment.

5.4.3 Shared Intelligence

Simulation games create a learning environment where groups of people share experience and intelligence, construct meaning, and propagate ideas and skills as a norm. They do that by continuously probing for those cognitive and emotional elements that might constitute an effective, innovative, and mutually satisfactory solution. They also greatly enhance and facilitate communication among the key stakeholders, resulting in a shared understanding of the need and direction of change, as well as in the increased propagation of ideas, best practices, and solutions.

Recent concoctions of good energy governance have yielded emerging research into the *Governance of Smart Energy Systems* (Katina et al. 2021). First, it has been suggested that if a "problem" is defined as the difference between a preferred state and an undesired status quo, the function of governance is "problem-solving" in the sense of moving to desired states (Katina et al. 2021; Schneider and Bauer 2007). In this case, governance is related to regulation such that the realization of desired long- and short-term goals is enabled.

Moreover, governance involves three attributes: direction, oversight, and accountability. Direction includes sustaining a coherent identity and vision that supports consistent decisions, actions, interpretations, and strategic priorities (Katina et al. 2021). Oversight involves providing for control, communication, and integration of systems and their parts/entities. Accountability for system development is focused on ensuring efficient utilization of resources, monitoring performance, and exploration of aberrant conditions (Keating and Katina 2016). The triad of governance (i.e. direction, oversight, and accountability) is one basis for complex system governance with implications for the governance of smart energy systems:

- Direction: governance for smart energy systems must include sustaining a coherent identity and vision that supports consistent decisions, actions, interpretations, and strategic priorities.
- Oversight: governance for smart energy systems must provide for control, communication, and integration of systems and their parts/entities.
- Accountability: governance for smart energy systems must provide for smart energy system development focused on ensuring efficient utilization of resources, monitoring of performance, and exploration of aberration conditions.

Additionally, governance relates to a "governing structure" in the form of principles, norms, rules, and procedures that guide (and restrain) formal and informal organizational processes (Katina et al. 2021; Nye and Donahue 2000; Yolles 2006). In this case, the governing structure ensures that members under the structure adhere to specific regulations. Under the concept of complex system governance (Keating et al. 2014), good energy governance also implies the design, execution, and evolution of the metasystem functions necessary to provide control, communication, coordination, and integration of a complex system (Katina et al. 2021).

Furthermore, complex system governance involves the nine governance functions of the metasystem, including four primary functions and five subfunctions (Keating and Katina 2019; Keating et al. 2022). The metasystem functions find their intellectual roots in Beer's work (Beer 1981) in management cybernetics and the Viable System Model. These interrelated governance functions must be performed if a system is to remain viable (continue to exist) under conditions of internal flux and external turbulence. Finally, communication and its channels account for the flow of information and consistency in interpretation for exchanges within the metasystem and between the metasystem and external entities. The ten communication channels are adapted from the work of Beer (1981) and extensions of Keating and Katina (2016). Again, the metasystem must provide control, communications, coordination, and integration among the different constituent systems. In this relationship, the metasystem represents the "governing structure" for the smart energy system. In contrast, the individual constituent systems represent the "governed entities" of the energy system, such as petroleum, natural gas, etc. In this case, the governed entities are also complex in their own right. However, they are seen as subsystems at the metasystem level. The smart energy metasystem ensures the overall system performs as a unified whole, which permits establishing and maintaining system coherence (identity) and cohesion (unity). Clearly therefore, the concoctions of good energy governance in the sense of governance of smart energy systems cannot be brought about effortlessly but rather through purposeful design, even if in a game mindset!

5.5 Concluding Remarks

To be sure, the model behind the game is no more (and probably far less) conducive to absolute maxima/minima than advanced linear/nonlinear programming models. However, this model produces extremal values which, even if relative, are convincing enough that designing proper energy mixes is a part of energy strategies and planning. While it can be difficult to control every aspect of the multi-attribute process, which is sometimes rippled by random perturbations – physical or human in origin – and perhaps requires a twist of "good instinct" for gambling it is, nevertheless, an attainable goal.

The goal of the original research and the model was to promote energy efficiency and renewable energy sources together with the securing of adequate protection of CIs by developing an energy security strategy for the nation of Romania. And while the research can be used to revise and update existing Romanian strategies, we suggest a larger vision: *focus on energy efficiency and renewable energy sources at any level, as well as new developments in energy security and CIs protection at tribal, regional, national, and international stages.*

An underlying message to all those who have found some pleasure in playing the mix game is that the science and art of modeling, simulation, and visualization (Katina et al. 2020; NSF 2006; Tolk 2019) is increasingly becoming a must in the risky business of designing sustainable futures – energy and all.

5.6 Exercises

1 Select a region of interest and develop your own mix game for energy resilience.
2 Discuss additional variables that can be added to a mix game to reduce stress in energy systems.
3 How can good energy governance enhance the resilience of a city?
4 How does "shared intelligence" enhance the resilience of a city?
5 How can you create an "understanding of the big picture" for a city of millions?

References

Beer, S. (1981). *The Brain of the Firm: The Managerial Cybernetics of Organization*. Wiley.

Center for Strategic and International Studies. (2022). *The Energy Weapon – Revisited*. https://www.csis.org/analysis/energy-weapon%E2%80%94revisited.

Depetris, D.R. (2022, 28). Weaponizing energy will hurt Russia the most. *Time*. https://time.com/6217385/weaponizing-energy-will-hurt-russia-the-most.

European Commission. (2007). An energy policy for Europe: Communication from the Commission to the European Council and the European Parliament (2007). Commission of the European Communities. http://www.europarl.europa.eu/meetdocs/2004_2009/documents/com/com_com(2007)0001_/com_com(2007)0001_en.pdf.

Gheorghe, A., Vamanu, D.V., Katina, P. et al. (2018). *Critical Infrastructures, Key Resources, Key Assets: Risk, Vulnerability, Resilience, Fragility, and Perception Governance*. Springer International Publishing.

Katina, P.F., Keating, C.B., Zio, E. et al. (2021). Governance of smart energy systems. In: *Handbook of Smart Energy Systems* (eds. M. Fathi, E. Zio, and P.M. Pardalos), 1–20. Springer International Publishing.

Katina, P.F., Tolk, A., Keating, C.B. et al. (2020). Modelling and simulation in complex system governance. *International Journal of System of Systems Engineering* 10 (3): 262–292. https://doi.org/10.1504/IJSSE.2020.109739.

Keating, C.B. and Katina, P.F. (2016). Complex system governance development: A first generation methodology. *International Journal of System of Systems Engineering* 7 (1/2/3): 43–74. https://doi.org/10.1504/IJSSE.2016.076127.

Keating, C.B. and Katina, P.F. (2019). Complex system governance: Concept, utility, and challenges. *Systems Research and Behavioral Science* 36 (5): 687–705. https://doi.org/10.1002/sres.2621.

Keating, C. B., Katina, P. F., & Bradley, J. M. (2014). Complex system governance: Concept, challenges, and emerging research. *International Journal of System of Systems Engineering*, 5 (3): 263–288. https://doi.org/10.1504/IJSSE.2014.065756.

Keating, C.B., Katina, P.F., Chesterman, C.W. et al. (eds.) (2022). *Complex System Governance: Theory and Practice*. Springer International Publishing.

NSF. (2006). *Simulation-based Engineering Science: Revolutionizing Engineering Science Through Simulation* (pp. 1–66). National Science Foundation. https://www.nsf.gov/pubs/reports/sbes_final_report.pdf.

Nye, J.S. and Donahue, J. D. (2000). *Governance in a Globalizing World*. Brookings Institution Press.

Royal, T. (May 2, 2019). No one understands the weaponization of energy better than Russia and Iran. Modern Diplomacy. https://moderndiplomacy.eu/2019/05/02/no-one-understands-the-weaponization-of-energy-better-than-russia-and-iran.

Schneider, V. and Bauer, J. M. (2007). Governance: Prospects of complexity theory in revisiting systems theory. Annual Meeting of the Midwest Political Science Association (pp. 1–36). https://www.uni-konstanz.de/FuF/Verwiss/Schneider/ePapers/MPSA2007Paper_vs_jmb.pdf.

Tolk, A. (2019). Limitations and usefulness of computer simulations for complex adaptive systems research. In: *Summer of Simulation: 50 Years of Seminal Computer Simulation Research* (eds. J. Sokolowski, U. Durak, N. Mustafee et al.), pp. 77–96. Springer International Publishing.

Yolles, M. (2006). *Organizations as Complex Systems: An Introduction to Knowledge Cybernetics*. Information Age Publishing.

6

Urban Planning Simulation Using "SimCity 2013®" Game

6.1 Introduction

A fundamental goal of playing SimCity® is to build a city (Electronic Arts 2013; Vasuthanasub 2019). It may sound like a simple task, yet just like any game, there is a learning curve. When starting a new city, neither the best strategy nor specific technique can be used routinely – one needs to pay close attention to details. The game provides a lot of freedom in what the player can build, so many people tend to construct essential infrastructures and service facilities without pre-designing city layouts. In this case, a systematic approach to urban planning is unavoidable for non-entertainment purposes.

In SimCity 2013®, the player assumes the role and duties of a city mayor. The central aspect of this character is construction and zoning, which comprise a wide range of responsibilities, including laying down the roads, manipulating the land areas, providing the essential facilities, maximizing the service capacities, and otherwise balancing between the demand and supply of resources. Most of the time, the player will work with the main menu bar across the lower end of the interface. This menu bar contains fourteen buttons with fourteen different options. Each of them is distinguished by the symbols, such as a lightning bolt, plumbing, trash can, firefighter helmet, and police badge, as depicted in Figure 6.1. The interface will display the features in its particular category by clicking each button. When playing the game, icons will remain dark blue in case all services and systems in the city are operationally functional. On the other hand, if there is any concern, incident, or disruption in the city, the icon will switch to yellow, indicating a minor issue, or red, indicating a major problem.

Sections 6.2 and 6.3 give an overview of each option, along with how they can facilitate the development of a simulation city. First, we provide basic information about the game.

6.2 About SimCity 2013®

6.2.1 Features

The game includes several features meant to tap into creativity. For example, a player can control multiple cities. With multi-city play, players can interact and influence an entire region of cities – alone or with friends! Cities can share services and resources, working together to build Great Works projects benefiting all areas. Other features enable players to create their cities with new zoning and design tools. Buildings can also be customized to reveal additional functionality and unlock gameplay benefits.

Gamification for Resilience: Resilient Informed Decision-Making, First Edition.
Adrian V. Gheorghe and Polinpapilinho F. Katina.

6.2.2 Edition Comparison

Currently, two editions of SimCity® exist: the standard and the complete edition. Table 6.1 compares and contrasts these two editions.

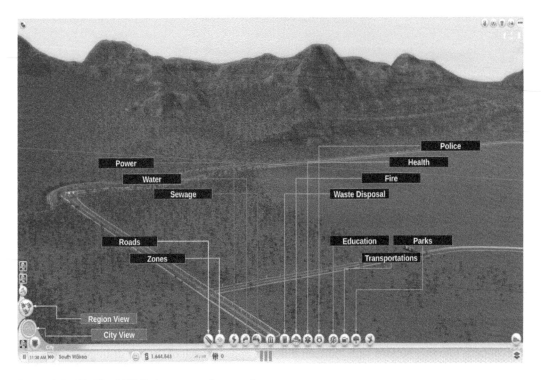

Figure 6.1 SimCity 2013®'s in-game main menu bar.

Table 6.1 SimCity® edition comparisons.

Capability	Capability description	Standard edition	Complete edition
Base game	Do you have what it takes to build a metropolis from scratch? Find out in SimCity®, a game that tasks you with planning the layout and infrastructure of a fully simulated city. Create a single city or up to 16 cities at once, then track the education, wealth, happiness, and more of your region and the Sims that live in it. Anyone can build a city – but it takes an excellent mayor to make one thrive.	Yes	Yes
Plumbob Park	Drop this scenic park anywhere in your city and watch your Sims revel in the great outdoors! Make your Sims happier, entice more to come to your city, and improve your rating as mayor.	Yes	Yes
Cities of Tomorrow	What kind of future will you build for your city? The Cities of Tomorrow expansion lets you decide, evolving your cities with futuristic tech and all-new city specializations. Want to create an environmentally friendly metropolis that runs on clean technology? No problem. Or create the ultimate resource-hungry mega-corporation to transform your city into a huge money-making machine. Just keep an eye out for giant, destructive robots. They are not fond of cities.	No	Yes

Table 6.1 (Continued)

Capability	Capability description	Standard edition	Complete edition
Heroes and Villains Set	With the Heroes and Villains Set, you can place and upgrade the Evil Villain Lair to unleash a crime wave or create your own Super Hero HQ to keep your Sims safe. One can order mayhem with the Evil Dr. Vu or MaxisMan to combat crime and save the day.	No	Yes
City Sets	The game contains several city sets: • British City Set: place your own Big Ben and watch the nearby buildings adopt England's classic Georgian-style architecture. Sensible and practical, these boxy brick buildings bring a classic British feel to your town. Plop in some iconic red double-decker buses and your miniature London will be ready for hordes of tourists. • French City Set: place the iconic Eiffel Tower and watch your city adopt the renowned architecture that makes Paris one of the most recognizable cities in the world. With warm stone facades and familiar circular layouts, this authentic French feeling really brings the decadent "City of Light" to your town. • German City Set: place the renowned Brandenburg Gate and see your city transform to the look and feel of classic German architecture. These buildings mesh together an old gothic look with the half-timbered look that makes Germany's colorful, red-roofed architecture so iconic. With all kinds of flowers and boutiques calling out from windows and shops, tourists are sure to stop by this quaint little section of town.	No	Yes
Airships Set	Take to the skies! Float tourists into your city with the Airship Hangar or add the Commuter Airship Mooring to help the morning commute. Your city will soar to new heights with enormous airships drifting through your city. Two included Hot Air Balloon Parks will lift your Sims' spirits and raise the neighborhood's land values. Gasp in wonderment as lumbering blimps hover above your stadiums during events. Fill your city with airships with the Airships set and see your city really take off.	No	Yes
Amusement Park	Build thrills. Create your own customized, fun-filled amusement park! Using amusement park paths, build your park around your city's terrain and layout. Your amusement park will benefit locals and tourists as they fill your park, riding all the rides and shopping at the concessions. Take your pick from three themed entrances to bring Sims into your amusement park. Draw tons of tourists to your theme park city, watch them stay in your hotels, and spend money in your shops!	No	Yes

6.3 Critical Infrastructure System Options

The city's critical infrastructure (CI) systems are presented as options with SimCity®. In this case, these represent physical and cyber systems and assets that are so vital to the city that their incapacity or destruction would have a debilitating impact on our physical or economic security or public health or safety.

6.3.1 Roads

The most crucial aspect of city planning is the roads. Roads play the most significant role and are considered the heart of SimCity®. In the game, roads are differentiated by using two properties: the number of lanes and the level of supported densities. Roads are blood vessels connecting the city to other cities, providing access to the buildings, distributing power, water, and sewage to Sims, and allowing Sims to travel from one location to another. Designing them wrong or with too many flaws will waste money, limit the building sizes and densities, and cause unfavorable traffic conditions. Figure 6.2 provides an example of a SimCity® visualization of traffic density.

In the case of traffic, congestion is an unavoidable problem that naturally occurs with increased populations. Moreover, congestion events can have many indirect effects on city operations. For instance, if emergency services, like ambulances or fire engines, cannot get to the location or scene on time, the Sims will die, or the buildings will burn down. For this reason, an effective road pattern is key to overall success. Finding the right proportion of street connections and avenue intersections is vital to keeping the traffic flowing smoothly into, out of, and around the city. Then, with the combination of adequate road network planning and intuitive management of mass transit infrastructures, the player can minimize traffic congestion to practically nothing, even with a population of over 100,000 Sims.

6.3.2 Zones

The zoning administration is the second most important task of the SimCity® mayor. After finishing the construction of the roads, the player has to determine which areas will be reserved for what purposes. By selecting the zones button, the menu bar will expand and display the zoning tools, which only contain four options: residential zone, commercial zone, industrial zone, and dezone. In this version of SimCity®, zones are extremely simplified. The residential zone is the area of residences and apartments where Sims live. The commercial zone is the place of shopping arcades or business centers where Sims shop. The industrial zone is the site of manufacturing factories or processing plants where Sims work. Lastly, the dezone is a tool that can be used to unmark zones. With those three assigned zones, Sims will start populating their buildings based on three factors: road type, available space, and land value. However, it should be noted that in the early stage of

Figure 6.2 SimCity®'s road network and density.

starting a new city, all buildings will normally be simulated under the rudimentary principles of low density and low wealth. Moreover, newly developed buildings have to be supplied with basic resources, including the likes of power, water, sewage, and parks.

6.3.3 Power

Nearly every building in SimCity® needs electric power to function. Energy is the first CI and essential service the mayor must provide to run the city. So without a power plant, the city will not grow. The third option on the toolbar is the power production tool. In the latest edition, there are several types of power plants. Each is radically distinct in terms of technological advancements, from an old-fashioned dirty generator like a coal power plant, to a modern, clean reactor such as a nuclear power plant. Each of them has advantages and disadvantages. However, most are undoubtedly expensive, and some are unquestionably polluted. Notice that when a player builds a power plant, all roads automatically serve as the power lines that distribute and deliver electricity to the city's buildings, as shown in Figure 6.3. This concept applies to all types of roads without exceptions. Furthermore, since the electric power moves along the road network in real-time, the buildings closer to the power station will gain the service before the buildings farther down the plant.

6.3.4 Water

Even in real life, clean water is another basic need for living. It is a prerequisite for maintaining public health and supporting life activities. It is widely considered part of the CI systems (Gheorghe et al. 2018). In a like manner to SimCity®, water is an essential resource, and a clean water production plant is the second vital service facility. Within SimCity®, Sims cannot survive without water.

The map switches to the data mode when the fourth button (on the menu bar) is clicked and selects either the water tower or water pumping station. This mode displays the entire water table directly underneath the land area. To maximize freshwater production in the long term, the mayor needs to place the building on the groundwater sources with the deeper blue color on the map. In

Figure 6.3 SimCity®'s electric power distribution.

the matter of providing the services, the idea is similar to electric power distribution. Roads also act as underground water pipes that deliver water to the buildings in the city (Figure 6.4). A potential issue with the water infrastructure is ground pollution. If the buildings nearby the water station pollute the area, the groundwater source will be contaminated. The incident can cause water contamination and lead to indirect problems for Sims (i.e. sickness). To eliminate this concern, the player must construct the water-pumping plant in a clean place or far away from polluters.

6.3.5 Sewage

The third utility service is a wastewater treatment system. Like living humans, all Sims consume clean water and then produce wastewater. In the game, if sewage is not adequately dealt with, it can cause ground pollution (affecting the nearby area with germ problems), leading to other consequences, particularly Sims sickness.

In the game, there are two simple solutions to handle sewage. First is the sewage outflow pipe and second is the sewage treatment plant. Both have the same purpose, which is to collect the sewage, but they do not process the sewage in the same way. The outflow pipe accumulates the sewage and later dumps it into the ground with a significant amount of pollution. The treatment plant stores the wastewater and slowly cleans it before replenishing the surrounding groundwater table with clean water. Figure 6.5 depicts how sewage service in SimCity® works when any one of the facilities is in operation. Noteworthy is the fact that the second option does not mean that the city is safe from pollution. In fact, the game recognizes that sewage treatment stations can also cause an increase in ground pollution footprint if they are running at overcapacity, understaffed, or underpowered. Therefore, the SimCity® mayor (i.e. the player) must stay vigilant to such issues in the game.

6.3.6 Waste Disposal

The next option in this evaluation, notably the seventh button on the toolbar, is waste disposal. Besides the management of the sewage treatment system, another two categories of waste collection services that the mayor must take into account are garbage and recycling. In SimCity®, both

Figure 6.4 SimCity®'s water supply distribution.

Figure 6.5   SimCity®'s wastewater management.

are grouped in the same category, but they are different things that each necessitate a specific service facility to manage. Garbage is waste that needs a garbage dump to consolidate and dispose of it. The dump station is the only solution to the city's trash disposal problem. Recyclables are materials that require a recycling center to claim and process them; they can then be used to produce valuable commodities, such as plastic, metal, and alloy, to make extra profit. The recycling plant should be built to reduce the accumulated amount of waste in the city without any pollution and to augment the city's expansion and prosperity.

By having at least one facility for both services, the garbage dump trucks and recycling collection trucks will leave the garages at their stations every day in the morning and circle around the city to collect trash and recyclables, as depicted in Figure 6.6. The trucks head back to their stations and drop off all collections at the end of the day. In addition to the collection performance of garbage

Figure 6.6   SimCity®'s garbage and recyclables collection.

dump trucks, traffic condition is the most crucial variable that can directly affect this service's capacity. In other words, in SimCity® if the garbage trucks cannot get to the collection points on time (i.e. garbage goes uncollected), the remaining amount of trash will be converted into soil pollution at the site of the buildings that produced it. To prevent an issue, the player can either build a garbage dump where its trucks can easily journey to populated areas or dispatch sufficient resources to all neighborhoods.

6.3.7 Fire

In SimCity®, the increased population comes with problems and opportunities. Specifically, when the number of people in the city are over 400 Sims, various issues – including garbage, fires, health, and crimes – are triggered. A fire can be a nightmare; it can burn a city block or turn a city into ashes if the mayor is not paying enough attention. In the simulation, single fires or multiple events can start in any building and any zones in the city, but in most cases, they usually happen in the industrial zone. As a matter of fact, typical fires will require a basic fire truck, but the hazmat truck will be required for the hazmat fires. Without the hazmat truck, hazmat fires will be unstoppable. They will indefinitely spread until all nearby buildings are burned down.

A fire station is a cheap but effective solution in the early stage of developing a new city. It comes with a fire engine, which can provide normal fire protection. Up to four fire trucks can be added to improve service performance or to cover multiple fire incidents. One distinctive advantage of the fire station is the size of the building itself. A small physical footprint makes it a perfect support station, which can be used in areas with limited space. However, the fire risk will grow exponentially as the city expands (Figure 6.7). To control the situation across the city, a large fire station needs to be commissioned. This not only provides the same service as the small one but also more comprehensively. The large fire station comes with a handful of tools that can fight all types of fire incidents, namely normal, hazmat, single, and multiple events. The station also offers additional modules, such as a fire marshal and fire helipad, which allow it to lower the fire risk and expand the service coverage area.

Figure 6.7 SimCity®'s potential fire risks.

6.3.8 Health

In SimCity®, Sims can get sick, injured, and die like humans. When Sims get sick, it will trigger the risk of injury, and when Sims get injured, it will activate the risk of death. Injured Sims need ambulances to pick them up. Otherwise, they will die. Therefore, sick Sims must receive medical attention as soon as possible. In the ninth option, two simple alternatives for providing healthcare services are a clinic and a hospital.

The clinic's service concept and building configuration are quite similar to the fire station in many aspects. It is cheap and small but a worthy investment for a solid starting point and an undeveloped city. The clinic comes with one ambulance bay and ten patient rooms. Both modules can be upgraded to reduce response time for injury emergencies and increase room capacity for patient treatments. A hospital is a large medical center with extensive medical equipment and specialized facilities. The extra modules at the hospital, including wellness centers, emergency centers, diagnostic labs, and surgical centers, can significantly improve the sickness causes, recovery times, and survival rate of Sims across the city.

6.3.9 Police

As the city mayor, another essential responsibility is protecting citizens from harm and violence. Law and order must be upheld to retain the community's safety and happiness. In SimCity®, criminals are automatically simulated based on various factors, mainly educational background and unemployment. They will randomly appear in the residential zone or travel into the city in personal vehicles. Criminals have their own patterns and routines to follow. They will leave their place at night and head to the targeted zone or building where they intend to commit the crimes. The list of offenses and types of violence ranges from simple shoplifting to attempted murder. With each successful criminal act, they will gain a greater experience level, which leads to higher chances of succeeding in the next illegal activities. Consequently, criminal events can deteriorate the city's image and value.

To fight criminals and keep Sims safe, the police station and police precinct are the only two answers. In fact, both stations are identical in a case of functionality but different in terms of building scale, upgradability, and serviceability. Like the technical qualifications of fire station and clinic, the police station is a smaller and less upgradable facility that works for a new city within the initial development stage. It prevents crimes and arrests criminals by dispatching patrol cars to secure its coverage area. If any crimes are in progress, the patrol officers will respond to the report and try to catch the perpetrators as fast as possible. Then, the arrested criminals will be transported back to the police station and imprisoned. To expand the police force on the street as well as to support the growing number of prisoners, additional patrol car lots can be authorized to boost the number of police cars, and the prison blocks can be renovated to raise the number of jail cells. Nevertheless, the true fighting against crimes will begin when the police precinct is founded. A precinct can cover an extensive patrol area, as illustrated in Figure 6.8. It also comes with unique modules, notably the detective wing and crime prevention center, that allow the mayor to actively track down criminals and passively reduce the crime rate. Also, detectives can be commissioned to investigate criminals' hiding locations and then arrest them before they have started committing crimes. Additionally, crime prevention agents can be assigned in a proactive approach to teaching kids in the education system about the value of being a good citizen.

6.3.10 Education

If the road network is the primary component in attaining overall success, education is a secondary element for breaking through to the next level of accomplishment. Schooling makes the life quality

Figure 6.8   SimCity®'s law enforcement and safety service coverage.

of Sims better in many practical ways. It reduces crime, health issues, fire risk, garbage, and water and electricity consumption. As a result, educated Sims are likely to save resources, more likely to produce recycles, less likely to cause fires and get sick, and unlikely to become criminals. Although educational facilities do not generate any income, they do increase the happiness and knowledge levels of residents in the city (Figure 6.9) as well as the technology level of manufacturers in the industrial zone. Building any educational facilities in the residential zone will also raise the land value of the surrounding area to the medium-wealth level. In the eleventh option on the toolbar, there are five educational facilities. A completed list of each type can be described as follows:

Figure 6.9   SimCity®'s educated Sims in the city.

- *Grade school:* a grade school is an ideal educational facility that provides basic education to young Sims. It increases the education level of the city's residents and the overall number of skilled workers.
- *High school:* this type of school functions with the same purpose as the grade school, although larger and more expensive. High schools favor the community by helping kids stay off the street, keeping them out of trouble, and educating them. So much so that they will not become criminals.
- *Community college:* the exclusive benefit of a community college is that it intentionally boosts the technology level of industrial buildings to level 2 (medium-tech) or occasionally even level 3 (high-tech). Industrial factories with these two tech levels pay higher taxes and produce less air pollution. In SimCity®, a community college is not accredited. However, operational costs are cheaper and its building size is a lot smaller when compared to a university.
- *University:* the university provides Sims with the highest level of education. It is a facility that enables industrial buildings to advance and maintain level 3 technology faster. Most of the research projects can be initiated and performed to unlock high-tech modules at this place, but the completion time will depend on the number of enrolled students.
- *Public library:* when Sims cannot afford to go shopping, they spend time at the library instead. Hence, the education level of the city's residents will slightly increase as Sims become more educated. Unlike the previous four educational facilities, a public library can be accessible by Sims of all ages.

In the game, even though each academic institution can offer varying degrees of education, this does not mean that all of them must be constructed in one city. In other words, Sims will be taken by school bus to neighboring cities to attend schools if there are not enough desks in their city. In the case of higher education, Sims will drive or use public transportation to colleges or universities in nearby cities (Vasuthanasub 2019).

6.3.11 Mass Transit

Mass transit is a vital CI that allows the mayor to improve traffic flow and prevents traffic congestion. It helps Sims move around the city and connects them to other regional cities. The following are five primary transportation systems in the mass transit option (the button with a bus icon):

- *Buses:* buses are the most basic public transportation infrastructure in SimCity®. As displayed in Figure 6.10, the system can operate as long as the road network is completed and the bus stops

Figure 6.10 SimCity®'s mass transit system (Buses).

are assigned. In this option, there are two types of bus stations. First is a shuttle-bus depot and second is a bus terminal. They perform the same service: transport low- and medium-wealth Sims. A noticeable difference between them is that the shuttle-bus depot provides a service for locals only, while the bus terminal is responsible for both local and regional services.

- *Streetcars:* to build a streetcar depot requires high-density streetcar avenues. With this specific condition, some mayors may not consider the streetcars to be a practical solution since the investment is costly. However, this type of public transportation is indispensable when the population is over 100,000 Sims. The streetcars not only reduce the traffic density by lessening the number of cars on the roads, they also enhance the service performance of a whole mass transit system by sharing the number of low- and medium-wealth commuters with the bus system. An example of functional streetcars service is depicted in Figure 6.11.
- *Trains:* unfortunately, trains are not serviceable transit systems in all cities since a regional heavy rail track network is required to connect stations. Passenger trains are carriers that allow regional commuters and shoppers to travel into or out of the city. They also provide ideal public transportation for low- and medium-wealth tourists.
- *Boats:* similar to the construction requirement of train stations, ferry terminals need a specific geographical condition for construction, especially along a shoreline. Therefore, water transportation is not an option in some cities. Notwithstanding, if available, the passenger ferry dock and cruise ship port can transport low- and medium-wealth workers from other regions and bring in medium- and high-wealth tourists to the city.
- *Planes:* a municipal airport is the only air transportation infrastructure and the last type of mass transit system in the game. It is a second alternative to transporting more medium- and high-wealth tourists into the city. The airport can be built and operated on any flat terrain. It is not expensive but requires a large area. One extra benefit of having the airport is that it boosts the productivity of nearby factories by shipping the industrial freight out on cargo planes.

Figure 6.11 SimCity®'s mass transit system (streetcars).

Figure 6.12 SimCity®'s land values and wealth level.

6.3.12 Parks

The final option in this evaluation is the thirteenth button on the main menu bar, the parks tool. Parks come with three levels of wealth but in a variety of sizes. They purposely function as spaces for relaxation and leisure activities. Sims visit parks to enjoy their free time and return home happy.

Parks provide comfort zones for residents, kids, and tourists. Moreover, parks are also an attribute that specifies land value. Land value is a standard in the game that characterizes wealthy areas, as shown in Figure 6.12. The wealth level of areas is a measure that determines the social class of Sims – mainly through residential and commercial zones. Thus, the idea of building parks is to relieve Sims' stress and designate the wealthy levels of residents, workers, and merchants in the city. Sims will play their role based on their associated social class. For example, low-wealth workers will fill the positions at the manufacturing factories and medium-wealth employees will get jobs in the business offices.

6.4 SimCity®: Limitations

SimCity® is not without its flaws. From its inception, the city-building and urban-planning simulation multiplayer online game has been plagued by many technical issues (BBC 2013; Edwards 2013; MacManus 2013). In this section, we expand on these limitations through the lens of CI sectors.

First, SimCity® utilizes a small section of sectors that define CI systems. For example, in the United States, the National Infrastructure Protection Plan (NIPP) represents the CI sectors and establishes sixteen essential sectors of infrastructure – i.e. chemical, commercial facilities, communications, critical manufacturing, dams, defense industrial base, emergency services, energy, financial services, food and agriculture, government facilities, healthcare and public health, information technology, national monuments and icons, nuclear reactors, materials, and waste, transportation systems, water and wastewater systems (US Department of Homeland Security 2013). This level of detail is still missing in SimCity®.

Second, an analysis of the current state of the CIs domain suggests that (Katina and Keating 2015):

- Critical infrastructures encompass physical (hard) systems such as roads and highways, hospitals, electrical systems, and water systems (Moteff et al. 2003; White House 2003) and soft systems such as supervisory control and data acquisition (SCADA) and information and telecommunication systems (GAO 2004).
- Threats to the sustained performance of CIs stem from natural events such as earthquakes, hurricanes, and heat waves as well as manufactured acts such as human error, accidents, acts of terrorism, and sabotage (Kröger and Zio 2011).
- Critical infrastructures operate primarily in the open and therefore are exposed in ways that make them vulnerable and susceptible to attacks (Wolf et al. 2011).
- Ubiquitous computing and the increasing use of information technologies create interdependencies among infrastructures (Anderson 2002; Katina et al. 2014; Kröger and Zio 2011). These interdependencies increase the probability that the seemingly isolated and inane events can cause cascading failures away from the point of origin (Calida and Katina 2012).
- As modern society evolves, creating new social changes (e.g. demand for quality products, goods, and services, globalization, and private–public governance policies), traditional concepts of protection, management, and controlling of infrastructures are also evolving (Gheorghe et al. 2006; Klaver et al. 2008).
- Infrastructure systems are critical because daily societal activities revolve around their continued operations. The distinction between critical and non-critical infrastructures can be difficult to pinpoint especially since the goods and services they provide are always restored as quickly as possible to support public well-being (Macaulay 2009).

From this summary, we offer the following conclusions regarding SimCity®. First, SimCity® does not address the distinction between physical (hard) systems (e.g. roads and highways) and soft systems such as SCADA and information and telecommunication systems. Moreover, there may be a need to extend threat analysis to include natural events (e.g. earthquakes) as well as manufactured acts such as human error, acts of terrorism, and sabotage. Such an analysis might expand the discussion on the openness of infrastructures and concepts of vulnerability and susceptibility. Again, ubiquitous computing and the increasing use of information technologies have created interdependencies among infrastructure systems. These interdependencies increase the probability that the seemingly isolated and inane events can cause cascading failures away from the point of origin. SimCity® has an opportunity to expand the concept of interdependence in the game.

Modern society includes many social changes (e.g. demand for quality products, goods, and services, globalization, and private–public governance policies) that can influence traditional concepts (e.g. education). SimCity® has an opportunity to expand these concepts. For example, education and learning can be asynchronous and synchronous. These forms of learning can influence other aspects of the game and the associated values. Moreover, there remains a debate on the distinction between CIs and non-CIs. In the game setting, this remains a challenge for SimCity® as there is still a need to evaluate essential systems of infrastructure.

In summary, critical infrastructures operate under conditions of ambiguity (i.e. lack of clarity and situational understanding), complexity (i.e. large numbers of richly interdependent and dynamically interacting elements with behavior difficult to predict), emergence (i.e. behavior, structure, or performance not deducible from constituent elements and only coming about through operational interactions of the system), interdependence (i.e. mutual influence among infrastructures through which the state of each infrastructure influences, and is influenced by, the state of interrelated infrastructures), and uncertainty (i.e. incompleteness in understanding, prediction, or control). Under these conditions, it is impossible to develop a game that can replace reality. However, SimCity® provides a learning environment where certain scenarios could be explored for learning to improve reality.

6.5 Concluding Remarks

SimCity® provides visualization for sophisticated investigation. Players can create a settlement that can grow into a city by zoning land for residential, commercial, or industrial development and building and maintaining public services, transport, and utilities. This chapter discusses the features of SimCity® (i.e. the game) as well as its view of CI systems. Notice that the purpose of experimentation is to examine and verify the potential use of a simulation computer game in combination with technical high-level analysis and assessment. In this case, the researcher set the gameplay mode in four experimental tests as a gentler version called "Sandbox." A sandbox is an ideal option, especially for easing in players with no experience with SimCity®'s mechanism or trying out creative management strategies. By applying this setting, the game unlocks most of the features. This setting disables all disasters since building a new city. Moreover, the scope of evaluation covers only the existing technological inventions in the real world. Therefore, improvements can be made to the game innovations, including adding nonexistent innovations and improving the game's present features.

Among these improvements, we suggest dealing with missing features and robust categories (i.e. different sectors that define CI). At the very least, chemical, commercial facilities, communications, critical manufacturing, dams, defense industrial base, emergency services, energy, financial services, food and agriculture, government facilities, healthcare and public health, information technology, national monuments and icons, nuclear reactors, materials, and waste, transportation systems, water/wastewater systems are needed in the game. Moreover, a robust analysis of CI must account for the ambiguity, complexity, emergence, and uncertainty associated with infrastructure systems, operations, and their landscape.

Again, beyond the game's technical issues, there remains potential for using SimCity® as a basis for informed decision-making, especially in the understanding of and guidance on sustainable and resilient city development in particular with regard to CI development and decision-making.

6.6 Exercises

1 Discuss aspects of CI that are missing in the SimCity® game.
2 What games can be combined with SimCity® to enhance infrastructure system design?
3 Discuss ways to enhance the limitations of SimCity®.
4 How can SimCity® be used to influence resilient city development?
5 How can urban planners use SimCity® to educate the next generation of city planners?

References

Anderson, P.S. (2002). Critical infrastructure protection in the information age. In: *Networking Knowledge for Information Societies: Institutions & Intervention* (eds. R. Mansell, R. Samarajiva, and A. Mahan), pp. 188–194. DUP Science, Delft University Press.

BBC. (8 March, 2013). Amazon suspends sales of SimCity video game. *BBC News.* https://www.bbc.com/news/technology-21712910.

Calida, B.Y. and Katina, P.F. (2012). Regional industries as critical infrastructures: A tale of two modern cities. *International Journal of Critical Infrastructures* 8(1): 74–90. https://doi.org/10.1504/IJCIS.2012.046555.

Edwards, T. (12 April 2013). How EA could repair SimCity's disastrous launch. *PCGamesN.* https://www.pcgamesn.com/simcity/how-ea-could-repair-simcitys-disastrous-launch.

Electronic Arts. (2013). Buy SimCity™ – PC and Mac – EA. Electronic Arts Inc. https://www.ea.com/games/simcity/simcity.

GAO. (2004). *Critical Infrastructure Protection: Challenges and Efforts to Secure Control Systems* (pp. 1–47). US Government Accountability Office.

Gheorghe, A., Vamanu, D.V., Katina, P. et al. (2018). *Critical Infrastructures, Key Resources, Key Assets: Risk, Vulnerability, Resilience, Fragility, and Perception Governance* (Vol. 34). Springer International Publishing.

Gheorghe, A.V., Masera, M., Weijnen, M.P.C. et al. (eds.). (2006). *Critical Infrastructures at Risk: Securing the European Electric Power System* (Vol. 9). Springer.

Katina, P.F. and Keating, C.B. (2015). Critical infrastructures: A perspective from systems of systems. *International Journal of Critical Infrastructures* 11(4): 316–344. https://doi.org/10.1504/IJCIS.2015.073840.

Katina, P.F., Pinto, C.A., Bradley, J.M. et al. (2014). Interdependency-induced risk with applications to healthcare. *International Journal of Critical Infrastructure Protection* 7(1): 12–26. https://doi.org/10.1016/j.ijcip.2014.01.005.

Klaver, M.H.A., Luiijf, H.A.M., Nieuwenhuijs, A.H. et al. (2008). European risk assessment methodology for critical infrastructures. *2008 First International Conference on Infrastructure Systems and Services: Building Networks for a Brighter Future (INFRA)* (pp. 1–5). IEEE.

Kröger, W. and Zio, E. (2011). *Vulnerable Systems.* Springer-Verlag.

Macaulay, T. (2009). *Critical Infrastructure: Understanding Its Component Parts, Vulnerabilities, Operating Risks, and Interdependencies.* CRC Press.

MacManus, C. (7 March 2013). SimCity launch a complete disaster. CNET. https://www.cnet.com/culture/simcity-launch-a-complete-disaster.

Moteff, J.D., Copeland, C., and Fischer, J. (2003). *Critical Infrastructures: What Makes an Infrastructure Critical?* (pp. 1–17). The Library of Congress.

US Department of Homeland Security. (2013). *NIPP 2013: Partnering for Critical Infrastructure Security and Resilience.* US Department of Homeland Security. https://www.dhs.gov/publication/nipp-2013-partnering-critical-infrastructure-security-and-resilience?topics=all.

Vasuthanasub, J. (2019). The resilient city: A platform for informed decision-making process. Dissertation, Old Dominion University. https://digitalcommons.odu.edu/emse_etds/151.

White House. (2003). Letter to congressional leaders reporting on the executive order regarding appointments during national emergency. *Weekly Compilation of Presidential Documents* 39(51): 1816–1822.

Wolf, T., Tessier, R., and Prabhu, G. (2011). Securing the data path of next-generation router systems. *Computer Communications* 34(4): 598–606. http://dx.doi.org/10.1016/j.comcom.2010.03.019.

7

A Platform for ReIDMP

7.1 Introduction

This research proposed the Resilient-Informed Decision-Making Process (ReIDMP) platform for developing resilient city systems. The ReIDMP platform consists of two practical approaches: first is a simulation computer game, SimCity 2013®, deployed under the concept of serious gaming. The second approach is the analysis and assessment that must take place to address risk and vulnerability. Risk and vulnerability are integrated into evaluation guidelines and methodologies provided by the International Atomic Energy Agency (IAEA) and the Science Applications International Corporation (SAIC). This initiative has evolved to enable stakeholders to conduct various risk and vulnerability assessment (VA) based on their own design in a simulated city in a real-world situation to enhance the efficacy of learning experiences relating to the knowledge of risk and vulnerability. The chapter expounds on the approaches undertaken to understand the simulation mechanism of SimCity® and the productive application of its visualization for sophisticated investigation.

7.2 Design and Development of City Simulation Using SimCity 2013®

To ensure the sustainment and resilience of existing and next-generation critical infrastructure (CI) systems, decision makers and stakeholders must be well-informed about past and current problems (Vasuthanasub 2019). Decision makers and stakeholders also need the knowledge and tools to help them analyze, assess, and design a viable implementation plan for long-term development. The result or output of studies and research must be able to apply to the decision-making process and resource allocation for solving real-world problems. Figure 7.1 depicts the structured methodology (i.e. platform) for analyzing the technical strategies and actions required for CI system resilience. Sections 7.2.1–7.3.4 describe the four phases of the ReIDMP platform/model, which can serve as a standard practice when developing resilient city systems.

7.2.1 Phase I: Project Planning and Management

Project management is a systemic process of planned and organized endeavor to meet a specific requirement, achieve a particular objective, or accomplish a specific goal (Meredith et al. 2013).

Gamification for Resilience: Resilient Informed Decision-Making, First Edition.
Adrian V. Gheorghe and Polinpapilinho F. Katina.

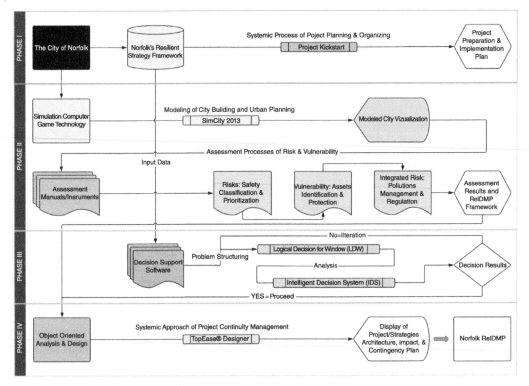

Figure 7.1 A framework of the RelDMP model.

A body of knowledge usually refers to developing critical phases under management science, including initiating, planning, executing, controlling, and closing. Project management is not trivial as it informs activities that are focused on achieving expected results effectively for individuals, organizations, or society. With this in mind, successful project planning and management are another two critical components of success.

Whether for a simple or unique project – like launching a new product or constructing a megastructure – decision makers, stakeholders, project managers, or team members need clear direction, organized operational procedures, consistently streamlined processes, and a user-friendly approach to maximize their full potential. Frequently, many projects have suffered from inadequate planning, inaccurate information, and unclear roles and responsibilities due to a lack of a decent starting framework. The consequences of those poor performances can be severe or unacceptable (Katina 2020; Stumpe and Katina 2019). Therefore, success does not come easily in project management. However, being better prepared for "what will be coming next?" is not always impossible. Project KickStart Pro 5 is a project management-based software that incorporates intuitive planning and managing processes, offering users a smooth sequence of functions to develop a project plan with precise descriptions and a deeper understanding of goals, obstructions, risks, and solutions. Users can define roles and responsibilities with their features and capabilities and assign each team member tasks accordingly. Then, a planner can perform essential project management tasks, such as assignment tracking, project costs, deadlines, or even personalized objectives. However, the whole team needs to have a say in a project's key milestones and it's execution plan.

Overall, Project KickStart Pro 5 helps a project manager to create an innovative, efficient, and organized plan from start to finish. The software can be helpful in one way or another, but in particular it will get project teams on board and unmistakably keep all members on the same page without leaving confusion about roles, responsibilities, expectations, and deadlines.

7.2.2 Phase II: Learning by Doing Through Gaming Strategy

While expertise in risk and vulnerability management of complex interdependent systems is not necessary, it is essential to know the basics of risks and vulnerabilities, infrastructure systems, and gaming. This base knowledge can also include energy generation and distribution or public transportation systems; a learning goal of risk and VA materials is to analyze potential risks and their impacts due to adverse events or pollution activities. Moreover, by fully reviewing and understanding those presented activities within a city or region, stakeholders (be it students or otherwise) should be able to determine the societal risks and asset vulnerabilities for individuals living in the given area. Figure 7.2 depicts Phase II elaborating on using computer game technology to enhance stakeholder engagements and practical experiences in quantifying the resiliency of infrastructure systems.

The following proposed procedures utilize a combination of serious gaming concepts in conjunction with risk analysis and VA techniques. Three specific documents are referred to here. First is the *Manual for the Classification and Prioritization of Risks Due to Major Accidents in Process and Related Industries*. This manual aims to introduce methods and procedures to classify hazardous activities in a region or city of interest by categorizing consequences and probabilities of occurrence. An assessment applies to the risks due to major accidents with off-site consequences in fixed installations

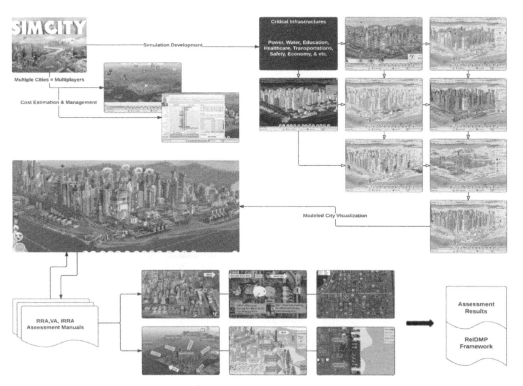

Figure 7.2 Deployment of the SimCity® application.

handling, storing, and processing dangerous substances and transporting hazardous materials by road, rail, pipeline, and inland waterway (International Atomic Energy Agency 1996). Figure 7.3 is based on this document and depicts the procedural steps of rapid risk assessment.

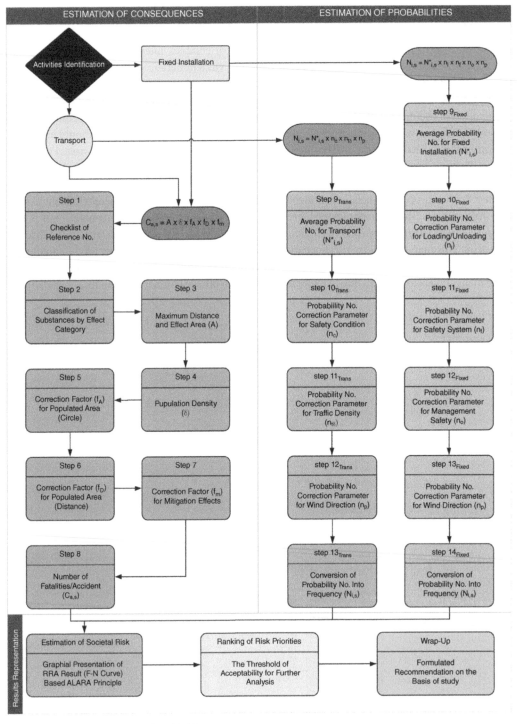

Figure 7.3 Procedural steps of rapid risk assessment.

The second is *A Guide to Highway Vulnerability Assessment for Critical Asset Identification and Protection*. The adoption of this guidebook presents the standard procedures for assessing the vulnerabilities of physical assets, such as roadways, highways, tunnels, bridges, and inspection and traffic operation facilities, among others. It provides a holistic set of steps to identify and mitigate the consequences of transportation routes from terrorist threats or attacks (Science Applications International Corporation 2002). Figure 7.4 is based on this document and depicts the procedural steps of vulnerability assessment.

The third is the *Guidelines for Integrated Risk Assessment and Management in Large Industrial Areas*. The purpose of using this document is to provide practical guidance and a technical

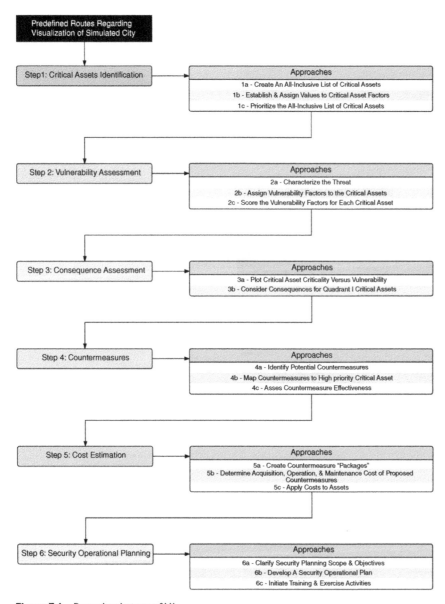

Figure 7.4 Procedural steps of VA.

reference for the proceeding of integrated health and environmental risk assessment studies and environmental management strategies in large industrial areas. The methodologies and techniques are best suited to geographical regions that accommodate several industrial and related activities of a hazardous and/or polluting nature (International Atomic Energy Agency 1998). Figure 7.5 is based on this document and depicts the procedural steps of VA.

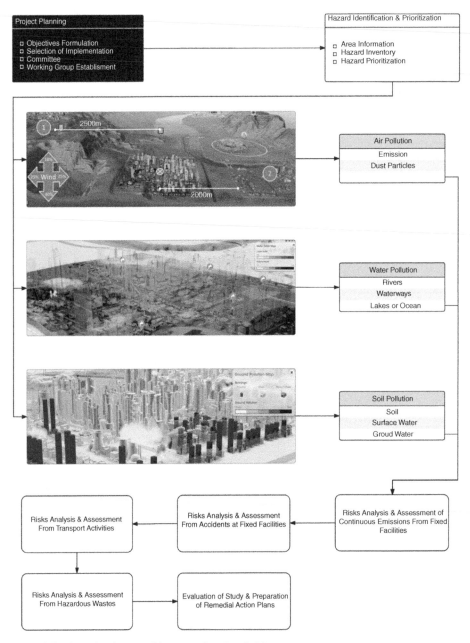

Figure 7.5 Procedural steps of integrated regional risk assessment.

Again, SimCity 2013® is a simulation game of organized play, which has a set of stated rules and purposes to guide players to the goals, and the goals can be either fanciful or purposeful. If the requirements are specified and supervision is provided to enable focus on learning outcomes, while preserving playfulness, then a serious learning experience is possible. With this intention, a simulation will allow players to play with complex computer models, interact with each other, and experience revolutionary or evolutionary changes. Ideally, this approach must be made before deciding or implementing a policy. And since this is a simulation, there are no effects on the real world. It also intends to benefit stakeholders – they can better understand and manage infrastructure resilience.

Moreover, researchers have seen real benefits, even with university students. For example, an experimental design was prepared and implemented by the authors for one year with students in a graduate course at Old Dominion University. SimCity® was included in the course syllabus as a required tool and other course materials in Spring 2015. During each experimental session, students, under the supervision of the senior faculty researcher, developed a city under the foundational concepts of sustainable development and infrastructure resiliency. Later that year, the original version of the experimental design was revised and upgraded as a result of a funded Faculty Innovator Grant Program, with the goal of creating a gaming laboratory to enable learning (Vasuthanasub 2019).

7.2.3 Phase III: Multi-Criteria Decision Analysis

Theoretically, decision-making can be considered a logical thinking process for selecting suitable alternatives under different criteria or factors. In the process of decision analysis, decision makers and stakeholders must assess all possible positive and negative impacts and should also be able to judge the consequences of that decision. Multi-criteria decision analysis (MCDA) or multi-criteria decision-making (MCDM) is a framework of analytical techniques that helps decision makers choose between multiple options when multiple objectives have to be pursued. It is a systematic and pragmatic process involving various criteria in rational decision-making. MCDA allows the users to determine a selection as valuable and as efficient as possible, to preserve a degree of consistency within the search, or at least to provide the inconsistencies, if they occur, without imposing unnecessary variables and unjustifiable structure in the decision-analysis process (Stewart 1992). With this in mind, the primary purpose of using MCDA is to assist the decision maker in discovering the most preferred solution to a problem. The application has widely supported many complex decision dilemmas, such as in business, government, and medicine, especially in situations with conflicting criteria (Belton and Stewart 2002).

There are many methods for implementing the MCDM approach. In this research, the decision models of multiple criteria, attributes, and alternatives are structured and presented with the implementation of two distinct MCDA methods through decision support system (DSS) tools.

7.2.3.1 Multi-Attribute Utility Theory

Deciding on complex problems in the real world is challenging; decision makers are often challenged by multiple objectives, various stakeholders, future or long-term consequences, and risk and adverse effects (Nikou 2011). In particular, when the problems are bound with the constraint, namely uncertainty, one of the most effective forms of approach for dealing with this type of problem is using "expected utility." In MCDA, this technique is formally called multi-attribute utility theory, or MAUT (Li et al. 2009). It was invented to ease the difficulty in solving the problem under uncertainty and aims to answer the question: Which alternative is the best option? The method offers users the steps to assign scores and to compare possible alternatives in which, afterward, all of them can be identified and analyzed. It also allows a group of stakeholders to search and examine the consequences in different ways for evaluating the options (Nikou 2011).

A core concept of MAUT is based on the theoretical foundation that the decision maker's preferences can be transformed and represented by a function called the utility "U" (Ishizaka and Nemery 2013). This utility function is being used to replace the value associated with each criterion for providing a degree of satisfaction to the decision maker. The MAUT method works best when a decision maker consciously tries to optimize the performance of alternatives under a set of conditions and points of view (Ishizaka and Nemery 2013). Thus, the preferred desirability of a particular alternative depends on how its associated attributes are being considered and judged. Similar to other MCDA methods, MAUT methodology consists of four key steps:

- Constructing a decision problem by specifying the objectives and identifying the attributes that need to be measured.
- Setting up the alternatives and exploring the potential consequences caused by each of them in terms of the attributes identified.
- Determining the preferences of the decision maker and stakeholders and assigning the weight of attributes reflecting their importance to the decision.
- Synthesizing the results by assessing the impact of a certain criterion of the decision and lastly comparing the alternatives.

In this research, a DSS tool, called Logical Decisions for Windows (LDW), will be utilized to assist the processes of problem modeling, calculation, and analysis. LDW is the MAUT-based decision-support software package that helps a decision maker and stakeholders to evaluate and select the best option under difficult circumstances and restricted constraints. A package combines features between spreadsheet and database programs that allow a user to organize data and information for all possible prospects at the same time.

The following are the basic required steps in completing the decision model and decision analysis with LDW:

- A decision maker can initialize the process by either manually inputting hard (number) and soft (detail or explanation) data or electronically importing prepared spreadsheets and database files. The software will convert an ordinary data table into a sophisticated hierarchical structure and link all the detailed information and specific preferences to overall goals. It can simply turn a set of incomprehensible numbers into a detailed roadmap that guides a decision maker to achieve the best outcome.
- Using the MAUT, the value judgments are a crucial stage of the process. LDW makes this phase easier by providing a variety of methods, such as Smarter (easy-to-use), Tradeoff (sophisticated), and AHP (popular), for making the judgments and assigning the weights. The user can select and use one method based on the appropriateness of the decision model.
- For the final step, the presentation of analysis results is designed to provide insights with interactive displays. A decision maker can rank the best to the worst alternatives, associating any goal or evaluation measures and comparing a particular option against the others to understand the differences.
- Significantly, a group of stakeholders can also revise the weight of importance to assume the effect of changes in the overall ranking results and conduct a sensitivity analysis to see the effects of uncertainty on the ranking results.

Last but not least, the MAUT method is usually adopted in a group situation. Frequently, a necessary level of detail and specification during a discussion on the determination of attributes and their weights can turn into conflicts or arguments rather than moving toward common ground. This restriction may result in wasting time or even worse. So much so that to implement MAUT through LDW effectively, a decision maker and all stakeholders must be able to agree on a set of attributes and a range of weights to be used in a model.

7.2.3.2 Evidential Reasoning

When dealing with problems under fuzzy weights and utilities, Zhou et al. (2010) suggest that "various types of criteria must be taken into account, which may be quantitative, measured by numerical values with certain units, or qualitative, assessed using subjective judgments with uncertainties." Consequently, this research employs evidential reasoning (ER) as a second MCDA method to tackle problems of uncertainty and subjectivity. The technique is the latest development and a technical breakthrough in handling hybrid MCDA problems, which can be in either hierarchical or non-hierarchical conditions (Xu and Yang 2001). Essentially, the ER approach is different from other conventional MCDA methods. Its algorithm was developed based on the fundamental principle of decision theory and the combination rule of Dempster–Shafer evidence theory (Xu and Yang 2001; Yang 2001; Zhou et al. 2010). When solving a problem with this method, the weights of importance are not necessary for assembling attributes in the model. Instead of aggregating average scores, it uses a belief structure, formally called the "degrees of belief," to represent an assessment and to reach a conclusion as a distribution. This belief degree is the level of expectation that can be purposely managed to obtain a decision maker's preferences.

Recent developments in ER algorithms have resulted in DSS tools, including the Intelligent Decision System, or IDS (Xu et al. 2006; Xu and Yang 2003; Yang and Xu 2002; Xu and Yang 2001; Yang and Xu 2004). IDS is an ER-based decision-support software designed to assist large-scale MCDA problems. The application has a unique capacity to handle thousands of attributes. IDS is also considered a flexible and versatile tool since it can be applied to various types of information, like deterministic numbers, random numbers, and subjective judgments in different formats (Xu et al. 2006; Xu and Yang 2003; Vasuthanasub 2019).

To support a decision-making process with a standard ER approach through IDS, Xu et al. (2008) suggest five required basic steps: (i) model implementation, (ii) data collection, (iii) group information and opinion, (iv) assessment aggregation, and (v) analysis results presentation.

- *Problem modeling*: a model implementation in IDS implies identifying the alternative courses of action, or simply choices, criterion weights, and evaluation scales for assessing selections on criteria (Xu et al. 2008). Using the software, the construction of an assessment criterion tree is straightforward. After a tree is constructed, a user needs to define each criterion accordingly. At this point, it is important to note that the IDS software was designed to use the five-point grading scale as a standard estimation for assessment procedures, which means all criteria are assessed as qualitative measurements. The highest grade is five. For this reason, whether it is a quantitative or a qualitative criterion, descriptions are required for both types of criteria. Meanwhile, the number of grades or points must be included as well. In addition to a default setting in IDS, relative attribute weights can be assigned through either pairwise comparison or an interactive chart, where the bars can be instantly dragged up and down to adjust the desirable criteria weight. A function is considered a useful feature since a user can observe the differentiation of individual viewpoints or group decision standpoints on criterion importance early on. At the end of this step, a user may administer an assessment model to individual participants to initiate the next phase.

- *Data collection*: practically, the assessment in this step involves a number of activities, such as evidence collection, comparison, judgment resolution, and determining the grade (Xu et al. 2008). With a completed problem structure in model implementation individual participants can assess each option and record their scores and opinions. Each of them needs to verify the grades, then the ER algorithm will automatically generate a degree of belief next to each answer. This degree of belief represents the strength level of describing an alternative to the criterion. Yet, in our research, there was not enough detail or information for the participant group to make accurate judgments; this is the case where there isn't a clear majority. Participants could only select a grade that was most appropriate based on their knowledge without worrying about the distribution of the belief degrees (Xu et al. 2008). IDS will handle a process by equally dividing 100% of the degrees of belief and automatically allocating them to the checked items.
- *Group decision support*: when utilizing IDS, individual participants may independently record and anonymously register their assessments of each alternative to prevent the risk of potential disagreement among them. Consequently, individual lists can be either separately reviewed or privately imported as a single file. After collating all inputs, a user will have two options to select from: comparing assessment data via a function of graphical representations or generating collective assessment information for each alternative (Xu et al. 2008).
- *Assessment aggregation*: again, the aggregation process of assessment information from lower-level to higher-level criteria is analyzed through the ER algorithm. With IDS functionality, this compilation is automatic and updated in real-time in the background whenever either initial assessment data is modified or an additional detail is entered for any criterion (Xu et al. 2008). Thus, a user should be able to obtain the original outcomes promptly if nothing is changed or to see the updated reports at any stage of revision, even before the assessment on some criteria is finished.
- *Assessment results presentation*: IDS can generate different types of analysis results in graphical formats to support decision communication, such as performance ranking, performance score range, and performance distribution. However, while the ranking and score graphs present general results information, the distribution chart provides more insight. The selected alternatives can be compared to each other through all those diagrams and distinguished from any preferred areas in different levels of the assessment hierarchy (Xu et al. 2008). Moreover, the properties and appearances of those graphs can be configured and then exported to MS Word documents or MS PowerPoint files. The software also provides a search function to help a decision maker identify strengths and weaknesses. Afterward, a model can be used to study the effect of action plans when simulating various improvement scenarios.

7.2.4   Phase IV: Object-Oriented Programming

In computer science engineering, object-oriented programming (OOP) is called "structured programming." It involves a set of procedural programming that administers a logical structure in the program being written to allow it greater efficiency while being easier to understand and modify. OOP is described by Eck (2014) as the approach of structured programming thus:

> To solve a complex problem, break the problem into several pieces and work on each piece separately; to solve each piece, handle it as a new problem respectively which itself can be broken down into a smaller piece of problems again; eventually, you will work your way down to problems that can be solved directly, without further decomposition.

However, the OOP paradigm may best be addressed by its corresponding alternate, Object-Oriented Analysis and Design (OOAD). OOAD was derived from adopting the fundamental concept of OOP, and it may be adequately concluded that it is an analytic method that illustrates an information system by identifying things called "objects." In this case, an object represents a real person, place, event, or system. The end product of object-oriented analysis is an object model, which represents the information system regarding the purpose and object-oriented concepts. It gives researchers an easier way to express or present the important pieces of information and essential features of the application to the stakeholders than any other approach does.

Booch et al. (2007) indicate four main processes for characterizing an object-oriented model's conceptual framework: abstraction, encapsulation, modularity, and hierarchy.

- *Abstraction/discovery*: the first technique refers to a simplified representation of a system. One that captures only those relevant characteristics or essential aspects with regard to the perspective of the researchers.
- *Encapsulation/visualization*: this component refers to the hidden details in an object's internal composition and work. Encapsulation acts as a protector to limit user access to an object's internal data. Also, it offers a means to reduce system complexity (Booch et al. 2007; Pulfer and Schmid 2006).
- *Modularity/mapping*: this process involves partitioning objects into sub-objects called modules. Especially for complex and large-scale system design, thus modularity helps in managing complexity by disintegrating a huge intractable solution into smaller and more manageable ones, which are interconnected and composed of the required large-scale solution.
- *Hierarchy/model and analysis*: the last step refers to rank allocation. Since encapsulation manages the hiding of detail or the prioritization of the relevant details to understand the problem at hand, it is necessary to have a hierarchy, as different levels of detail may be required to solve problems (Booch et al. 2007).

OOP can be applied using a tool called TopEase® Designer. TopEase® is a software product that was designed to allow organizations to model the impact of adverse events on every dimension of their business, understand which elements need to be restored within what timeframe, create and maintain organization disaster response plans, and identify any gaps where response plans do not yet exist. In the same way, all its capabilities, including discovery, visualization, mapping, and particularly model and analysis, enable the researchers to design and model a complex or large system structure and then perform a comprehensive system analysis. Figure 7.6 depicts the main window of TopEase®.

The original developers of TopEase® suggest that it can be viewed as a combination of comprehensive methodology and integrated tool (Pulfer and Schmid 2006). Moreover, TopEase® and TopEase® XBench offer complete support for sustainable corporate development. The TopEase® approach is probably the most comprehensive framework available for corporate engineering. The traditional approach comes with a box of a wide variety of diverse and (if at all) most loosely coupled and integrated techniques. The framework has an open design and enables other process models to be embedded into the model or the framework after modeling, like Catalyst, Prince, V-Model, Hermes, RUP, etc. (Pulfer and Schmid 2006). The approach is also integrative in that it allows for managing the whole life cycle, from the first development iteration to operations, disposal of the initial system, and the next iteration cycle. The framework is integrated into operations (via the development of systems and control of workflow engines). It provides corporate management with the company's current data (KPI/risk-/compliance-control) in the form of measurements, hence supporting sustainability concepts.

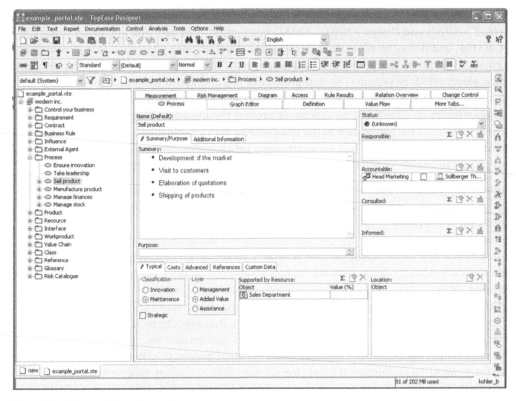

Figure 7.6 TopEase®'s main window.

7.3 Concluding Remarks

This chapter outlines the phases of a platform (ReDMP) necessary to create resilient cities. First, project planning and management emphasize the basics of project and project management. Second is the issue of learning where gaming strategies are necessary, especially if one attempts to address the risk and vulnerability of complex interdependent CI systems without impacting physical, economic security, public health, and safety. Third, there is a need for MCDA and other approaches supporting decision-making, involving alternatives selection under different criteria or factors. Finally, and due to complexity, it is necessary to break the problem into several pieces and work on each part separately while considering the whole; a capability provided by OOP.

However, offering a cautionary tale about the articulated platform/model is essential. A familiar aphorism in statistics is that "all models are wrong the scientist cannot obtain a 'correct' one by excessive elaboration" (Box 1976, p. 792). This chapter postulates that this is a fair criticism of engineered models. Moreover, it is suggested that the developed ReIDMP model carries assumptions that potential users must understand. Nevertheless, these assumptions do not make the model "useless." Rather, the model is useful in the "context" in which it is developed. And those that *understand* the model can always improve it. Someone who has experience of studying a map will be able to use maps with ease and yet "A map is not the territory it represents, but, if correct, it has a similar structure to the territory, which accounts for its usefulness" (Korzybski 1994, p. 58). Similarly, the ReIDMP model, *while wrong, can be useful in the hands of a skilled modeler*. In fact, Chapter 8 shows how a skilled modeler can use the proposed model to perform risk and VA in a game-like situation.

7.4 Exercises

1 Discuss how ReIDMP helps in the development of a resilient city.
2 Discuss how project management influences the ReIDMP platform.
3 What areas of assessment can be developed to enhance the ReIDMP platform?
4 Apply the ReIDMP to the city of your choice.
5 Feedback is not "explicit" in ReIDMP. Discuss why it is "implied" in the ReIDMP platform?

References

Belton, V. and Stewart, T. (2002). *Multiple Criteria Decision Analysis: An Integrated Approach.* Kluwer Academic Publishers.

Booch, G., Maksimchuk, R.A., Engle, M.W. et al. (2007). *Object-Oriented Analysis and Design with Applications* (3rd ed.). Addison-Wesley Professional.

Box, G.E.P. (1976). Science and statistics. *Journal of the American Statistical Association* 71(356): 791–799. https://doi.org/10.2307/2286841.

Eck, D. J. (2014). *An Introduction to Programming Using Java* (7th ed.). Hobart and William Smith Colleges.

International Atomic Energy Agency. (1996). *Manual for the Classification and Prioritization of Risks Due to Major Accidents in Process and Related Industries.* http://www-pub.iaea.org/books/IAEABooks/5391/Manual-for-the-Classification-and-Prioritization-of-Risks-due-to-Major-Accidents-in-Process-and-Related-Industries.

International Atomic Energy Agency. (1998). *Guidelines for Integrated Risk Assessment and Management in Large Industrial Areas.* http://www-pub.iaea.org/books/IAEABooks/5391/Manual-for-the-Classification-and-Prioritization-of-Risks-due-to-Major-Accidents-in-Process-and-Related-Industries.

Ishizaka, A. and Nemery, P. (2013). *Multi-Criteria Decision Analysis: Methods and Software* (1st ed.). Wiley.

Katina, P.F. (2020). System acquisition pathology: A comprehensive characterisation of system failure modes and effects. *International Journal of Critical Infrastructures* 16(3): 255–292. https://www.inderscienceonline.com/doi/abs/10.1504/IJCIS.2020.108499.

Korzybski, A. (1994). *Science and Sanity: An Introduction to Non-Aristotelian Systems and General Semantics.* Wiley.

Li, H., Apostolakis, G.E., Gifun, J. et al. (2009). Ranking the risks from multiple hazards in a small community. *Risk Analysis* 29(3): 438–456. https://onlinelibrary.wiley.com/doi/abs/10.1111/j.1539-6924.2008.01164.x.

Meredith, J.R., Mantel, S.J., Shafer, S.M. et al. (2013). *Project Management in Practice* (5 ed.). Wiley.

Nikou, T. (2011). Application of multi-attribute utility theory to heating and cooling system selection for a sustainable building project. Thesis, Clemson University. https://tigerprints.clemson.edu/all_theses/1114.

Pulfer, R. and Schmid, U. (2006). *Control Your Business: The Balance Between Principles and Pragmatism.* Pulinco.

Science Applications International Corporation. (2002). *Guide to Highway Vulnerability Assessment for Critical Asset Identification and Protection.* Transportation Policy and Analysis Center.

Stewart, T. (1992). A critical survey on the status of multiple criteria decision making theory and practice. *Omega* 20(5): 569–586. https://doi.org/10.1016/0305-0483(92)90003-P.

Stumpe, F. and Katina, P.F. (2019). Multi-objective multi-customer project network: Visualising interdependencies and influences. *International Journal of System of Systems Engineering* 9(2): 139. https://www.inderscienceonline.com/doi/abs/10.1504/IJSSE.2019.100338.

Vasuthanasub, J. (2019). The resilient city: A platform for informed decision-making process. Dissertation, Old Dominion University. https://digitalcommons.odu.edu/emse_etds/151.

Xu, D.-L., McCarthy, G., and Yang, J.-B. (2006). Intelligent decision system and its application in business innovation self assessment. *Decision Support Systems* 42(2): 664–673. https://doi.org/10.1016/j.dss.2005.03.004.

Xu, D.-L. and Yang, J.-B. (2003). Intelligent decision system for self-assessment. *Journal of Multi-Criteria Decision Analysis* 12(1): 43–60. https://doi.org/10.1002/mcda.343.

Xu, D.L., Yang, J.B., Carle, B. et al. (2008). Application of an intelligent decision system to nuclear waste repository option analysis. *International Journal of Nuclear Governance, Economy and Ecology* 2(2): 146. https://www.inderscience.com/info/inarticle.php?artid=18333.

Xu, L. and Yang, J.-B. (2001). Introduction to multi-criteria decision making and the evidential reasoning approach (Working Paper No. 106). University of Manchester Institute of Science and Technology.

Yang, J. and Xu, L. (2004). Intelligent decision system for supplier assessment. *DSS2004: The 2004 IFIP Conference on Decision Support Systems*. Monash University. https://www.research.manchester.ac.uk/portal/en/publications/intelligent-decision-system-for-supplier-assessment(999748c6-ceb6-403c-8a9b-8ed874ee3724)/export.html.

Yang, J.-B. (2001). Rule and utility based evidential reasoning approach for multiattribute decision analysis under uncertainties. *European Journal of Operational Research* 131(1): 31–61. https://doi.org/10.1016/S0377-2217(99)00441-5.

Yang, J.-B. and Xu, D.-L. (2002). On the evidential reasoning algorithm for multiple attribute decision analysis under uncertainty. *IEEE Transactions on Systems, Man, and Cybernetics – Part A: Systems and Humans* 32(3): 289–304. https://doi.org/10.1109/TSMCA.2002.802746.

Zhou, M., Liu, X.B., and Yang, J.B. (2010). Evidential reasoning based nonlinear programming model for MCDA under fuzzy weights and utilities. *International Journal of Intelligent Systems* 25(1): 31–58. https://onlinelibrary.wiley.com/doi/10.1002/int.20387.

Part III

Applications

8

Analysis and Assessment of Risk and Vulnerability via Serious Gaming

8.1 Introduction

Risk and vulnerability assessments (VAs) are performed in many areas of engineering and technology. The goal of evaluating them is to be able to analyze potential impacts that can result in occurring of adverse events. In this research, the second phase of the Resilient-Informed Decision-Making Process (ReIDMP) is utilizing a product from SimCity as an applied visualization for technical analysis of risk and vulnerability. The specific techniques and procedures adopted in this investigation include assessments on potential accidents of hazmat processing at fixed installations and during transport activities, assessments on possible transportation routes regarding the critical assets, and assessments on health and environmental impacts from polluted byproducts generated by the industrial sector within the city and region. Altogether these analysis efforts improve the conceptual understanding of risks and vulnerabilities that are present in everyday society and how those exposures may affect the larger society as a whole. After the preceding stages, an informed decision-making process can be formalized to initiate and supervise a comprehensive plan promoting the city's resilience.

8.2 Rapid Risk Assessment

To concurrently review rapid risk assessment (RRA) and modeled environment in SimCity application, the approach in *Manual for the Classification and Prioritization of Risks due to Major Accidents in Process and Related Industries*, (International Atomic Energy Agency 1996) is used. This document is also known as "IAEA-TECDOC-727 (Rev.1)." It represents the means to manage the risk of accidents regarding hazardous activities, such as fixed installations or transportation in the city or region of interest. The assessment method relies heavily on tables that have been developed based on historical information and input from subject matter experts (International Atomic Energy Agency 1996). By completing methodological procedures, the assessment results can give decision makers a holistic view of incentive information about the significant risks within the selected region.

Gamification for Resilience: Resilient Informed Decision-Making, First Edition.
Adrian V. Gheorghe and Polinpapilinho F. Katina.

8.2.1 Applications and Algorithm of RRA Methodology

According to the International Atomic Energy Agency (1996) IAEA-TECDOC-727 (Rev.1), the assessment process of each activity requires two calculating approaches to estimate the casualties per incident (consequence) and probabilities of occurrence (frequency). In the case of consequences, the estimation is defined by the number of fatalities. The number of fatalities is established using Equation 8.1 and the tables in IAEA-TECDOC-727 (Rev.1), as shown in Figure 8.1. Figure 8.2 is the continuation of the information in Figure 8.1.

$$C_{A,S} = A * D * \prod_{i=1}^{3} CF_i \tag{8.1}$$

where:

A = area affected by the incident (circle area)

D = population density within the affected area

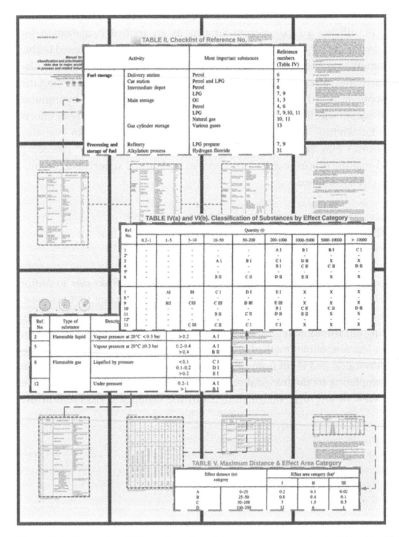

Figure 8.1 Example of information from tables used consequence estimation of major accidents.

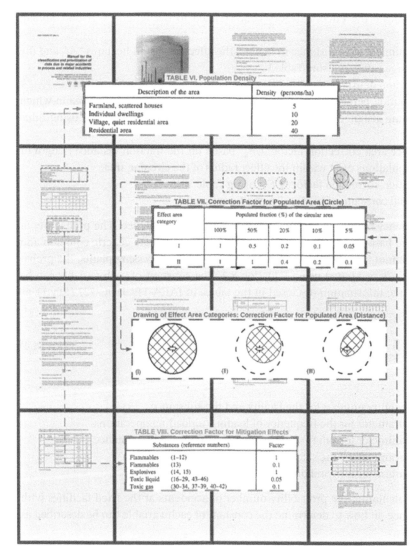

TABLE VI. Population Density

Description of the area	Density (persons/ha)
Farmland, scattered houses	5
Individual dwellings	10
Village, quiet residential area	20
Residential area	40

TABLE VII. Correction Factor for Populated Area (Circle)

Effect area category	Populated fraction (%) of the circular area				
	100%	50%	20%	10%	5%
I	1	0.5	0.2	0.1	0.05
II	1	1	0.4	0.2	0.1

Drawing of Effect Area Categories; Correction Factor for Populated Area (Distance)

(I)　　　(II)　　　(III)

TABLE VIII. Correction Factor for Mitigation Effects

Substances (reference numbers)		Factor
Flammables	(1–12)	1
Flammables	(13)	0.1
Explosives	(14, 15)	1
Toxic liquid	(16–29, 43–46)	0.05
Toxic gas	(30–34, 37–39, 40–42)	0.1

Figure 8.2 Example of information from tables used consequence estimation of major accidents (continued).

CF_1 = correction factor for the populated area (part of circle area)
CF_2 = correction factor for the distance of effect category (radius of the circle)
CF_3 = correction factor for mitigation at the selected facility

The following set of procedures is the sequential steps to obtain the constant of each variable in the equation of consequence estimation:

1) Classify the activity using Table II and indicate reference numbers for Table IV(a) or IV(b).
2) Determine the hazardous substance in each activity. Note that if multiple hazmats are presented in one location, both cannot be considered simultaneously. Alternatively, if hazardous materials are different in terms of effect area categories, such as flammable and toxic, they must be analyzed separately.
3) Estimate the quantity of substances in each hazardous activity.

4) Using Table IV, indicate the effect category code (related to the letters A–H and Roman numerals I–III).
5) Indicate the maximum effective distance in meters, the affected area in hectares "*A*," and the shape of the effect area category using Table V.
6) Estimate the population density "*D*" within the affected area using Table VI.
7) Estimate the distribution percentage of the existing population in the circular area in which radius is the maximum distance of effect. Then, obtain the correction factor "CF_1" using Table VII.
8) Estimate the distance area correction factor "CF_2" based on the fraction distance (length or depth) in which populations exist within the effect radius of the circular area.
9) Estimate the mitigation correction factor "CF_3" using Table VIII.
10) Calculate the external consequences "$C_{A,\,S}$" using Equation 8.1.

The estimation of frequency is different from the estimation of consequence. The probability of occurrences is calculated based on the type of hazmat activities. The same generic equation and estimated procedures cannot assess both. For fixed installations or processing plants, the probability of a major accident is computed using Equation 8.2. The constant of each variable can be obtained by evaluating the information disclosed in the tables in IAEA-TECDOC-727 (Rev.1), as illustrated in Figure 8.3.

$$N_{Fixed} = N_{Fixed}^* + \sum_{i=1}^{4} CP_i \qquad (8.2)$$

where:
N_{Fixed}^* = average probability number for the facility and the substance
CP_1 = correction parameter for the frequency of loading/unloading operations
CP_2 = correction parameter for safety systems in cases of flammable substance
CP_3 = correction parameter for the safety level at the facility
CP_4 = correction parameter for wind direction toward a populated area

To proceed further in calculating the probability number of accidents at the fixed facilities with Equation 8.2, the guidance on how to determine the constant of each variable can be described as follows:

1) Estimate the average probability number of an accident N^*_{Fixed} using Table IX.
2) Estimate the probability number correction parameter for loading/unloading operations "CP_1" using Table X.
3) Using Table XI, estimate the probability number correction parameter for safety systems for flammable substances "CP2."
4) Estimate the probability number correction parameter for organizational and safety management aspects "CP_3" using Table XII.
5) Using Table XIII, estimate the probability number correction parameter for the wind direction toward populated areas "CP4."
6) Calculate the probability number "N_{Fixed}" using Equation 8.1.
7) Convert the probability number "N_{Fixed}" into the frequency value "$P_{i,s}$" for the number of accidents per year using Table XIV.

In the cases of hazmat transportation, the probability number of a significant accident is calculated using Equation 8.3 and tables in IAEA-TECDOC-727 (Rev.1), as exhibited in Figure 8.3. Figure 8.4 is a continuation of Figure 8.3.

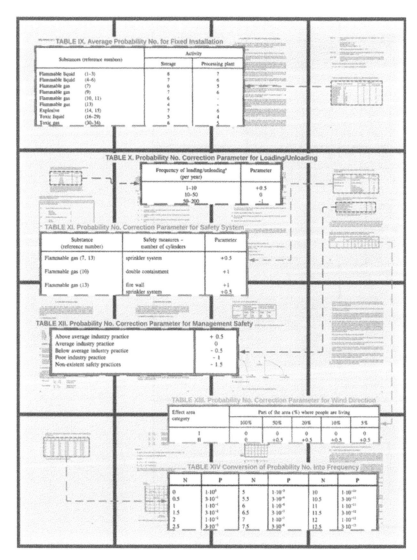

Figure 8.3 Example of table information for estimating probability of major accidents for fixed installations of hazmat or dangerous goods.

$$N_{Transport} = N_{Trans}^* + \sum_{i=5}^{7} CP_i \qquad (8.3)$$

where:

N_{Trans}^* = average probability number for the transportation of the substance

CP_5 = correction parameter for the safety conditions of substance transportation

CP_6 = correction parameter for traffic density of the transportation route

CP_7 = correction parameter for wind direction toward a populated area

The steps in defining numerical values in Equation 8.3 are similar to Equation 8.2. They are straight-forward. The following are the instructions on how to assign the constant of each variable:

1) Estimate the average probability number of transport category "N_{Trans}^*" using Table XV or XVI.

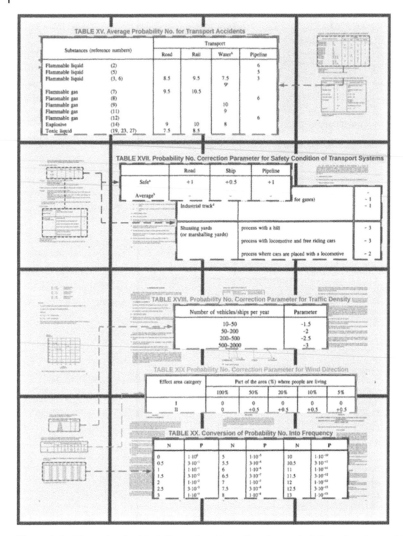

Figure 8.4 Example of table information for estimating probability of major accidents for transportations of hazmat or dangerous goods (continued).

2) Estimate the probability number correction parameter for the transport system "CP5" safety using Table XVII.
3) Estimate the probability number correction parameter for traffic density "CP_6" using Table XVIII.
4) Estimate the probability number correction parameter for the wind direction toward populated areas "CP_7" using Table XIX.
5) Calculate the probability number "$N_{Transport}$" using Equation 8.3.
6) Using Table XX, convert the probability number "NTransport" into the frequency value "Pi,s" for the number of accidents per year.

Once the consequence value and frequency number of all potential accidents are calculated, the outputs of each activity need to be plotted on the chart to represent and quantify the state of risks. For this RRA manual, the samples of assessing information, diagram drawing, calculation procedure, and result representation from classroom experimentation are shown in Figures 8.5a–8.5d.

Rapid Risk Assessment (continued)

Estimate of Consequences

1. **Asset – Trade Port**

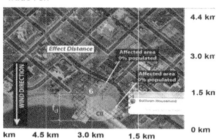

Description	Location	Ref. No. (Table II)	Amount (tonnes)	Effect Category (Table IV)	Physical Effect (Table V)		Population Density (δ) (Table VI)	Correction Factor (f$_A$) (Table VII)	Correction Factor (f$_d$) (Table VII)	Correction Factor (f$_m$) (Table VIII)
					Distance (m)	Area (ha)				
1. Trade Port Storage of oil in barrels near residential area.	Asset 6	Oil storage Ref 3	6000 Barrels (approx. 840 tonnes)	CI Wind direction not considered	50-100	3	40	1	0% of effect area populated	1
		Coal storage (coal ash) Ref 30	100	CII Wind direction considered	100-200	1.5		0.2	0% of effect area populated	0.1
Consequence 1	3(ha) x 40 (persons/ha) x 1 x 0 x 1 = 0 fatalities *(good placement limits fatalities)*									
Consequence 2	1.5(ha) x 80 (persons/ha) x 0.2 x 0 x 0.1 = 0 fatalities *(good placement limits fatalities)*									

1. **Asset – Water Treatment/Pumping Station**

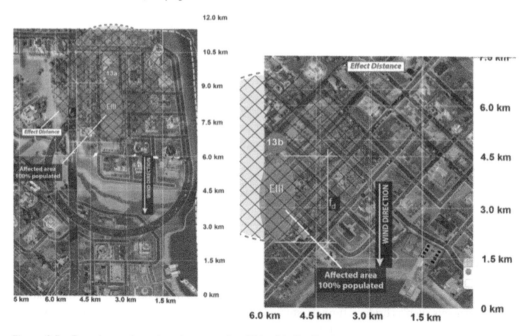

Figure 8.5 Experimental results – incorporating RRA with SimCity 2013.

RESULTS

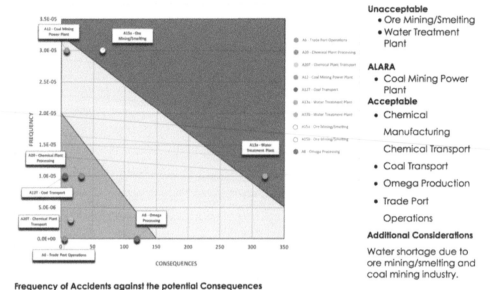

Frequency of Accidents against the potential Consequences

Unacceptable
- Ore Mining/Smelting
- Water Treatment Plant

ALARA
- Coal Mining Power Plant

Acceptable
- Chemical Manufacturing
- Chemical Transport
- Coal Transport
- Omega Production
- Trade Port Operations

Additional Considerations

Water shortage due to ore mining/smelting and coal mining industry.

Classification of Activities

Ref. No	Ref. Name	Activity		Substance	Ref. No. (Table IV)	
FIXED INSTALLATION						
1 Asset 6	Trade Port (Harbor)	Fuel (storage)	Depot/main station	Oil	3	< 100 m from population
		Coal (storage)	Intermediate depot	Coal ash	30	< 10,000 m from population
2 Asset 20	Chemical Manufacturing	Specific Chemicals	Drugs/	Chlorine	32	< 10,000 m from population
			Pharmaceuticals	Solvents	4	< 10,000 m from population
3 Asset 12	Coal Mining/Power Plant	Coal (processing)	Furnaces	Carbon Monoxide	31	< 10,000 m from population
		Coal (processing)	Mining	Sulphur oxides	45	< 10,000 m from population
		Coal (Storage)	Mining	Coal ash	30	< 10,000 m from population
4 Asset 13	Water Treat/ Pumping Station (1)	Public Utility (processing)	Waterworks	Chlorine	32	< 10,000 m from population
	Water Treat/ Pumping Station (2)	Public Utility (processing)	Waterworks	Chlorine	32	< 10,000 m from population
5 Asset 14	Sewage Plant	Public Utility (processing)	Sewage treatment	Various	8	< 10,000 m from population
6 Asset 15	Ore Mining/ Smelting (1)	Metallurgical (processing)	Furnace	Carbon Monoxide	31	< 10,000 m from population
				Ammonia	31	< 10,000 m from population
	Ore Mining/ Smelting (2)	Metallurgical (processing)	Furnace	Carbon Monoxide	31	< 10,000 m from population
				Ammonia	31	< 10,000 m from population
7 Asset 8	Omega Production	Metallurgical (processing)	Furnace	Carbon Monoxide	31	< 10,000 m from population
				Ammonia	31	< 10,000 m from population
8 Asset 21	Ferry Port	Harbor Facilities (storage)	Tanks	Various	4	< 1,000 m from population
TRANSPORTATION						
9 Asset 20	Chemical Manufacturing	Specific Chemicals (transport)	Drugs/	Chlorine	6	< 1,000 m from population
			Pharmaceuticals	Solvents	6	< 1,000 m from population
10 Asset 12	Coal Mining/Power Plant	Coal (transport)	Coal product	Coal Ash	30	< 3,000 m from population

Figure 8.5 (Continued)

8.3 Vulnerability Assessment

The second process of the analysis portion is the vulnerability of transportation corridors relating to physical assets such as bridges, tunnels, storages, complexes, and headquarters. The assessment technique utilized in the experiment was developed from the original instructions in *A Guide to Highway Vulnerability Assessment for Critical Asset Identification and Protection* (Science Applications International Corporation 2002). The development of this handbook was funded and commissioned as joint research, called Project 20–07/Task 151B, under the supervision of the National Cooperative Highway Research Program and the American Association of State Highway and Transportation Officials. The method involves multiple steps for conducting a vulnerability assessment (VA) and identifying cost-effective countermeasures to deter or compromise the vulnerability of dangerous goods and potential threats. The guidelines reference recommended approaches that apply to a wide range of assets in general and to any state department of transportation in particular.

8.3.1 Applications and Algorithm of VA Methodology

As proposed in Chapter 7 (Section 7.2.2), the assessment process for the vulnerability of highway transportation initially consists of six primary steps. However, the one delineated in this ReIDMP platform development is a slightly modified version. To be more specific, the process has been redefined to accommodate the limited availability of data parameters in SimCity. One additional sub-procedure was incorporated as a supplementary approach at the beginning of the whole process to complement any alternate routes analysis. Further, the critical assets chosen in this process were focused on essential infrastructures and service facilities instead of road elements. The reason for this adaptation was the homogeneous nature of the streets and avenues within the simulation model. There are just a few variations in roads, bridges, and tunnels. Therefore, concentrating on roadway elements may not provide enough information to generate and differentiate the accurate VA results between routes. In contrast, focusing on facilities along routes would render a more considerable degree of disparity between routes, such that the significant differences between the vulnerability of each route could be identified. Sections 8.3.1.1–8.3.1.7 give the detail of each assessment step as it applies to transportation routes within the simulated city.

Step 1: identification of routes and critical assets
This step aims to create an inclusive list of critical assets. Those assets can be infrastructures, facilities, equipment, and personnel that deem vital to the transportation system. To develop a comprehensive list of critical assets, the assessor must determine which routes will be analyzed, as illustrated in Figure 8.6. Then, when the potential routes have been verified and selected, one can proceed further in locating the prominent assets along each route, as depicted in Figure 8.7.

Step 2: assessments of critical asset scoring and criticality factors
The next task of the assessment process is to identify and prioritize critical assets. In this step, fourteen critical asset factors will be used as the criterion to determine the assigned value of each asset on the list. The factors are the conditions, scenarios, and consequences that may result in the loss of the

Figure 8.6 Determination of potential routes using simulation city from SimCity 2013.

Figure 8.7 Identification of critical assets using simulation city from SimCity 2013.

asset. The values range from "less" (1) to "extremely" (5), which indicate the degree of importance. Nonetheless, it should be noted that the scoring assignment of these factors is binary. The values of (1) to (5) can be assigned just in case the factor applies to the asset. Otherwise, the number must be replaced with the value of (0). A hypothetical example, based on research by Science Applications International Corporation (2002), of assigning values to the critical asset factors is presented in Table 8.1. A more robust yet general set of "criticality" factors is suggested by Katina and Hester (2013).

After the scoring assignment of all listing critical assets is completed, it is time to fulfill the core requirements of this procedure. First is the calculation of the total score, and second is the computation of the criticality coordinate. These two estimations can be implemented by using Table 8.2, where the assigned critical asset factor values have been entered in corresponding with the critical asset factors recorded in Table 8.1. The sum of these values represents that asset's total score (x). The highest number among the critical asset total scores ranking is the maximum possible criticality value (C_{max}). Then, both values, (x) and (C_{max}), are substituted as the constants in the criticality equation to calculate the coordinate (X).

Step 3: assessments of vulnerability factor scoring and vulnerability coordinate

The third approach in the VA process is the calculation of vulnerability. This procedure particularly involves applying the vulnerability factors to analyze the inherent vulnerabilities of critical assets. The factors are classified into three categories: visibility and attendance, accessibility, and susceptibility. Each of them comprises two sub-elements, which will be utilized to evaluate the default value and later calculate the vulnerability score and coordinate in the end. In the case of the vulnerability factor default values, the scoring scale is essentially the same as it was used to determine the critical asset factors. The values range from (1) to (5). They indicate the degree of importance associated with the specific definition for that factor. At this time, a hypothetical example of assigning values to the vulnerability factor is shown in Table 8.3 based on Science Applications International Corporation's (2002) research.

When the default values of the vulnerability factor on all selected critical assets are assigned, those recorded numbers can be transferred into one table using the Matrix of Vulnerability Factor Scoring and Vulnerability Coordinate (Table 8.4). To calculate the total score (y) for each critical asset, the sub-element scores in the same category are multiplied by each other, like visibility and

Table 8.1 Assigning values to critical asset factors.

	Critical asset factor		Description
Deter and defense	A. Protection providing ability	1	Does the asset lack a system of measures for protection?
	B. Relative attack vulnerability	2	Is the asset relatively vulnerable to an attack?
Loss and damage	C. Casualty risk	5	Is there a possibility of serious injury or loss of life resulting from an attack on the asset?
	D. Environmental impact	1	Will an attack on the asset have an ecological impact of altering the environment?
	E. Replacement cost	3	Will significant replacement cost be incurred if the asset is attacked?
	F. Replacement/down time	3	Will an attack on the asset cause significant replacement/down time?
Consequence to public services	G. Emergency response function	5	Does the asset serve an emergency response function, and will the action or activity of emergency response be affected?
	H. Government continuity	5	Is the asset necessary to maintain government continuity?
	I. Military importance	5	Is the asset important to military functions?
Consequences to general public	J. Alternative availability	4	Is this the only asset that can perform its primary function?
	K. Communication dependency	1	Is communication dependent upon the asset?
	L. Economic impact	5	Will damage to the asset have an effect on the means of living, or the resources and wealth of a region or state?
	M. Functional importance	2	Is there an overall value of the asset performing or staying operational?
	N. Symbolic importance	2	Does the asset have symbolic importance?

Table 8.2 Matrix of critical asset scoring and criticality factors.

	Critical asset factor														Total Score (x)	CriticalityX = $(x/C_{max})100$
Critical asset	A	B	C	D	E	F	G	H	I	J	K	L	M	N		
Asset 1	1	2	5	1	3	3	5	5	5	4	1	5	2	1	**43**	100
Asset 2	1	2	5	0	3	3	0	0	0	4	1	5	2	1	27	63
Asset 3	1	2	5	1	3	3	0	5	0	4	1	5	2	0	32	74
Asset 4	0	2	5	0	3	3	5	5	5	4	1	5	2	1	41	95
Asset 5	1	2	5	0	3	3	0	0	0	4	0	5	2	1	26	60
Asset 6	0	2	5	0	3	3	5	5	5	0	1	5	2	0	36	84
Asset 7	0	2	5	1	3	3	0	0	5	4	0	5	2	0	30	70
Asset 8	0	2	5	1	3	3	0	0	0	4	0	5	2	0	25	58
Asset 9	1	2	5	1	3	3	5	5	5	4	0	5	2	1	42	98
Asset 10	1	0	5	0	3	3	0	5	0	4	1	5	2	1	30	70

Table 8.3 Assigning values to the vulnerability factor.

Vulnerability factor			Vulnerability factor definition
Visibility and attendance	(A) Recognition level	-	Largely invisible in the community
		-	Visible by the community
		-	Visible statewide
		4	Visible nationwide
		-	Visible worldwide
	(B) Attendance and users	-	< 10
		-	10–100
		3	100–1000
		-	1000–3000
		-	> 3000
Asset accessibility	(C) Access proximity	-	No vehicle traffic and no parking within 50 ft
		-	No unauthorized vehicle traffic and no parking within 50 ft
		-	With vehicle traffic but no parking within 50 ft
		4	With vehicle traffic but no unauthorized parking within 50 ft
		-	With open access for vehicle traffic and parking within 50 ft
	(D) Security level	-	Controlled and protected security access with a response force
		2	Controlled and protected security access without a response force
		-	Controlled security access but not protected
		-	Protected but not controlled security access
		-	Unprotected and uncontrolled security access
Potential/specific hazard	(E) Receptor impacts	-	No environmental or human receptor effects
		-	Acute or chronic toxic effects on the environmental receptor(s)
		3	Acute and chronic effects on the environmental receptor(s)
		-	Acute or chronic effects on the human receptor(s)
		-	Acute and chronic effects to environmental and human receptor(s)
	(F) Volume	-	No materials present
		-	Small quantities of a single material present
		-	Small quantities of multiple material present
		4	Large quantities of a single material present
		-	Large quantities of multiple material present

Table 8.4 Matrix of vulnerability factor scoring and vulnerability coordinate.

Critical asset	Vulnerability factor							
	(A x B)		+ (C x D)		+ (E x F)			
	A	B	C	D	E	F		
	1–5	1–5	1–5	1–5	1–5	1–5	Total Score (y)	Vulnerability Y = (y/75)100
Asset 1	4	3	4	2	3	4	32	43
Asset 2	4	3	4	2	3	5	35	47
Asset 3	3	3	4	3	5	5	46	61
Asset 4	2	3	4	1	2	3	16	21
Asset 5	2	3	4	3	1	1	19	25
Asset 6	2	2	5	5	1	1	30	40
Asset 7	2	1	3	5	1	1	18	24
Asset 8	3	3	5	5	1	3	37	49
Asset 9	2	3	5	4	3	5	41	55
Asset 10	1	2	4	3	4	3	26	35

attendance (A1 × A2), accessibility (B1 × B2), and susceptibility (C1 × C2). Then, the three resulting numbers are summed. Finally, the value of factor (y) is used as the constant in the vulnerability equation to calculate the coordinate (Y) for that asset respectively.

Step 4: representation of consequence results
The purpose of result representation, in fact, basically refers to the reviewing of consequence assessment. This step will help identify which assets possess the most significant concerns in terms of their criticality to a specific set of circumstances and conditions and their vulnerability to undesirable outcomes. For real-world projects or case studies, this assessment must also be performed in conjunction with the pieces of advice from subject matter experts, such as the reliability of data collection, the credibility of threats, or specifically identified vulnerabilities.

Once the coordinates of criticality (X) and vulnerability (Y) for each asset are calculated, they are adopted as defined points and plotted on a scatter diagram called the Matrix of Criticality versus Vulnerability, as indicated in Figure 8.8. The matrix is divided into four quadrants (I, II, III, and IV). The chart analyzes the critical assets by prioritizing the level of consequence based on the critical asset factors and vulnerabilities default values estimated in Steps 2 and 3. Any assets that fall into Quadrant I (high criticality and high vulnerability) are considered critical to the city or region and judged to be vulnerable to the identified hazards and potential threats (Science Applications International Corporation 2002). The consequences of disruptions depend on the nature of the intervention and the impact of the loss of assets. The possible damages may vary from the loss of life and property to the loss of transportation infrastructures or even a completed shutdown of transporting system functionality.

Step 5: development of potential countermeasures
While assessing the critical assets along the routes and their susceptibility to potential threats decreases the vulnerability of those assets, designing the typical countermeasures will enhance

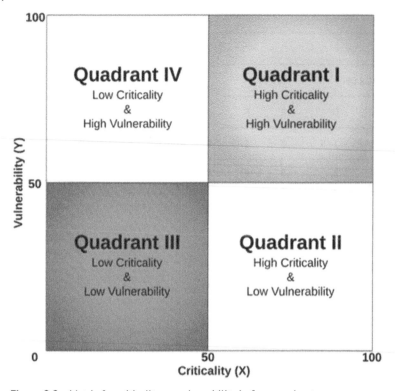

Figure 8.8 Matrix for criticality vs. vulnerability in four quadrants.

security and improve resilience for the community at the core. For this reason, developing these protection protocols ideally requires effective collaboration between stakeholders, subject matter experts, and regional governance bodies. Assembling the right team and tasking it with the right job will ensure that the challenges are correctly identified and precisely addressed within the scope of the assessment process.

Theoretically, countermeasures must be developed based on the focus on three primary attributes – deterrence, detection, and defense:

- *Deterrence*: the protective measures deter an attacker either by making it difficult for the aggressor to access the facility or causing the aggressor to perceive a risk of being caught.
- *Detection*: the surveillance measures discover the potential attack and alert the security response team or emergency response units.
- *Defense*: the defensive measures protect the asset by delaying the attacker's movement toward the asset, keeping the attacker away from gaining access to the facility, and mitigating damage from the attacks, especially weapons and explosives.

The definitions of these terminologies are used as relative terms to identify a collection of countermeasures considered applicable to protecting physical assets and their functionalities. Table 8.5 is based on Science Applications International Corporation's (2002) research and outlines the potential countermeasures. It should be noted that the effectiveness of the listed countermeasures is subjectively measured by considering how well the strategies reduce the probability of occurrences (or consequences) of attacks on assets with specific threats and vulnerabilities.

Table 8.5 Potential countermeasure for asset protection.

Potential countermeasures	Deter	Detect	Defend
Install motion detected cameras with infrared technology Cameras should include an automatic alarming trigger to notify response team	x	x	
Place active barriers at vehicle entry point. Barriers should be able to be rapidly deployed and be capable of stopping large commercial vehicles	x		x
Construct fences or gates to block bystanders from instantly accessing the buildings			x
Replace external windows with safety glass to prevent broken glass from explosions or shrapnel			x
Hire a private security force to continually monitor the facility and surrounding area	x	x	x
Build a reinforced, well-ventilated area for facility residents to take refuge in the event of an attack			x
Restrict all parking and vehicle traffic in close proximity to the facility to authorized vehicles only	x		
Install redundant power systems (e.g. emergency generators) to maintain critical systems and communication networks			x
Upgrade exterior lighting and emergency phone stations at walkways, entrances, exits, and parking lots	x	x	
Limit access to restricted buildings or area through the issuance of a security badge with specific access identification and key card	x	x	

Step 6: estimation of countermeasure costs

The idea of cost estimation in the VA process is to calculate the range of aggregate expenditures for implementing the countermeasures identified in Step 5. The investment plan must be drafted to package countermeasures in ways that are operationally rational and strategically cost-effective. With these intentions, the productive countermeasure packaging will allow the assessment team to review all possible alternative solutions, namely equipment, technologies, and structures, for maximizing vulnerability reduction. Nevertheless, countermeasure implementation expenses, such as capital investment, annual operation, maintenance costs, and life-cycle costs, can vary. The relative cost ranges for each transportation agency are very subjective and depend on many variables. Table 8.6 displays an example of sample values as a general guideline for estimating the countermeasure costs in each category. These figures, when applied to the countermeasures, are described as high (H), medium (M), or low (L), as shown in Table 8.7.

Table 8.6 Potential countermeasure relative cost range.

	Sample countermeasure relative cost range		
	Capital investment	Annual operating cost	Annual maintenance cost
Low	< $150K	< $75K	< $35K
Medium	$150K–$500K	$75K–$250K	$35K–$150K
High	> $500K	> $250K	> $150K

Table 8.7 Potential matrix of countermeasure cost estimation.

Countermeasure description	Function			Cost		
	Deter	Detect	Defend	Capital	Operating	Maintenance
Install motion-detector cameras with infrared technology: cameras should include an automatic alarming trigger to notify response team	X	X		H	L	L
Place active barriers at vehicle entry point: barriers should be able to be rapidly deployed and be capable of stopping large commercial vehicles	X		X	M	L	L
Construct fences or gates to block bystanders from instantly accessing the buildings.			X	L	L	L
Replace external windows with safety glass to prevent broken glass from explosions or shrapnel			X	M	L	L
Hire a private security force to continually monitor the facility and surrounding area	X	X	X	M	M	L
Build a reinforced, well-ventilated area for facility residents to take refuge in the event of an attack			X	H	L	M
Restrict all parking and vehicle traffic in close proximity to the facility to authorized vehicles only	X			L	M	L
Install redundant power systems (e.g. emergency generators) to maintain critical systems and communication networks			X	H	L	M
Upgrade exterior lighting and emergency phone stations at walkways, entrances, exits, and parking lots	X	X		M	L	L
Limit access to restricted buildings or area through the issuance of a security badge with specific access identification and key card	X	X		M	M	L

This step practically refers to balancing the unit price of the countermeasure packages with the critical assets. The team can group the assets into categories and adjust the appropriate budget and cost per unit for countermeasures to the number of critical assets in each category. However, the analyst needs to know that it is possible to have one asset fit with multiple countermeasures. And in other cases, several assets could be considered applicable to just a particular countermeasure. The nature of these circumstances will frequently require cost–benefit analyses and trade-off studies.

Step 7: development of security operational planning

Security operational scope, objectives, and management are a final vital part of VA. Awareness and preparedness must begin with comprehensive plans, standard policies, and stringent regulations. The smart initiatives will help improve critical assets' security against imminent threats and potential consequences. Unfortunately, no example of a completed security operational plan is provided at this time since it is considered beyond the scope of ReIDMP platform development. However, to establish the roles and responsibilities and maximize the support and services in crisis or emergency situations, substantial resources and mandatory requirements can be developed using the general outline of operational security planning (Vasuthanasub 2019).

The experimental results of the present research are given in Figures 8.9a–8.9f. These figures were developed from an in-class experimentation assessment.

8.4 Integrated Regional Risk Assessment

Another method of risk assessment utilized in this analysis portion of the ReIDMP platform development is Integrated Regional Risk Assessment (IRRA). This method was adapted from the *Guidelines for Integrated Risk Assessment and Management in Large Industrial Areas*. The guidelines

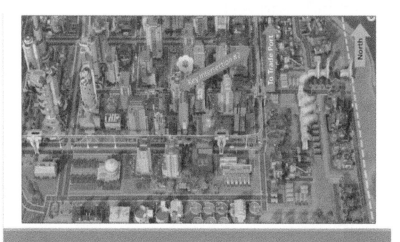

Figure 8.9 Experimental results on incorporating VA with SimCity 2013.

Critical Asset Number	Critical Asset	Critical Asset Factors Route 1													Total Score (x)
		A	B	C	D	E	F	G	H	I	J	K	L	M	N	
1	Police Station	0	2	5	0	3	3	5	5	5	4	1	5	2	1	41
2	Fire Station	0	2	5	0	3	3	5	5	5	4	1	5	2	1	41
4	Big Ben	1	2	5	0	3	3	0	0	0	4	0	5	2	1	26

Critical Asset Number	Critical Asset	Vulnerability Factors Route 1						Total Score (y)
		(A * B)	+	(C * D)	+	(E * F)	
		1-5 * 1-5	+	1-5 * 1-5	+	1-5 * 1-5	
1	Police Station	2	2	5	1	4	3	21
2	Fire Station	2	2	5	2	4	3	26
4	Big Ben	3	3	5	5	1	3	37

Critical Asset Number	Critical Asset	Total Score (x)			Total Score (y)			Criticality (x)		Vulnerability (Y)
1	Police Station	41			21			100	(41/41)*100	28	(21/75)*100
2	Fire Station	41			26			100	(41/41)*100	35	(26/75)*100
4	Big Ben	26			37			63	(26/41)*100	49	(37/75)*100

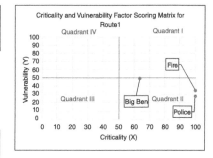

(Ref SAIC Manual,2002.)

Figure 8.9 (Continued)

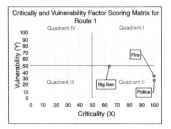

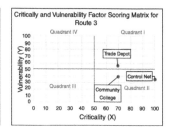

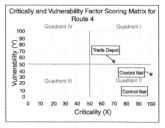

(Ref SAIC Manual, 2002.)

Summary:

• Routes 2 through 5 each have at least one critical asset that is identified in Quadrant I. These assets are as follows:

  • Route 2: Quadrant I Critical Assets 3 (Hospital) and 12 (Trade Depot)

  • Route 3: Quadrant I Critical Asset 12 (Trade Depot)

  • Route 4: Quadrant I Critical Asset 12 (Trade Depot)

  • Route 5: Quadrant I Critical Assets 11 (Trade Port) and 12 (Trade Depot)

• The only route without critical assets in Quadrant I is Route 1.

  • Route 1 still passes Critical Assets 1 (Police Station), 2 (Fire Station), and 4 (Big Ben).

• Recommended that hazardous materials transported along Route 1 to the greatest extent possible.

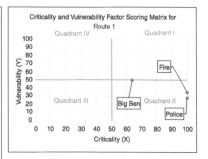

(Ref SAIC Manual, 2002.)

Figure 8.9 (Continued)

were a collaborative product of the Inter-Agency Program on the Assessment and Management of Health and Environmental Risks from Energy and Other Complex Industrial Systems. It was a jointly sponsored project, issued under the International Atomic Energy Agency's supervision in 1998, and is also known as "IAEA-TECDOC-994" (International Atomic Energy Agency 1998). The manual introduces the compilation of procedures and techniques to assist in planning and conducting the integrated health and environmental risk assessment at the regional level. The guidelines also include a reference framework for developing and evaluating the formulation of appropriate risk management strategies. Overall, the IRRA method focuses on assessing the risk due to continuous emissions instead of the risk due to major accidents. These concerns usually do not pose an immediate effect or loss of life, but they often lead to high morbidity rates in the long term. In other words, the individuals may not experience sudden death, yet their life expectancy will slowly be shortened because of the severe sickness propensity or chronic health condition caused by the duration of exposure to emissions.

8.4.1 Applications and Algorithm of IRRA Methodology

By summarizing the contents in chapter 4 of IAEA-TECDOC-994 within the research scope of ReIDMP platform development, the IRRA process incorporates three main areas of study: air emissions, soil contamination, and water pollution – and it consists of six primary methodological steps.

Step 1: identification of continuous emission sources

The initial step of the assessment process is identifying the emissions sources. Estimations of sources, types, and quantities of any emission categories, including solid, liquid, and gas, are needed to evaluate their risks and adverse effects on human health and environmental hazards. Table 8.8 is adapted from the International Atomic Energy Agency (1998), outlining a list of possible sources of information.

Step 2: characterization of emission source inventory

Collected emission sources data must be characterized and compared with relevant emission standards. The correct numbers of emission quantities and physical or chemical properties are essential to increase the accuracy of the risk assessment efforts. The International Atomic Energy Agency (1998) suggested that four fundamental approaches can be implemented to initiate the process:

- *First approach:* if monitoring is available, then estimate all required emission data from operational sources by direct measurement.

Table 8.8 Possible sources of information.

Type of data	Sources
Industrial activity	Ministry of industry or commerce
	National planning/economic development agencies
Electronic energy minister, authority, or company	Internal revenue agencies
	Local governments
	Industry associations
Fuel consumption	Ministry of energy
	Ministry of industry
Rail and road traffic activity	Ministry of transportation
Air traffic activity	Airport authorities
	Ministry of transportation
Shipping activity	Port of authorities
	Ministry of transportation
Air emissions	Ministry of health or environment
	Air pollution control authorities
Water emission	Ministry of health or environment
	Water pollution control authorities

- *Second approach*: if monitoring is not available or not technically feasible, then calculate the emission quantities and other associated input values from pollutants using theoretical or empirical equations correlating operating parameters.
- *Third approach*: if the direct measurement is unavailable and input constants are not calculable, then utilize the compilation of comparative data and values from similar situations or existing literature to estimate the emission values.
- *Fourth approach*: if none of the abovementioned approaches are applicable, the only last option is to rely on expert advice and judgment.

In the ReIDMP platform, the SimCity environment's application capability still has limitations in simulating some specific information required as input data. Consequently, the second approach is selected to overcome those constraints and to proceed further in the investigation process. All in all, the calculation in this second option converts the estimated emission quantity into input values by using emission coefficients. An example list of conversion factors and specific information on five conventional air pollutants in the United States required to practice this step is displayed in Table 8.9, as suggested by the International Atomic Energy Agency (1998). Also, to better understand characterizing emission sources inventory, an approach for recalculating input values is provided in Equation 8.4.

Table 8.9 Emission coefficients of five conventional air pollutants.

| Energy industry | Air pollutants | | | | | Activity |
	SO_x	NO_x	CO	HC	TSP	
Coal						
Fluidized bed, bituminous	1440.0	366.00	56.00	15.00	138.00	Steam plant with emission controls
Fluidized bed, subbitumen	1700.0	582.00	90.00	30.00	146.00	Steam plant with emission controls
Coal/oil power plant	1297.0	648.00	40.00	18.00	144.00	40/60 mixed by weight of coal/oil
Petroleum						
Primary oil Extraction	13.60	18.60	0.50	10.60	3.50	Emission from drilling/ production
Enhanced oil recovery	207.00	71.00	4.00	2.00	24.00	Recovery via steam injection
Oil-fired power plant	3720.0	432.00	49.30	9.80	410.00	Steam plant with emission controls
Gas						
Offshore gas extraction	1425.0	84.70	1.90	0.60	1.90	120 gas wells
Natural gas purification	0.01	40.90	0.00	0.36	0.16	Treatment prior to transmission
Liquefied natural gas tanker	7.42	5.84	0.41	0.52	2.44	63,460 DWT ton tanker

(Continued)

Table 8.9 (Continued)

Energy industry	Air pollutants					Activity
	SO$_x$	NO$_x$	CO	HC	TSP	
Nuclear						
Open pit uranium mining	0.43	0.25	0.00	0.02	0.27	Mining of ore for fuel
Underground uranium mining	0.02	0.32	0.19	0.03	0.01	Mining of ore for fuel
Solar						
Residential wood stoves	32.30	134.65	29.10	28.15	565.00	Steam boiler with emission controls
Industrial wood-fired boiler	70.00	162.00	1300.0	325.00	79.60	Steam boiler with emission controls

To recalculate input data into metric ton/GW * Year

$$n\frac{TONS}{10^{12}\,BTU} = 27n\frac{MT}{GWa} \tag{8.4}$$

where $MT = 1000$ kg, $a = 365$ days

Case 1: oil-fired power plant – sulfur oxide (SO$_2$)

$$27 * 3720 * \left(\frac{1\,MT}{GW}\right) * \left(\frac{1}{365\,days}\right) * \left(\frac{1{,}000{,}000\,kg}{1\,MT}\right) = 275{,}178.2 \text{ kg/GW}$$

Case 2: coal/oil power plant – sulfur oxide (SO$_2$)

$$27 * 1297 * \left(\frac{1\,MT}{GW}\right) * \left(\frac{1}{365\,days}\right) * \left(\frac{1{,}000{,}000\,kg}{1\,MT}\right) = 95{,}942.5 \text{ kg/GW days}$$

Step 3: determination of pathway for analysis

The investigation of human exposure to hazardous materials and substances frequently concentrates on the four following factors (International Atomic Energy Agency 1998):

- The sources and mechanisms of releasing pollutants to the environment
- The transfer amounts and rates of pollutants through the environment
- The exposure duration of human subjects to contaminated particles or polluting substances
- The moving directions of the pollutant

When analyzing continuous emissions, as far as the release mechanisms have existed and human activities are concerned, the moving path of the pollutants from the source to the receptors (dermal, inhalation, eating, and drinking) is needed to be determined and evaluated. Pathways are the condition that indicates the numbers of population average exposures and maximum individual exposures. Each of them also represents a unique mechanism of exposure.

Step 4: selection of model for dispersion value calculations

Suppose the direct measurements of pollution exposures from continuous emissions and hazardous wastes are absent. In that case, the pollutant concentrations must be quantified using analytical models that roughly simulate the passage, distribution, and transformation of materials in the environment. These models can range from simple hands-on calculations with the graphical calculator to complex computerized systems or software that solve coupled partial differential equations. IAEA-TECDOC-994 recommended that IRRA requires a decent selection of appropriate mathematical models for describing natural phenomena and effects of pollution exposure (International Atomic Energy Agency 1998). The choice of models must depend heavily on the availability of information and the purpose of the study. Combining highly sophisticated models with inadequate data is unquestionably the worst decision. Last but not least, it is crucial to remember that the final product of IRRA is supposed to be a list of corrective measures which is rational, practical, and favorable to social and economic objectives (International Atomic Energy Agency 1998).

8.4.2 Atmospheric Dispersion Models

The idea of applying atmospheric dispersion modeling within the IRRA process is to estimate the pollutant concentrations as a function of time since release and to construct the dispersal pattern of hazardous emissions concerning the source (International Atomic Energy Agency 1998). Some models can be developed in the form of simple mathematical formulas. The uncomplicated ones may be exercised with an intermediate level of calculation proficiency, but the advanced models will need considerable levels of skill and experience. Various meteorological dispersion models, such as Gaussian plume, physical, or regional air quality models, could be employed but they must be adopted with appropriate judgment (International Atomic Energy Agency 1998):

- *Gaussian plume models:* Gaussian plume modeling is one of the simplest ways to calculate the dispersion if the air is the medium. It is commonly used and relatively suitable for evaluating the concentration of pollutants as a time function with dispersion distances of 50–80 km from a large point of emission source (International Atomic Energy Agency 1998). This technique simulates an estimated concentration distribution in the form of the Gaussian plume model as a function of a few sources and meteorological characteristics. The input data of its mathematical descriptions require only a source term, an atmospheric stability category, wind speed, and wind direction. However, to analyze a simple air pollution model with Gaussian plume modeling, one of the most convenient approaches is to implement an online-based atmospheric dispersion model calculator. Figure 8.10 depicts the interface of Gaussian plume calculation from California State University, Northridge (2018). The mathematical formula and physical characteristics of dispersion in wandering plumes are programmed as a calculator application package. The user enters the value of all required input variables in the fields of section 1. Then, the program instantly generates the sigma values in section 2, and the results are displaced in section 3 of the calculator.
- *Physical models:* physical models are choices of meteorological dispersion concept, which can simulate the wind and temperature patterns and predict the exact behavior of single or several plumes. They can provide qualitative results comparable with other sophisticated plume computerization methods (International Atomic Energy Agency 1998). Nonetheless, this type of model can only be used if a precise representation of topography is available.

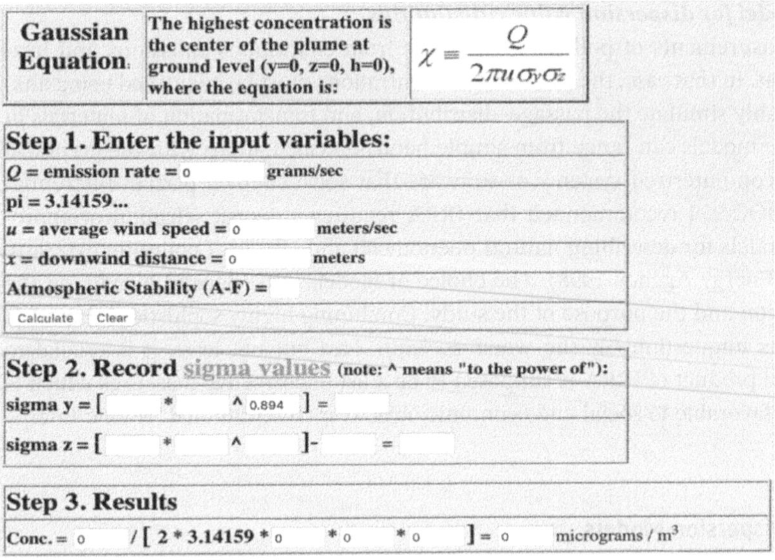

Gaussian Equation	The highest concentration is the center of the plume at ground level (y=0, z=0, h=0), where the equation is:	$\chi = \dfrac{Q}{2\pi u \sigma_y \sigma_z}$

Step 1. Enter the input variables:

Q = emission rate = o   grams/sec

pi = 3.14159...

u = average wind speed = o   meters/sec

x = downwind distance = o   meters

Atmospheric Stability (A-F) =

Calculate   Clear

Step 2. Record sigma values (note: ^ means "to the power of"):

sigma y = [*   ^ 0.894   ] =

sigma z = [*   ^   ]-   =

Step 3. Results

Conc. = o   /[2 * 3.14159 * o   * o   * o   ] = o   micrograms / m^3

Figure 8.10 California State University, Northridge's Gaussian plume calculator.

- *Regional air quality models:* the air quality models require simple data and are easy to use. They adopt a concept of a linear relationship between average regional emissions and regional average concentrations, which is, however, only helpful when the changes happen in the smaller range from the observations and for pollutants with uncomplicated atmospheric chemistry conditions. The mechanisms of this model implementation are pretty strict and cannot be adjusted for new case requirements.

8.4.3 Aquatic Dispersion Models

The aquatic environment can be sorted into various media, such as lakes, rivers, bays, oceans, rain, and flood water. All have different characteristics, and each requires a particular way of approach. The aquatic dispersion models are considered moderately to highly complicated. They are usually analyzed using a computer software package that can be configured for modeling specific bodies of water, complex aquifers structures, and intricate flow patterns (International Atomic Energy Agency 1998).

- *Surface models:* surface models deal with the contamination of surface water. Choices of models are mainly either steady-state or time-dependent. Both are distinct in term of complexity, namely two or three dimensions, with or without convection, and with or without sinks (International Atomic Energy Agency 1998). Many water quality models tend to be highly site-specific. They were designed to prohibit real-time condition changes and not deviate from their intended functional purposes. Thus, straightforward models are as good as solutions for estimating pollutant concentrations in streams and rivers. In contrast, the complex ones are more appropriate for computerizing dispersion patterns in lakes, reservoirs, and any other bodies of water with complicated situations.
- *Subsurface models:* subsurface models deal with pollutant concentrations deep in the water level. They are simple in concept but quite challenging in execution compared to surface models.

The contamination modeling procedures have two phases and usually involve the potential complexity of the subsurface structures. The first stage investigates a vertical movement of pollutants through the unsaturated zone above an aquifer. The second stage is examining plume formation and the flow rate of pollutants through the aquifer. On the whole, the modeling implementation of subsurface aquifer contamination requires a comprehensive collection of data and must be done using advanced computer software packages.

8.4.4 Food Chain Models

The evaluation of food chain pathways is typically determined by examining diets, sources of products, and potential exposure pathways (International Atomic Energy Agency 1998). Many conceptual frameworks and computerized models have been developed to investigate pollutant dispersions and contamination activities. Food chain models are categorized as both terrestrial and aquatic. They are distinguished in terms of ecosystems but do not differ in concept (International Atomic Energy Agency 1998). These models were primarily appropriated for the assessment of long-term releases. However, they can also be applied to the cases of accidental releases, yet the result may possess considerable degrees of uncertainty.

Step 5: evaluation of health impact on population
The necessity of estimating the dose–response relationship is tied directly to quantitative risk assessment. The International Atomic Energy Agency (1998) recommended that it is a mandatory requirement that aids the assessment team and stakeholders in avoiding irrational planning and decision-making. The conventional method usually consists of hazard identification, followed by parallel steps of exposure quantification and dose–response assessment. This procedure is purposely concerned with evaluating and quantitative characterization of the relationship between the exposure level and health impact.

8.4.5 Elements of Exposure

As previously stated, IRRA deals with multiple intermediaries of exposure, including air, water, and soil. Even with the same concentration of pollutants, exposure to different environmental mediums could result in a significantly different dose at the tissue level. The exposure–response function will highly depend on the subject's exposure. Elements of exposure include:

- *Exposure and dose:* a clear distinction between exposure and dose is a significant element in understanding the dose–response relationship and its use in risk assessment. Exposure is the amount of pollutant or state of harmful condition in the environment to which an individual is exposed. The dose is the pollutant concentration that causes the impacts or problems to the human body's organ, tissue, or specific cell. These two technical terms are bound under a principle of causality (cause and effect). Even so, their connection is interposed by simple factors, such as breathing rate, complex metabolism, and pharmacokinetic processes. These systems in the human body can intervene between the initial point of exposure and the issue of interest. They are challenging to understand and could be involved in substantial interspecies variation.
- *Averaging time:* in short, the average duration of exposure measurement ranges from seconds to a day or even longer and also varies depending on the environmental conditions. Moreover, people who stand in one spot for a certain period will be endangered from continually varying exposure. And yet a person who moves around in their daily activities will be exposed to even more extensive exposure variations.

- *Exposure time regimen:* in assessing the risk of health impact on the population, the duration of exposure was perceived to be an uncertain variable. Regimen were often introduced in the assessment processes by applying dose–response functions based on two examination forms. First are the epidemiological and occupational studies on humans, in which daily workers were exposed for eight hours a day, five days a week, while normal persons had continued exposure. Second is toxicological experiments on whole mammals in which the animals were exposed for five days a week.
- *Complex mixtures:* nobody is exposed to a single substance or pure chemical. Even in a specific time and place, both humans and animals are habitually at risk of exposure to multiple compounds of pollutants. Nevertheless, it should be remembered that dose–response functions always represent the effects in terms of either a single pure state or an index of a mixture only.
- *Measurement techniques:* technically, the considerations in measuring exposure, dose, and effect are usually unnecessary in most cases.

8.4.6 Elements of Effects

Many conclusions on health impacts or issues are available for dose–response functions and applications for risk assessment. Most end-points regularly focus on diseases with significant concern, such as cancer, heart disease, reproductive toxicity, and even genetic disorders in future generations. These potential effects are a severe matter regarding human wellness, which decision makers can easily understand:

- *Sensitive populations:* in some cases, the predominant effects can be unaccountable in large population studies, if they occur only in a small group or sensitive subgroups.
- *Morbidity:* morbidity means the condition of being diseased. In a manner of IRRA, this terminology is regularly expressed by technical terms, either "incidence" (number of new cases per thousand people in a population each year) or "prevalence" (number of existing cases per thousand people in a population at a given time or place). The first expression was widely used for its appropriateness in emphasizing the implication of dose–response relationships.
- *Mortality:* the definition of mortality in IRRA refers to the total number of deaths in a given time or place. This variable is frequently served as an end-point in the dose–response function. An essential consideration for risk assessment in this element includes length, quality, or value of life lost. Overall, the fundamental purpose of mortality studies is not to investigate a cause of death but to resolve concerns about the unnecessary shortening of life expectancy.

8.4.7 Sources and Implication of Data

In principle, there are three basic ways to compile the data for analyzing dose–response functions:

- Epidemiological and clinical studies of human populations
- Toxicological studies on whole mammals
- Laboratory studies on of human/mammal cells or tissues

All studies from those sources that mean to provide the basis of the dose–response function must include information on both exposure activities and immune responses. They should also be verified with reliable literature before applying them to determine an effective dose–response relationship.

8.4.8 Interpretation of Dose–Response Relationship

A dose–response relationship is a factor that signifies an increase in a particular health effect as well as an increase in exposure to a pollutant. The result of this interaction may be concluded in absolute terms (number of increasing cases per thousand people per unit of exposure) or relative terms (number of increasing percentages in background rate per unit of exposure). Dose–response relationships are usually developed by applying a mathematical model in combination with data from epidemiological, toxicological, and clinical studies. However, it is essential to remember that the mathematical model was only used to simplify the underlying biological mechanisms and provide theoretical assumptions that are experimentally unverifiable.

8.4.9 Level of Aggregation

Each individual will respond differently when exposed to environmental pollution. Thus, the collectible population data must be sorted out into groups with similar characteristics. Each group's degree of detail should also primarily rely on available exposure and dose–response information. This suggests that the more detail available in the dose–response function, the more flexibility and reliability are possible in the assessment process and result. The three basic criteria of grouping are as follows:

- *Demographic factors:* age, gender, and ethnicity
- *Constitutional factors:* genetic predispositions, pre-existing disease, immune deficiency, and health conditions
- *Intermediary factors:* exposure level, specific agent, and other additional conditions (e.g. diet, smoking, and concurrent occupational or environmental exposures).

Some of the aforementioned factors, especially age, gender, diet, and smoking, are considered extremely useful in a risk assessment and strongly recommended to include in a dose–response function. On the other hand, some information, such as genetic disorders or chromosomal abnormalities, might be difficult to obtain due to privacy rights.

8.4.10 Uncertainty

Discussing the dose–response functions, particularly at low-level exposures, it is unavoidable that the cases may possess considerable uncertainty. This concern is a sensitive subject since the uncertainties can cause misleading results and conclusions derived from using the dose–response function. Therefore, anytime that a model is put into practice, analysts must take two critical aspects of uncertainty into account:

- Uncertainty in the appropriate form functionality of the dose–response model
- Uncertainty in the parameter setting validity of that model

Moreover, since IRRA relies heavily on knowledge from the field of science and the use of 95% confidence levels is widely accepted in the scientific community, 95% is thus the common value that often adopts as the confidence level in risk assessment. In practical terms, this recommended approach will also help provide sufficient information on the dose–response function's uncertainty. With such supplemental details, the decision makers would have a better understanding of a particular analysis and should be able to conclude by their judgment.

Step 6: evaluation of continuous emission impact on the environment

Assessment of environmental impacts is much more complex and requires more extensive knowledge than human health impacts. Extensive knowledge involves a large variety of living organisms and physical entities. Moreover, there must be toxicological data and a maintaining of "control" of other ecological factors, including relationships and interactions. The assessment usually focuses on four specific areas (Area I, Area II, Area III, Area IV) of critical environmental issues (Science Applications International Corporation 2002; Vasuthanasub 2019).

Finally, integrating the redefined version of applications and algorithms developed from IRRA assessment documents along with the visualizations of the simulated city results in different mappings for group pollution (Figure 8.11), water pollution (Figure 8.12), air pollution (Figure 8.13), and overall pollution mapping (Figure 8.14). Figures 8.11–8.14 are from in-class experimentation assessment results.

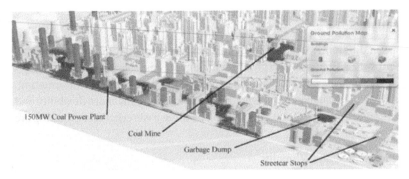

Figure 8.11 Group pollution from experimental data incorporating IRRA with SimCity 2013.

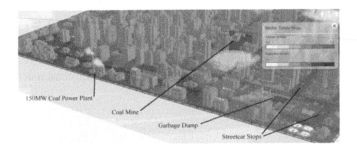

Figure 8.12 Water pollution from experimental data incorporating IRRA with SimCity 2013.

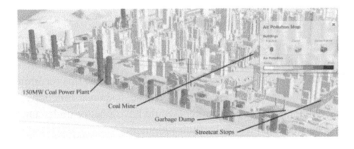

Figure 8.13 Air pollution from experimental data incorporating IRRA with SimCity 2013.

Activity	Pollutant	Soil pollutant emissions (PPB)	Air pollutant emissions (PPM)	Local Impact	Regional Impact	Global Impact
150MW Coal Power Plant	Sulfur dioxide, carbon dioxide, mercury compounds, others	6.7	1.8	Moderate	Low	Contributor
Coal Mine	Hydrocarbons, sulfur dioxide, carbon dioxide, mercury compounds, others	15.1	0.1	Moderate	Low	Contributor
Garbage Dump	Residual chlorides, nitrates, phosphates, dissolved solids, heavy metals, others	0	0	Low	0	Contributor
Industrial Manufacturing	Brown ooze, black smoke	158.2	4.7	Moderate	Low	Contributor
Streetcars	Smugness	0	Oppressive	Moderate	Low	Contributor

Figure 8.14 Overall pollution mapping from experimental data incorporating IRRA with SimCity 2013.

8.5 Concluding Remarks

Some of the more elementary assessments in engineered systems involve risk and vulnerability, aiming to understand potential impacts and develop mitigation factors. However, these assessments are rarely used in visualizations meant for the development of resilient cities. In this chapter, we illustrate how ReIDMP can be utilized in conjunction with SimCity as an applied visualization for technical risk and vulnerability analysis. The specific techniques and procedures adopted in this investigation include RRA for classifying and prioritizing risks due to major accidents in processes and related industries. Second is the process of the analysis portion of the vulnerability of transportation corridors relating to physical assets such as bridges, tunnels, storages, complexes, and headquarters. Together, these analysis efforts improve the conceptual understanding of risks and vulnerabilities that are present in everyday society and how those exposures may affect the larger society as a whole. Following that, an informed decision-making process can be formalized to initiate and supervise a comprehensive plan promoting the city's resilience. A set of sequential steps for obtaining the constant of each variable in the equation of consequence estimation is provided along with means for calculating the probability number of accidents at the fixed facilities.

Detailed instructions for each VA step as it applies to transportation routes within the simulated city are also articulated. Another approach to risk assessment is utilized in conjunction with the ReIDMP platform IRRA to focus on assessing the risk due to continuous emissions. However, the use of RRA, VA, and IRRA in ReIDMP is only part of the story; there remains a need for models that can help enhance decision-making. Chapter 9 reviews and application of decision-making processes involving multiple criteria.

8.6 Exercises

1 Discuss the importance of RRA in evaluating and developing resilient cities.
2 Discuss the importance of VA in evaluating and developing resilient cities.

3 Discuss the importance of IRRA in evaluating and developing resilient cities.

4 Identify and discuss other assessments that can be used in evaluating and developing resilient cities.

5 Discuss the role of aleatory and epistemic uncertainty in the analysis and assessment of risk and vulnerability.

References

California State University, Northridge. (2018). Gaussian Dispersion Model [Online Calculator]. http://www.csun.edu/%7Evchsc006/469/gauss.htm.

International Atomic Energy Agency. (1996). *Manual for the Classification and Prioritization of Risks Due to Major Accidents in Process and Related Industries*. http://www-pub.iaea.org/books/IAEABooks/5391/Manual-for-the-Classification-and-Prioritization-of-Risks-due-to-Major-Accidents-in-Process-and-Related-Industries.

International Atomic Energy Agency. (1998). *Guidelines for Integrated Risk Assessment and Management in Large Industrial Areas*. http://www-pub.iaea.org/books/IAEABooks/5391/Manual-for-the-Classification-and-Prioritization-of-Risks-due-to-Major-Accidents-in-Process-and-Related-Industries.

Katina, P.F. and Hester, P.T. (2013). Systemic determination of infrastructure criticality. *International Journal of Critical Infrastructures* 9(3): 211–225. https://doi.org/10.1504/IJCIS.2013.054980.

Science Applications International Corporation. (2002). *Guide to Highway Vulnerability Assessment for Critical Asset Identification and Protection*. Transportation Policy and Analysis Center.

Vasuthanasub, J. (2019). The resilient city: A platform for informed decision-making process. Dissertation, Old Dominion University. https://digitalcommons.odu.edu/emse_etds/151.

9

MCDA Application via DSS Software

9.1 Introduction

This chapter focuses on applying multiple-criteria decision analysis (MCDA) through a decision support system (DSS), a computerized program used to support determinations, judgments, and courses of action in an organization or a business. MCDA is a series of systematic approaches intended to support the analysis process of decision-making involving multiple criteria and conflicting objectives, often conflicting objectives. DSS is a collection of decision support software products that use those analytical techniques in the MCDA framework to aid decision makers and stakeholders in solving complex decision problems in a much better and more comprehensive way. They are conventionally interactive computer-based systems that can be applied to various contexts of complex decision scenarios. The tools adopt models or algorithms from data processing, mathematical programming, and logic modeling. Some DSS applications even incorporate a multitude of MCDA methods and come with a preliminary preference setting that allows users to (Vasuthanasub 2019):

- break down a problem into a set of more manageable components
- define and structure individual components in systematic ways
- weigh and measure each component, and then
- combine all evaluated results to identify the preferable solutions

When applying MCDA in group decision-making, the framework will help people express their thoughts, judgment, and decision opportunity in a way that the values of each viewpoint are as crucial as the others.

In the third phase of the ReIDMP platform, the details from the NRS or Norfolk Resilient Strategy (City of Norfolk 2015) document are used again as input data for designing and evaluating the decision models. Specific pieces of information, particularly the "NRS: Framework," were synthesized to fit appropriately with two selected MCDA methods: MAUT and evidential reasoning (ER). For this decision model testing, three key goals of the NRS project are transformed into three primary areas of interest: environment, economy, and society. Each goal consists of its associated strategies and corresponding proposed actions, which will serve as attributes and alternatives. In the case of proposed actions, the original propositions of each strategy in the NRS document have been intentionally revised and clustered into a single item at this time to comply with the MCDA framework requirement. Table 9.1 describes the selected strategies and the proposed actions for the City of Norfolk.

Gamification for Resilience: Resilient Informed Decision-Making, First Edition.
Adrian V. Gheorghe and Polinpapilinho F. Katina.
© 2023 John Wiley & Sons, Inc. Published 2023 by John Wiley & Sons, Inc.

Table 9.1 Resilient goals, strategies, and actions for the City of Norfolk.

Aspects (goals)			
Selective strategies (criteria/attributes)		**Proposed actions (alternatives)**	
Environmental aspect: design the coastal community of the future			
EVS1	Creative vision for Norfolk City's future	EVA1	Development of next generation water management strategies
EVS2	Innovative infrastructure for water management	EVA2	Comprehensive studies of flood risk and control
		EVA3	Global practice on water innovation and integrated flood management solutions
EVS3	Ideal place for living and working	EVA4	Norfolk collaboratory and live Norfolk programs
EVS4	Tools and regulations for vision accomplishment	EVA5	Partnership with academia and experts on the future of land use
		EVA6	Long-term recovery plan and rapid housing recovery
Economic aspect: create economic opportunity by advancing efforts to grow existing and new sectors			
ECS1	Multi-pronged economic development strategy	ECA1	Economic development plan and job creation capital (EB-5)
ECS2	City's entrepreneurial ecosystem	ECA2	Business community support and resilience lab
ECS3	Workforce development initiative	ECA3	Regional career technical school and workforce development center
		ECA4	Early childhood care and education systems
ECS4	Neighborhood revitalizations	ECA5	Lots of Opportunity program and affordable housing trust fund
ECS5	Innovative financing methods	ECA6	Creative risk reduction bond and local business investment fund
Societal aspect: advance initiatives to connect communities, deconcentrate poverty, and strengthen neighborhoods			
SCS1	Citizen's information access	SCA1	Bank on Norfolk and resilience dashboard programs
SCS2	Community-building support through technology	SCA2	Helping hands and emergency response programs
SCS3	Community connection channels	SCA3	Neighborhood asset mapping and open lines of communication

9.1.1 The Description of Selective Strategies and Proposed Actions

9.1.1.1 EVS1–EVA1

To create and preserve the coastal community, The City of Norfolk is committed to defining its future through a collaborative visioning process. A campaign focuses on facilitating a citizen-led discussion to address "what is important for Norfolk" and to identify "what principles should be adopted by or would be the best option for the city" (City of Norfolk 2015). This idea aims to generate an innovative plan for living with water now while making a long-term investment for future growth.

9.1.1.2 EVS2–EVA2 and EVA3

Securing the future of Norfolk's coastal community requires innovative water management approaches and infrastructures that can respond to both present and future risk events (City of Norfolk 2015). The city intends to conduct a comprehensive study of flooding in partnership with the US Army Corps of Engineers and to create integrated flooding management solutions by combining human-made and natural systems, such as green infrastructure and seawall upgrades, to better control flooding. The City of Norfolk is also teaming up with a group of global experts to provide peer critiques and explore how multiple benefits can be achieved successfully from flood mitigation investments.

9.1.1.3 EVS3–EVA4

Coastal access is a key advantage for Norfolk. This fundamental value attracts people in terms of residential dwellings and business investments (City of Norfolk 2015). Therefore, while protecting the coastline and core area through infrastructure investment, the City of Norfolk strives to brand itself with a strong identity as a vibrant place for inhabitants and investors.

9.1.1.4 EVS4–EVA5 and EVA6

People are at the beginning of change, but to form better change together the city must redesign the government process and redefine the regulatory environment that aligns with the resilient actions (City of Norfolk 2015). New tools and regulations, especially zoning code, land use, rapid housing model, and long-term recovery plan, should be user-friendly and encourage future project developments in sustainability and resiliency.

9.1.1.5 ECS1–ECA1

To create more economic opportunity, Norfolk has investigated its economic situation and identified the potential disciplinary approaches and drivers for existing and new sectors to boost economic prosperity (City of Norfolk 2015). The city is committed to incorporating knowledge into a new comprehensive economic development strategy for future growth. The development plan will include information, such as business recruitment, expansion, retention, and creation, focusing on capturing markets outside the region. The City of Norfolk also collaborates with the US Citizens and Immigration Service to establish an EB-5 regional center, where direct investments from foreign investors will be allowed to fund the regional projects.

9.1.1.6 ECS2–ECA2

Norfolk has become a burgeoning center for entrepreneurs over the past few years. These small businesses and growing enterprises are bringing energy and excitement into the city. With this in mind, the city believes that to accelerate and maintain overall growth, Norfolk must address the key challenge of access to capital and talent. The need for these requirements is to invent a resilience lab/accelerator platform that connects problems, solutions, and products.

9.1.1.7 ECS3–ECA3 and ECA4

Highly qualified human resources are another key to the future success of Norfolk's economy. Thus, a strong workforce must be built, starting with the youth (City of Norfolk 2015). Providing training opportunities for residents and nurturing the necessary skill sets to strengthen future economic growth is the apparent answer to crafting resilience. The City of Norfolk intends to pave the way for consistent growth and ensure ongoing access to education and opportunity through adulthood. The city also plans to open the first regional career technical school and workforce development center, which will help students and transitioning workers gain more knowledge or technical competency for higher-level employment.

9.1.1.8 ECS4–ECA5

It is inevitable that the expansion and prosperity of Norfolk's future economy are tied directly to the vitality of neighborhoods. The social disparities, like concentrated poverty, social isolation, and lack of educational or career training opportunities, limit the economic growth rate in many city areas. To resolve these issues as well as secure future resilience, the City of Norfolk means to collapse those disparities by launching poverty support programs called "Lots of Opportunity" and "Affordable Housing Trust Fund" (City of Norfolk 2015). The former was invented to target households in the low to moderate median income range with the condition that they must be first-time homebuyers. The latter was founded to establish the operating principles and long-term sustainable funding sources for the fund.

9.1.1.9 ECS5–ECA6

Funding is one of the primary challenges for the NRS project. Resourcing resilience solutions require a tremendous amount of investment. The City of Norfolk not only intends to focus on existing resource allocations but also plans to develop new financing methods for the implementation of forty-five proposed resilience actions. To raise more funding resources, however, Norfolk's Departments of Budget and Strategic Planning and Finance have worked with its partner in seeking innovative ways to leverage the financial benefits from investments of risk reduction bonds or social impact bonds.

9.1.1.10 SCS1–SCA1

Accessing accurate information promptly is critical to an individual in making an informed decision. So much so that all key data, such as buildings, permits, code violations, flood risks, storm damages, and calls for service, must be integrated into a single system and can also be disseminated into actionable information. The City of Norfolk has partnered with Palantir (https://www.palantir.com), a global data integration company, to develop the building blocks for information-based decision-making. This new resilience module will enhance the city's ability to serve and respond to citizens.

9.1.1.11 SCS2–SCA2

City of Norfolk (2015) claimed that a city with well-connected communities would withstand better and recover quicker from disruptive events. Technology advancements can help citizens connect more efficiently and build a more extensive network of people. The City of Norfolk aims to bring communities together and increase their attachment to one another by engineering new smartphone applications and networking technologies that are capable of connecting vulnerable populations with communities and services.

9.1.1.12 SCS3–SCA3

The City of Norfolk strives to improve communication methods for connecting people with each other and their government. The city believes that citizens who share the same vision will be essential to fulfilling that vision (City of Norfolk 2015). The city's Department of Neighborhood Development works closely with local communities and residents to map their neighborhood's physical, social, and economic assets. This effort will help the city to understand those core values that make neighborhoods strong and to provide support in times of emergency.

9.1.2 Summary

This section has provided data parameters that work with two DSS software programs (LDW and IDS), briefly discussed in Chapter 7. However, the decision analysis will be implemented with a two-step approach to represent well-defined decision modeling structures. First, each area of interest (i.e. environment, economy, and society) will be modeled individually to explore a ranking of proposed actions (alternatives) regarding their associated strategies (i.e. attributes) and targeted objectives (i.e. goal). Second, the top-three priority of alternatives on each goal will be adopted and combined as a complete version of the decision model to analyze the prioritization of alternatives concerning twelve attributes and three goals. Third, inform the purpose of implementing DSS in this study. Again, the aim is to demonstrate the benefits of the MCDA approach through DSS tools and especially to present examples of analysis results from an academic research viewpoint. Any findings from either LDW or IDS are not to be taken as the final product or absolute answer. People, and not tools, make decisions.

9.2 Logical Decisions® for Windows

LDW is a DSS software designed to support the processes of decision-making analysis (Georgescu et al. 2019; Howard 1968; Kim and Ambler 2002; Vasuthanasub 2019). It allows decision makers and stakeholders to address and solve complex problems by considering many variables at once, separating facts from value judgments, and explaining the choice to others. The tool captures differences by evaluating each alternative on a set of attributes called "measures" and analyzes the importance of those differences by incorporating value judgments, known as preferred levels, into the measures. Once the preferred levels have been assigned, LDW can apply the implications of those defined judgments to particular data and information and then provide alternative ranking results based on preference settings. All in all, the software is capable of handling a large number of attributes and manipulation of multiple utility curves (Kim and Ambler 2002). Adding objects, such as goal, sub-goal, attribute, sub-attribute, and alternative, requires only a few keystrokes. The configuration of utility functions for those attributes is automated. The application also comes with various methods for assessing attribute weights, displays many results, and enhances users' experiences with a number of sophisticated features. Perhaps the most useful element of LDW is its capability to support rapid changes in values, with results that can be viewed immediately.

Structuring decision models and specifying the data parameters are the most important aspects of using a DSS tool. LDW facilitates the beginning step by providing a pre-outlined hierarchical structure for modeling a decision problem. This default hierarchy is comprised of two levels. The first level is a goal, and the second level is a measure. In LDW, a goal is a set of measures and other goals that form a hierarchy of decision problems. Each analysis always needs at least one goal, initially called the "overall goal." Additionally, to identify which objects are the goal component and which objects are the measure component, LDW distinguishes them using basic shapes. The rectangle represents goals or sub-goals, and the oval depicts attributes or sub-attributes. While Chapter 10 discusses data input into the LDW, this chapter addresses the construction of hierarchical structure of decision models regarding the three individual goals (i.e. environment, economy, and society) Figures 9.1–9.3 depict LDW hierarchical structure models for the environment, the economy, and society, respectively. The integrated version of all three goals is depicted in Figure 9.4.

Each goal has certain measures that are used to define how well an alternative meets the goal. Thus, adding measures is slightly more complicated than goals. Measures require inputting the most or least preferred levels and scale with units for each measure. The input of most and least

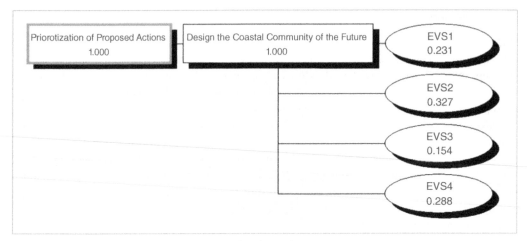

Figure 9.1 A LDW hierarchical structure model for the environment.

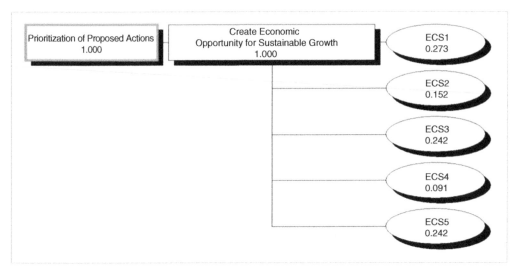

Figure 9.2 A LDW hierarchical structure model for the economy.

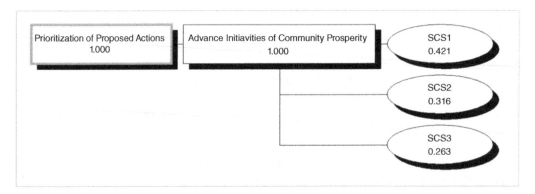

Figure 9.3 A LDW hierarchical structure model for society.

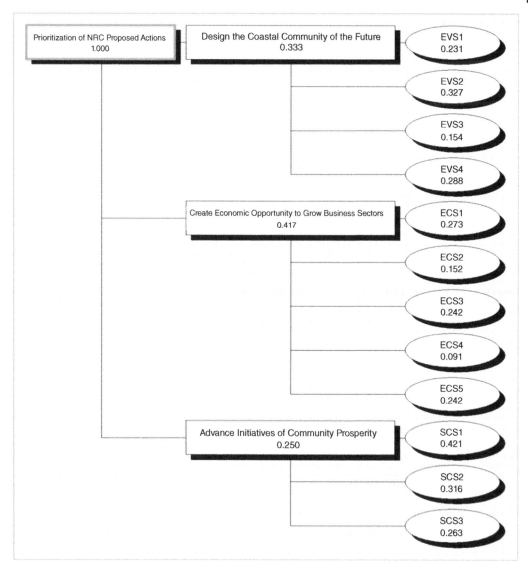

Figure 9.4 An integrated LDW hierarchical structure model for all goals.

preferred values is a significant characteristic since this is how the application detects that a goal is designed to maximize or minimize a specific weight. LDW also allows label scales for particular attributes and numerical values. This function is a distinctive feature of the application as often; many attributes cannot be characterized in numerical units. As for this decision analysis, a scale of five priority levels (i.e. lowest, low, moderate, high, and highest) is selected for every model's attributes. Figure 9.5 depicts the setting for designated units, while Figure 9.6 depicts the assigned labels of lowest, low, moderate, high, and highest.

Alternatives are a collection of choices that decision makers and stakeholders expect to rank in the order of best to worst in the analysis and mean to select after obtaining the result. However, when implementing decision analysis with LDW, the set of proposed alternatives will not be included or illustrated graphically in the hierarchical structure of the decision model. It will be

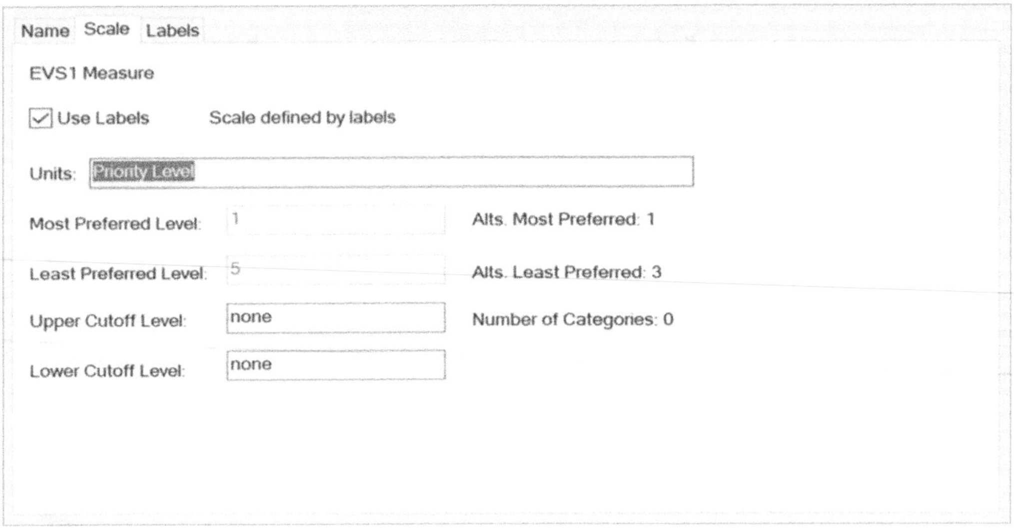

Figure 9.5 Using label scales in LDW for the designation of units.

Figure 9.6 Using label scales in LDW for the nomination of label scales.

displayed separately in another window. The user can navigate the model/program to reach that alternative registration window by clicking on the tab bar, namely "Matrix: Name of Overall Goal," located at the top of the LDW main activity window. The list of alternatives for the NRS was used in the scoring judgment matrix concerning the set measures within the NRS decision-making process. For example, Table 9.2 depicts the LDW matrix of alternatives for the priority level of the proposed environmental actions. Table 9.3 depicts the LDW matrix of alternatives for the priority level of proposed economic actions. Table 9.4 depicts the LDW matrix of alternatives for the priority level of societal proposed actions.

Each of NRS's three primary goals is modeled individually to investigate the possible ranking of alternatives on each goal. Later, the top-three alternatives in each ranking result will be adopted

Table 9.2 Using label scales in LDW for the nomination of label scales for proposed environmental actions.

	EVS1	EVS2	EVS3	EVS4
EVA1	Highest	High	Moderate	High
EVA2	High	Highest	High	High
EVA3	Moderate	Highest	High	High
EVA4	Low	Low	Highest	Moderate
EVA5	Moderate	Moderate	Lowest	Highest
EVA6	Moderate	Lowest	High	Highest

Table 9.3 Using label scales in LDW for the nomination of label scales for proposed economic actions.

	ECS1	ECS2	ECS3	ECS4	ECS5
ECA1	Highest	Moderate	High	Moderate	High
ECA2	High	Highest	Low	Lowest	Moderate
ECA3	High	Moderate	Highest	Moderate	Moderate
ECA4	Moderate	Low	Highest	High	Moderate
ECA5	Lowest	Low	Moderate	Highest	High
ECA6	Moderate	Low	Low	Moderate	Highest

Table 9.4 Using label scales in LDW for the nomination of label scales for societal proposed actions.

	SCS1	SCS2	SCS3
SCA1	Highest	Moderate	Low
SCA2	Moderate	Highest	Moderate
ASC3	Low	High	Highest

and put together to develop a comprehensive version of the integrated decision model. Note that just two alternatives from the ranking result of Goal III will be selected at this time since its original strategies and proposed actions are fewer in numbers than the activities listed in Goals I and II – Chapter 11 discusses goals in greater detail. In this step, each alternative's priority level must correspond with each attribute to generate a certain amount of utility that will contribute to the overall goal. So much so that the assigned priority level has to accurately indicate how the alternative performs with respect to that measure. Each pairwise will have different priority levels; some might be more or less favorable than others. Eventually, each of these measures must be mutually independent, meaning that an increase in one measure's value will not change the value of another.

The assessment of common units is a function wizard of LDW that was ideally designed to convert the level for each measure to common units of utility. In principle, this step is mandatory and always subjected to be evaluated if a set of measures utilizes different types of scale, either quantitative (numerical) or qualitative (label). In LDW, multiple conversion methods are available to assess common units, such as Analytic Hierarchy Process (AHP), SUF, AHP SUF, Balance Beam SUF, Adjusted AHP, Ideal AHP, and Direct Assessment. By default, most are risk neutral and assume that scales are equally distributed (i.e. 0, 0.25, 0.50, 0.75, and 1). The user can individually edit the utility of each scale using these conversion methods. The feature converts a measure's level into utility, which can be linear or exponential. However, when any measure's levels in the decision model use labels as a unit, only four methods, including AHP, Adjusted AHP, Ideal AHP, and Direct Assessment, will be applicable to perform the conversion assessment. This rule is applied to the current situation since all measures in the decision models were characterized to use the label scales of priority level. Hence, the Adjusted AHP was chosen to accommodate the conversion process of common units. Theoretically, this method is essentially the same as the original AHP. Both versions define the relative performances by comparing the performance ratio on each possible pair of alternatives or labels. However, the difference is that the Adjusted AHP function wizard provides a simpler approach to assigning values, in which the least preferred has a utility of 0 and the most preferred has a utility of 1. Figure 9.7 depicts the adjustment of performance ratios used in this decision analysis. The same values are repeatedly assigned to each measure since they all use the label scales.

The final stage of any decision analysis with multiple attributes is the assessment of weights. This step aims to define how the utilities of an active set of goals and their members (measures) are combined into the utility for a higher-level or overall goal. The assessment is usually completed by using a weighted average of the utilities. Similar to the common unit assessment step, LDW provides several options for weight assessment for each of the measures. The available methods include AHP, Smart, Smarter, Tradeoffs, Balance Beam, Direct Entry, and Pairwise Weight Ratios. For this experimental evaluation, the Smart Method (swing weights) option was adopted to determine the preferred level of importance of any attributes. This method was selected as it is the most straightforward approach among the weight assessment options, which renders an easy understanding as well as flexible adjustment. By selecting the swing weight function, the user can directly enter the value, ranging from the least preferred (0) to the most preferred (100), to adjust each attribute's relative weight of importance. The swing weight values administered in the three individual decision models (environmental, economic, and societal attributes) are presented in Figures 9.8–9.10.

Once the components of goals, attributes, and alternatives are correctly transformed into the decision models, the conversions of a common unit on all of the measures are appropriately established, and the assessment of weight distribution on an active set of goals and their members is precisely verified. LDW will calculate the results based on those settings and configurations.

I-max = 5.237 C.I. = 0.059 C.R. = 0.0535	Highest	High	Moderate	Low	Lowest
Highest	1.000	3.000	5.000	7.000	9.000
High	0.333	0.476	3.000	5.000	7.000
Moderate	0.200	0.333	0.199	3.000	5.000
Low	0.143	0.200	0.333	0.063	3.000
Lowest	0.111	0.143	0.200	0.333	0.000

Figure 9.7 LDW common unit assigned values in Adjusted AHP.

Regarding the result representations, LDW offers a variety of features to present the analysis results in different formats. However, the most common and simplistic one is the Rank Alternatives. With a selection of this function wizard, the application will generate a graphical chart, which displays the relative utility scores and the stacked bar comparing each of the alternatives. The utility values

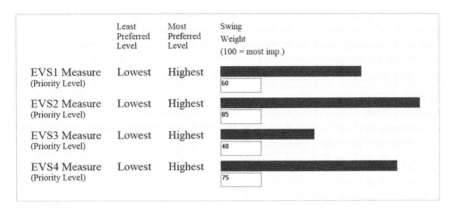

Figure 9.8 LDW weight assessment for the weight distribution on environmental attributes.

Figure 9.9 LDW weight assessment for the weight distribution on economic attributes.

Figure 9.10 LDW weight assessment for the weight distribution on societal attributes.

are the determinant that indicates the length of the stacked bar. The higher the number of total utilities, the longer the length of the bar.

Additionally, each stacked bar represents the accumulated utility ratios obtained from each measure. As a result, each alternative could be compared to the other to see exactly how the utility of each measure factored into the final decision – the results of the alternative ranking for each area of interest (environmental, economic, and societal goals) are depicted in Figures 9.11–9.13.

Modeling each of NRS's goals individually is only a first-step approach to examining the alternative rankings based on their goal. New screening sets of proposed actions include EVA2, EVA3, EVA1, ECA1, ECA4, ECA3, SCA1, and SCA2.

With the finding of eight selective proposed actions, an inclusive version of the decision model will be executed by using this set of alternatives. In the second-step approach, three NRS goals were incorporated into a larger-scale model by demoting goals to sub-goals. In contrast, the associated strategies of each goal remain as indicated in Table 9.1. The label scale judgments of priority levels previously determined for each pairwise (Tables 9.2–9.4) are mapped and combined with any new possible pair of proposed actions and strategies, as shown in Table 9.5. Regarding the assessment of

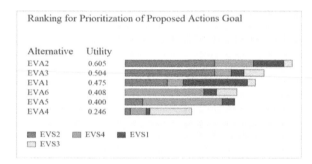

Figure 9.11   LDW alternative ranking result for environmental goal.

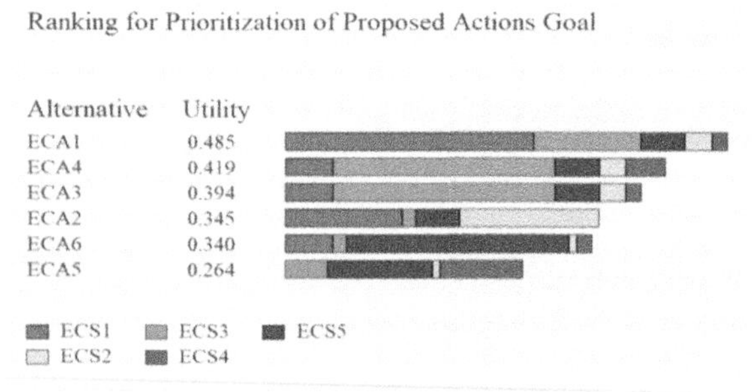

Figure 9.12   LDW alternative ranking result for economic goal.

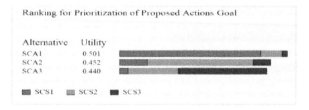

Figure 9.13   LDW alternative ranking result for societal goal.

Table 9.5 LDW matrix of alternatives for priority level of selected proposed actions.

	EVS1	EVS2	EVS3	EVS4	ECS1	ECS2	ECS3	ECS4	ECS5	SCS1	SCS2	SCS3
EVA1	Highest	High	Moderate	High	Moderate	Moderate	Lowest	High	Moderate	Low	Moderate	Lowest
EVA2	High	Highest	High	High	Low	Low	Low	High	Low	Moderate	Moderate	Moderate
EVA3	Moderate	Highest	High	High	Low	Low	Low	High	Low	Moderate	Moderate	Low
ECA1	High	Low	Moderate	Moderate	Highest	Moderate	High	Moderate	High	Moderate	Low	Low
ECA3	High	Low	High	Low	High	Moderate	Highest	Moderate	Moderate	Moderate	Low	Low
ECA4	High	Lowest	High	Moderate	Moderate	Low	Highest	High	Moderate	Moderate	Low	Low
SCA1	Moderate	Low	Low	Moderate	Low	Moderate	Low	Moderate	High	Highest	Moderate	Low
SCA2	Moderate	Lowest	High	Moderate	Lowest	Lowest	Low	High	Low	Moderate	Highest	Moderate

common units, neither custom configuration in the conversion method nor specific adjustment on the performance ratios were changed. The same set of values demonstrated earlier in the matrix of common unit conversion by Adjusted AHP (Figure 9.7) was still applied in the larger-scale modeling case. There is also no change in either the selection of weight assessment method or determination of swing weight values regarding any measures. However, the only additional correction in the setting at this time was the ratio of weight distributions on each of the city's three primary goals. The adjustments of weight distribution and new utility ratios are exhibited in Figure 9.14.

According to the description of a stacked bar chart disclosed in Figure 9.15, the prioritization of proposed actions is ranked as follows: (1) ECA1, (2) EVA2, (3) ECA3, (4) EVA3, (5) EVA1, (6) ECA4, (7) SCA1, (8) SCA2. To sum up, ECA1, ECA3, and ECA4 were ranked first, third, and sixth respectively; EVA2, EVA3, and EVA1 were ranked second, fourth, and fifth; and SCA1 and SCA2 somehow were outranked by the others and dropped to seventh and eighth. This ranking of priorities could imply that the priority level of proposed actions in economic and environmental aspects may appear to be distinguishable in terms of scoring performance. Still, they are critical to achieving the overall goal of the city. From a societal viewpoint, its proposed actions may seem to have less priority than the others, yet they are important and need to be accomplished as well. However, Phase III of the ReIDMP platform

	Least Preferred Level	Most Preferred Level	Swing Weight (100 = most imp.)
Environmental Aspect Goal (Utility)	0	1	80
Economic Aspect Goal (Utility)	0	1	100
Societal Aspect Goal (Utility)	0	1	60

Figure 9.14 LDW weight assessment for the adjustment of weight distribution on three goals.

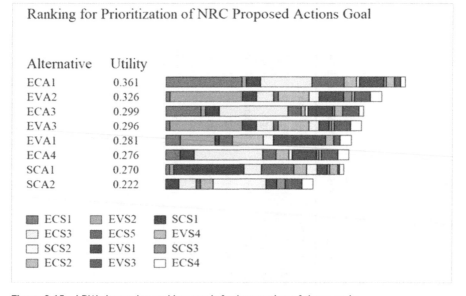

Ranking for Prioritization of NRC Proposed Actions Goal

Alternative	Utility
ECA1	0.361
EVA2	0.326
ECA3	0.299
EVA3	0.296
EVA1	0.281
ECA4	0.276
SCA1	0.270
SCA2	0.222

ECS1 EVS2 SCS1
ECS3 ECS5 EVS4
SCS2 EVS1 SCS3
ECS2 EVS3 ECS4

Figure 9.15 LDW alternative ranking result for integration of three goals.

was purposely designed to be developed using two different MCDA techniques through two specific DSS software packages, so much so that this prioritization list was not a final answer. The result merely provides an initial assumption and overall idea of the priority level of proposed alternatives. A summary of points based on the finding will be reviewed and finalized after implementing the decision model with IDS. Incidentally, besides the Ranking Alternative function, additional options providing informative result representations are Dynamic Sensitivity and Compare Alternatives.

Figure 9.16 depicts the sensitivity analysis graph for NRC (i.e. NRS) and gives insight into how the ranking of alternatives could change if the weight of specific attributes is altered. The user can

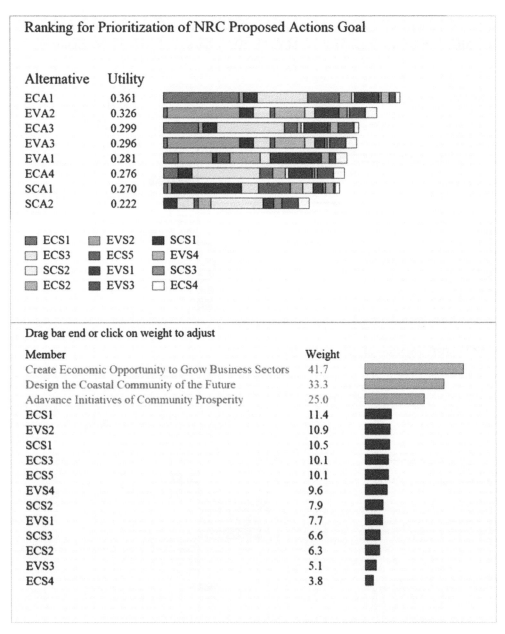

Figure 9.16 LDW dynamic sensitivity.

adjust the weight by directly dragging the blue color bar or clicking on the current weight to enter the new value at the lower section of the LDW main activity window. In LDW, the user can also compare each alternative's performance against the others. By selecting this function, the user chooses two alternatives to create a pair that needs to be examined. Examples of Compare Alternative charts are provided in Figures 9.17 and 9.18.

9.3 Intelligent Decision System

Like LDW, Intelligent Decision System (IDS) is a DSS software developed to assist decision makers and stakeholders in facing a complicated decision problem. Moreover, while the other DSS use traditional MCDA methods (e.g. AHP or MAUT), IDS adopts a theory of ER approach. An

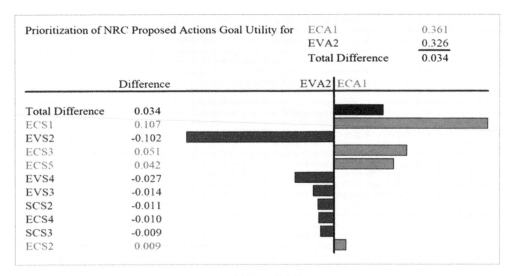

Figure 9.17 LDW comparison of alternatives (ECA1 vs. EVA2).

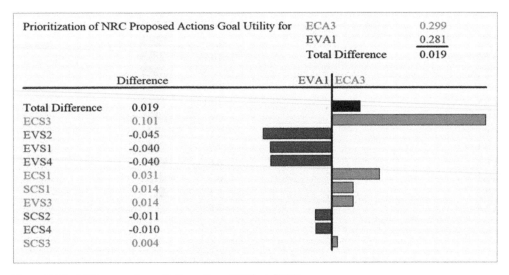

Figure 9.18 LDW comparison of alternatives (ECA3 vs. EVA1).

evidence-based reasoning process deals with complex decision problems, particularly for quantitative and qualitative criteria with uncertainties (Xu and Yang 2001, 2003, 2005; Yang and Xu 2002, 2004). In IDS, the MCDA problem is modeled and analyzed using an extended decision matrix in which each pairwise attribute and alternative is assessed with a two-dimensional variable, namely possible criteria referential values and their associated degree of belief (Xu and Yang 2003, 2004; Zhou et al. 2010). The tool has significant advantages over conventional methods, allowing the user to improve consistency, transparency, and objectivity during the execution process. Overall, the software is considered a flexible application that is not only capable of handling different types of data (e.g. probability uncertainty, incomplete information, subjective judgments, and interval data) but also offers various informative analysis results, including alternatives' scores, performance diversity, strengths and weaknesses, and profile and graphical representation.

Regarding software implementation, constructing decision models and defining the necessary data is the most important aspect of utilizing a DSS product. The interface and usability of IDS are quite similar to LDW, yet somewhat more user-friendly and straightforward. In IDS, the main menu bar and basic function shortcut bar are located at the top of the main application wizard, and below those two bars is the modeling activity window. This window consists of two sections: the right side is the tree view window for illustrating a hierarchical structure of the decision problem, particularly goals and criteria. The left side is the list view window to display possible alternatives that need to be assessed (Yang and Xu 2004). The data parameter will remain unchanged for this decision model testing with IDS. The two-step approach used in LDW is still applied.

Eventually, by mapping the same input data set into the IDS with its function wizard, the hierarchical structure of decision models regarding three individual goals (environmental, economic, and societal) and the integrated version of all three goals are presented in Figures 9.19–9.22.

However, in addition to representing the decision model in the tree and list view as described earlier, IDS also offers another viewing option for visualizing a holistic view of the decision model. This mode is called "Dialog Box View" and can be found and operated by selecting the fifth icon on the basic function shortcut bar. Within this mode, the yellow-colored boxes represent the alternatives (proposed actions). The light blue colored boxes portray the attribute (strategies). Each also

Figure 9.19 Creating an IDS tree for list views of decision model of environmental goal.

Alternative Name	⊟ ▦ Economic Aspect: Create Economic Opportunity for Sustainable Growth
▤ECA1	▦ ECS1 - Multi-Pronged Econimic Development Strategy
▤ECA2	▦ ECS2 - City's Entrepreneurial Ecosystem
▤ECA3	▦ ECS3 - Workforce Development Initiative
▤ECA4	▦ ECS4 - Neighborhood Revitalizations
▤ECA5	▦ ECS5 - Innovative Financing Methods
▤ECA6	

Figure 9.20 Creating an IDS tree for list views of decision model of economic goal.

Figure 9.21 Creating an IDS tree for list views of decision model of societal goal.

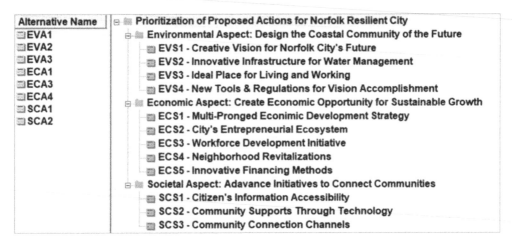

Figure 9.22 Creating an integrated IDS tree for list views of decision model of all goals.

presents brief information about the decision component. For the alternative box, the name is at the top, the ranking is in the bottom left, and the utility value is in the bottom right. For the attribute object, the name is at the top, the weight is in the bottom left, and the value (quantitative case) or average utility value (qualitative case) is in the bottom right. Figures 9.23–9.25 are the IDS Dialog Box Views of the environmental, economic, and societal goals, respectively. Figure 9.26 is the IDS Dialog Box View of the integrated goals.

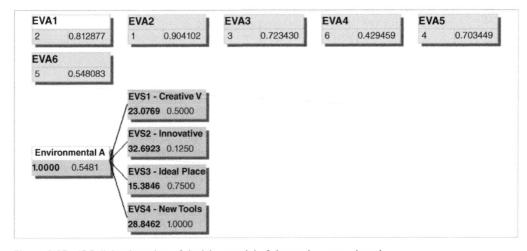

Figure 9.23 IDS dialog box view of decision model of the environmental goal.

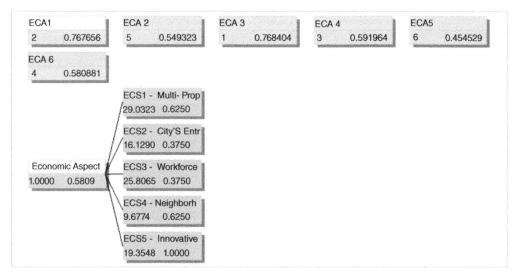

Figure 9.24 IDS dialog box view of decision model of the economic goal.

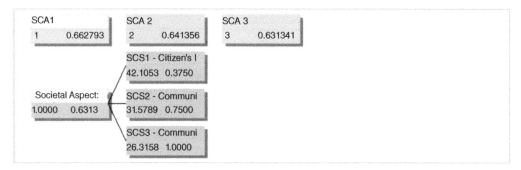

Figure 9.25 IDS dialog box view of decision model of the societal goal.

Defining a set of assessment grades for each attribute is imperative when using IDS to conduct a decision analysis on the MCDA problem. Each grading set must be separately determined, so the software can understand how each attribute is being assessed. In the dialog setting window, the attribute can be defined as qualitative or quantitative with whether certain or uncertain conditions. As for the case of NRC decision model testing, since the selected strategies and proposed actions were meant to be assessed with the label scale of five priority levels, an option of the qualitative attribute was selected at this time. The five evaluation grades are indicated in Figure 9.27. The associated grades are labeled (1) lowest, (2) low, (3) moderate, (4) high, and (5) highest, as indicated in Figure 9.28. Furthermore, to keep the configuration settings of this model testing comparatively identical as well as relatively consistent with the previous modeling implementation in LDW, it is assumed that the utility values of five priority grades are linearly distributed, which are 0, 0.25, 0.50, 0.75, and 1, as indicated in Figure 9.29.

Judging the score or assigning the grade for each of the alternatives corresponding with each of the attributes in IDS differs from LDW and other DSS applications. In IDS, the software does not offer an option of visualizing all possible combinations between alternatives and attributes in a comparison table or a matrix format. Each alternative and each attribute must be manually paired and individually evaluated one-by-one at a time. Moreover, on the condition that ER assesses the

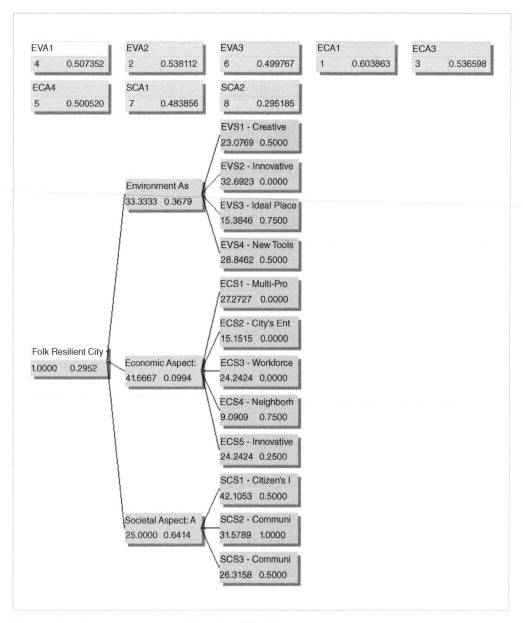

EVA1		EVA2		EVA3		ECA1		ECA3	
4	0.507352	2	0.538112	6	0.499767	1	0.603863	3	0.536598

ECA4		SCA1		SCA2	
5	0.500520	7	0.483856	8	0.295185

EVS1 - Creative
23.0769 0.5000

EVS2 - Innovative
32.6923 0.0000

Environment As
33.3333 0.3679

EVS3 - Ideal Place
15.3846 0.7500

EVS4 - New Tools
28.8462 0.5000

ECS1 - Multi-Pro
27.2727 0.0000

ECS2 - City's Ent
15.1515 0.0000

Folk Resilient City
1.0000 0.2952

Economic Aspect:
41.6667 0.0994

ECS3 - Workforce
24.2424 0.0000

ECS4 - Neighborh
9.0909 0.7500

ECS5 - Innovative
24.2424 0.2500

SCS1 - Citizen's I
42.1053 0.5000

Societal Aspect: A
25.0000 0.6414

SCS2 - Communi
31.5789 1.0000

SCS3 - Communi
26.3158 0.5000

Figure 9.26 IDS dialog box view of decision model of the integrated goals.

IDS Dialog: Define An Attribute — □ ×

Attribute Name: EVS1 – Creative Vision for Norfolk City's Future

Attribute Type: Quantitative or Qualitative
○ Quantitative   ⦿ Qualitative

Number of Grades:
[ ]

Define Grades Now?
Yes   No

OK
Cancel
Describe
Help
Advanced

Figure 9.27 IDS dialog window defining name and number of grades.

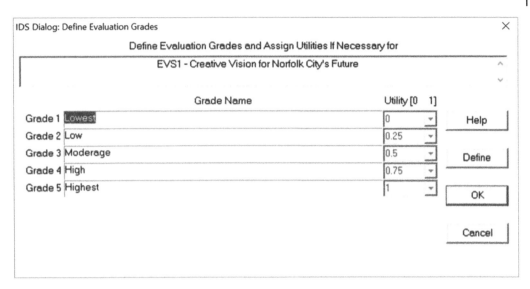

Figure 9.28 IDS dialog window defining qualitative grades.

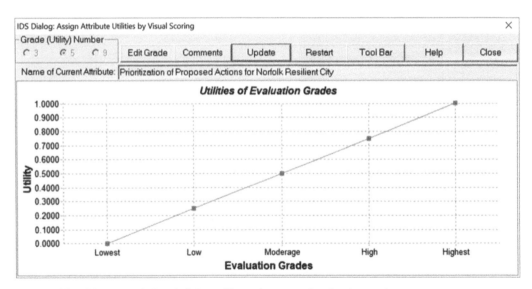

Figure 9.29 IDS dialog window defining utility assignment of evaluation grades.

qualitative attributes by using both grades and a degree of belief. Consequently, instead of assigning just a single value of scores or determining one level of importance, the user can choose one or more preferred grades with different degrees of belief. Figures 9.30–9.32 provide examples of how the grades can be assigned to some of each possible pair of the alternative and attribute.

One additional annotation to these figures is the implication of a degree of belief in the field on the right of a checkbox. Technically, this variable represents the strength with which an answer is believed to be true. The value can be less than or equal to one (1). This means that when only one answer is selected, a belief degree would equal (1). However, suppose that two or more answers were chosen. In that case, the values of a belief degree will either be equally average based on the number of checked answers by IDS or be instantly adjustable with an exact number by the user,

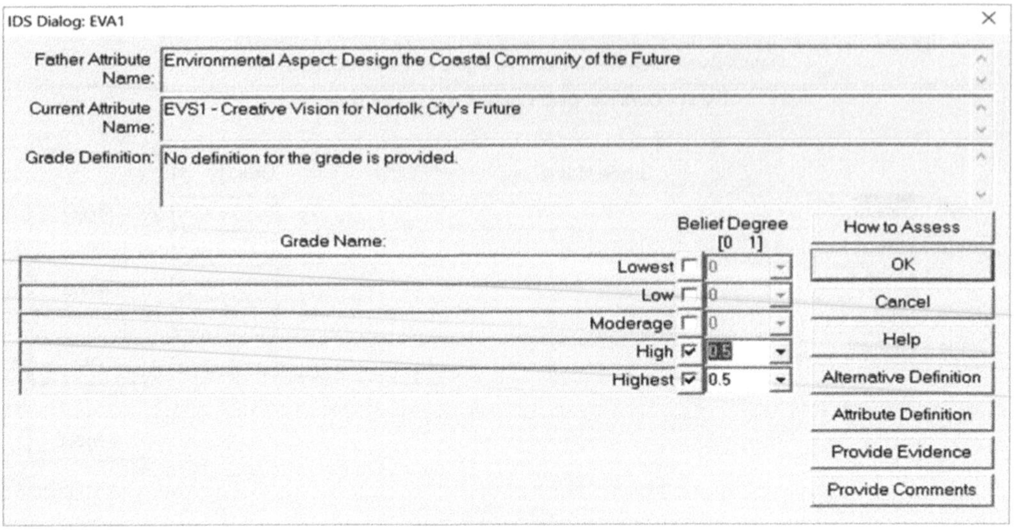

Figure 9.30 IDS dialog window for pairing alternatives (EVA1–EVS1).

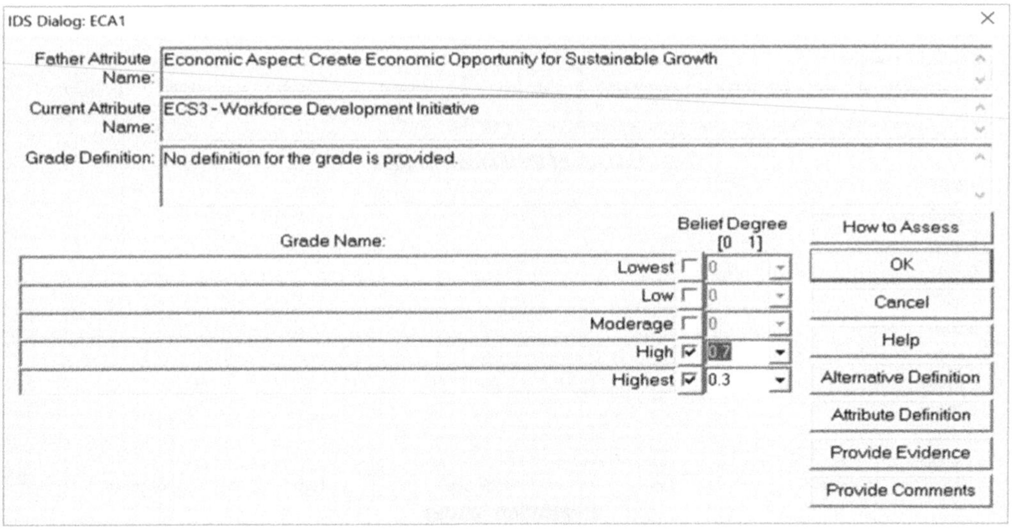

Figure 9.31 IDS dialog window for pairing alternatives (ECA1–ECS3).

which in the end must in total be equal to one (1) as indicated in Figures 9.31 and 9.32. At any rate, this distinctive feature is an outstanding benefit that sets IDS apart from other DSS tools. It possesses unique flexibility in handling MCDA problems with subjective information and judgmental uncertainty simultaneously.

Another mandatory requirement in developing the decision model with IDS is the determination of relative weights for each attribute. In IDS, the software provides a few options for the assessment method, notably visual scoring, and pairwise comparisons, to assist the user in assigning weights to the attributes. The former seems to be a suitable method in this decision analysis since the latter requires additional knowledge and opinions from subject matter experts. By selecting the visual scoring option, the function wizard allows the user to administer the weight distribution to each attribute by dragging an interactive bar graph up and down to reach a preferred limit or entering an exact value in the weight edited field. For example, Figures 9.33–9.35 depict the weight distribution for values assigned to environmental, economic, and societal attributes, respectively. In all cases, the visual scoring approach is performed with the normalized condition to ensure that the sum of the weights on all attributes is equal to 1.

With the completed set of three required modeling procedures, the software should be ready to analyze the decision model and produce the output information. In IDS, the most frequently used function in processing the result representation is "Graph Ranking." The user can reach the command by either selecting "Report Graph Ranking" on the main menu bar or directly clicking the twentieth icon on the basic shortcut bar within the IDS window. By opting in for this function wizard, the software will generate a graphical chart, which displays the relative utility scores and the vertical bar comparing each of the alternatives. Again, the utility values are the determinant that indicates the height of the bar. The more significant the number of utilities, the taller the bar's

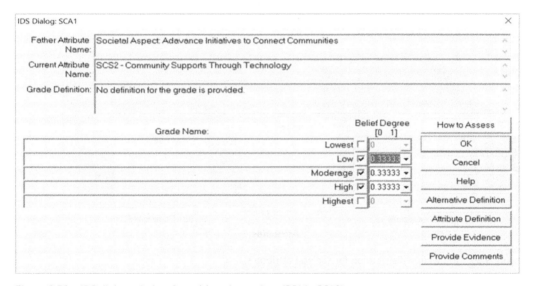

Figure 9.32 IDS dialog window for pairing alternatives (SCA1–SCA2).

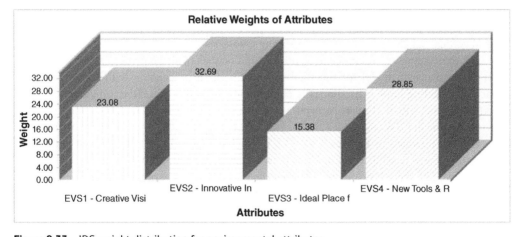

Figure 9.33 IDS weight distribution for environmental attributes.

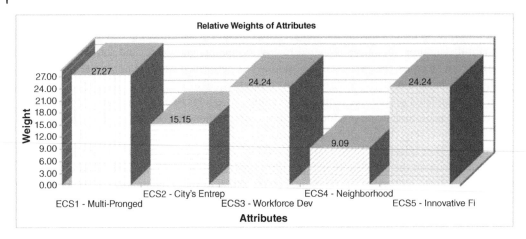

Figure 9.34 IDS weight distribution for economic attributes.

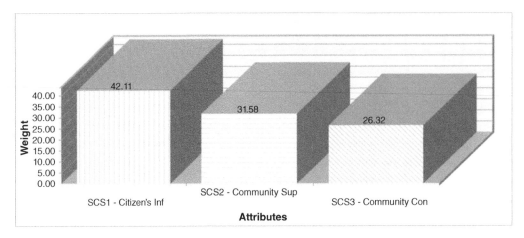

Figure 9.35 IDS weight distribution for societal attributes.

height. For example, Figure 9.36 shows the rankings for the environmental alternatives in vertical bar charts, with EVA2 being the tallest. Figure 9.37 indicates the economic options rankings in vertical bar charts, with ACA1 appearing tallest. Figure 9.38 shows the orders for the societal alternatives in vertical bar charts, with SCA1 appearing tallest.

Likewise, this finding was intended to be utilized as a new set of alternatives in a comprehensive version of the decision model for the final prioritization. In proceeding with the second-step approach of modeling implementation, the components in each of the three individual decision models (see Figures 9.19–9.21) were incorporated into a larger-scale model with the same condition as previously done in LDW (Figure 9.22). The grading of priority levels for each pair of alternatives and strategy, as provided in Figures 9.30–9.32, were characterized and consolidated with additional grading of new possible combinations between proposed actions and strategies. In the case of attributes' weight, there is no change in either the selection of assessment method or evaluation of distribution ratios. The task was completed by applying the same sets of weight values through a visual scoring function (see Figures 9.33–9.35). The only additional configuration in the setting at this time was the weight distribution ratios on three NRC targeted objectives. Figure 9.39 presents the adjustments of weight distribution and new utility ratios.

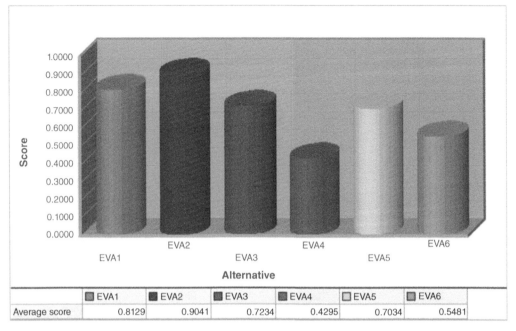

Figure 9.36 IDS alternative ranking for environmental attributes.

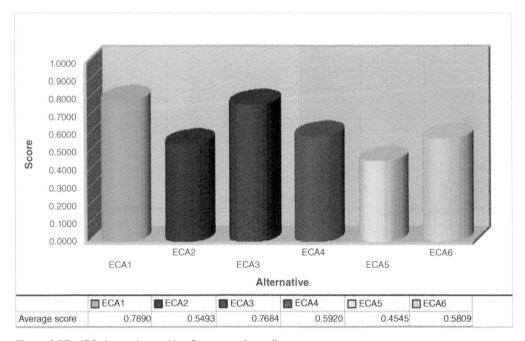

Figure 9.37 IDS alternative ranking for economic attributes.

By integrating three primary goals and analyzing them as a comprehensive model, the final output in Figure 9.40 shows that the prioritization of proposed actions is ranked as follows: (1) ECA1, (2) EVA2, (3) ECA3, (4) EVA1, (5), ECA4, (6) EVA3, (7) SCA1, (8) SCA2. Comparing this result to the one obtained from LDW, both are the same in terms of the top three and the

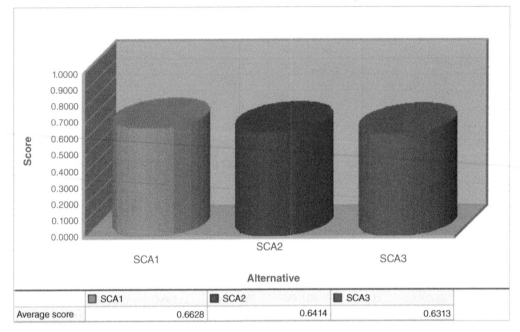

	SCA1		SCA2		SCA3
Average score	0.6628		0.6414		0.6313

Figure 9.38 IDS alternative ranking for societal attributes.

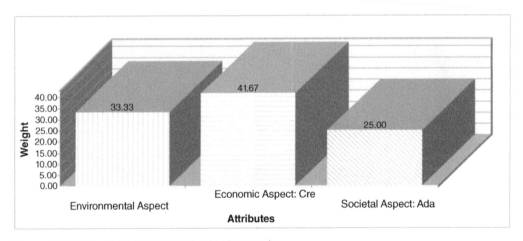

Figure 9.39 IDS weight distribution for the three goals.

last two priorities but slightly different in the fourth, fifth, and sixth ranks. With the application of the ER approach, ECA1, EVA2, and ECA3 still rank first, second, and third on the prioritization list. EVA1 and ECA4 scored higher than the previous decision analysis and earned fourth and fifth place.

On the contrary, as EVA1 and ECA4 have pushed themselves one rank up, ECA4 has dropped down to the sixth. While SCA1 and SCA2 are relevant in the decision-making process, they have somehow been outranked by the others, falling to seventh and eighth again.

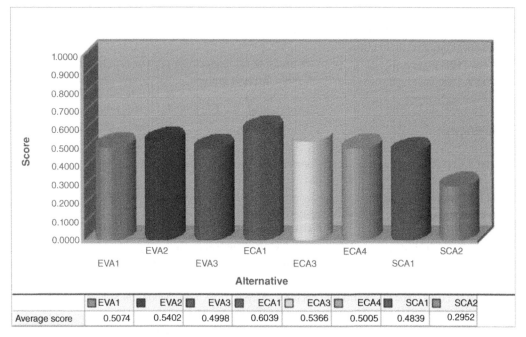

	EVA1	EVA2	EVA3	ECA1	ECA3	ECA4	SCA1	SCA2
Average score	0.5074	0.5402	0.4998	0.6039	0.5366	0.5005	0.4839	0.2952

Figure 9.40 IDS prioritization of the integrated goals.

9.4 Concluding Remarks

At any rate, the earlier analysis can be summarized as follows: to transform Norfolk into a resilient city, there is a need to create economic opportunities in the city, which requires a development plan, capital for job creation, and a technical school and workforce development center that align with existing businesses and future directions. In the meantime, designing the coastal community for the future requires a comprehensive study on flood risk and flooding control before developing integrated flood management solutions and next-generation water management strategies. Both environmental preservation and economic development are correspondingly significant and must be arranged simultaneously. As for societal reformation, connecting the communities, deconcentrating the poverty, and strengthening the neighborhoods are considered just some of the essential elements needed to accomplish an overall goal. The analysis suggests that societal reformation is just a little less vital in execution priority than the others. Even though societal reformation activities are ranked second to last and last in both lists of priority ranking, those indications do not imply that the proposed actions are of less importance or that they should be ignored.

Again in offering a cautionary tale about the articulated analysis, we report a familiar aphorism: "all models are wrong the scientist cannot obtain a 'correct' one by excessive elaboration" (Box 1976, p. 792). The engineered analysis is "useful" in the "context" in which it is developed. And those that *understand* the model can continually improve it.

9.5 Exercises

1 Discuss the importance of MCDA in evaluating and developing resilient cities.
2 Discuss the importance of LDW in evaluating and developing resilient cities.

3 Discuss the importance of IDS assessment in evaluating and developing resilient cities.

4 Identify and discuss other DSS that can enhance the decision-making process for evaluating and developing resilient cities.

5 In the NRS project, the three primary areas of interest are the environment, economy, and society. Discuss whether these are sufficient areas of interest.

References

Box, G.E.P. (1976). Science and statistics. *Journal of the American Statistical Association* 71 (356): 791–799. https://doi.org/10.2307/2286841.

City of Norfolk. (2015). *Norfolk Resilience Strategy*. The Norfolk City Manager's Office of Resilience. https://www.norfolk.gov/3612/Office-of-Resilience.

Georgescu, A., Gheorghe, A.V., Piso, M.-I. et al. (2019). CSI – A Complex System Governance Approach. In: *Critical Space Infrastructures: Risk, Resilience and Complexity* (eds. A. Georgescu, A.V. Gheorghe, M.-I. Piso et al.), pp. 281–320. Springer International Publishing. https://doi.org/10.1007/978-3-030-12604-9_12.

Howard, R.A. (1968). The foundations of decision analysis. *IEEE Transactions on Systems Science and Cybernetics* 4 (3): 211–219. https://doi.org/10.1109/TSSC.1968.300115.

Kim, H.-M. and Ambler, T. (2002). Using logical decision in DFT method selection. In: *Proceedings, IEEE AUTOTESTCON*, 634–639. https://doi.org/10.1109/AUTEST.2002.1047945.

Vasuthanasub, J. (2019). The resilient city: A platform for informed decision-making process. Dissertation, Old Dominion University. https://digitalcommons.odu.edu/emse_etds/151.

Xu, D.L. and Yang, J.-B. (2005). Intelligent decision system based on the evidential reasoning approach and its applications. *Journal of Telecommunications and Information Technology* 3: 73–80.

Xu, D.-L. and Yang, J.-B. (2003). Intelligent decision system for self-assessment. *Journal of Multi-Criteria Decision Analysis* 12 (1): 43–60. https://onlinelibrary.wiley.com/doi/10.1002/mcda.343.

Xu, L. and Yang, J.-B. (2001). Introduction to multi-criteria decision making and the evidential reasoning approach (Working Paper No. 106). University of Manchester Institute of Science and Technology.

Yang, J. and Xu, L. (2004). Intelligent decision system for supplier assessment. In: *DSS2004: The 2004 IFIP Conference on Decision Support Systems*. Manchester University Press. https://www.research.manchester.ac.uk/portal/en/publications/intelligent-decision-system-for-supplier-assessment(999748c6-ceb6-403c-8a9b-8ed874ee3724)/export.html.

Yang, J.-B. and Xu, D.-L. (2002). On the evidential reasoning algorithm for multiple attribute decision analysis under uncertainty. *IEEE Transactions on Systems, Man, and Cybernetics – Part A: Systems and Humans* 32 (3): 289–304. https://doi.org/10.1109/TSMCA.2002.802746.

Zhou, M., Liu, X.B., and Yang, J.-B. (2010). Evidential reasoning based nonlinear programming model for MCDA under fuzzy weights and utilities. *International Journal of Intelligent Systems* 25 (1): 31–58.

10

Representing System Complexity Using Object-oriented Programming

10.1 Introduction

Representing complex phenomena – whether in language, film, computer modeling, or other media – affects our understanding and remains a challenge for researchers, even in the twenty-first century (Katina et al. 2020; Steiner 2013). While this chapter does not directly address this challenge, it shows how a complex system can be represented via object-oriented programming (OOP). OOP is a programming paradigm that uses "objects" to design applications and computer programs. This body of knowledge was created based on several concepts and techniques, including abstraction, encapsulation, modularity, and inheritance (see Chapter 7, Section 7.2). In OOP, the objects may contain data, in the form of fields (attributes) and code, in the form of procedures (methods). They can interact with one another by receiving messages, processing data, and sending information to others. Each acts as an independent unit with distinctive roles and responsibilities (Ancel 2011). Overall, the paradigm aims to support the development of efficient data structures and target real-world elements' behaviors within the digital environment.

The present research uses a specialized tool, "TopEase® Designer," to handle OOP-related activities. TopEase® Designer software allows the user to manage critical information of focused systems and visualize those entities in a holistic view of a complex system (Pulfer and Schmid 2006). A Swiss company named Action4Value developed the tool. It is a commercial software product intentionally designed to handle business processes and initially used in various fields of the business sector, such as financial institutions, healthcare providers, and real estate firms. The software, which has been used for nearly twenty-five years as a business application tool, comes with the capability to provide methodological procedures to capture a desirable end-state of the organization, company, or enterprise while highlighting the gap between the current "system as is" and desired "system to be" states. The idea behind the development of the software was to establish a balance between principles and pragmatism. This fundamental concept is laid on four axioms:

- *1 – Methodology:* The software utilizes only one methodology, which attempts to accomplish its targets or goals based on a pragmatic solution and a balanced manner.
- *2 – Layers:* In TopEase®, There are three layers, including definition, support, and implementation. This feature assists the user in obtaining a target audience-related business structure.
- *3 – Models:* The models allow inputs and data structures to be modeled, documented, and elaborated. With a system analysis and design through TopEase®, the output can be validated through

Gamification for Resilience: Resilient Informed Decision-Making, First Edition.
Adrian V. Gheorghe and Polinpapilinho F. Katina.
© 2023 John Wiley & Sons, Inc. Published 2023 by John Wiley & Sons, Inc.

value chains and questions in case all required elements are modeled appropriately. The five models are business, resource, information, delivery, and change.

- *4 – Questions:* This function supports interpreting the connections between three layers and five models. It helps the user to determine and verify interrelationships among nodes and objects that are constructed. These questions are about cost, benefit, risk, quality, feasibility, manageability, and impact.

The recent version of TopEase® offers even more flexibility with powerful features at every step of the analysis and design processes to assist the user in achieving continuous improvements and meaningful results. The tool aims to provide sustainable solutions to system problems by concentrating on the management of system complexity, transparency of data structure, and control of transformation processes. Phase IV of the ReIDMP (Resilient-Informed Decision-Making Process) platform development aims to present the benefits of adopting the OOP paradigm to address and visualize the system's complexity. Therefore, this chapter focuses on how the OOP-based software approach could be useful in handling emergency management operations as enterprise management processes, mainly through study and investigation.

10.2 Hampton Roads: Critical Infrastructure Resilience

The safety of critical infrastructure (CI) systems is one of the highest priority tasks for national security. Service interruption on any one or more of them due to either man-made threats or natural disasters, such as terrorist attacks, pandemics, hurricanes, and earthquakes, could result in catastrophic failure, not only for the region but also for the entire nation. For example, after 9/11 and Hurricane Katrina, it was obvious that the "protection plans" were insufficient (Georgescu et al. 2019; Gheorghe et al. 2006, 2018; Katina et al. 2014; US Department of Homeland Security 2005, 2009, 2013). It emerged that new paradigms were necessary. For instance, it transpired that there was a need for emphasis on resilience and creating resilient infrastructures that are able to minimize extreme impacts and withstand damages (or disruptions) from both expected and unexpected events. However, the main problem in enhancing the resilience capacity of CI systems is that it requires a comprehensive approach and an appropriate tool to incorporate existing protection plans with emergency preparedness actions.

Security and protection of CI systems have received significant attention and have become a major concern for the United States and nations worldwide (Katina and Keating 2015). Numerous research projects on the risk and vulnerability of CI systems have been funded to address the key issues and find pragmatic solutions. Among those developments, one of the projects, "Critical Infrastructure Resilience for the Hampton Roads Region (CIRHRR)," involved analyzing and assessing the factors that could affect the functionality, reliability, security, and resiliency of four particular CI sectors in the region: energy, water and wastewater, transportation, and communications. The study introduced a strategic risk assessment process using the International Risk Governance Council's (2017) "Risk Governance Framework" to identify systemic risks of imminent threats or adverse events. It then employed an object-oriented instrument to demonstrate a multi-dimensional complexity of interconnection and interdependence between two or more large-scale infrastructure systems. The project's goal was to develop high-level risk management on economic and social impacts from identified threats and to create a risk assessment model that can be implemented as standard procedural security and countermeasure for other regions.

Hampton Roads is a region consisting of a body of water and the surrounding metropolitan areas in the southeastern United States. The area comprises sixteen jurisdictions, including nine cities and seven counties, with a population of over 1.7 million. Hampton Roads has a unique characteristic and is highly critical to national security. It is home to the world's largest naval complex station and the second-largest port on the Atlantic Coast. Besides its prominence as the economic hub and one of the US military strongholds, the region's location is low-lying in terms of geographic condition, so it is more susceptible to floods and vulnerable to the effects of seasonal hurricanes and occasional tornadoes. Taking those characteristics and identities of a region into consideration, the Port of Hampton Roads, also officially known as "Port of Virginia," is a key CI in the Hampton Roads region (Gheorghe et al. 2008). Concerning the Port of Virginia, it is a natural deep-water harbor with a depth of 50 feet with unobstructed channels and berths. Consequently, an autonomous agency is the only major operating port on the US east coast that receives congressional authorization for 55-feet depth channels (Virginia Port Authority 2017). It is located just 2.5 hours from the open sea and operates on a year-round schedule due to ice-free conditions. Most activities and services are facilitated by a total of 22 Suez-class ship-to-shore cranes port-wide and almost 7 miles of on-dock rail track (Virginia Port Authority 2018).

Furthermore, there are four principal facilities: Norfolk International Terminals (NIT), Portsmouth Marine Terminal (PMT), Newport News Marine Terminal (NNMT), and Virginia International Gateway (VIG). The waterways and coastal areas are occupied with military assets, nuclear power plants, oil refineries, fuel tanks, pipelines, chemical plants, cargo terminals, and passenger terminals. The very nature of these systems suggests that they have inherent security vulnerabilities (Gheorghe et al. 2008; Vamanu et al. 2016). Each facility is relatively spacious and easily accessible by water and land. The terminal is also located in the crowded industrial zone and connected with a transportation network that stretches throughout the nearby metropolitan areas, including Norfolk, Portsmouth, Newport News, Hampton, Virginia Beach, Chesapeake, and Suffolk (US Department of Homeland Security 2005). This transportation system consists of infrastructures and assets, such as roads, railroads, bridges, tunnels, and hundreds of highway miles. Under these circumstances, the bridges and tunnels are considered vulnerable spots in the area, which pose a significant threat during any emergency and crisis situation (Gheorghe et al. 2008).

As a CI and key resource, the Port of Virginia is a vital part of the complex systems necessary for public well-being, national security, and the global economy. The port and its facilities along with the vessels and barges that sail through the harbor of Hampton Roads are indispensable components in supporting the free movement of goods and passengers into and out of the United States and the world. Some physical and virtual assets of the port and other associated infrastructures are also tied to the resistance function and countermeasure ability of the US defense infrastructure systems. A single unexpected attack by terrorists on one or more parts of this CI may cause temporary disruption, massive casualties, or economic damages. In the worst-case scenario, the action could even result in catastrophic failure of the entire system (US Department of Homeland Security 2005). In addition to man-made threats, natural disasters are another threat in Hampton Roads, a region that borders the Atlantic Ocean. So much so that the region is no stranger to storm surges and flash floods. In this area, most flooding is the result of surges, heavy rains, rainstorms, or hurricanes. These events have been known to bring traffic to a grinding halt and to affect underpasses, tunnels, and bridges, which can lead to activity discontinuation and service interruptions between the main facilities and branch locations. As a result, the availability of the Port of Virginia must be constantly assured for national security operations. Addressing the risks and mitigating their potential impacts should remain a priority for the general public, Hampton Roads policy, and decision-makers.

10.3   CIRHRR Through TopEase® Designer Implementation

In this section, the US Department of Homeland Security's funded project, "CIRHRR" (Critical Infrastructure Resilience for the Hampton Roads Region), is used as a test case for implementation using TopEase® Designer. First, we suggest that resilient infrastructures include components, facilities, assets, or systems, whether physical or virtual, that can withstand disruption and damage but, if affected, can be readily recovered or cost-effectively restored (Gheorghe et al. 2008). Second, to establish a regional disaster mitigation, response, and recovery plan as well as enhance regional security and resiliency of Hampton Roads, a complex set of management and policy issues have to be addressed. Third, a complete list of critical assets and essential public and private resources must be integrated as a regional model. Finally, all involved facilities, relationships among them, and their dependencies over one another must also be analyzed to determine the capabilities of response and recovery in each of the jurisdictions during emergencies (Gheorghe et al. 2008). Moreover, with the complication of diversity in local authorities, federal agencies, and private organizations in multiple jurisdictions, the City of Hampton was selected as a model city to develop its Emergency Operation Plan (EOP). The idea of using TopEase® in the CIRHRR project is to convert the EOP of the City of Hampton into a digital model for illustrating the interdependencies among CI systems.

Again, the Hampton Roads region has unique characteristics and is strategically critical to national security, especially the economy and military. For this reason, multiple jurisdictions, military assets, and private utility facilities require an analytical solution through the system of system technology. To analyze the current state of an emergency plan, the process was initiated within TopEase® by outlining four primary CI systems as layers. Each represents a specific sector and selected infrastructures, including electric power, water and wastewater, transportation and military, and communication. Figure 10.1 depicts the primary CI sectors as layers. The functionalities of these integrated CI layers and EOP against different threats are cross-cut as predefined issues. Figure 10.2 depicts the selected CI systems and their associated threats.

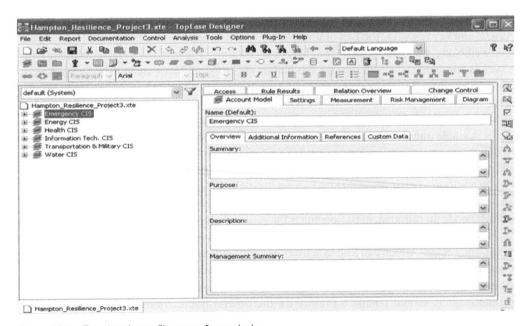

Figure 10.1   The six primary CI sectors for analysis.

The next example of implementation is modeling the organizational chart and the visualization of complexity among entities. At this point, it should be noted that when using TopEase® to develop models, every output result needs the input data. In other words, the user must enter all details and information and construct the data structure to generate the models. Figure 10.3 depicts the data structure of the organization – accounting for employees, roles, and responsibilities. TopEase® uses this data to produce a graphical output model that shows the relationship between objects and the complexity of emergency management in a process support diagram, as shown in Figure 10.4.

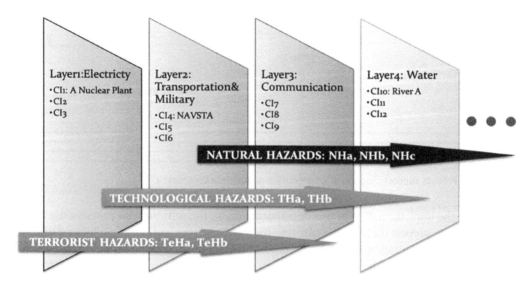

Figure 10.2   Selected CI and their associated threat.

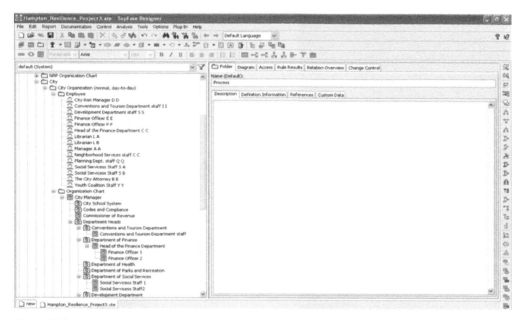

Figure 10.3   A data structure with employees, roles, and responsibilities.

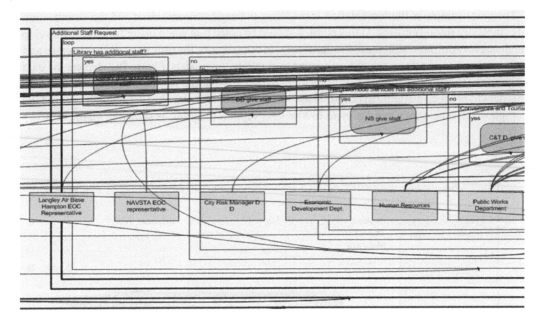

Figure 10.4 Process support diagram of emergency management complexity.

Regarding the implementation of this organization chart, the software also provides the RACI matrix feature to support the user in evaluating the characteristics and responsibilities of various positions in the organization chart. In TopEase®, "RACI" refers to Responsible, Accountable, Concerned, and Informed. The overall RACI matrix is depicted in Figure 10.5. This function facilitates the process by mapping all detail and information in the data structure, which allows the user to analyze the entire organization chart and to identify the influence factors and interdependencies

Object	R	A	C	I
The Governor declares a state of emergency.	Governor			
Direction of the Director or the Coordinator of EM	Coordinator of Emergency Management/ Manager A A		The City Attorney/ The City Attorney B B	Police Chief/ Police Chief Z Z
A disaster threatens or occurs in the city	City Manager/ Manager A A		The City Attorney/ The City Attorney B B	
Provide initial warning and alerting	Police Chief/ Police Chief Z Z			
Backing-up computers, automated data systems, and data regularly	Information Technology Department			
Ensure adequate communications	Information Technology Department			
Coordinating State	Director of Emergency Management/ Manager A A			
Activation of the EOC	Director of Emergency Management/ Manager A A Emergency Management Coordinator of Police Dept./ Police Cpt-HQ	Police Chief/ Police Chief Z Z		
Order of EOC Activation	Director of Emergency Management/ Manager A A			
Public Information Function	Public Inf. Officer for Fire Dept./ Public Inf. Officer for Fire Dept. M M Public Inf. Officer for Police Dept./	Director of Emergency Management/ Manager A A		

Figure 10.5 The overall RACI matrix output.

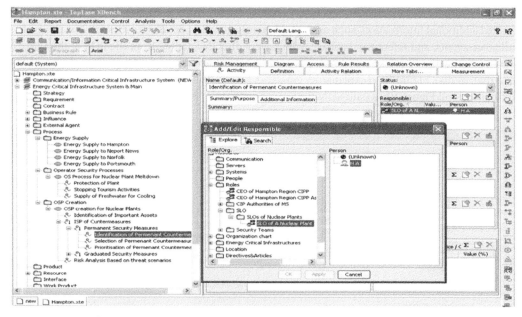

Figure 10.6 The "Responsible" RACI Matrix Function Wizard.

among the objects. For example, Figure 10.6 depicts RACI Matrix Function Wizard for "Responsible." While Figure 10.7 illustrates RACI Matrix Function Wizard for "Informed."

In complex situations, managing emergency operations is not for the lazy. For example, delayed responses – for example, due to overlapping authority and uncleared instructions – to incidents in minutes (or seconds) could lead to costly consequences. The plan must identify and include all

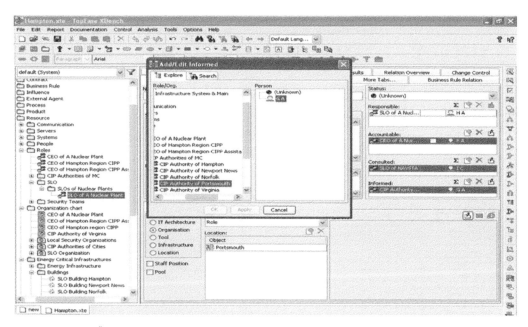

Figure 10.7 The "Informed" RACI Matrix Function Wizard.

possible external factors to avoid unnecessary confusion and errors. In CIRHRR, this step has incorporated additional information, such as the explanatory glossary, detail activities, process life cycle, influence agents, and reference database, which were directly adapted from the EOP of the City of Hampton into the TopEase®. Examples of additional information are depicted in Figure 10.8 (external agents), Figure 10.9 (explanatory glossary), Figure 10.10 (reference database), Figure 10.11 (influence), and Figure 10.12 (sub-activities).

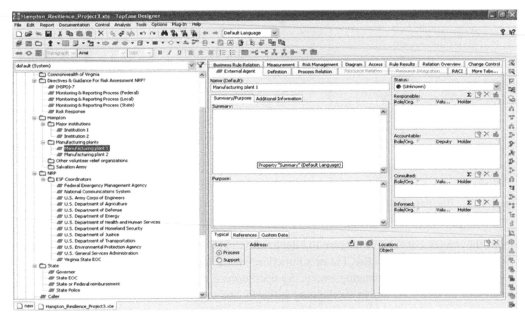

Figure 10.8   Data structure for additional information (external agents).

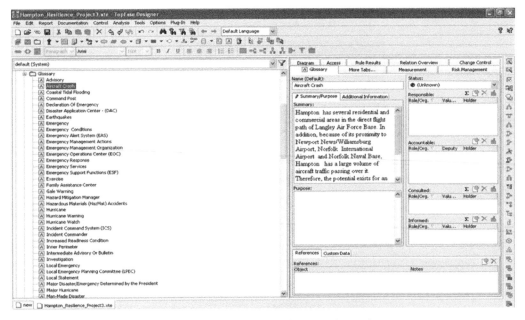

Figure 10.9   Data structure for additional information (explanatory glossary).

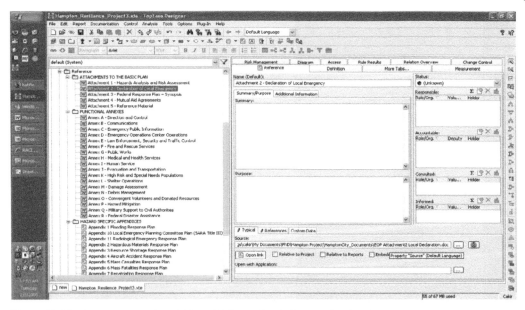

Figure 10.10 Data structure for additional information (reference database).

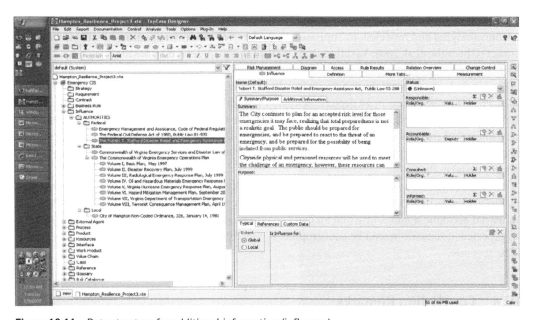

Figure 10.11 Data structure for additional information (influence).

The aforementioned additional data structures allow the software to create an inclusive visualization of a model that includes activities, processes, roles, responsibilities, and people in the same diagram. Figure 10.13 is a partial example of a visual output depicting activities, processes, roles, and responsibilities.

In addition to the capability of creating models and graphic representations, TopEase® also comes with the risk catalog function. This feature can handle any definable risk to the system that

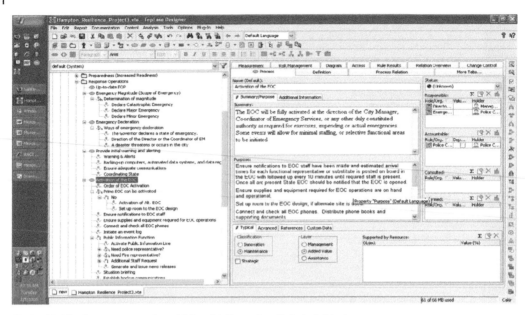

Figure 10.12 Data structure for additional information (Sub-Activities).

is being analyzed and modeled. In TopEase®, the risk is defined by two parameters: likelihood and impact (Gheorghe et al. 2008; Vasuthanasub 2019). Table 10.1 depicts scales associated with risk in the software.

The results suggest that Hampton Roads is vulnerable to man-made disasters and natural catastrophes. For example, Figure 10.14 depicts the region's overall landscape of disaster risk. In the study, the risk numbers for different disasters are generic (thus the approach and model are adaptable to new sources of data). These numbers are the basis for the effects on CI operations. Figure 10.15 depicts the disaster "earthquake" being applied to different energy-critical systems (i.e. nuclear power plants) in the region.

There are different ways of representing risk (e.g. risk matrix or interdependency diagram). For example, Figure 10.16 shows the likelihood of different types of disasters (i.e. a cyber attack, an industrial accident, a meltdown, and an earthquake) happening in the same nuclear power plant. As expected, a scenario would be catastrophic. Figure 10.17 provides another way of viewing the same scenario.

10.4   Concluding Remarks

Object-oriented programming (OOP) is a programming paradigm that uses "objects" to design applications and computer programs. TopEase® Designer implements the OOP approach by allowing the user to manage critical information of focused systems and visualize those entities in a holistic view of a complex system. Several conclusions can be drawn from the application in this chapter. However, emphasizing the idea most pertinent to the present research, TopEase® OOP

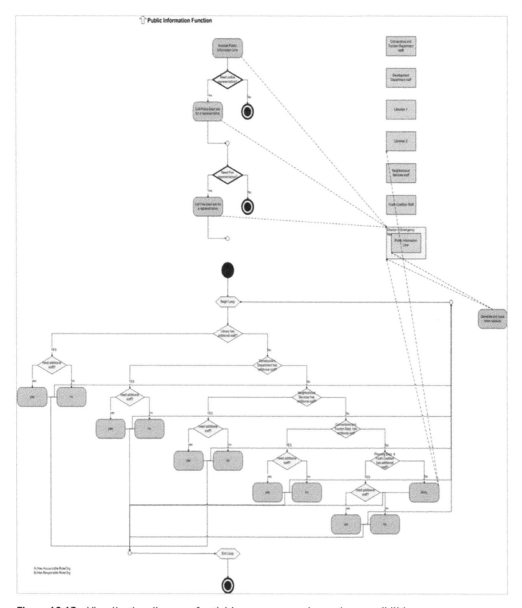

Figure 10.13 Visualization diagram of activities, processes, roles, and responsibilities.

analysis suggests that Hampton Roads is vulnerable to man-made disasters and natural catastrophes. In TopEase®, the assigned risk can be represented with different options, including a risk matrix and interdependency diagram. Moreover, it was possible to generate different kinds of disasters.

While TopEase® is not free of technical issues, there remains a need for research that can take advantage of the additional features of the TopEase® OOP approach. Additional features include:

Table 10.1 Likelihood and impact categories for TopEase®.

Likelihood ranking			Impact severity		
Description	**Frequency of occurring event**	**Probability of 1-off event**	**Description**	**Safety**	**Security**
Improbable	Once every 10,000 years	1 in 1,000	Minor	Minor injuries	Minor breach
Remote	Once every 1,000 years	1 in 100	Moderate	Major injuries	Major breach
Occasional	Once every 100 years	1 in 10	Significant	Single fatality	
Probable	Once every 10 years	Likely	Substantial	Multiple fatalities (10+)	
Frequent	Once every year	Certain	Mega	Multiple fatalities (100+)	

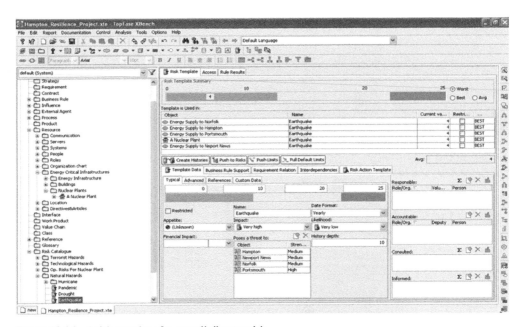

Figure 10.14 A risk template for overall disaster risk.

- *New web architecture for enhanced WebExplorer functionality* – TopEase® V6.3. comes with a new web architecture based on AJAX and JavaServer Faces (JSF). With the new web architecture, various interactive features, such as dynamic filters, editing of texts and data, creation of object relations, web graphics editor, etc., were integrated into the TopEase WebExplorer.
- *New toolbars in the WebExplorer* – Toolbars in the WebExplorer provide access to various interactive functions such as creating and modifying charts, changing text, creating and modifying RACI relationships, entering values, making comments, etc.
- *The graphic editor is now also available in the WebExplorer* – TopEase users who have not installed TopEase designer on their system can now create or modify charts employing the graphic web editor, which is integrated into the WebExplorer.

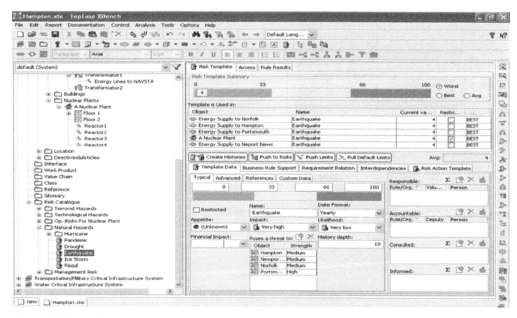

Figure 10.15 A risk template for "earthquake" applied nuclear power plants.

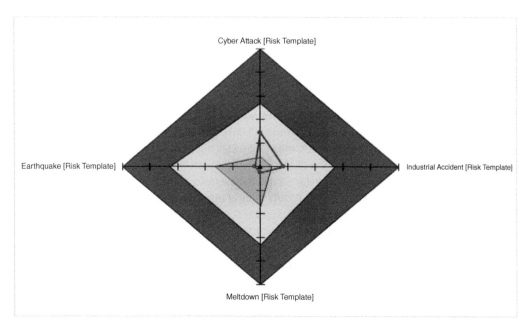

Figure 10.16 Scoring multiple risks affecting one CI.

- *Advanced TopEase MyZone* – TopEase MyZone comes with an additional tab for all objects where the user is registered as responsible, accountable, or consulting and with a tab for all organizational units in which the user is registered as a member.
- *Graphical representation and modeling of class diagrams* – Class diagrams, modeled in TopEase® Designer, can now be displayed in UML-compliant notation in TopEase® Designer and WebExplorer. Modeling changes are easy to perform through the use of the integrated graphics editor.

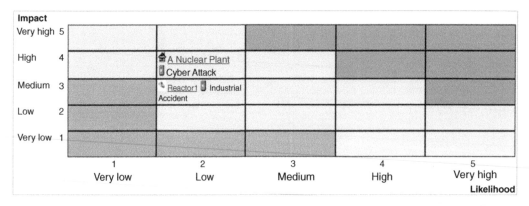

Figure 10.17 A different view of multiple risks affecting one CI.

10.5 Exercises

1 Discuss the importance of OOP in evaluating and developing resilient cities.
2 What aspects of critical interdependent infrastructure systems are difficult to implement using OOP and why?
3 Identify and discuss a city of your choice from a CI viewpoint.
4 Discuss the importance of TopEase® in evaluating and developing resilient cities.
5 What aspects of TopEase® are critical in evaluating and developing resilient cities?

References

Ancel, E. (2011). *A Systemic Approach to Next Generation Infrastructure Data Elicitation and Planning Using Serious Gaming Methods*. PhD, Old Dominion University. http://search.proquest.com.proxy. lib.odu.edu/docview/896960555/abstract/C4484A36FA444018PQ/5.

Georgescu, A., Gheorghe, A.V., Piso, M.-I. et al. (2019). *Critical Space Infrastructures: Risk, Resilience and Complexity*. Springer International Publishing. https://www.springer.com/us/book/9783030126032.

Gheorghe, A., Vamanu, D.V., Katina, P. et al. (2018). *Critical Infrastructures, Key Resources, Key Assets: Risk, Vulnerability, Resilience, Fragility, and Perception Governance* (Vol. 34). Springer International Publishing. https://www.springer.com/us/book/9783319692234.

Gheorghe, A.V., Masera, M., Weijnen, M.P.C et al. (eds.). (2006). *Critical Infrastructures at Risk: Securing the European Electric Power System* (Vol. 9). Springer.

Gheorghe, A.V., Tokgoz, B.E., Cakir, V. et al. (2008). *Critical Infrastructure Resilience for the Hampton Roads Region: Policy Analysis for Regional Resilience*. Internal Report, Department of Engineering Management and Systems Engineering, Old Dominion University.

International Risk Governance Council. (2017). *Introduction to the IRGC Risk Governance Framework: Revised Version*. International Risk Governance Center. https://irgc.org/risk-governance/irgc-risk-governance-framework.

Katina, P.F. and Keating, C.B. (2015). Critical infrastructures: A perspective from systems of systems. *International Journal of Critical Infrastructures* 11 (4): 316–344. https://doi.org/10.1504/IJCIS.2015.073840.

Katina, P.F., Pinto, C.A., Bradley, J.M. et al. (2014). Interdependency-induced risk with applications to healthcare. *International Journal of Critical Infrastructure Protection* 7 (1): 12–26. https://doi.org/10.1016/j.ijcip.2014.01.005.

Katina, P.F., Tolk, A., Keating, C.B. et al. (2020). Modelling and simulation in complex system governance. *International Journal of System of Systems Engineering* 10 (3): 262–292. https://doi.org/10.1504/IJSSE.2020.109739.

Pulfer, R. and Schmid, U. (2006). *Control Your Business: The Balance Between Principles and Pragmatism*. Pulinco.

Steiner, F. (2013). Representing Complexity. *Landscape Architecture Frontiers* 1 (6): 44–63. https://journal.hep.com.cn/laf/EN/Y2013/V1/I6/44.

US Department of Homeland Security. (2005). *The National Strategy for Maritime Security*. The White House. https://www.hsdl.org/?view&did=456414.

US Department of Homeland Security. (2009). *NIPP 2009: Partnering for Critical Infrastructure Security and Resilience*. US Department of Homeland Security. https://www.cisa.gov/publication/nipp-2009-partnering-enhance-protection-resiliency?topics=all.

US Department of Homeland Security. (2013). *NIPP 2013: Partnering for Critical Infrastructure Security and Resilience*. US Department of Homeland Security. https://www.dhs.gov/publication/nipp-2013-partnering-critical-infrastructure-security-and-resilience?topics=all.

Vamanu, B.I., Gheorghe, A.V., and Katina, P.F. (2016). *Critical Infrastructures: Risk and Vulnerability Assessment in Transportation of Dangerous Goods: Transportation by Road and Rail*. Springer International Publishing. https://www.springer.com/us/book/9783319309293.

Vasuthanasub, J. (2019). *The Resilient City: A Platform for Informed Decision-making Process*. Dissertation, Old Dominion University. https://digitalcommons.odu.edu/emse_etds/151.

Virginia Port Authority. (2017). *Big-Ship Ready: Fiscal Year 2017 Annual Report*. Virginia Port Authority. http://www.portofvirginia.com/wp-content/uploads/2017/11/The-Port-of-Virginia-FY17-Annual-Report.pdf.

Virginia Port Authority. (2018). *Capabilities*. Virginia Port Authority. https://www.portofvirginia.com/capabilities.

11

ReIDMP

Implications, Limitations, and Opportunities

11.1 Introduction

Transforming the City of Norfolk into a resilient city is a significant undertaking, yet it remains achievable based on three strategic goals: (i) design the coastal community of the future, (ii) create economic opportunity by advancing efforts to grow existing and new industry sectors, and (iii) advance initiatives to connect communities, deconcentrate poverty, and strengthen neighborhoods. These goals are the basis for the Norfolk Resilient Strategy, or NRS (City of Norfolk 2015).

11.1.1 Goal I: Design the Coastal Community of the Future

In the face of rising sea levels, Norfolk, one of the international hubs of a global trading system, is committed to maintaining the most significant responsibility in ensuring seamless movements through its port and supporting US Navy Forces' readiness. The City Manager's Office of Resilience acknowledges that a physical transformation of the city is needed to sustain economic vitality and social cohesion. Over the decades, the city has worked hard to design and build several protective systems to preserve Norfolk's coastline and keep itself safe and dry. Those constructions include seawalls, sophisticated dune landscapes, and other gray and green infrastructure types. With its success in transforming into a new kind of coastal community, Norfolk's achievement can be used as an implementation model to demonstrate how other coastal cities around the world can learn to live, adapt, and thrive along with the water. Figure 11.1 depicts goal I of Norfolk's resilience strategy (Office of Resilience 2022; Vasuthanasub 2019).

11.1.2 Goal II: Create Economic Opportunity by Advancing Efforts to Grow Existing and New Industry Sectors

The Naval Station Norfolk and the Port of Virginia are central pillars of Norfolk's economy. Unfortunately, with an uncertain future of government policy and geopolitical context, as well as the declining trend in consumer spending and job investments, it is unlikely that traditional naval activities alone will support the economic growth in a region. Indeed, it is true that the Port of Virginia is expected to grow gradually. However, if a city can still not maximize its advantageous position as an international hub, all input efforts would be worthless. As well as creating the

Gamification for Resilience: Resilient Informed Decision-Making, First Edition.
Adrian V. Gheorghe and Polinpapilinho F. Katina.
© 2023 John Wiley & Sons, Inc. Published 2023 by John Wiley & Sons, Inc.

opportunity for living-wage employment in the area to revitalize the economy, the city will also direct its development attention to expanding existing businesses, assisting potential investors, and promoting local workforces to strengthen and attract more industrial enterprises. Figure 11.2 depicts goal II of the NRS (Office of Resilience 2022; Vasuthanasub 2019).

11.1.3 Goal III: Advance Initiatives to Connect Communities, Deconcentrate Poverty, and Strengthen Neighborhoods

As the directions of change point to the new ways of living and working, the City of Norfolk commits to being a place where all residents are connected to the available resources, they need to be successful. Connecting people means creating stronger neighborhoods. They will communicate and support each other to make the city safer, elevate a higher quality of life, and protect themselves better in emergencies. For this reason, the city has initiated a Neighbors Building Neighborhoods program. This initiative was built based on the fundamental belief that people are the most influential catalyst for their community changes. A campaign seeks to complement and support the missions already accomplished. The tasks are still underway and aim to strengthen and help the communities become more resilient at the individual, neighborhood, and city levels. Figure 11.3 depicts goal III of the NRS (Office of Resilience 2022; Vasuthanasub 2019).

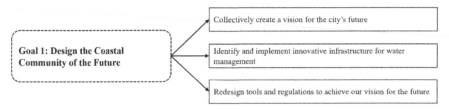

Figure 11.1 Goal I of the NRS.

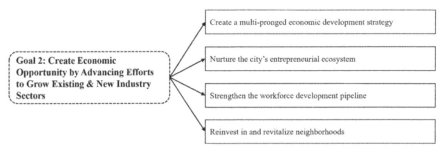

Figure 11.2 Goal II of the NRS.

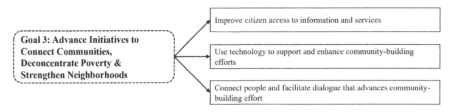

Figure 11.3 Goal III of the NRS.

11.2   Initializing the ReIDMP for the City

Armed with the NRS goals, the researchers were primed for further project planning.

11.2.1   Project Execution Plan

To professionally tackle a sophisticated project, such as resilient city development, Project KickStart (https://www.projectkickstart.com) is selected to render essential study and extensive examination in Phase I (Project Planning and Management). The information presented in the NRS report was input data to develop and evaluate an ideal platform framework.

Project KickStart is desktop project management software created by Experience in Software, Inc. in Berkeley, California. The program uses a wizard-like interface for project planning. Project KickStart's wizard prompts users to identify phases, goals, obstacles, and personnel assignments for projects and uses a calendar to produce a Gantt Chart that features the project's phases and the goals, tasks, and assignments for each of them (Ahlvin 2008).

Project KickStart is equipped with nine wizard functions, while its planning process requires seven major steps. The software's user interface and operating procedure are straightforward. The software features provide a more convenient way to administer the work structure and increase the management efficiency to monitor the ongoing progress and resource requirements until the project completion. The subsections concisely describe how to outline and detail (i.e. a list of phases, tasks, responsibilities, and timeframe) an execution plan for Norfolk Resilient City (NRC) as a development project with Project KickStart implementation. Moreover, KickStart's project files can be exported into several software packages, including Microsoft's Project, Outlook, Word, Excel, or PowerPoint, as well as ACT!, Milestones Professional, MindManager, and WBS Chart.

11.2.2   Project Name

Each project has a name; therefore naming a project is the first mandatory step for planning with Project KickStart. Figure 11.4 depicts the initial layout of the project in Project KickStart. Since the project objective is to create a resilience development plan for the City of Norfolk, the name of this project is "Norfolk Resilient City Development."

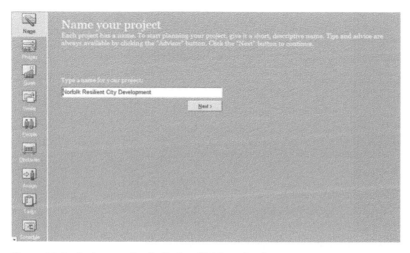

Figure 11.4   Project naming in Project KickStart Pro 5.

11.2.3 Project Phases and Tasks

"Phases" wizard helps create major grouping while "Tasks" wizard helps to help tasks. Each task is then associated with each phase. A planner can begin a process by using a predefined phase library shortcut or manually entering specific details. As a result, by linking and integrating inputs from the NRS report with predesigned methodologies in a proposed ReIDMP framework (see Chapter 7). Figure 11.5 depicts the extracted information grouped into six project phases.

After creating the phase library, we move to the next sub-procedure known as "task identification." The software wizard cycles through those six phases, one at a time, asking a planner to enter tasks for each phase. It is important to note that phases are organized in sequence as they are created. However, it is not always necessary for a planner to register tasks to the phases by following that sequence.

While Project KickStart allows for linear planning, it was also designed for systemic non-linear thinking – meaning that if a planner thinks of a new task while working on a different phase, it is possible to add a new task to a different phase using a drop-down. The planner can then return to the current phase. In the present study, most of the listing tasks were concisely determined and precisely associated with each phase based on the obtained information from the NRS report and the methodological approaches in the proposed ReIDMP platform framework. Figure 11.6 indicates the completed list of phases and tasks for NRC. Notice that Figure 11.6 includes an additional listing of tasks (i.e. Analysis and Assessment of Risk, Vulnerability, and Integrated Risk). This list provides predefined extension works for potential future studies to enhance the ReIDMP platform framework development and provides further analysis for the City of Norfolk.

11.2.4 Project Goals

Entering project goals is essentially the same as entering project phases. This wizard function has a first-level verification for a more profound understanding of the project phases and structuring of tasks. The milestones, goals, and targeted accomplishments of a project can be identified in this step to suggest any necessary phases or tasks that the planner has not thought of yet. As previously indicated, the City of Norfolk strives to accomplish three primary goals (see Figures 11.1–11.3). A set of strategies accompanies each goal, and then each strategy encompasses a set of actions.

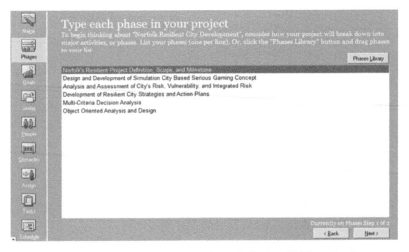

Figure 11.5 Creating NRC development phases in Project KickStart Pro 5.

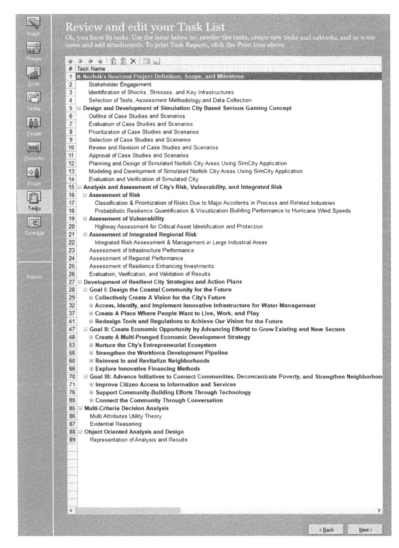

Figure 11.6 Project phases and tasks for NRC development.

However, the three primary goals of NRC are already mapped in the previous step; there are no additional phases or tasks to enter in Project KickStart Pro 5.

11.2.5 Project Obstacles

Project KickStart also offers a feature that allows a planner to identify potential risks or issues in the project planning stage. In this wizard, the planner can key in a list of obstacles that may occur during the project timeframe and then prepare the encounter measure as additional phases/tasks. The NRS report does not address this aspect of research. However, to develop the ReIDMP platform, several obstacles were assumed and added for project elaboration and execution.

11.2.6 Task Assignment

Project KickStart provides a simple and direct way of assigning tasks or responsibilities to team members. There are two ways a planner can deal with resources: (i) manually key in the resource names (e.g. team members, individuals, and organizations) to the main window or (ii) use an automated resource list wizard "People Library," to store the resource information by registering them one-by-one or importing those data from Microsoft Outlook. The distinction between these two options is that the software will save all information in its resource list if the second option is selected. Then the planner can reuse that stored information when similar resources are required for planning a new project.

The present research implemented the second option since it provides more flexibility during the planning review process and faster access in case resource revisions are necessary later in the project. Figure 11.7 illustrates the tasks and resources needed for the ReIDMP platform development. For example, since the NRS report was prepared by the City Manager's Office of Resilience, the staff members are listed as resources. The specific roles are based on verified information from the City Manager's Office of Resilience website (Office of Resilience 2022).

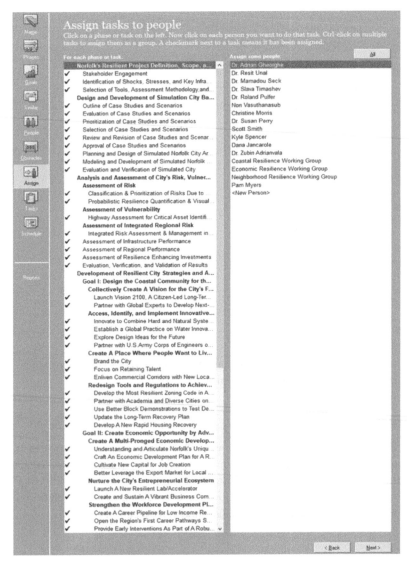

Figure 11.7 Project resources for NRC development.

Once the project task list is constructed and the project team members are identified, the planner can start assigning the tasks to each resource responsible for that task. Again, the planner must select each person, one at a time, to assign a task. If one resource (e.g. consultants) is needed for multiple tasks, the planner can choose those tasks as a group and then assign them all at once to that person. Figure 11.8 depicts the assignment of the tasks. Many of the assignments are based on the NRS report.

11.2.7 Task Management

Step six in Project KickStart is not only about reorganizing and editing the project phases and tasks, but it can also be seen as a second-level verification of phase determination and task identification. This wizard contains the features that allow the planner to (i) move up and down any task or any phase and its tasks, (ii) promote a sub-task to a task and demote a task to a sub-task, (iii) add a new task and add a new sub-task under an existing task, and (iv) delete any task and sub-task or any phase and its tasks.

During the implementation of this step, after reviewing the existing structure of project phases and tasks, minor modifications were made to avoid the potential confusion of listing tasks in the development of the "Resilient Strategies and Actions Plan." For example, three primary goals were inserted into the list as the three sub-phases, and the associated strategies of each goal were demoted under the sub-phase as the individual task. Then again, the proposed actions of each strategy were demoted under the task as the individual sub-tasks. The same correction concept was also applied to the "Analysis and Assessment of Risk of City's Risk," "Assessment of Vulnerability," and "Assessment of Integrated Regional Risk." These assessment areas were promoted from the main tasks to the sub-phases, and each domain's analysis and assessment methods were re-associated to their sub-phase as individual tasks.

Figure 11.8 Task assignment for NRC development.

11.2.8 Project Timeline

The final wizard's primary purpose is to present the project timeline visually. The software uses the Gantt Chart feature, which allows the planner to edit start/finish dates and durations, work with weekends and holidays, and adjust tasks according to resource availability. In Project KickStart, the default duration of tasks is set to one day. The planner can either key in the exact number of days or select the start/finish date fields in the calendar to indicate each task's duration.

The NRS report was released in October 2015. It was then assumed that most of the predefined actions were also ready to be implemented around that time. Hence, fall 2015 was adopted as the set-point to complement the estimation of task durations in prior or later phases. When the information from the NRS report was merged with the methodological approaches in the proposed ReIDMP platform framework, it was estimated that at least seven months would be required in advance to prepare and develop strategies and actions. Figure 11.9 depicts the overall project timeline and task durations. Project KickStart set the motion for the research articulated in Chapters 6, 7, 8, 9, and 10.

11.3 Overview of the Research

In the view of the "100 Resilient Cities" project, "resilience" is the ability of a system, entity, community, or person to absorb and withstand any shock or stress while maintaining its essential functions, structures, and identity, and to recover quickly and effectively (ARUP 2012; Rockefeller Foundation 2014, 2015). Therefore, building a city's resilience is about making people, communities, and systems better prepared to survive, adapt, and thrive through catastrophic events. In this context, resilience means more than coping with possible contingency or short-term survival. This notion aims to sustain and enhance adaptability to face and resist uncertainties or shocks. Ultimately, resilience is an attribute that can be learned and a skill that must be gained through experience (Rockefeller Foundation 2014).

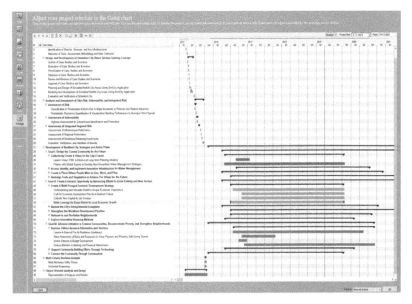

Figure 11.9 Project timeline and task durations for NRC development.

Resilience thinking is a paradigm that implicitly challenges the idealistic principle of stability and resistance to change in sustainable development. However, when it comes to improving city resilience, the city must be perceived as a mega-scale system with multidimensional complexity and embedded critical systems. In other words, the city resilience-building process is challenging and requires a holistic approach (Collier et al. 2013; Gheorghe and Katina 2014; Hernantes et al. 2019; Jabareen 2013; Katina and Gheorghe 2023). There is a pressing need for new tools or examples of the practical sequential steps that any city could adopt as effective guidance for developing city resilience (Hernantes et al. 2019; Jabareen 2013; Weichselgartner and Kelman 2015). Most frameworks in the scholarly literature still do not focus on providing a systemic roadmap with a detailed sequence that can be implemented to advance the resilience-building process (Cavallo and Ireland 2014; Collier et al. 2013; Hernantes et al. 2019). The challenge was to develop a *resilience quantification platform-based informed decision-making process* resulting in better understanding and guidance on sustainable and resilient development of critical infrastructure (CI) systems – *et hoc fecimus*. We now list implications, limitations, and directions.

11.3.1 ReIDMP Implications

A targeted objective of this was the development of a generic platform, ReIDMP, that supports the planning and management process for the resilient city project. The development intends to propose a practical approach to building or enhancing the capacity of resilience for the city systematically and reliably. The platform is grounded in several concepts and techniques adopted from academic disciplines and industrial practices, including project management, serious gaming, risk analysis, vulnerability assessment, multiple-criteria decision analysis (MCDA), and object-oriented programming (OOP). The ReIDMP consists of four primary phases:

- *Phase I – project planning and management.* The first step of resilient city transformation – definition, scope, and tasks – is indispensable. To reach significant milestones and achieve resilience, a definition must be clearly articulated, the scope must be explicitly established, and the tasks must be comprehensively designated. Overall, the example of a resilient city project plan outlined in Project KickStart software allows the planners, stakeholders, and decision-makers to capture the procedural step of project execution in sequential order, track the progress of tasks, and control the ongoing development process.

- *Phase II – development of a simulation city and management of risk and vulnerability.* This phase is divided into two parts. First is the utilization of a commercial computer simulation game under serious gaming. Second is the application of risks and vulnerability management. SimCity 2013® was selected and employed to support the process of modeling cities. Then, the simulated outputs are incorporated with a set of assumed scenarios to conduct the analysis and assessment under the selected technical manuals of risk, vulnerability, and integrated regional risk (International Atomic Energy Agency 1996, 1998; Science Applications International Corporation 2002). Indeed, serious gaming methodology experimentations can successfully be adapted to the classroom environment and have delivered learning experiences to students at different educational levels. In this research, most students grasped using SimCity 2013® for non-entertainment purposes and manipulating the simulation city-building mechanisms.

- *Phase III – evaluation of alternatives using MCDA.* This phase demonstrates how to transform the identified alternatives into decision problems and how those decision components can be analyzed. In this regard, a specific part of the information in the NRS report (Resilient Strategies and Actions) was used as input data in this research. Later, the decision models were implemented using two distinct techniques in MCDA framework through two decision-support system tools: Logical

Decisions® for Windows via Multi Attribute Utility Theory LDW (MAUT) and Intelligent Decision System via Evidential Reasoning. All in all, these two MCDA techniques can handle the decision problems involving a large group of stakeholders. The examples of results obtained from both software reveal that they can be applied in parallel to compare the difference in alternative prioritization.

- *Phase IV – representation of project complexity.* Due to city resilience's complexity and dynamic nature, a tool that can provide a holistic view at the time of planning and execution is required. The final phase of the ReIDMP framework relates to implementing and presenting management complexity for the resilient city transformation processes. The software, TopEase®, grounded in an OOP paradigm, was adopted to handle large-scale data structures and model the resilient city's different objects.

The approach presented in this research contributes to the current body of knowledge by proposing four frameworks that support the practical development of resilient cities. In addition to the intended functions of assisting the planning process and execution management for building a resilient city, this ReIDMP platform can also be used as a decision analysis toolkit. The platform enables the decision-makers and stakeholders to assess the current problem, identify the solutions and strategies, and evaluate the alternatives. It also enables the capturing of interrelationships, interconnection, and interdependencies between city entities as a whole system.

11.3.2 ReIDMP Limitations

The use of serious gaming in commercial and industrial sectors is widely accepted to be a promising strategy for training employees and promoting customer experiences and satisfaction. Even though this technique has proven to provide considerable success in marketing practices and business management, adopting this technique in the academic field, notably higher education, to teach specific knowledge or to encourage learning experiences poses challenges. For example, choosing a game that can benefit learning experiences and measuring the outcomes can be a challenge. Moreover, the first part of Phase II was introduced with the application of SimCity 2013®. Various versions of this simulation city-building game have proven valuable within the formal classroom setting at both school and university levels, yet they are limited in pedagogical contents and features.

In the development of the ReIDMP platform framework, the first part of Phase II was introduced with the application of SimCity 2013®. Various versions of this simulation city-building game have proven valuable within the formal classroom setting at both school and university levels, yet they are limited in pedagogical contents and features. Bereitschaft (2016) and Gaber (2007) assert that when using SimCity® for an educational purpose, particularly at the university level, the limitations and inaccuracies of the game limit its utility for understanding the complexity of urban planning processes. While professional urban planners and theorists familiar with the required knowledge or experiences could understand the underlying principle by themselves, most players without the proper training will be influenced by contextualized biases woven by the game mechanism. This criticism is valid in the present research. For example, during the experimentation periods, students involved in this research would start the modeling process without laying out the road pattern or conditioning the zones even though the completed basic instructions were presented in a classroom setting. Therefore, to optimize the percentage of success in SimCity 2013® under serious gaming, it is necessary to provide clear instructions with comprehensive demonstrations.

Besides the limitation of the pedagogical tool embedded in the game itself, participants' mindset could also be a concern. Frequently, when serious gaming is included in the coursework as a learning tool, gamers (students) will try to master the game context and mechanism for experiencing the learning contents. However, non-gamers with less or no digital gaming experience will spend more time and effort figuring out how to play the game than trying to understand the intended learning material. Situations such as these make it harder for the participant to benefit from serious gaming (Heeter et al. 2011; Vasuthanasub 2019). Feeling lost or incompetent while attempting to play the game could cause negative impacts that create performance deficiencies, resulting in negative consequences on learning.

Another limitation of this research is using data and information from the NRS report as input in Phase III. The purpose of adopting the NRC project as a case study is to provide an example of how the decision analysis in Phase III of the ReIDMP could be functional and helpful in real situations. However, the current case application does not involve subject matter experts. The involvement of subject matter experts could potentially have yielded a more comprehensive platform framework. Unquestionably, validating this kind of research study requires great effort from stakeholders, decision-makers, and the people involved in the actual project implementation.

11.3.3 ReIDMP Future Direction

Management of risk and vulnerability is fundamental to building a resilient city. The ReIDMP platform covers this underlying implication by including those activities in the second part of Phase II. In this development, three analysis and assessment methods are performed and provided as examples to delineate some specific aspects of risk and vulnerability, including: (i) prioritization of risks due to the major accidents-related industries, (ii) integrated risk management in large industrial areas, and (iii) highway vulnerability for critical asset protection. Moreover, a few selected methods are used in the analysis and assessment of different risk areas, and vulnerability can be incorporated. There remains room for additional analysis methods and tools that extend the platform. Such a study will render extra advantages in analyzing the entire community's resilience and identifying strategies and actions to cope with risk and hazards.

11.4 Concluding Remarks

The emergence of city resilience is a relatively new domain of research. It became prominent following the "100 Resilient Cities" project initiated by the Rockefeller Foundation (2013). Under this circumstance, building a resilient city might mean making the concept of resilience more meaningful beyond its theoretical context. Nonetheless, making this attribute tangible and practical is still not only complicated but also challenging.

The background information provides ample detail for those interested in furthering the present research, especially in the case of applications that lead to the refinement of the proposed framework. Moreover, in actual circumstances, a comprehensive study of the city's problems and the identification of possible alternatives is necessary. This research is essential as it directly influences the city's resilience through implementation – *the city is only as resilient as the methods used to develop its resiliency.*

11.5 Exercises

1 Discuss the need that the ReIDMP platform is emerging to address.
2 Discuss the nature of goals that must be developed for the ReIDMP platform.
3 Implement Sections 11.2.1–11.2.8 for your selected city.
4 Explain the ReIDMP implications and limitations.
5 Discuss another possible area of research that can improve the ReIDMP platform.

References

Ahlvin, K. (2008, September 28). *Project Kickstart Pro 4 Launches with Professional Gantt Chart Dependencies Feature*. PR-USA.Net. https://web.archive.org/web/20080928092138/http://www.pr-usa.net/index.php?option=com_content&task=view&id=104001&Itemid=34.

ARUP. (2012). *Visions of a Resilient City*. Engineers Without Borders-UK. https://www.arup.com/en/perspectives/publications/research/section/visions-of-a-resilient-city.

Bereitschaft, B. (2016). Gods of the city? Reflecting on city building games as an early introduction to urban systems. *Journal of Geography* 115(2): 51–60. https://doi.org/10.1080/00221341.2015.1070366.

Cavallo, A. and Ireland, V. (2014). Preparing for complex interdependent risks: A System of Systems approach to building disaster resilience. *International Journal of Disaster Risk Reduction* 9: 181–193. https://doi.org/10.1016/j.ijdrr.2014.05.001.

City of Norfolk. (2015). *Norfolk Resilience Strategy*. The Norfolk City manager's office of resilience. https://www.norfolk.gov/3612/Office-of-Resilience.

Collier, M.J., Nedović-Budić, Z., Aerts, J. et al. (2013). Transitioning to resilience and sustainability in urban communities. *Cities* 32: S21–S28. https://doi.org/10.1016/j.cities.2013.03.010.

Gaber, J. (2007). Simulating planning: SimCity as a pedagogical tool. *Journal of Planning Education and Research* 27(2): 113–121. https://journals.sagepub.com/doi/10.1177/0739456X07305791.

Gheorghe, A.V. and Katina, P.F. (2014). Editorial: Resiliency and engineering systems – Research trends and challenges. *International Journal of Critical Infrastructures* 10(3/4): 193–199.

Heeter, C., Lee, Y.-H., Magerko, B. et al. (2011). Impacts of forced serious game play on vulnerable subgroups. *International Journal of Gaming and Computer-Mediated Simulations* 3(3): 34–53. https://doi.org/10.4018/jgcms.2011070103.

Hernantes, J., Maraña, P., Gimenez, R. et al. (2019). Towards resilient cities: A maturity model for operationalizing resilience. *Cities* 84: 96–103. https://doi.org/10.1016/j.cities.2018.07.010.

Jabareen, Y. (2013). Planning the resilient city: Concepts and strategies for coping with climate change and environmental risk. *Cities* 31: 220–229. https://doi.org/10.1016/j.cities.2012.05.004.

Katina, P.F. and Gheorghe, A.V. (2023). *Blockchain-Enabled Resilience: An Integrated Approach for Disaster Supply Chain and Logistics Management* (1st ed.). CRC Press.

Office of Resilience. (2022). *Norfolk Resilient City*. Office of Resilience. https://www.norfolk.gov/3612/Office-of-Resilience.

Rockefeller Foundation. (2013). *100 Resilient Cities*. Rockefeller Foundation. https://www.rockefellerfoundation.org/100-resilient-cities.

Rockefeller Foundation. (2014). *City Resilience Framework*. Rockefeller Foundation/ARUP. https://www.rockefellerfoundation.org/wp-content/uploads/City-Resilience-Framework-2015.pdf.

Rockefeller Foundation. (2015). *City Resilience and the City Resilience Framework*. Rockefeller Foundation/ARUP. https://www.rockefellerfoundation.org/report/city-resilience-framework.

Vasuthanasub, J. (2019). *The Resilient City: A Platform for Informed Decision-making Process*. Dissertation, Old Dominion University. https://digitalcommons.odu.edu/emse_etds/151.

Weichselgartner, J. and Kelman, I. (2015). Geographies of resilience: Challenges and opportunities of a descriptive concept. *Progress in Human Geography* 39(3): 249–267. https://doi.org/10.1177/0309132513518834.

12

Portland

Risk and Vulnerability Assessment

12.1 Introduction

Risks and vulnerabilities exist throughout every city. These risks and vulnerabilities have to be prioritized based on their consequence and frequency to decide best how to decrease the effects on the city. Critical assets throughout the city must also be identified and prioritized so that concerns for attacks on those assets can be managed. Risks in cities can also relate to emissions released by certain activities across the city. Most risks in a city can be controlled or brought down to a more tolerable effect. Several assessments can be performed, including rapid risk assessment (RRA), vulnerability assessment (VA), and integrated regional risk assessment (IRRA) to determine the most critical risks to a city. When developing a comprehensive implementation plan to solve a problem, it is essential to account for resiliency. This will allow for a developed system, or solution, capable of preventing and mitigating risks and recovering from failures. In these a ReIDMP can be helpful. This chapter aims to illustrate how the ReIDMP can be combined with readily available manuals, guidelines, assessments, and tools to better understand a city in terms of risks and vulnerabilities to mitigate their effects in a realistic case. To achieve this aim, this chapter is organized as follows: First, it articulates ten different risks in the selected city, Portland, Oregon (USA), using the RRA methodologies from *Manual for the Classification of Prioritization of Risks Due to Major Accidents in Process and Related Industries* (International Atomic Energy Agency 1996). Vulnerability of certain critical assets along transportation routes is then conducted using the VA methodologies from *Guide to Highway Vulnerability Assessment for Critical Asset Identification and Protection* (Science Applications International Corporation 2002). Air, water, and soil emissions analyses are then conducted throughout the city, and the effects on citizens in the area are addressed using the IRRA methodologies from *Guidelines for Integrated Risk Assessment and Management in Large Industrial Areas* (International Atomic Energy Agency 1998). The effects of electromagnetic pulse (EMP) blasts at varying heights above a city are suggested. Finally, a ReIDMP for Portland is then provided to indicate the transportability of the model. Unless otherwise noted, Google Earth Pro v.7.3.4. (https://earth.google.com) is used to visualize the city.

In this realistic case, the actual City of Portland, is impacted by fixed risks and the transportation of hazardous goods. In addition, many of the city's critical assets are susceptible to attacks, and the city houses many sources of continuous emissions. All these aspects increase risks throughout the city and endanger the health and safety of those living in and visiting the city. City officials would

Gamification for Resilience: Resilient Informed Decision-Making, First Edition.
Adrian V. Gheorghe and Polinpapilinho F. Katina.
© 2023 John Wiley & Sons, Inc. Published 2023 by John Wiley & Sons, Inc.

like various assessments to be completed to identify risks and vulnerabilities throughout the city to make the city safer for those in and around the city. Due to budgets, city officials are looking for prioritized lists of risks and vulnerabilities. Multiple assessments, including the RRA, VA, IRRA, and EMP, will be completed to assist with the requests of the city officials. In addition, the city officials request a ReIDMP model to assist with developing resilient systems. After completing these assessments, city officials hope to make Portland a safe place for its citizens and visitors. A short, concise problem statement for this issue can be written as follows:

> *The city of Portland, OR is experiencing high levels of risk and vulnerability throughout the city. This issue is affecting the safety and health of hundreds-of-thousands citizens and visitors in and around the city as evidenced by observations, studies, and assessments.*

12.2 Rapid Risk Assessment

RRA aims to identify possible risks throughout a specified area, determine the consequence and frequency of each risk, and prioritize each risk. The *Manual for the Classification of Prioritization of Risks Due to Major Accidents in Process and Related Industries* (International Atomic Energy Agency 1996) is used to perform the RRA for the chosen area of Portland. This manual includes detailed instructions for each step, which are discussed and summarized throughout this section. Figure 12.1 depicts the selected analysis area in Google Earth Pro v.7.3.4.

RRA consists of five main steps: (i) classification of type of activities and inventories, (ii) estimation of consequences, (iii) estimation of probabilities, (iv) estimation of social risks, and (v) prioritization of risks. The risks evaluated in this assessment include both fixed installations and the transportation of hazardous goods.

12.2.1 Classification of Types of Activities and Inventories

A total of ten risks are assessed. Each risk, the type of risk, and its associated substances causing risk are listed in Table 12.1. Figure 12.2 depicts the location of risks throughout the city.

Figure 12.1 The selected analysis area of Portland.

Table 12.1 Risks in Portland and the associated substances.

Risk	Associated substance	Type
Ice rink	Ammonia	Fixed
Bus garage	Petrol	Fixed
Competition pool	Chlorine	Fixed
Forge	Carbon monoxide	Fixed
Pest control service	Phosgene	Fixed
Sugar refinery	Sulfur dioxide	Fixed
Composite wood manufacturer	Formaldehyde	Fixed
Gas distribution center	Petrol	Fixed
Gas transportation	Petrol	Transportation
Chlorine transportation	Chlorine	Transportation

Figure 12.2 The location of risks.

12.2.2 Estimation of Consequences

Step 2 involves estimating the consequence of each risk event. Equation (12.1) is used to assess consequences.

$$C_{a,s} = A * \delta * f_A * f_d * f_m \tag{12.1}$$

where:

A = affected area (ha)

δ = population density in a defined populated area (persons/ha)

f_A = correction factor for the populated area (part of circle)

f_d = correction factor for the populated area (distances)

f_m = correction factor for mitigation effects

Using this equation allows you to solve for $C_{a,s}$, which is the number of consequences (number of fatalities/accident) of an accident caused by the substance (subscript s) for each identified activity (subscript a). The consequence for each risk will be detailed in Sections 12.2.3–12.2.6.

12.2.3 Estimation of Probabilities

Step 3 is the estimation of the probability, or frequency, of each risk for both fixed installations and transportation risks. To calculate the frequency ($P_{i,s}$, number of accidents per year) of accidents involving a hazardous substance (subscript s) for each hazardous *fixed installation* (subscript i), it is necessary to calculate the related probability number, $N_{i,s}$. $N_{i,s}$ can be calculated using Equation (12.2).

$$N_{i,s} = N_{i,s}^* + n_l + n_f + n_o + n_p \tag{12.2}$$

where:

$N_{i,s}^*$ = average probability number for the installation and substance

n_l = probability number correction parameter for the frequency of loading/unloading operations

n_f = probability number correction parameter for the safety systems associated with flammable substances

n_o = probability number correction parameter for the organizational and management safety

n_p = probability number correction parameter for the wind direction toward the populated area

The relationship between $N_{i,s}$ and $P_{i,s}$ can be represented by Equation (12.3).

$$N = \left| \log_{10} P \right| \tag{12.3}$$

Therefore, once N is known, it is possible to solve for P, the frequency. International Atomic Energy Agency (1996) also includes a lookup table for common values of N, which gives us the corresponding P value.

Similarly, to calculate the frequency ($P_{t,s}$, number of accidents per year) of accidents during the *transportation* (subscript t) of a hazardous substance (subscript s), it is also necessary to calculate the related probability number, $N_{t,s}$, which can be calculated using Equation (12.4).

$$N_{t,s} = N_{t,s}^* + n_c + n_{t\delta} + n_p \tag{12.4}$$

where:

$N_{t,s}^*$ = average probability number for transportation of the substance

n_c = probability number correction parameter for the safety conditions of the transport system

$n_{t\delta}$ = probability number correction parameter for the traffic density

n_p = probability number correction parameter for wind direction toward the populated area

Again, the relationship between $N_{t,s}$ and $P_{t,s}$ can be represented by Equation (12.3), and the same table in International Atomic Energy Agency (1996) can be used to look up P values for common values of N. The frequency of each risk will be detailed in Sections 12.2.4–12.2.6.

Finally, once the estimated consequence and frequency are determined for each risk, those values can be used to determine the societal risk of each incident, and from there, the risk incidents can be prioritized. To address societal risk and prioritization of all dangers, a case application is necessary – this is addressed in Section 12.2.4, along with recommendations.

12.2.4 Illustrated Example: Classification of Types of Activities and Inventories

12.2.4.1 Risk Scenario #1: Ice Rink

The ice rink is selected since it serves as storage for ammonia. Ammonia is needed because it is used in the mechanical refrigeration system in ice rinks (US Environmental Protection Agency 2018). A Montreal ice rink claims they could bring their ammonia charge down to 175 lbs (O'Shea 2021). Ice rinks must report annual chemical inventory to the state if they have more than 500 pounds of ammonia. Ice rinks with more than 10,000 pounds of ammonia must prepare a risk management plan (US Environmental Protection Agency 2018). In this case, we assume the charge of 175 lbs is per month. Therefore, since 1 ton is equal to 2,000 lbs, the rink uses 1.05 tons of ammonia per year. The conversion for this weight is 175 lbs per month * 12 months per 1 year * 1ton per 2,000 lbs = 1.05 tons per year. Figure 12.3 depicts the location of the ice rink in Portland.

Before solving for the consequence, numerical values for the variables in Equation (12.1) must be solved first. Various tables from International Atomic Energy Agency (1996) are used to find these values. To begin, Table II is used to find the reference number for the substance of interest in relation to the fixed installation. From the table, the reference number for ammonia in relation to an ice rink is 31. The next step is to find the effect category for the risk. By knowing the weight in tons, and the reference number, Table IV could be used to find the effect category, which in this case is CII. With the effect category, Table V can be used to find the maximum effect distance and effect area, which in this case is 100 m and 1.5 ha (A), respectively. From there, table VI can be used to estimate the population density in the area of interest. In this situation, it is estimated that the populated density, δ, is 80 ha since the ice rink is in a busy residential area and an ice rink is a busy place with a lot of people entering and exiting daily.

Once the effect category and maximum effect distance are known, an fA & fd Diagram can be created to solve for those two values and fm. In the diagram, it is best to draw your area of interest, which has a radius of the maximum effect distance, found in Table V. Then, draw the affected area. For an effect category of CII, the affected area is a circle with a diameter of approximately the maximum effect distance. RRA focuses on the worst-case scenario of all situations. Therefore, in this diagram, the wind blows the affected area toward the highest population. fA is determined by

Figure 12.3 Ice rink location.

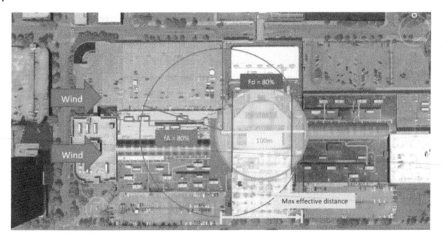

Figure 12.4 Ice rink indicating wind, fA, fd and effective distance.

estimating the average angle of the populated area within the circular area of interest, then by taking that estimated angle and the effect category to find the value of fA using table VII. In this case, fA is estimated to be about 80% of the area of interest, and for an effect category of CII, table VII shows that the value for fA is 1.0. fd is an estimation of the fraction of the "length or depth" of the populated density compared with the radius of the area of interest. In this case, it is estimated that the length of the population covered approximately 80% of the length of the radius. Therefore, fd is 0.8. As for fm, proposed values for fm can be found in table VIII. For this case, fm is estimated to be 0.1. Figure 12.4 depicts the fA & fd diagram of the ice rink. By using the abovementioned values, the consequence can be calculated by using Equation (12.1). Solving this equation gives you a value of 9.6 fatalities or accidents.

The next step is to solve for the values needed to find the frequency. Again, various tables from International Atomic Energy Agency (1996) are used to see these values. Since the reference number is already known, Table IX could be used to find the average probability number for fixed installations, $N^*_{i,s}$. For the ice rink, this value is 6. The ammonia is assumed to be loaded/unloaded one to two times per month. With that information, it is estimated that ten to fifty loadings/unloadings per year are done, so by using Table X, n_l is estimated to be 0. To solve for n_f, Table XI is used. After looking at this table, it is determined this value is not applicable since the substance of focus is not a flammable gas. Therefore, a value of 0 is used for nf in Equation (12.2) when solving for frequency. It is assumed that the ice rink has an average industry practice relating to safety, so n_o is 0 according to Table XII. Finally, n_p is estimated to be 0.5, using Table XIII, since this risk has an effect area category of CII and less than 100% of the area in the effect area is where people live. By substituting these values into Equation (12.2), $N_{i,s}$ is found to be 6.5. By using Table XIV, $P_{i,s}$ is found to be $3*10^{-7}$ events per year. Table 12.2 is a summary of constants and values for the ice rink scenario. Due to the limited space allocated to this research, the rest of the risk scenarios are summarized.

12.2.4.2 Risk Scenario #2: Bus Garage
The bus garage is chosen because of its petrol storage. Petrol is needed to fuel the buses stationed there after they get back from a route or before leaving for another. Table 12.3 summarizes the constants and values for the bus garage scenario.

Table 12.2 A summary of constants and values for the ice rink scenario.

Description	Ice rink	Location	1
Reference number (Table II)	31	Average probability number, N^*i,s (Table IX)	6
Weight (tons)	1.05	Correction parameter for frequency of load/unload, n (Table X)	0
Effect category (Table IV)	CII	Correction parameter for safety systems of flammable substances, n (Table XI)	0
Effective max distance (m) (Table V)	100	Correction parameter for the organizational and management safety, n_o (Table XII)	0
Effective area, A (ha) (Table V)	1.5	Correction parameter for wind direction in area, n_p (Table XIII)	0.5
Population density, δ (persons/ha) (Table VI)	80	Probability number, $N_{i,s}$ $N_{i,s}$ $= N^*_{i,s} + n_1 + n_f + n_o + n_p$	6.5
Correction factor for distribution of main populated area(s), f_A (Table VII)	1	Frequency, $P_{i,s}$ (accidents/year) (Table XIV)	3.0E−07
Correction factor for mitigation, f_m (Table VIII)	0.1		
Area correction factor, $1/8$	0.8		
Consequence, $C_{a,s}$ (fatalities/accident) $C_{a,s} = A * \delta * f_A * f_d * f_m$	9.6		

12.2.4.3 Risk Scenario #3: Competition Pool

The competition pool is chosen because of its storage and usage of chlorine. Chlorine is needed to keep the pool water clean and healthy. Table 12.4 summarizes the constants and values for the competition pool scenario.

12.2.4.4 Risk Scenario #4: Forge

The forge is chosen because of its production of carbon monoxide. A blast furnace can be found in forge. A blast furnace is used to extract iron from iron ore and converts raw iron from the furnace into other kinds of steel. Table 12.5 summarizes the constants and values for the forge scenario.

12.2.4.5 Risk Scenario #5: Pest Control Service

The pest control service center is selected because it uses and stores phosgene. Phosgene is one of the main ingredients used to produce pesticides. Table 12.6 summarizes the constants and values for the pest control service scenario.

12.2.4.6 Risk Scenario #6: Sugar Refinery

Sugar refinery is selected because it uses and stores sulfur dioxide. Sulfur dioxide is used as a decolorizer in sugar. It is used to minimize color in food processing and fruit and vegetable storage. Table 12.7 summarizes the constants and values for the sugar refinery scenario.

Table 12.3 A summary of constants and values for the bus garage scenario.

Description	Bus garage	Location	2
Reference number (Table II)	6	Average probability number, N^*i,s (Table IX)	7
Weight (tons)	350	Correction parameter for frequency of load/unload, n_I (Table X)	0.5
Effect category (Table IV)	DII	Correction parameter for safety systems of flammable substances, n_f (Table XI)	0
Effective max distance (m) (Table V)	200	Correction parameter for the organizational and management safety, n_o (Table XII)	0
Effective area, A (ha) (Table V)	6	Correction parameter for wind direction in area, n_p (Table XIII)	0.5
Population density, δ (persons/ha) (Table VI)	20	Probability number, $N_{i,s}$ $N_{i,s} = N^*_{i,s} + n_1 + n_f + n_o + n_p$	8
Correction factor for distribution of main populated area(s), f_A (Table VII)	0.6	Frequency, $P_{i,s}$ (accidents/year) (Table XIV)	1E–08
Correction factor mitigation, f_m (Table VIII)	1		
Area correction factor, f_d	0.5		
Consequence, $C_{a,s}$ (fatalities/accident) $C_{a,s} = A*\delta*f_A*f_d*f_m$	36		

Table 12.4 A summary of constants and values for the competition pool scenario.

Description	Competition pool	Location	3
Reference Number (Table II)	32	Average probability Number, $N^*_{i,s}$ (Table IX)	6
Weight (tons)	0.147	Correction Parameter for Frequency of Load/Unload, n_I (Table X)	0.5
Effect Category (Table IV)	CII	Correction Parameter for Safety Systems of Flammable Substances, n_f (Table XI)	0
Effective Max Distance (m) (Table V)	100	Correction parameter for the Organization and management safety, n_o (Table XII)	0
Effective Area, A (Ha) (Table V)	1.5	Correction parameter for Wind Direction in Area, n_p (Table XIII)	0.5
Population Density, δ (persons/Ha) (Table VI)	40	Probability Number, $N_{i,s}$ $N_{i,s} = N^*_{i,s} + n_1 + n_f + n_o + n_p$	7
Correction Factor for Distribution of Main populated Area(s), f_A (Table VII)	1	Frequency, $P_{i,s}$ (accidents/year) (Table XIV)	1.00E – 07
Correction Factor for Mitigation, f_m (Table VIII)	0.1		

Table 12.4 (Continued)

Description	Competition pool	Location	3
Area Correction Factor, f_d	0.9		
Consequence, $C_{a,s}$ (fatalities/accident) $C_{a,s} = A * \delta * f_A * f_d * f_m$	5.4		

Table 12.5 A summary of constants and values for the forge scenario.

Description	Forge	Location	4
Reference number (Table II)	31	Average probability number, $N^*_{i,s}$, (Table IX)	6
Weight (tons)	168437.5	Correction parameter for frequency of load/unload, n_I (Table X)	0.5
Effect category (Table IV)	**HIII**	Correction parameter for safety systems of flammable substances, n_l (Table XI)	0
Effective max distance (m) (Table V)	10000	Correction parameter for the organizational and Management safety, n_0 (Table XII)	0
Effective area, A (ha) (Table V)	1000	Correction parameter for wind direction in area, n_p (Table XIII)	0
Population density, δ (persons/ha) (Table VI)	80	Probability number, $N_{i,s}$, $N_{i,s} = N^*_{i,s} + n_I + n_f + n_0 + n_p$	6.5
Correction factor for distribution of main populated area(s), f_A (Table VII)	1	Frequency, $P_{i,s}$ (accidents/year) (Table XIV)	3.00E−07
Correction factor for mitigation, f_m (table VIII)	0.1		
Area connection factor, f_d	1		
Consequence, $C_{a,s}$ (fatalities/accident) $C_{a,s} = A * \delta * f_A * f_d * f_m$	8000		

Table 12.6 A summary of constants and values for the pest control service scenario.

Description	Pest control service	Location	5
Reference number (Table II)	33	Average probability number, $N^*_{i,s}$ (Table IX)	6
Weight (tons)	4.16	Correction parameter for frequency of load/unload, n_I (Table X)	0.5
Effect category (Table IV)	EIII	Correction parameter for safety systems of flammable substances, n_f (Table XI)	0
Effective max distance (m) (Table V)	500	Correction parameter for the organizational and management safety, n_0 (Table XII)	0

(Continued)

Table 12.6 (Continued)

Description	Pest control service	Location	5
Effective area, A (ha) (Table V)	8	Correction parameter for wind direction in area, n_p (Table XIII)	0
Population density, δ (persons/ha) (Table VI)	40	Probability number, $N_{i,s}$ $N_{i,s} = N^*_{i,s} + n_I + n_f + n_o + n_p$	6.5
Correction factor for distribution of main populated area(s), f_A (Table VII)	1	Frequency, $P_{i,s}$ (accidents/year) (Table XIV)	0.0000003
Correction factor for mitigation, f_m (Table VIII)	0.1		
Area correction factor, f_d	0.9		
Consequence, $C_{a,s}$ (fatalities/accident) $C_{a,s} = A * \delta * f_A * f_d * f_m$	28.8		

12.2.4.7 Risk Scenario #7: Composite Wood Manufacturer

The composite wood manufacturer is selected because it uses and stores formaldehyde. Formaldehyde is a colorless, flammable, strong-smelling chemical that is used in resins (i.e. glues) used in the manufacture of composite wood products (i.e. hardwood plywood, particleboard, and medium-density fiberboard). Table 12.8 summarizes the constants and values for the composite wood manufacturer scenario.

Table 12.7 A summary of constants and values for the sugar refinery scenario.

Description	Sugar refinery	Location	6
Reference number (Table II)	31	Average probability number, $N^*_{i,s}$ (Table IX)	6
Weight (tons)	21	Correction parameter for frequency of load/unload, n_I (Table x)	0.5
Effect category (Table IV)	DIII	Correction parameter for safety systems of flammable substances, n_f (Table XI)	0
Effective max distance (m) (Table V)	200	Correction parameter for the organizational and management safety, n_o (Table XII)	0
Effective area, A (ha) (Table V)	1	Correction parameter for wind direction in area, n_p (Table XIII)	0.5
Population density, δ (persons/ha) (Table VI)	40	Probability number, $N_{i,s}$ $N_{i,s} = N^*_{i,s} + n_I + n_f + n_o + n_p$	7
Correction factor for distribution of main populated area(s), f_A (Table VII)	1	Frequency, $P_{i,s}$ (accidents/year) (Table XIV)	1.00E–07
Correction factor for mitigation, f_m (Table VIII)	0.1		

Table 12.7 (Continued)

Description	Sugar refinery	Location		6
Area correction factor, f_d	0.6			
Consequence, $C_{a,s}$ (fatalities/accident) $C_{a,s} = A * \delta * f_A * f_d * f_m$	2.4			

Table 12.8 A summary of constants and values for the composite wood manufacturer scenario.

Description	Composite wood manufacturer	Location	7
Reference number (Table II)	32	Average probability number, $N^*_{i,s}$, (Table IX)	6
Weight (tons)	0.7	Correction parameter for frequency of load/unload, n_l (Table X)	0
Effect category (Table IV)	CII	Correction parameter for safety systems of flammable substances, n_f (Table XI)	0
Effective max distance (m) (Table V)	100	Correction parameter for the organizational and management safety, n_o (Table XII)	0
Effective area, A (ha) (Table V)	1.5	Correction parameter for wind direction in area, n_p (Table XIII)	0.5
Population density, δ (person/ha) (Table VI)	40	Probability number, $N_{i,s}$ $N_{i,s} = N^*_{i,s} + n_l + n_f + n_o + n_p$	6.5
Correction factor for distribution of main populated area(s), f_A (Table VII)	1	Frequency, $P_{i,s}$, (accidents/year) (Table XIV)	3.00E–07
Correction factor for mitigation, f_m (Table VIII)	0.1		
Area correction factor, F_d	0.5		
Consequence, $C_{a,s}$ (fatalities/accident) $C_{a,s} = A * \delta * f_A * f_d * f_m$	3		

12.2.4.8 Risk Scenario #8: Gas Distribution Center

The gas distribution center is selected because it uses and stores petrol. Petrol must be held at a distribution center to then distribute to gas stations throughout the city. Table 12.9 summarizes the constants and values for the gas distribution center scenario.

12.2.4.9 Risk Scenario #9: Gas Transportation

Gas transportation is selected because of the risk involved with carrying large amounts of petrol in one vehicle. In this gas transportation route, petrol is transported from the gas distribution center to local gas stations throughout this city. One centrally located gas station is chosen for this assessment, as suggested in Figure 12.5. The red path shows the path from the distribution center to the gas station and the yellow section shows the most populated 1 km area along the path, which will be the area of focus. The most populated and busy intersection is selected within that yellow section to continue the assessment. Table 12.10 summarizes the constants and values for the transportation scenario.

Table 12.9 A summary of constants and values for the gas distribution center scenario.

Description	Gas distribution center	Location	8
Reference number (Table II)	6	Average probability number, $N^*_{i,s}$ (Table IX)	7
Weight (tons)	4871	Correction parameter for frequency of load/unload, n_l (Table X)	0
Effect category (Table IV)	EII	Correction parameter for safety systems of flammable substances, n_f (Table XI)	0
Effective max distance (m) (Table V)	500	Correction parameter for the organizational and management safety, n_o (Table XII)	0
Effective area, A (ha) (Table V)	40	Correction parameter for wind direction in area, n_p (Table XIII)	00.5
Population density, δ (persons/ha) (Table VI)	40	Probability number, $N_{i,s}$ $N_{i,s} = N^*_{i,s} + n_l + n_f + n_o + n_p$	70.5
Correction factor for distribution of main populated Area(s), f_A (Table VII)	1	Frequency, $P_{i,s}$ (accidents/year) (Table XIV)	3E–08
Correction factor for mitigation, f_m (Table VIII)	1		
Area correction factor, F_d	1		
Consequence, $C_{a,s}$ (fatalities/accident) $C_{a,s} = A^* \delta^* f_A {}^* f_d {}^* f_m$	1600		

Figure 12.5 The gas transportation route.

Table 12.10 A summary of constants and values for the gas transportation scenario.

Description	Gas Transportation	Location	N/A
Reference Number (Table II)	6	Average Probability Number, $N^*_{t,s}$ (Table XV)	8.5
Weight (tons)	32	International Transport code (Table XVI)	Combination first digit 3 and a digit 3
Effect Category (Table IV)	BII	Correction Parameter for Safety Conditions, n_c (Table XVII)	0
Effective Max Distance (m) (Table V)	50	Correction Parameter for Traffic Density, $n_{t\delta}$ (Table XVIII)	−3
Effective Area, A(Ha) (Table V)	0.4	Correction parameter for Wind Direction, n_p (Table XIX)	0
Population Density, δ (persons/Ha) (TableVI)	80	Probability Number, $N_{t,s}$ $N_{t,s} = N^*_{t,s} + n_c + n_{t\delta} + n_p$	5.5
Correction Factor for Distribution of Main Populated Area(s), f_A (Table VII)	1	Frequency, $P_{t,s}$ (accidents/ year) (Table XX)	3.00E−06
Correction Factor for Mitigation, f_m (Table VIII)	1		
Area Correction Factor, f_d	1		
Consequence, $C_{a,s}$ (fatalities/ accident) $C_{a,s} = A^* \delta^* f_A^* f_d^* f_m$	32		

12.2.4.10 Risk Scenario #10: Chlorine Transportation

Chlorine transportation is selected because of the risk involved with carrying large amounts of chlorine in one vehicle. In this chlorine transportation route, chlorine is transported from the trade port to pools throughout this city. For this assessment, one centrally located competition-sized pool is chosen. The red path shows the path from the trade port to the competition pool, and the yellow section shows the most populated 1 km area along the path, which will be the area of focus. The most populated and busy intersection is selected within that yellow section to continue the assessment, shown in Figure 12.6. Tank trailers used to transport chlorine on roads and highways have a capacity of 15–20 tons (SafeRack 2022). The worst-case scenario is used for this risk assessment, so a capacity of 20 tons of chlorine per truck will be used. Table 12.11 summarizes the constants and values for the chlorine transportation scenario.

12.2.5 Societal Risk and Prioritization

The International Atomic Energy Agency (1996) suggests that the estimation of societal risk can be done as follows: (i) by classifying each activity using a scale of consequence classes and a scale of probability classes (the scales are shown in the manual), (ii) if certain activities present risks to the public from different substances, which can each cause accidents independently of each other, then sum up the risk from the substances that have the same class of consequences, and (iii) map all activities on a frequency vs. consequence matrix. Table 12.12 summarizes each risk activity's classification based on each risk's consequence and probability. After classifying each activity in Table 12.12, Step 1 of RRA is complete. And since only one substance for each activity is selected, we can skip Step 2.

Step 3 involved plotting the consequence and frequency of each activity in terms of the consequence vs. frequency matrix. The overall results are depicted in Figure 12.7.

Figure 12.6 The chlorine transportation route.

Table 12.11 A summary of constants and values for the chlorine transportation scenario.

Description	Chlorine transportation	Location	N/A
Reference number (Table II)	32	Average probability number, $N^*_{t,s}$ (Table XV)	9.5
Weight (tons)	20	International transport code (Table XVI)	26 265 266
Effect category (Table IV)	Elll	Correction parameter for Safety Conditions, n_c (Table XVII)	0

Table 12.11 (Continued)

Description	Chlorine transportation	Location	N/A
Effective max distance (m) (Table V)	500	Correction parameter for traffic density, $n_{t\delta}$ (Table XVIII)	−2.5
Effective area, A(ha) (Table V)	8	Correction parameter for wind direction, n_p (Table XIX)	0
Population density, δ(persons/ Ha) (Table VI)	80	Probability number, $N_{t,s}$ $N_{t,s} = N^*_{t,s} + n_c + n_{t\delta} + n_p$	7
Correction factor for distribution of main populated area(s), f_A (Table VII)	1	Frequency, $P_{t,r}$ (accidents/year) (Table XX)	1.00E−07
Correction factor for mitigation, f_m (Table VIII)	0.1		
Area correction factor, f_d	1		
Consequence, $C_{a,s}$ (fatalities/ accident) $C_{a,s} = A * \delta * f_A * f_d * f_m$	64		

Table 12.12 Societal risk classification.

Risk#	Risk	Type	Location	$C_{a,s}$ (fatalities/ accident)	Consequence class	$P_{i,s}$ OR $P_{t,s}$ (#of accidents/ year)	Probability class
1	Ice rink	Fixed	1	9.6	0–25	3.0E−07	3.0E−07
2	Bus garage	Fixed	2	36	26–50	1.0E−08	1.0E−08
3	Competition Pool	Fixed	3	5.4	0–25	1.0E−07	1.0E−07
4	Forge	Fixed	4	8000	>500	3.0E−07	3.0E−07
5	Pest control service	Fixed	5	28.8	26–50	3.0E−07	3.0E−07
6	Sugar refinery	Fixed	6	2.4	0–25	1.0E−07	1.0E0−07
7	Composite wood manufacturer	Fixed	7	3	0–25	3.0E−07	3.0E−07
8	Gas distribution center	Fixed	8	1600	>500	3.0E−08	3.0E−08
9	Gas transportation	Transportation	N/A	32	26–50	3.0E−06	3.0E−06
10	Chlorine transportation	Transportation	N/A	64	51–100	1.0E−07	1.0E−07

Figure 12.8 displays a zoomed-in result capturing the bottom left side as indicated by the rectangle in Figure 12.7. In this case, gas transportation has a very high frequency compared to other elements. Forge risk has a very high consequence compared to the others. Pest control service, ice rink, and the transportation of chlorine have the highest frequency. Also, this diagram shows that the gas distribution center risk has the next highest consequence. The rest of the risk activities have relatively low frequency and consequence. The ALARA (As Low As Reasonably Achievable) principle can determine the societal risk. Thresholds are drawn in Figure 12.8 to depict tolerable risks, intolerable risks, and the ALARA region. The ALARA region needs more information before risks can be considered tolerable or intolerable. The threshold for acceptability is established by accounting for the probability class and consequence rather than just one or the other.

To prioritize risks, first, the risks in the intolerable region must be addressed. Then, the risks in the ALARA region should be evaluated further to decide if they can be deemed tolerable for reasons such as impractical mitigation methods or cost of correction exceeding improvements gained. ALARA risks deemed intolerable should be corrected next. Lastly, risks in the tolerable region do not need any modifications unless the consequence or frequency increases. Risks in the tolerable region only need to be monitored to ensure they do not worsen and cross into the ALARA or intolerable region. Table 12.13 depicts risks, their region, and a description of the risk, consequence, and frequency value.

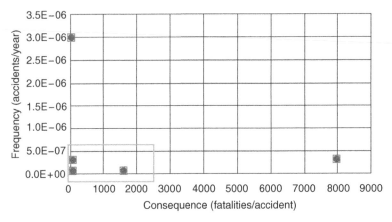

Figure 12.7 Overall societal risk consequence vs. frequency (original).

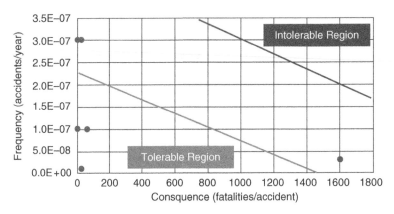

Figure 12.8 Overall societal risk consequence vs. frequency (zoomed).

Table 12.13 A table for overall societal risk.

Region	Risk	Type	Risk description	Consequence (fatalities/ accident)	Frequency (accidents/ year)
Intolerable	Forge	Fixed	Carbon monoxide, CO, is the main reducing agent in blast furnace gas	8000	3.0E–07
Intolerable	Gas transportation	Transportation	Gas (petrol) is transported from the gas distribution center to gas stations across the city	32	3.0E–06
ALARA	Pest control service	Fixed	Phosgene is a main ingredient in pesticides	28.8	3.0E–07
ALARA	Composite wood manufacturer	Fixed	Formaldehyde is used in the manufacture of composite wood products	3	3.0E–07
ALARA	Gas distribution center	Fixed	Gas (petrol) is stored to be distributed to gas stations around the city	1600	3.0E–08
ALARA	Ice rink	Fixed	Ammonia is used in the refrigeration system	9.6	3.0E–07
Tolerable	Bus garage	Fixed	Petrol is used and stored to fuel buses	36	1.0E–08
Tolerable	Competition pool	Fixed	Chlorine is used and stored to keep the pool water clean and healthy	5.4	1.0E–07
Tolerable	Sugar refinery	Fixed	Sulfur dioxide is used as a decolorizer in sugar	2.4	1.0E–07
Tolerable	Chlorine transportation	Transportation	Chlorine is transported from the port and delivered to pools across	64	1.0E–07

12.2.6   Recommendations

The following recommendations are based on the results of the assessment and risk prioritization in Section 12.2.5:

12.2.6.1   Forge

The forge has a high risk because it has a very high consequence. Therefore, the focus should be on lowering the consequence of an accident. With the current capacity and production of blast furnace gas (BFG), even if BFG is disposed of daily, the amount of carbon monoxide produced would still be above 10,000 tons, meaning an effect category of HIII. To reduce the amount of BFG produced, the forge should slow down production, thus reducing the BFG produced and changing the effective category, decreasing the maximum effective distance and area. In addition, the forge could also find a way to reuse the BFG, minimizing the amount of BFG created. If the amount of carbon monoxide and BFG produced can be decreased from over 16,000 tons to 10,000 tons or less, the effect category would be GIII rather than HIII, thus reducing the maximum effective distance from 10,000 m to 3,000 m. Also, the affected area will decrease from 1,000 ha to 300 ha. This could bring the consequence from 8,000 fatalities per accident to 2,400 fatalities per accident. Alternatively, if neither of those can be done, or results are insufficient, the forge should move and open a new location in a large area with a low population. Ideally, this area should be at least 10,000 m away from the nearest town since that is the current maximum effect distance. If these changes could be accomplished, this risk would then be in the ALARA region.

12.2.6.2 Gas Transportation

This transportation route has a high frequency of accidents, so the focus should be on lowering this. To lower the frequency of accidents, the route the truck drives could be changed to divert the truck to less busy roads with little to no traffic, increasing the safety of areas with large populations in the city. This change will increase the probability correction parameter for wind direction toward populated areas (n_p) and the safety conditions of transport systems (n_c). Currently, n_p has a value of 0 because people live in most of the effect area. However, a better path can be found where the part of the area where people are living only covers 50% or less of the effect area, n_p can increase from a value of 0 to +0.5. In addition, diverting the route to a less populated area could increase n_c from a value of 0 to +1. These increases in value would bring $N_{t,s}$ from 5.5 to 7, decreasing P from 3E–06 to 1E–7. If these changes could be achieved, this risk would be in the tolerable region.

12.2.6.3 Pest Control Service

The risk related to the pest control service is in the ALARA region for risk because of its frequency. If this risk is determined to be tolerable, nothing will be done. However, suppose this risk is determined to be an intolerable risk. In that case, the accident frequency can be decreased by having the company implement more safety measures in their facility, thus increasing their probability number correction parameter for organizational safety (n_o). Currently, the pest control service only practices the average industry safety standards. If the company can increase its safety regulations to above the industry standard, it can increase their n_o from 0 to +0.5. This increase would bring their $N_{t,s}$ from 6.5 to 7, decreasing their P value from 3E–7 to 1E–7. If this is not possible, the company could move its location to farther outside the city, diminishing the population in the affected area and increasing the probability number correction parameter for wind direction toward populated areas in the affect zone, n_p. Currently, n_p has a value of 0 because most of the affected area has a population living there. If the company moves to a place where 50% or less of the population lives in the affected area, the n_p value could increase from 0 to +0.5, +1, or +1.5. These values would increase $N_{t,s}$ from 6.5 to 7, 7.5, or 8, respectively, thus decreasing P from 3E–7 to 1E–7, 3E–8, or 1E–8, respectively. This risk would be in the tolerable region if these changes could be accomplished.

12.2.6.4 Composite Wood Manufacturer

The risk caused by the composite wood manufacturer is in the ALARA region for risk because of its higher frequency. If this risk is determined to be tolerable, nothing will be done. However, if this risk is considered intolerable, a few changes can be made. Like the pest control service, the composite wood manufacturer could implement higher safety measures in the facility, bringing the value of n_o from 0 to +0.5. Again, this increase would increase their $N_{t,s}$ from 6.5 to 7, decreasing their P value from 3E–7 to 1E–7. This risk would be in the tolerable region if these changes could be accomplished.

12.2.6.5 Gas Distribution Center

The risk caused by the gas distribution center is in the ALARA region because of its high consequence. If this risk is determined to be tolerable, nothing will be done. However, if this risk is determined to be an intolerable risk, a few changes can be made. To decrease the risk, the center could be forced to lower the amount of petrol they can have at a time, lowering the effective category, which also reduces the maximum affected distance and area. Currently, the amount of petrol stored is 4,871 tons, leading to an effect category of EII. If the amount of petrol stored can be decreased to 200–1000 tons, the new effect category would be DII. With this category, the maximum effect distance would drop from 500 m to 200 m, and the effect area would decrease from 40 ha to 6 ha. This change would bring the consequence from 1,600 fatalities per accident to 240 deaths per accident. This risk would be in the tolerable region if these changes could be accomplished.

12.3 Vulnerability Assessment

The Vulnerability Assessment (VA) aims to assess the vulnerabilities of physical assets throughout the city, develop countermeasures, estimate costs, and develop a better plan to protect the city and its citizens against future attacks. The *Guide to Highway Vulnerability Assessment for Critical Asset Identification and Protection* (Science Applications International Corporation 2002) is used to perform the VA for the selected area of Portland. This approach consists of six main steps:

1) identification of critical routes and assets
2) assessment of vulnerabilities
3) assessment of consequences
4) identification of countermeasures
5) estimation of countermeasure costs
6) security operational planning development

12.3.1 Step 1: Identify Critical Routes and Assets

The comprehensive plan vision for Portland is as follows (City of Portland 2022):

> Portland is a prosperous, healthy, equitable and resilient city where everyone has access to opportunity and is engaged in shaping decisions that affect their lives

Taking this mission statement, five critical routes are identified. Two different routes from the trade port to a pool are identified, as well as three routes from the gas distribution center to a popular gas station. Figure 12.9 depicts the routes involved. These routes involve the transportation of hazardous goods.

These five routes all cross over one intersection, so this intersection is evaluated in more detail. Four critical assets relating to the mission statement surround this intersection, including a bank, school, bus station, and hospital, thus making this intersection a critical intersection. Therefore, there are now five essential assets of this area, which will be evaluated in further detail throughout this assessment. Figure 12.10 shows the location of each critical asset.

Once identified, each critical asset is categorized as infrastructure, facilities, equipment, or personnel, as suggested in Table 12.14. The critical infrastructure (CI) – bus station, school, hospital, and bank – will be the main focus throughout this assessment. Still, the equipment and personnel of those facilities will be used for more detailed analysis when necessary.

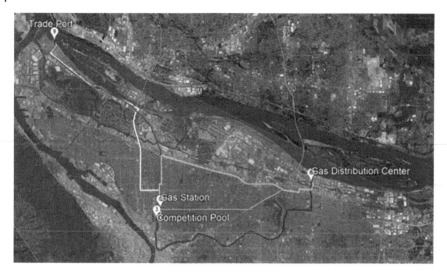

Figure 12.9 Identification of critical routes.

Figure 12.10 Identification of critical assets.

Once critical routes and assets are identified, critical asset scoring must be completed. This is done through established critical asset factors and a value assigned to each factor. The value assigned to each factor will be ranked on a scale of 1 to 5, 1 being of very little importance and 5 being extremely important. Using Science Applications International Corporation's (2002) guide, Table 12.15 is developed to show each critical asset factor, its value, and a description of the factor. Next, each of the five main critical assets is scored against the factors established in Table 12.15, as suggested in Table 12.16, indicating the most critical assets. And in this case, the hospital is the most critical, followed by the school and the critical intersection. The bus station and the bank are the least critical. This concludes Step 1 of the VA.

Table 12.14 Categorization of critical assets of the city.

Critical city assets			
infrastructure	Facilities	Equipment	Personnel
Critical intersection	Bus station	Public buses	Bus drivers
	School	School buses	Teachers
	Hospital	Ambulances	Bank tellers
	Bank		Doctors/ Nurses

Table 12.15 Critical assets factors.

Critical asset factor	Value	Description
Deter/defend factors		
A) Ability to provide protection	1	Does the asset lack a system of measures?
B) Relative vulnerability	2	Is the asset relatively vulnerable to an attack?
Loss and damage Consequences		
C) Casualty risk	5	Is there a possibility of serious injury or loss of life resulting from an attack on the asset?
Consequence to public services		
D) Emergency response function	5	Does the asset serve an emergency response function and will the action or activity of the emergency response be affected?
E) Transportation	1	Will an attack on the asset affect the ability for transportation around the city?
Consequence to general public		
F) Economic impact	4	Will damage to this asset have an effect on the means of living, resources or wealth of the city and those in
G) Health and care	4	Does this asset serve to assist with the health and care for citizens of the city?
H) Education	1	Will an attack on this asset affect access to education?

Table 12.16 Scoring critical assets.

Critical asset factor	Value	Description
Deter/defend factors		
A) Ability to provide protection	1	Does the asset lack a system of measures?
B) Relative vulnerability	2	Is the asset relatively vulnerable to an attack?
Loss and damage consequences		
C) Casualty risk	5	Is there a possibility of serious injury or loss of life resulting from an attack on the asset?

(Continued)

Table 12.16 (Continued)

Critical asset factor	Value	Description
Consequence to public services		
D) Emergency response function	5	Does the asset serve an emergency response function and will the action or activity of the emergency response be affected?
E) Transportation	1	Will an attack on the asset affect the ability for transportation around the city?
Consequence to general public		
F) Economic impact	4	Will damage to this asset have an effect on the means of living, resources, or wealth of the city and those in nearby areas
G) Health and care	4	Does this asset serve to assist with the health and care for citizens of the city?
H) Education	1	Will an attack on this asset affect access to education?

12.3.2 Step 2: Assess Vulnerabilities

Step 2 identifies and evaluates critical assets regarding their weaknesses and other vulnerabilities. Each critical asset is scored against multiple vulnerability factors. These vulnerability factors included visibility and attendance, access to the asset, and site-specific hazards. Each of these three factors is broken into two sub-elements. Factors and their sub-elements are as follows:

- Visibility and attendance
  - Level of recognition (A)
  - Attendance/users (B)
- Access to the asset
  - Access proximity (C)
  - Security level (D)
- Site-specific hazards
  - Receptor impacts (E)
  - Volume (F)

Each asset's vulnerability is scored on a scale of 1 to 5 based on a table in Science Applications International Corporation's (2002) research, which described each level of the scale for each vulnerability factor sub-element. Once each critical asset's vulnerability is scored against the six sub-elements, the total vulnerability score, y, is calculated using Equation (12.5).

$$Vulnerability(y) = (A * B) + (C * D) + (E * F) \tag{12.5}$$

Table 12.17 depicts the results from the vulnerability factor scoring. These results show that the bus station is the most vulnerable asset, followed by the hospital, intersection, school, and bank, consecutively. This concludes Step 2.

Table 12.17 Vulnerability factor scoring.

Critical asset	Vulnerability factor (A * B)		+ (C * D)		+ (E * F)		Total score(y)
	1–5	1–5	1–5	1–5	1–5	1–5	
School	4	3	5	3	2	3	33
Bus station	2	2	5	5	4	4	45
Hospital	4	5	5	2	4	3	42
Bank	5	3	5	1	2	3	26
Critical intersection	2	2	4	5	4	4	40

12.3.3 Step 3: Assess Consequences

Step 3 is to identify assets with the most significant risk based on the asset's criticality and vulnerability. The critical asset scoring completed in Step 1 and the vulnerability factor scoring in Step 2 are used to determine the criticality and vulnerability assets. Equations (12.6) and (12.7) are used to plot the criticality vs. vulnerability of each asset.

$$X = Criticality = (x / C_{max}) * 100 \tag{12.6}$$

$$Y = Vulerability = (y / 75) * 100 \tag{12.7}$$

where x is the critical asset score for each critical asset, C_{max} is the maximum critically score (which in this case is 23), and y is the vulnerability score for each critical asset. By using these equations, X and Y for each asset could be calculated. These calculations are shown in Table 12.18.

A criticality and vulnerability matrix with four quadrants is then developed. Critical assets located in Quadrant I have high criticality and high vulnerability. Assets in Quadrant II have low criticality and high vulnerability. Assets in Quadrant III have low criticality and low vulnerability. Assets in Quadrant IV have high criticality and low vulnerability. Figure 12.11 depicts the criticality and vulnerability matrix. This concludes Step 3.

12.3.4 Step 4: Identify Countermeasures

Step 4 is to identify typical countermeasures to protect critical assets against an attack. Table 12.19 depicts a list of proposed countermeasures, the corresponding critical asset category, and the countermeasure function adapted from Science Applications International Corporation (2002).

Table 12.18 Criticality and vulnerability of assets.

Critical asset	x	X = (x/C_{max})*100	Y	Y = (y/75)*100	Quadrant
School	13	57	33	44	II
Bus station	12	52	45	60	I
Hospital	21	91	42	56	I
Bank	12	52	26	35	II
Critical intersection	13	57	40	53	I

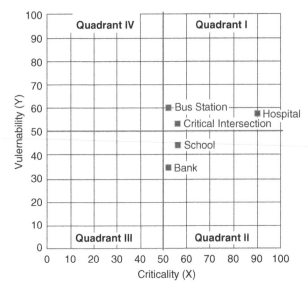

Figure 12.11 Criticality vs. vulnerability matrix.

12.3.5 Step 5: Estimate Countermeasure Costs

Step 5 estimates the capital, operating, and maintenance costs of the countermeasures proposed in Step 4. All countermeasures are broken down into "packages" based on the critical asset category that the countermeasure would assist. These "packages" are based on the "Critical asset category" column from Table 12.19. If a countermeasure is applied to a critical asset category, it is added to that critical asset category's package. Each type of cost is determined to be high (H), medium (M), or low (L) based on values from Science Applications International Corporation (2002). Costs are determined based on estimates and data from Science Applications International Corporation (2002). The countermeasure function column is the same as the information found in Table 12.19. Table 12.20 shows the countermeasure cost estimates for infrastructure. Table 12.21 shows the countermeasure cost estimates for facilities. Table 12.22 shows the countermeasure cost estimates for equipment. Table 12.23 shows the countermeasure cost estimates for personnel.

12.3.6 Step 6: Security Operational Planning Development

An operational security plan is meant to prevent potential risks and consequences. The plan includes developing countermeasures, such as training and exercises, as well as other security measures. The scope for an operational security plan for Portland would be as follows:

> To identify and prevent risks to protect personnel, deter criminal and/or terrorist activities and eliminate unauthorized access to critical assets.

Cloutier (2021) suggests a five-step process for operational security plans:

1) identify critical information
2) analyze threats
3) analyze vulnerabilities
4) assess the risk
5) determine countermeasures

Table 12.19 Countermeasures for critical assets.

Countermeasure	Critical asset category				Countermeasure function		
	Infrastructure	Facilities	Equipment	Personnel	Detect	Deter	Defend
Ensure there are full-time security guards on the property guarding all main entrances		X			X	X	
Keep all non-main access points locked and install motion-sensored security cameras around those access points		X			X	X	
Have a front desk by the main entrance that all guests/visitors have to sign in at		X		X		X	
Implement bag checks and install metal detectors at main entrances		X		X	X	X	
Install more light fixtures	X	X	X	X	X	X	
Install barriers around entrances / seating areas to prevent easy and quick access for vehicles		X	X	X		X	X
Install bullet-proof windows on counters/desks/vehicles that others may have easy access to		X	X	X		X	X
Add motion sensors to fences		X	X		X	X	
Implement frequent safety trainings for employees and customers in case of an emergency			X	X		X	
Limit access with building badges for employees and visitors		X	X	X		X	
Install full-time security cameras with video capability at critical assets	X	X	X	X	X	X	
Implement full-time surveillance at critical assets	X	X	X	X	X	X	

Table 12.20 Infrastructure countermeasure cost estimates.

Countermeasure	Critical asset category				Countermeasure function		
	Infrastructure	Facilities	Equipment	Personnel	Detect	Deter	Defend
Ensure there are full-time security guards on the property guarding all main entrances		X			X	X	
Keep all non-main access points locked and install motion-sensored security cameras around those access points		X			X	X	
Have a front desk by the main entrance that all guests/visitors have to sign in at		X		X		X	
Implement bag checks and install metal detectors at main entrances		X		X	X	X	
Install more light fixtures	X	X	X	X	X	X	
Install barriers around entrances / seating areas to prevent easy and quick access for vehicles		X	X	X		X	X
Install bullet-proof windows on counters/ desks/vehicles that others may have easy access to		X	X	X		X	X
Add motion sensors to fences		X	X		X	X	
Implement frequent safety trainings for employees and customers in case of an emergency			X	X		X	
Limit access with building badges for employees and visitors		X	X	X		X	
Install full-time security cameras with video capability at critical assets	X	X	X	X	X	X	
Implement full-time surveillance at critical assets	X	X	X	X	X	X	

Table 12.21 Facilities countermeasure cost estimates.

Critical asset group	Countermeasure	Countermeasurefunction			Estimated relative cost (H/M/L)		
		Detect	Deter	Defend	Capital	operating	Maintenance
Equipment: Public buses	Install more light fixtures	X	x		L	L	L
School buses Ambulances	Install barriers around entrances/seating areas to prevent easy and quick access for vehicles		x	X	L	L	L
	Install bullet-proof windows on counters/ desks/vehicles that others may have easy access to		x	X	M	L	**L**
	Add motion sensors to fences	X	x		L	L	L
	Implement frequent safety trainings for employees and customers in case of an emergency		X		L	L	L
	Limit access with building badges for employees and visitors		X		L	L	L
	Install full-time security cameras with video capability at critical assets	X	X		H	M	L
	Implement full-time surveillance at critical assets	X	X		H	**H**	**H**

These five steps are very similar to the steps in the VA. During these steps, critical information is identified by determining the critical assets of the area (VA Step 1). Threats are analyzed after establishing and assigning values to the critical asset factors (VA Step 1). Vulnerability is analyzed during the VA Step 2. The risk is assessed during the VA Step 3, where the consequence of risk on each critical asset is assessed. And finally, during the VA Steps 4–5, countermeasures are identified as well as the estimated cost for each countermeasure.

Now that those activities have been completed during this VA for Portland, the next step of the operational security plan is to implement the countermeasures. Once implemented, the success of the countermeasure would be evaluated to determine if the results are satisfactory or not. If the results are not satisfactory, these five steps would be repeated until the results are satisfactory.

Table 12.22 Equipment countermeasure cost estimates.

Critical asset group	Countermeasure	Countermeasure function			Estimated relative cost (H/M/L)		
		Detect	Deter	Defend	Capital	Operating	Maintenance
Facilities: Bus station School Hospital Bank	Ensure there are full-time security guards on the property guarding all main entrances	X	X		M	M	L
	Keep all non-main access points locked and install motion-sensored security cameras around those access points	X	X		H	M	L
	Have a front desk by the main entrance that all guests/visitors have to sign in		X		L	L	L
	Implement bag checks and install metal detectors at main entrances	X	X		L	M	L
	Install more light fixtures	X	X		L	L	L
	Install barriers around entrances/seating areas to prevent easy and quick access for vehicles		X	X	L	L	L
	Install bullet-proof windows on counters/desks/vehicles that others may have easy access to		X	X	M	L	L
	Add motion sensors to fences	X	X		L	L	L
	Limit access with building badges for employees and visitors		X		L	L	L
	Install full-time security cameras with video capability at critical assets	X	X		H	M	L
	Implement full-time surveillance at critical assets	X	X		H	H	H

Table 12.23 Personnel countermeasure cost estimates.

Critical asset group	Countermeasure	Countermeasure function			Estimated relative cost (H/M/L)		
		Detect	Deter	Defend	Capital	Operating	Maintenance
Personnel: Bus drivers Teachers Bank tellers Doctors/ nurses	Have a front desk by the main entrance that all guests/visitors have to sign in at		X		L	L	L
	Implement bag checks and install metal detectors at main entrances	X	X		L	M	L
	Install more light fixtures	X	X		L	L	L
	Install barriers around entrances/seating areas to prevent easy and quick access for vehicles		X	X	L	L	L
	Install bullet-proof windows on counters/ desks/vehicles that others may have easy access to		X	X	M	L	L
	Implement frequent safety trainings for employees and customers in case of an emergency		X		L	L	L
	Limit access with building badges for employees and visitors		X		L	L	L
	Install full-time security cameras with video capability at critical assets	X	X		H	M	L
	Implement full-time surveillance at critical assets	X	X		H	H	H

12.4 IRRA of Air, Water, and Ground Pollution

The IRRA aims to analyze continuous emission sources and evaluate their impact on the city's citizens' health. Dangerous goods and hazardous materials are some of the most significant pollution causes in a city like Portland. Unfortunately, the largest producers of those same dangerous goods and hazardous materials are the large manufacturers and consumer products within that city. The transportation of these dangerous goods and hazardous materials further adds to the pollution within the city. The manufacturing and transportation of these materials create emissions that can cause adverse amounts of pollution in the air, water, and soil in and around the city. The *Guidelines for Integrated Risk Assessment and Management in Large Industrial Areas*

(International Atomic Energy Agency 1998) are used to analyze continuous emissions in the city. These guidelines outline seven steps:

1) identify sources of continuous emission
2) characterize the emission source inventory
3) select a pathway for analysis organized according to the receiving media: air, water, soil
4) use models calculate dispersion values
5) (if necessary) evaluate the concentration of pollutants as a time-distance function by using atmospheric dispersion models
6) use air quality, water quality, and soil quality standards or dose–response relationships to estimate the risk to the population; evaluate the health impacts
7) use analytical methods, critical load concepts or expert judgment for environmental impact assessment

An in-depth analysis of emissions for Portland is outside the scope of the present research. Only three sources of continuous emissions in Portland are selected, as depicted in Table 12.24. In Sections 12.4.1–12.4.5, individual pollution maps for each source are unavailable, so multiple maps will be used to describe the emissions.

12.4.1 Airborne (Air Pollution)

Figure 12.12 is taken from AQICN (https://aqicn.org/city/usa/oregon/portland) and shows Portland's real-time air quality index as of Saturday, April 16, 2022 at 3 p.m. This map shows places where air quality is measured. As shown in the map, all the measurements in Portland are green, meaning the air quality is considered "good" and minimal pollutants are detected in the air.

AQICN also lists changes in air quality over the last forty-eight hours. Figure 12.13 breaks down pollution by different air pollutants and lists the minimum and maximum values for each. The overall air quality in Portland is an 18, which is considered "good." The lower the number, the better the air quality because fewer pollutants are detected. This figure also shows that the pollution consists of mainly fine particle matter ($PM_{2.5}$) and nitrogen dioxide (NO_2). NO_2 is found in pollution from all three sources of continuous emissions listed previously, which all contribute to the total emission count for the city.

AQICN also displays historical data related to air pollution. For example, Figure 12.14 shows the daily data for NO_2 from 2020 to April 16, 2022. This figure shows that over the last few years, a low amount of NO_2 has been detected in emissions. Therefore, despite many continuous emission sources throughout the city, they do not produce an overwhelming or dangerous amount of NO_2.

Table 12.24 Suggested continuous sources of emissions.

Source	Pollutant	Emission coefficient	Description
Gas distribution center	NO_2	136.98	Underground gas storage – 5000 acres 6 × 1010 scf/yr capacity
Landfill	NO_2	0.42	Commercial waste repository – construction and operations emissions
Power plant	NO_2	850.00	Coal-fired power plant, western coals – conv. steam plant; emissions controls

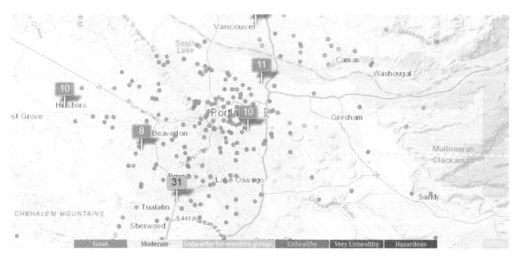

Figure 12.12 Real-time air quality in Portland.

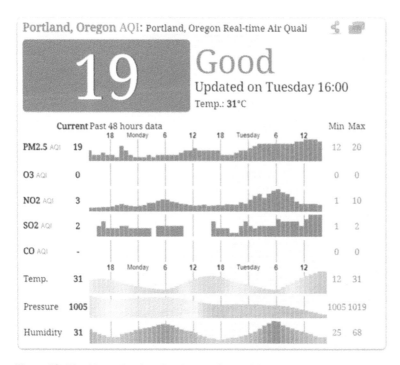

Figure 12.13 Air quality data for the past forty-eight hours.

12.4.2 Waterborne (Water Pollution)

EnviroAtlas (https://www.epa.gov/enviroatlas) shows water pollution throughout the Portland area. Figure 12.15 shows all impaired waterways in red, while Figure 12.16 shows the waterways that are assessed in blue. These waterways are assessed and determined to be impaired as they are degraded and do not meet the standards for many designated beneficial uses, such as aquatic life and drinking water.

Daily Data

PM₂.₅   PM₁₀   O₃   NO₂   SO₂   CO

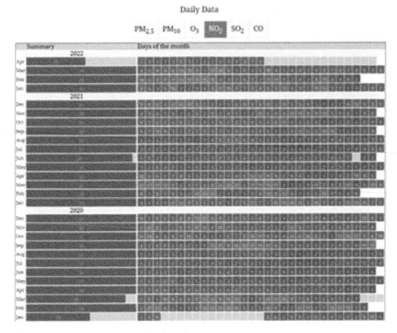

Figure 12.14   Annual air pollution data.

Figure 12.15   Impaired waterways.

Nitrate violations in surface water systems are also a concern. Again, higher values indicate a higher probability of a violation. This violation means more nitrate, such as NO_2, is in the surface water system than is allowed or safe. Overall, Portland has a better-than-average probability of a violation of nitrate in a surface water system, according to the scale in Figure 12.17. However, the northern outskirts of Portland have a higher probability, so the previously listed sources of continuous emissions, or similar sources, are likely found in those areas. Areas south of Portland have a lower probability of a violation, so there are likely not as many continuous emissions sources.

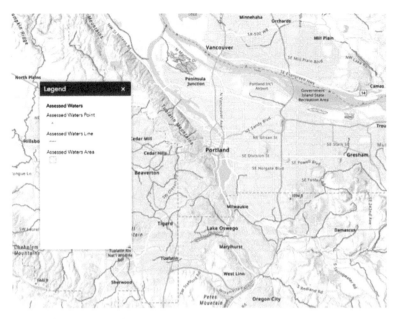

Figure 12.16 Assessed waterways.

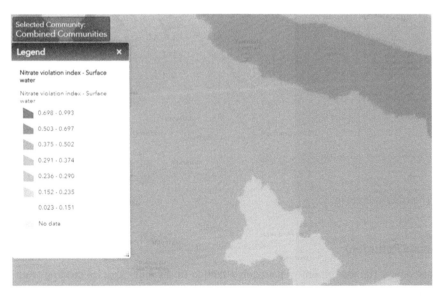

Figure 12.17 Surface water violation index.

Overall, there is little pollution in the surface water system in the center and other main areas of Portland, unlike the outskirts.

Figure 12.18 shows the nitrate violation in groundwater systems. A water quality index map from 2020 is shown in Figure 12.19. This map displays the water quality in certain areas in and around Portland and whether that measurement is better or worse or if there is no change from the previous year.

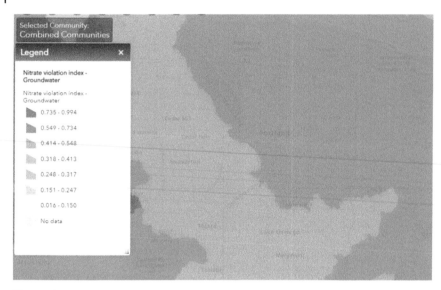

Figure 12.18 Groundwater violation index.

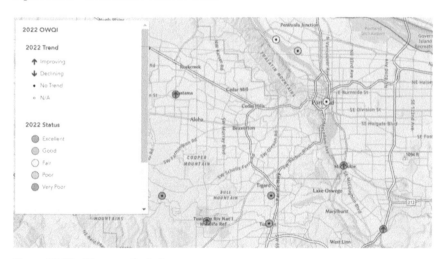

Figure 12.19 Water quality index map.

12.4.3 Soil (Ground Pollution)

EnviroAtlas can also show the movement of nitrogen attached to the soil particles eroding from the surface of agricultural fields, as depicted in Figure 12.20. Green areas have smaller amounts of nitrogen than blue or purple areas. High levels of nitrogen movement mean there is likely a high level of breakdowns of nitrates, meaning there could be a lot of pollution, such as NO_2 in the soil. Areas shaded in blue or purple have higher nitrogen levels, indicating a higher probability of pollution in the soil. NO_2 is found in the three sources of continuous emissions listed previously, meaning those sources or similar locations are likely located in the outskirts of Portland. Therefore, the soil on the edges of Portland has more pollution than the soil in the city's center. Again, this makes sense because the areas on the outer edges, specifically the northern area of Portland, are more commercial and industrial than the center of Portland, which is more residential.

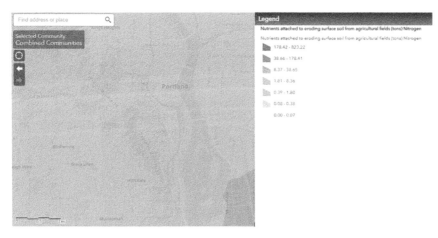

Figure 12.20 Surface soil pollution.

12.4.4 Risks and Associated Consequences

The more pollution in the environment (i.e. air, water, ground), the more at-risk the city's citizens are. These risks can lead to consequences, including mortality and morbidity. Air pollution is the most significant risk to the health of the citizens in the city. Citizens who spend the most time in risk areas are more likely to develop health problems in the future. Figure 12.21 shows the cancer risk per million due to cumulative air toxics. Figure 12.22 shows respiratory risk due to cumulative air toxics. Interestingly, these numbers suggest that all people in Portland have the same risk category (i.e. they all have the same risk of developing cancer and respiratory issues due to air toxics, including pollution). Figure 12.23 depicts the risk of developing a non-cancer neurological risk due to cumulative air toxics, including pollution. Figure 12.24 shows the risk of cancer due to formaldehyde air toxics. Figure 12.25 shows the respiratory risk due to formaldehyde air toxics.

Figure 12.21 Cancer risk due to cumulative air toxics.

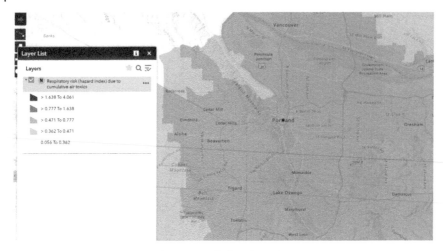

Figure 12.22   Respiratory risk due to cumulative air toxics.

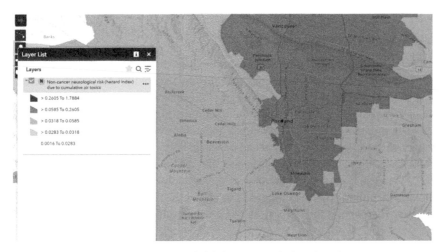

Figure 12.23   Non-cancer neurological risk due to cumulative air toxics.

Figure 12.24   Cancer risks due to formaldehyde air toxics.

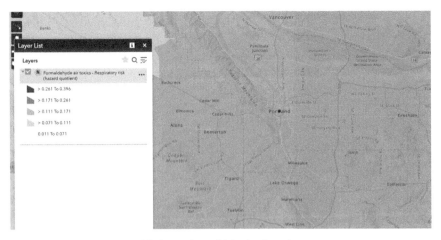

Figure 12.25 Respiratory risk due to formaldehyde air toxics.

Although the data in both figures use different data and units to create their scales, the same color codes represent similar risk levels. The majority of Portland is all the same color, meaning the same risk. This makes sense because all buildings, including residential homes, businesses, apartment buildings, etc. have floors and furniture made from composite wood. Assuming these items are dispersed equally throughout the city among all buildings, the entire city has the same risk. Therefore, all citizens in Portland have roughly the same chance of developing the two issues due to formaldehyde.

12.4.5 EMP Assessment

EMP Assessment (EMPA) assesses EMP in an area at varying heights. EMP is a pulse of high-intensity electromagnetic radiation generated especially by a nuclear blast high above the earth's surface and held to disrupt electronic and electrical systems (Zhang et al. 2022). EMP has the potential to affect extensive areas. If an area is affected, CIs will be severely impacted (National Coordinating Center for Communications 2019). EMP devices, including weapons and missiles, can explode in the air and release an electromagnetic wave, disrupting the electrical grid and causing damage to electronics such as computers, cell phones, radios, etc. (Cybersecurity and Infrastructure Security Agency 2022). Figure 12.26 visually represents how a high-altitude EMP detonation affects an area when it explodes (Security Team 2022).

The area that an EMP explosion covers depends on the height of the explosion. The EMP radius can be determined as long as the height of the burst (HOB) is known. The HOB and EMP radius are related using Equation (12.8) (EMPEngineering.com 2022; National Coordinating Center for Communications 2019).

$$EMP\ Radius = 100\sqrt{(HOB)} \tag{12.8}$$

The following analysis calculates how large the EMP radius would be if the HOB is at 25 km, 100 km, and 400 km above the center of Portland, and discusses which areas would be affected at each HOB. Since Portland is on the west coast, less land will be directly affected than if the blast occurred in a more central state, so the blast will also cover parts of the Pacific Ocean. If there are ships in the affected area, their electronics, such as radios, can be damaged too. Using Equation (12.8), a HOB of 25 km, the EMP radius is:

HIGH-ALTITUDE EMP DETONATION

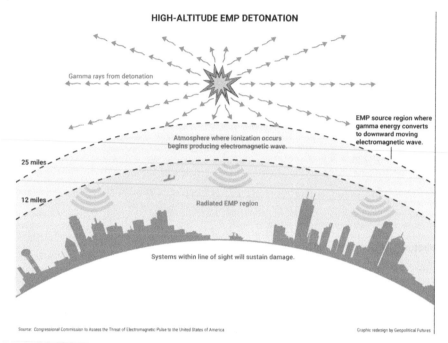

Figure 12.26 A high-altitude EMP detonation.

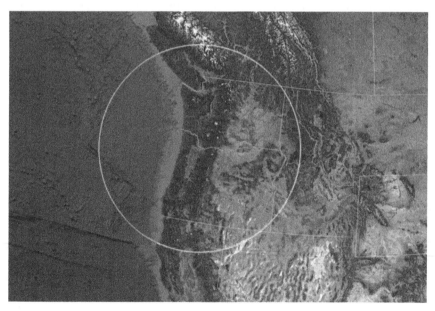

Figure 12.27 EMP detonation at a HOB of 25 km.

$$EMP\ Radius = 110\sqrt{25} = 550\ km$$

At the height of 25 km, the entire state of Oregon and Ishington area would be affected, including surrounding states as well as parts of Canada, as depicted by Figure 12.27.

At the height of 40 km, the entire state of Oregon and Ishington would be affected, including parts of Canada, Idaho, California, and Nevada, as suggested by Figure 12.28. At the height of 400 km, roughly 50% of the United States and Canada and Mexico would be affected, as suggested in Figure 12.29.

Figure 12.30 depicts EMP radius for the HOBs at 25 km, 40 km, 100 km, and 400 km, allowing for a better comparison of how the height affects EMP radius.

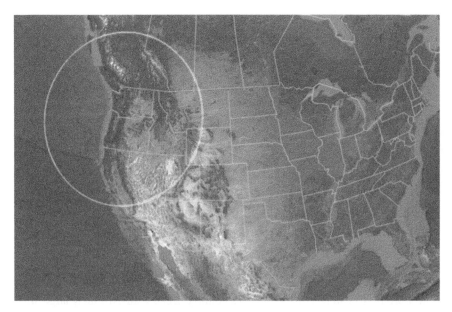

Figure 12.28 EMP detonation at a HOB of 100 km.

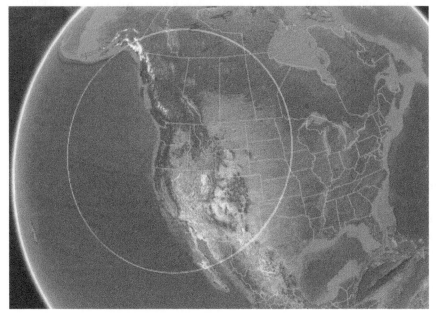

Figure 12.29 EMP detonation at a HOB of 400 km.

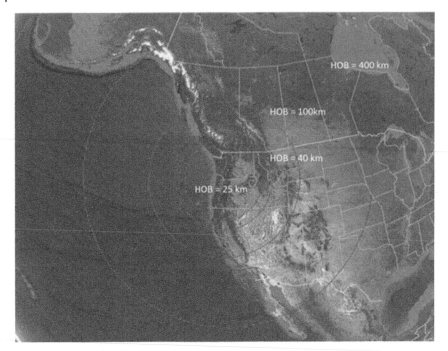

Figure 12.30 EMP radius for varying height of bursts.

From all these figures, it is easy to see how an EMP blast in Portland could affect many areas across the continent. EMP blasts can be detrimental to a country because an extremely large area can be affected by just one blast. More specifically, if the blast is released above a location more in the center of the country, such as Omaha, NE, the blast could have the potential to affect practically all of the contiguous United States, as well as parts of Canada and Mexico, if the blast occurred at 400 km, as suggested by Figure 12.31.

Preventing an EMP attack is impossible, and reducing its effects is challenging (Electromagnetic Pulse Commission 2008). However, the Department of Homeland Security mitigates risks (Cybersecurity and Infrastructure Security Agency 2022).

12.5 Comprehensive Implementation Plan for ReIDMP

Again, "resilience" has no single widely accepted definition (Gheorghe and Katina 2014; Katina and Gheorghe 2023; Vasuthanasub 2019). The goal of the design process is to develop a resilient system. This is important early in the design process, where informed decisions are made to ensure the developed system is resilient. Considerations of resilience must occur early in the design process because that is when there is the most freedom to explore design alternatives. A resilient developed system is capable of preventing/avoiding, mitigating, and recovering from failures, unlike reliability engineering, which only focuses on avoiding risks at all costs (Hulse 2019). The ReIDMP model is intended to develop a process that ends with a product/system that is created with resiliency in mind, including a city. Figure 12.32 depicts a simplified version of the ReIDMP presented in Chapter 7. The final product/system should be a resilient system capable of

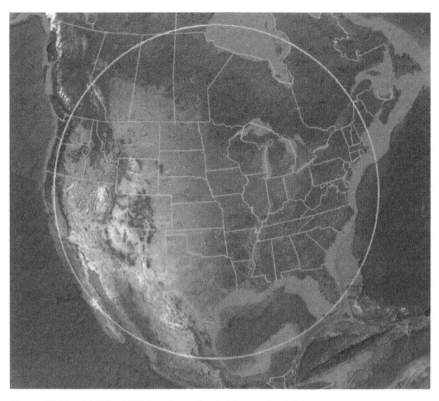

Figure 12.31 A HOB of 400 km above Omaha (approximately).

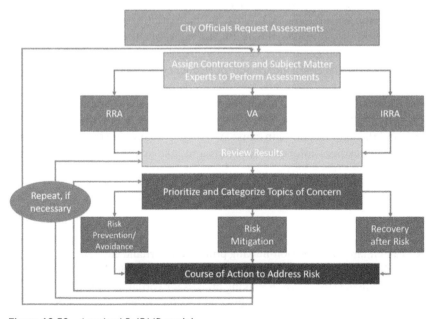

Figure 12.32 A revised ReIDMP model.

preventing, mitigating, and recovering from failures. Again, the ReIDMP model is grounded in RRA, VA, and IRRA and enables informed decisions for developing resilient systems.

The framework initially starts with city officials, and the same officials decide when the RRA, VA, and IRRA should be conducted. The same officials contact contractors and subject matter experts to conduct the three assessments – RRA, VA, and IIRA. Once RRA, VA, and IIRA are completed, the results are presented to the city officials, regional officials, other governance board members, and stakeholders, who will discuss topics of grave concern. Together, they will prioritize and categorize these concerns and determine whether they would need risk prevention, mitigation, and/or recovery after the risk occurs. A possible course of action is developed and implemented to address risks and vulnerabilities.

In this case, we can see that city officials can apply the ReIDMP to develop a resilient city with relative ease. Moreover, incorporating resilience into a solution or plan can lead to a more economical solution, especially for those involved in improving city safety through prevention, mitigation, and recovery (Hulse 2019).

12.6 Concluding Remarks

In this chapter, multiple assessments are performed on the City of Portland, including the RRA, VA, and IRRA. These assessments used the methodologies from the *Manual for the Classification of Prioritization of Risks Due to Major Accidents in Process and Related Industries* (International Atomic Energy Agency 1996), *Guide to Highway Vulnerability Assessment for Critical Asset Identification and Protection* (Science Applications International Corporation 2002), and *Guidelines for Integrated Risk Assessment and Management in Large Industrial Areas* (International Atomic Energy Agency 1998). These assessments help determine significant fixed risks and risks related to the transportation of hazardous goods, the vulnerability of critical assets, and the effect of different emissions throughout the city. With these assessments, risks are prioritized to determine which activities cause the most significant threats to the health and safety of citizens and visitors in the city. Prioritizing risk activities and vulnerabilities allows city officials to determine risks and implement viable solutions to decrease the consequence and/or frequency of risks – making a city safer and healthier.

An EPA is also performed to analyze the effects of an EMP blast at varying heights above Portland. Although reducing the effects of EMP blasts is difficult, it is important to understand how they work and the damage they can cause. We suggest that using these models can allow city officials to make resilient-informed decisions and take action to develop resilient cities.

12.7 Exercises

1 Discuss how RRA can enhance the decision-making process for Portland city leaders.
2 Discuss how VA can enhance the decision-making process for Portland city leaders.
3 Discuss how IRRA can enhance the decision-making process for Portland city leaders.
4 Discuss how EMPA can enhance the decision-making process for Portland city leaders.
5 Discuss how you would implement ReIDMP analysis results for the City of Portland.

References

City of Portland. (2022). *Portland's Vision for Growth and Progress [Portland.com]*. https://www.portland.gov/bps/planning/comp-plan/vision-growth-and-progress.

Cloutier, R. (2021, November 5). *What is Operational Security? The Five-step OPSEC Process [Cybersecurity]*. Security Studio. https://securitystudio.com/operational-security.

Cybersecurity and Infrastructure Security Agency. (2022). *Electromagnetic Pulse and Geomagnetic Disturbance*. https://www.cisa.gov/emp-gmd.

Electromagnetic Pulse Commission. (2008). *Report of the Commission to Assess the Threat to the United States from Electromagnetic Pulse (EMP) Attack: Critical National Infrastructures*. Prepper Press.

EMPEngineering.com (2022). *EMP/HEMP attacks*. EMP Engineering. https://www.empengineering.com/emp-hemp-attacks

Gheorghe, A.V. and Katina, P.F. (2014). Editorial: Resiliency and engineering systems – Research trends and challenges. *International Journal of Critical Infrastructures* 10 (3/4): 193–199. https://www.inderscience.com/info/dl.php?filename=2014/ijcis-4113.pdf.

Hulse, D. (2019). A framework for resilience informed decision making in early design. *Annual Conference of the PHM Society* 11 (1): Article 1. https://doi.org/10.36001/phmconf.2019.v11i1.913.

International Atomic Energy Agency. (1996). *Manual for the Classification and Prioritization of Risks Due to Major Accidents in Process and Related Industries*. International Atomic Energy Agency. http://www-pub.iaea.org/books/IAEABooks/5391/Manual-for-the-Classification-and-Prioritization-of-Risks-due-to-Major-Accidents-in-Process-and-Related-Industries.

International Atomic Energy Agency. (1998). *Guidelines for Integrated Risk Assessment and Management in Large Industrial Areas*. International Atomic Energy Agency. http://www-pub.iaea.org/books/IAEABooks/5391/Manual-for-the-Classification-and-Prioritization-of-Risks-due-to-Major-Accidents-in-Process-and-Related-Industries.

Katina, P.F. and Gheorghe, A.V. (2023). *Blockchain-enabled Resilience: An Integrated Approach for Disaster Supply Chain and Logistics Management* (1st ed.). CRC Press.

National Coordinating Center for Communications. (2019). *Electromagnetic Pulse (EMP) Protection and Resilience Guidelines for Critical Infrastructure and Equipment (Version 2.2)*. National Cybersecurity and Communications Integration Center. https://www.cisa.gov/sites/default/files/publications/19_0307_CISA_EMP-Protection-Resilience-Guidelines.pdf.

O'Shea, C. (2021, June). How Montreal made ammonia safe for its rinks. *HPAC Magazine*. Annex Business Media. https://www.hpacmag.com/features/how-montreal-made-ammonia-safe-for-its-rinks.

SafeRack. (2022). Chlorine handling design, loading, and installation. *SafeRack*. https://www.saferack.com/bulk-chemical/chlorine-loading-platforms.

Science Applications International Corporation. (2002). *Guide to Highway Vulnerability Assessment for Critical Asset Identification and Protection*. Transportation Policy and Analysis Center.

Security Team. (2022). *EMP: A Real Threat*. Aus Security Products. https://aussecurityproducts.com.au/blogs/posts/emp-a-real-threat.

US Environmental Protection Agency. (2018). *Ammonia Safety in New England Ice Rinks* (overviews and factsheets EPA-901-F-18-001). US Environmental Protection Agency. https://www.epa.gov/indoor-air-quality-iaq/ammonia-safety-new-england-ice-rinks.

Vasuthanasub, J. (2019). The resilient city: A platform for informed decision-making process. Dissertation, Old Dominion University. https://digitalcommons.odu.edu/emse_etds/151.

Zhang, M., Li, H., and Liu, Q. (2022). Deep exploration on fault model of electromagnetic pulse attack. *IEEE Transactions on Nanotechnology* 21: 598–605. https://doi.org/10.1109/TNANO.2022.3214341.

13

Smart Cities and Security of Critical Space Infrastructure Systems

13.1 Introduction

It is challenging to completely comprehend the current security risks to space systems due to a shortage of academic study in the area and the frequent secrecy around or classification of information concerning events harming vital infrastructure. Nevertheless, the literature in the field has highlighted the following vulnerabilities (Botezatu 2022):

- Remote sensing is gathering information about a research topic without directly contacting them. These devices are especially susceptible to laser assaults because electromagnetic weapons might be used to accomplish their primary goal.
- Communications satellites are necessary for aircraft and long-distance connections due to the planet's curvature impeding the line of sight. The destruction of these links might lead to a huge loss of life on Earth. According to studies, the Earth component of the satellite communications infrastructure is particularly susceptible to online assaults like jamming and spoofing (Steinberger 2008).
- Meteorological space facilities are essential for missions like forecasting severe weather. These satellites are frequently created only to send pictures and meteorological data to Earth. There isn't much published research on the vulnerabilities of meteorological satellites, but at a minimum, they probably have at least the same problems as other satellite systems.
- The Global Positioning System (GPS) and other satellite technologies are part of the Global Navigation Satellite System (GNSS). Jamming and spoofing are the two main ways GNSS is exposed by the literature (Faria et al. 2016; Ioannides et al. 2016).

13.2 Critical Space Infrastructure and Smart Cities

Space is very complex from a myriad of perspectives. First, the environment behaves differently. For example, laws governing motion and forces in space are different from ground systems. The rules of celestial mechanics make the space environment much more complex than what we have on the ground. Secondly, the uses of space are multiple. Initially referred to as dual-use technologies, the space infrastructures and services serve a multitude of actors, bluntly split among civil and military, but much more complex than that, ranging from governmental users to commercial ones. Lastly, different uses lead to various actors, institutions, and legislative framework constellations. These delineations of actors might not be equally valid in the cities on the ground. In scarce

Gamification for Resilience: Resilient Informed Decision-Making, First Edition.
Adrian V. Gheorghe and Polinpapilinho F. Katina.
© 2023 John Wiley & Sons, Inc. Published 2023 by John Wiley & Sons, Inc.

situations, the militaries are involved in smart city operations. Control rooms are managed by public–private entities, with security personnel when needed.

As opposed to any other finite surface on Earth, outer space is endless. Thus, any operation planning is different than on the ground. As an analogy, Earth's oceans contain 329 million cubic miles of water on and below the planet's surface. The volume of space between Earth and the Moon is 4.81097E+16 cubic miles. To achieve a comfortable degree of space control, one has to "control" 146,230,091 times the volume of Earth's oceans. It sounds like an impossible task, at least for the current level of development, since there aren't any geographic features in space. However, satellites cannot hide from Earth- or space-based sensor networks. And yet real satellites are "lost" all the time. For instance, in a satellite catalog published by the 18th Space Defense Squadron (Mattern 2021), nearly half of all space objects are classified as "Analyst Objects," meaning it is unknown what they are and who owns them. In addition, there are many means of hiding satellites in space. An additional problem is fully identifying the targets for space weapon systems. Moreover, even objects that are cataloged and tracked near a collision (less than 500 m) can sometimes get overlooked, as in the Iridium 33 collision with Cosmos 2251. Finally, there are so many pieces of uncatalogued debris in outer space that the space is obscured.

13.2.1 Responsible Actions in Space and Smart City Governance

While, according to the current international law, responsible actions in space are the prerogative of nation-states, and smart city governance requires a local-level approach, this research is attempting to make this connection visible (Botezatu 2022). Undoubtedly, the information and services offered by space technology are crucial to the success of smart cities. However, the specifics of this complex relationship and the degree of this dependency are the main subjects of this study. The capacity to describe the space environment and activities is known as space situational awareness (SSA), which entails monitoring space objects using both ground- and space-based sensors, such as radars or optical telescopes. The orbits of space objects are ascertained and future courses are predicted using a combination of tracking data from various sensors. Characterizing space objects, space weather, and pre-planned on-orbit operations are other crucial SSA elements.

Even though certain nations perform activities that may be categorized as space traffic management, there are presently no well-established international frameworks or common state practices (STM). The US government launched a program in 2010 to notify all satellite operators when an object is approaching them closely. Soon after, a few additional countries joined in and sent identical warnings to satellite providers. To improve the vital warnings and information governments provide, several satellite operators work with a third-party service, such as the Space Data Association (SDA) or their own national space agency. Additionally, studies have looked at the relationships between space aviation traffic and potential safety issues, and there have been worldwide political movements to look into voluntary laws or norms for enhancing the sustainability and safety of space operations. There is now no international framework to regulate space flight since, as far as these authors are aware, no study has been conducted that shows the importance of high politics to local politics. Although smart city governance can connect the population to the urban realms of decision-making, there remains a lack of connection to rural realms of decision-making. The rural realms are often unmanaged and left invisible.

13.2.2 Natural Threats from Space and Their Effects on Smart City Infrastructure

Those space assets currently in use are at risk of various dangers, such as collisions with space debris and the total amount of energy unleashed by space weather events. Over the last twenty-five years, multiple models for the causal chains connecting solar, wind, and geomagnetic disturbances, geomagnetic induced currents, and the sensitivity of the electrical grid have been investigated.

In the early 1990s, people began considering how space weather may affect the electricity system. Engineers at energy provider Hydro Quebec attributed the failure of their power grid in March 1989 to unusual solar activity (Australian Space Weather Forecasting Centre 2022). Six million people in Quebec were without power for more than nine hours due to the transformers' gradual failure and the electrical system's final collapse. The planet's first recognized geomagnetic storm reignited research into how the geomagnetic currents created influence activities on Earth. The incident clarified how crucial solar weather is to all ground-based electrical conductor systems, including pipeline, railroad, and telephone networks. Critical infrastructures in smart cities that rely on space-based assets may have issues during an electromagnetic storm. Many other types of damage might occur, so it is important to consider the storm's severity, timing, and geographic dispersion (CENTRA Technologies 2011). Relevant research has stressed the following effects to offer a framework for organizing the development of resilient systems.

A solar storm begins when one or more complex sunspot clusters are visible across the whole solar surface. One or more solar flares from these active regions might be seen on Earth eight minutes later utilizing radio, optical, and x-ray wavelengths. Extremely intense solar particles are then blasted at satellites and ground systems over a period of hours to days. During these stages, critical ground infrastructures from smart cities might experience significant repercussions and possibly damage, either directly, as with satellites, or indirectly as a consequence of cascade failures. Figure 13.1 depicts an array of infrastructure systems that could be affected in the case of solar storms (IFP Energies Nouvelles 2018).

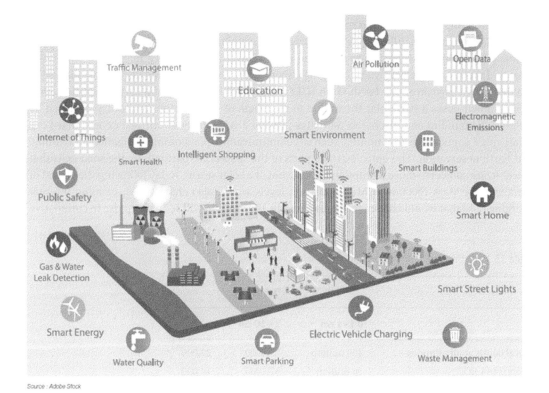

Source : Adobe Stock

Figure 13.1 Elements of a smart city that could be affected by solar storms. *Source:* Adobe Stock

Satellites, airplanes, and power grids are among the technological infrastructure systems that are impacted by space weather occurrences. The contemporary economy is particularly vulnerable to solar storms due to a web of interdependencies. Thus, critical goals are improving our understanding of the root causes of space weather and our capacity to anticipate it.

Impacts on the urban electrical power grid: the geomagnetic storm has the potential to damage several significant facilities. Due to conductors on the earth's surface acting as conduits for geomagnetic generated currents (GICs), electrical power networks are particularly susceptible. These GICs cause systemic issues by moving through the pipes and wires that make up the power transmission networks. Overloading the grid with GICs might cause major voltage control problems and even widespread power outages. Extra-high voltage transformers heated inside by GICs are also more prone to failure or perhaps irreparable harm (National Research Council 2008). Since the total collapse of the energy system would be such a catastrophic event for the people, infrastructure sectors, and trust in authorities, many more studies have concentrated on this probable course of action. According to a study by the North American Electric Reliability Corporation (2010), the geomagnetic hazard environment's potential extremes may be far more significant than previously believed. In fact, a one-in-one-hundred-year incident may lead the United States to face a catastrophic system failure that would take several years and billions of dollars to fix, according to Kappenman (2010). However, recent discussions indicate that voltage instability and a reduction in reactive power would likely be the consequences (North American Electric Reliability Corporation 2012). Additionally, during a solar storm, GICs may develop on extensive lengths of earthed electrical conducting material. In summary, disruption of the electrical grid caused by solar storms could impact smart cities very seriously. Table 13.1 indicates the number of confirmed orbital collisions involving active satellites. These dangers cannot be mitigated as solar weather is a natural phenomenon. Nevertheless, built-in resilience plays a fundamental role in withstanding such major disruption.

Radiation impacts on all satellite services: certain satellites may malfunction as a result of geomagnetic storms. According to the satellite's architecture, the rising microelectronic upset rates and the resulting electrostatic charging dangers may result in varying degrees of failure. For satellites in Geosynchronous Earth Orbit (GEO) and Medium Earth Orbit (MEO), Earth's outer radiation belt poses a particular threat due to the frequent irregularities and outages caused by electrostatic buildup and discharge. Satellites provide a wide array of critical services that keep smart cities' applications functioning, such as communication, positioning, navigation and timing, and Earth observation. The optoelectronic parts of the spacecraft, particularly the solar cells that power it, are subject to more disruption in the event of a solar storm. A day following the arrival of the Coronary Mass Ejection (CME), radiation levels would also sharply rise, creating internal charging risks that would endure for weeks. Finally, the satellite will see a sharp rise in cumulative

Table 13.1 Estimated debris in orbital.

	Debris size		
	0.1–1 cm	1–10 cm	>10 cm
Total debris at all altitudes	150 million	750,000	22,000
Debris in LEO	16 million	370,000	14,000
Debris from the Chinese ASAT	2 million	150,000	2,500

radiation damage (Cannon 2013). For instance, the geomagnetic storm of 2003 affected 10% of the world's satellites. It resulted in brief outages that lasted up to a few days, with older satellites needing to be replaced. Figure 13.2 depicts a list of significant satellite outages and their effect on ground technologies (Cannon 2013).

Impact on radio communication systems: during a space-weather event, mobile satellite communication may stop working altogether or provide weak performance. High-frequency radio communications will also likely stop working after a few days. If such a geomagnetic storm occurs, emergency communications may become inoperable. Secondary impacts, like loss of power and GNSS timing, might be problematic for terrestrial broadcasting.

Impacts on transoceanic communications cables: the geomagnetic event of March 1989 provided evidence that GICs may damage the cables that accompany the transoceanic fibers of the global communication network (Cannon 2013). It is crucial for these optical fiber cables to be constructed more sturdily since they transport most Internet and telephone traffic in addition to satellite communication (Georgescu et al. 2019).

Impact on urban transportation: solar storms might have varying effects on the transportation industry. On the one hand, a geomagnetic storm might result in greater radiation exposure for passengers and personnel on board aircraft. High-energy solar and cosmic ray particles are produced in vast numbers by nuclear reactions in the upper atmosphere as they travel toward Earth. Additionally, these particles generate secondary particles, whose flow peaks at a distance of around 18 km and is subsequently curbed by the atmosphere. At airplane cruising altitudes, the flow of ionizing radiation is approximately three hundred times larger than at sea level (Cannon 2013). The dose may increase a person's likelihood of acquiring cancer to one in a thousand in the event of a small incidence.

In avionics, electronic equipment may fail because of the intense solar particles' indirect charge on semiconductor materials. Secondary neutrons and protons are produced at ground level by the

Date	Event	Satellite	Orbit	Effects
8 March 1985	n/a	Anike D2	GEO	Outage
October 1989	CME storm	TDRS –1	GEO	Outage
July 1991	n/a	ERS –1	LEO	Instrument failure
20 January 1994	Fast solar wind stream	Anik E1: Anik E2: Intelast K	GEO	Outage
11 January 1997	Fast solar wind stream	Telstar 401	GEO	Total loss
19 May 1998	Fast solar wind stream	Galaxy 4	GEO	Total loss
15 July 2000	CME storm	Astro –D	LEO	Total loss
6 November 2001	CME storm	MAP	L2	Outage
24 October 2003	CME storm	ADEOS / MIDORI 2	LEO	Total loss
26 October 2003	CME storm	SMART - 1	HEO	Instrument failure
28 October 2003	CME storm	DRTS / Kodama	GEO	Outage(2 weeks)
14 January 2005	n/a	Intelsat 804	GEO	Total loss
15 October 2006	Fast solar wind stream	Sicral 1	GEO	Outage(Weeks)
5 April 2010	Fast solar wind stream	Galaxy 15	GEO	Outage(8 months)
13 March 2012	CME storm	Spaceway 3	GEO	Outage(hours)
7 March 2012	CME storm	SkyTerra 1	GEO	Outage(1 day)
22 March 2012	CME storm	GOES15	GEO	Outage(days)

Figure 13.2 Space weather satellite attributed outages and effects.

movement of solar energy particles (SEPs), which interact with semiconductor materials both on board and on the ground. Very little information is available on how solar energetic particles affect ground infrastructure. As will be underlined in Section 13.3, this is one of the instances when the importance of critical space infrastructures as suppliers of security, or at the very least as instruments for security decision-makers, has become clear. However, electromagnetic storms affect ground transportation systems on different planes. The GNSS system might become partly or totally useless for up to three days. Over many days, there can be multiple eruptions. After around twenty-four hours, the CME's accompanying plasma particles arrive and disrupt the ionosphere's electron density across a sizable planet region. These plasma particles result in the ionosphere developing large-scale, wave-like structures (10–1,000 km in size). Critical space infrastructure may experience scintillation from tiny constructions of less than 1 km. Scintillation in the phase critical space infrastructure disrupts the carrier phase and affects the receipt of crucial navigational data messages.

In the case of GNSS for navigation, the positioning and navigation from a single receiver will be considerably affected during the start of a solar event when the ionosphere is strongly perturbed. There may be major mistakes in position reporting since it is unlikely that all satellites will be monitored due to key space infrastructure scintillation. However, extremely severe electron density fluctuations will occur during the main event. There is a good chance that all positional and navigational solutions will be briefly but entirely lost. As a result, it is anticipated that all crucial infrastructures dependent on GNSS systems may malfunction for up to three days.

In summary, the web of interdependencies makes the modern economy especially sensitive to solar storms. Figure 13.3 depicts the overall technological effects of space weather events as suggested by the National Aeronautics and Space Administration (Zell 2015).

Although there has been an increase in public awareness of space weather and its possible effects, more research is still required to understand the concerns fully. Most of the research on the impact of space weather on nations, people, and owners and operators of infrastructure focuses on financial harm. However, there are further consequences. For instance, the OECD project on "Future Global Shocks" offered a framework for evaluating the threat of social unrest, which indicates broad dissatisfaction with the political system and manifests itself in unorthodox protest behavior (Renn et al. 2011). One potential underlying cause is identified as having inadequate infrastructure.

13.3 Interdependencies Between Urban Systems and Space Infrastructure

Regarding areas of interdependencies between critical space infrastructures and terrestrial critical or not-so-critical infrastructures that are the backbones of urban settlements, these encompass more or less all-important sectors of society (Katina et al. 2014). Sections 13.3.1–13.3.10 examine how nonfunctioning space-based technologies might affect terrestrial activities and services in smart cities.

13.3.1 Industry

According to the taxonomy of critical infrastructures developed by the European Programme for Critical Infrastructure Protection, two essential infrastructures need to be discussed: infrastructure for the energy sector and for the chemical and nuclear industries. First, the energy

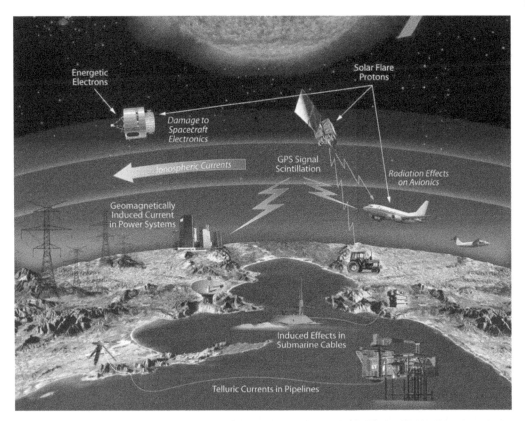

Figure 13.3 Overall technological effects of space weather events. Credit: NASA / Public Domain

infrastructure – electricity, gas, and oil – represents one of the most significant societal sectors on which our existing way of life depends. Numerous other crucial industries, including healthcare, banking, transportation, and food production, are in danger without a steady energy supply.

Space technologies like GNSS are used more often in energy infrastructure to monitor activity and keep an eye on smart grids. A complicated technology, intelligent power distribution needs accurate environmental monitoring given by GNSS and sophisticated interoperability protocols. Additionally, GNSS may monitor water reservoirs, and water flows in hydropower plants and assess the properties of certain energy sources, such as wind. For example, the 2003 power outage along the US East Coast may be an example of how remote sensing and weather satellites can be utilized to monitor environmental conditions in a specific metropolitan region.

Key space infrastructures are inextricably linked to these critical sectors in the chemical and nuclear industries. Because of this, failure indirectly impacts other crucial sectors, including: energy supply; health services; transportation due to the flow of radioactive materials; information and communication technologies (ICT); defense, public order, and national security; and access to food and water.

13.3.2 Finance

Because urban settlements are the true engines of national economies, the banking sector is an essential part of every nation-state that develops at the city level. The financial industry is vital in several ways, including: allocating capital to its most advantageous use; reducing knowledge asymmetry between economic parties; providing tools for balancing supply and demand; and creating a pricing process. To give a coherent large-scale system, the financial infrastructure – which consists of banks, insurance and finance businesses, national treasury and financial agencies, markets, trading platforms, and others – form a network of extensive connections. With space technologies, digital technologies have secured the system's ideal performance. Any danger, like the 2008 financial crisis (Calida and Katina 2015), may cascade globally due to the interconnectedness of the financial system.

It is crucial to distinguish between direct and indirect dependency concerning the relationship between the financial infrastructure and critical space infrastructures. The former describes physically linked databases and processes in which a service interruption brought on by a faulty power source renders a portion of the system unusable. Additionally, issues with communication satellites might cause problems with the banking system. Similarly, a crippled global navigation system might interfere with worldwide synchronization, leading to catastrophic losses in the financial infrastructure's ability to function and delays in the financial markets.

Space-based services that are not directly utilized by the constellation of financial systems, such as data gathered by Earth observation satellites that may be used for financial choices by insurance firms, might have an indirect influence. Additionally, the financial industry, which is essential to society, considers the early warning indicators provided by crucial space infrastructures (Krausmann et al. 2014).

13.3.3 Politics

The central government is a critical sector because of how vital it is to the operation of every nation-state. These governmental systems consider a broad range of structures, many of which are used by the public, as well as business, commercial, administrative, or recreational activities. The public administration infrastructure includes postal services, electronic components for identification, databases, access control systems, and CCTV. Satellites provide service tracking, imaging of different operational domains, and data on a nation's strategic logistics, including information on transport vehicles, critical locations, information and communications networks, demographic identification, and personal data. Thus, in the case of central administration infrastructure, critical space infrastructure is pivotal.

Less important for cities, unless they are city-states (e.g. Singapore) or are situated on borderlines (e.g. US–Mexico), is the acquisition of data on hazardous and inaccessible places and border regions. This data may be gathered via remote sensing for the defense and national security systems. In addition to GNSS services for monitoring cars and suspects or for rescue operations, satellites are indispensable to border control.

13.3.4 Transportation

In a linked world, the movement of resources and people depends on the transportation infrastructure. As transportation infrastructures become more intricate and connected with programs that address coordination, flow, and control issues, space technologies play a crucial role in laying the groundwork for a competitive transportation industry. Infrastructures for navigation and location, as well as those for weather monitoring and communications, are the key space applications employed in this industry.

The coordination and efficiency of logistics that GNSS service offers is vital to aviation, maritime, railways, and road transportation. In the air industry, GNSS services are essential for managing air traffic congestion or passenger- and luggage-related operations. In the case of maritime transportation, the GNSS offers the fastest and most accurate route, thus increasing the efficiency of transport and the trip's safety. For busy seaports, space infrastructures help to coordinate the movements of large vessels in narrow spaces, as well as automated container placement, pick-up, and the transfer of goods. In the case of road transportation, GNSS is useful for highway surveillance, vehicle location detection, and emergency operations. Equally important, railway transportation uses GNSS to track the movement of locomotives, control delays, and reduce operating costs by automatically adjusting train speed and re-routing rail traffic.

Finally, it is essential to mention the complex interdependencies between space technologies and transport infrastructures, directly or indirectly affecting other critical sectors. This includes the role of telecommunication infrastructures, the close relationship between the transportation and energy sector, and food and health, particularly in disease outbreaks and their spread across geographical space.

13.3.5 ICT/Communication

Communication satellites become essential for a city to thrive economically, socially, and culturally as well as to ensure community safety and security. Another complicated satellite constellation, wireless and wired service providers, and other technologies are required to transmit a complex universe of telecommunication and Internet services. Another component of spatial technology is bringing TV and radio information to areas that are not generally linked to landlines and other terrestrial networks. Nearly half of the world's population, especially in Latin America, Africa, and Asia, is thought to reside in places without broadband networks (Broadband Commission for Digital Development 2013).

Synchronization is crucial for communication applications. Mobile telephony and data networks are able to use GNSS to maintain synchronization, and digital broadband radio uses GPS to ensure that all radio station bits arrive at receivers in sync and with minimal delay.

13.3.6 Water Supply

The water sector is vulnerable to events ranging from contamination with deadly agents to cyber-attacks, which may cause many human illnesses or deaths. It is also a key sector especially for critical energy infrastructures and the nuclear industry, not to mention the security of citizens.

Regarding critical space infrastructure, communication satellites might be used for communications. Additionally, Earth observation satellites may be used for water supply, flood control reservoirs, flood predictions, and drinking water reserves. Indirectly, they in turn affect the food supply sector by providing information vital to a nation's survival.

13.3.7 Food Supply

In the food supply sector, space infrastructures are primarily vital for the production of food (i.e. precision agriculture). With GNSS, farmers can monitor their crops, animals, or aquaculture crops. Even in adverse conditions like rain, dust, or fog, work can be done when visibility is low thank to GPS. Precision agriculture also means a rational and needs-oriented distribution of fertilizers and pesticides and better control of the dispersion of these substances. Space technologies can provide accurate maps of areas – with precise information on crops, road infrastructure, and irrigation systems. Moreover, it can provide data on animal dangers, like outbreaks of diseases caused by particular viruses.

13.3.8 Healthcare Services

Healthcare is essential for a society's well-being because of its involvement in both the prevention and treatment of infectious disease epidemics as well as the response to

natural catastrophes (Katina et al. 2014). The networks of healthcare institutions are heavily reliant on other infrastructures, including information and telecommunications, administrative infrastructures, defense and national security, energy, food and water supply, and transportation, even when individual assets are handled locally (Karthikeyan et al. 2023).

There are interconnections between these crucial industries and space infrastructures. These involve how GNSS and GISs (geographic information systems) may manage disasters and identify air, water, and soil pollution (Katina and Gheorghe 2023). Additionally, space technologies are essential for tracking the spread of diseases during epidemics. By exploiting the localization capabilities of GPS and ensuring a timely reaction, correlated data among police, fire, and medical personnel may help save lives in the event of calamities.

Telemedicine, made possible by GIS and communication satellites, offers fresh approaches to enhancing human health. Healthcare may be provided remotely in settings with limited resources thanks to two-way communications technology, multimedia, and computer networks. Medical professionals can conduct teleconsultations and tele-diagnostics, and give remote training to share their medical experience – therefore moving the expertise rather than the individuals.

Space goods help to fuse medical data with environmental elements, assisting in the early detection of disease epidemics. Both healthcare practitioners and policy makers may benefit from multivariable interactive GIS maps that are produced by combining hospital admission information and police reports to understand the spread of health and sickness better. Medical applications now use materials and technologies that were first created for space purposes.

Another important subject in the healthcare sector is tele-epidemiology, which uses essential space infrastructure to study the transmission of diseases in humans and animals. Tele-epidemiology combines information from satellite observation and a wide range of diverse domains in the realm of space infrastructure (i.e. physical components like temperature or humidity, biological readings, health data, socioeconomic data, etc.). Space technology allows us to evaluate the mechanisms of the emergence, spread, and transmission of infectious illnesses by first looking at the linkages between climate, environment, and health, and then updating the links between infectious diseases and the habitats in which they occur. The ultimate objective is to provide public health stakeholders with tools, such as risk maps, that will enable them to foresee and monitor epidemics. Tele-epidemiology has space-based uses in emergency care and health monitoring.

13.3.9 Education

Access to education has been effectively increased by satellites especially in underdeveloped regions with little infrastructural development. One of these crucial projects is creating remote learning platforms particularly during emergencies (e.g. the COVID-19 pandemic), to provide access to courses and resources and promote contact among peers who would otherwise be unable to meet in person.

In 1975, India experimented with tele-education utilizing the India National Satellite System to broadcast tele-education and telehealth programs. India deployed the first satellite ever devoted to education in 2004. For elementary, secondary, tertiary, and specialized educational facilities, it provides broadcasts, interactive video conferencing, and web-based lessons. The African Virtual University is a satellite-based remote and e-learning effort that enables sub-Saharan African countries to offer professionals university-level education and specialized training. Similar alliances between satellite service providers and several other organizations have been established in South Africa and Brazil to increase educational accessibility.

13.3.10 Other Areas

Urban farming: the most significant population density is found in urban areas with the biggest regional food production needs. Space-based technology enables "precision agriculture" or "smart farming," helping urban farmers to effectively handle the financial, environmental, and social issues associated with food production (Gebbers and Adamchuk 2010). One essential component of precision agriculture is GNSS-based autonomous steering of agricultural equipment. Systems for controlling animals and growing specialty crops have both benefited from telemetry. The Earth observation satellite's thermal, optical, and radar imaging might provide valuable data on crops in a repeatable manner. This imaging might be used for agricultural inventory, watershed level planning, and gathering pertinent data on crop growth conditions (water, carbon, and nitrogen cycles). To boost soil productivity, it is thus valuable to receive and analyze data from several satellite platforms.

Human rights: since it is difficult to investigate and provide reports on human rights breaches, high-resolution satellite images from Earth observation satellite instruments may provide the foundation for such reports. Additionally, geospatial imaging is used particularly by non-governmental organizations (NGOs) to evaluate risks to human security, such as the gradual demolition of settlements, access to resources, and the monitoring of refugees, among others. For example, space-based technology discovered mass graves in Kosovo for the first time in 1999. Images captured from space during the second Chechen War served as proof of war crimes (Lyons 2012). Similarly, satellite images were able to show the international community the location of political jail camps in North Korea and intentional village burning in South Kordofan and Darfur, as well as mass graves (Botezatu 2022; Van 2008).

When gathering on-the-ground information is too risky or politically sensitive, especially in war zones, satellite photography may be utilized to monitor the condition of vital facilities. During the Arab Spring, residents in the impacted nations could communicate through satellite because they had access to mobile phones and the Internet. By avoiding government censorship, activists were able to update fellow citizens on their plans, human rights abuses, demonstration sites, and no-go zones.

13.4 Risk Scenarios

Critical space infrastructures differ from the other critical sectors due to the adverse environment in which they operate and the nature of attacks on their ability to function well (Georgescu et al. 2019). Consequently, three risk categories have been identified:

1) Risks related to natural phenomena, which in one form or another endanger, limit, or determine the failure of a particular technology or service, such as space weather or the re-entry into the atmosphere of any piece of debris or asteroid.
2) Risks related to the operational activities of satellites and sensors, mostly related to human errors from ground control stations, as well as various technical other issues.
3) Risks related to malicious intervention within the efficient functioning of space technologies and services, such as jamming, spoofing, using electronic weapons and lasers, as well as ASAT.

Any form of deliberate attack, such as cyberattacks, falls into this category. Figure 13.4 depicts operational risks related to natural phenomena; Figure 13.5 illustrates risks related to malicious interventions; and Figure 13.6 shows natural/environmental risks.

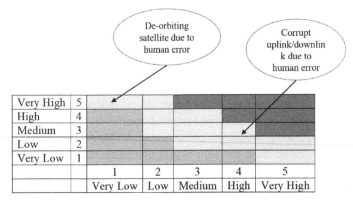

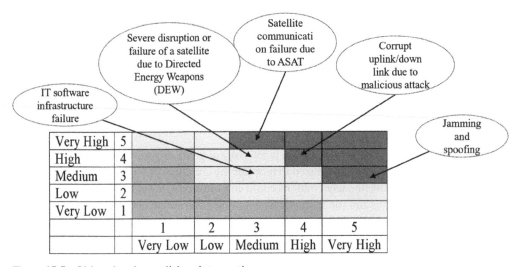

Figure 13.4 Operational risks related to natural phenomena.

Figure 13.5 Risks related to malicious interventions.

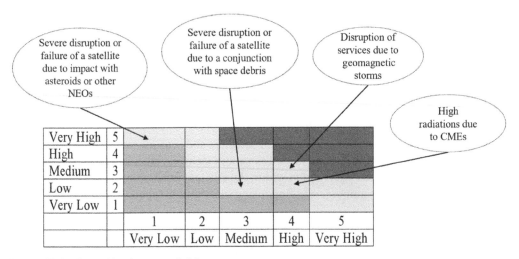

Figure 13.6 Natural/environmental risks.

13.4.1 The General Risk Multimodel

A rendering of a general risk multimodel through TopEase® software has been developed. TopEase® is a risk management tool that can be used in a wide range of cases, including risk management within critical infrastructure systems. Figure 13.7 provides a general risk multimodel. Notice that the highest risks are associated with malicious attacks, such as corrupt uplink/downlink or jamming and spoofing. At the other end of the spectrum, environmental threats such as near-Earth objects (NEOs) or space debris have lower values due to low probability. This general risk multimodel considers all dimensions of risks identified and presented earlier: operational, related to malicious intervention, and environmental. In this case, object-oriented programming, a programming paradigm based on the concept of "objects" that can contain data and code, was used to capture the challenging space environment and its significance for the resilience of vital space facilities. Efforts were then undertaken to emphasize interdependence between outer space and other crucial infrastructure sectors, including telecommunications, electricity, water, and food elements in smart cities.

Society takes the increasing number of technological developments for granted, such as in the case of PNT or GNSS services. However, the failure of such services highlights massive societal failures in critical services, such as healthcare or governmental communications. In the case of a collapse in the essential infrastructures of space, it is quite possible that businesses and governments would continue operating but at significantly reduced levels of efficiency. Airlines would have to revert to legacy systems and procedures that waste expensive jet fuel on inefficient routes. Cargo vessels entering harbors would slow to a crawl to ensure safety, or they might not be allowed to dock at all. Container cranes at ports would revert to cumbersome manual operations. Logistical supply-chain management systems would lose or degrade their ability to track the flow of parts to their factories and products from warehouses. Construction and mining projects would become

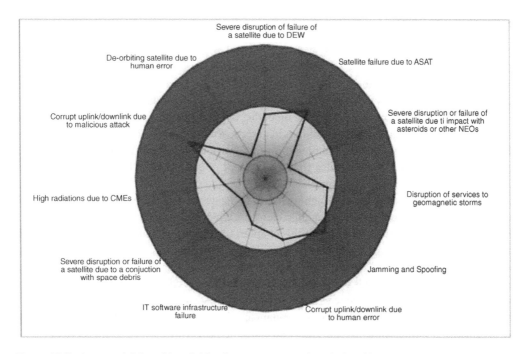

Figure 13.7   A general risk multimodel for the space–smart city relationship.

delayed as expensive manual labor replaced systems used to automate surveying, regrading, earth moving, and asset tracking. Farmers would lose the ability to operate twenty-four hours a day using automated machinery, and as a result, they may not be able to harvest all their crops before they spoil in the fields (Botezatu 2022; Georgescu et al. 2019; Nichols et al. 2022).

Furthermore, if a significant event – such as an earthquake, tsunami, forest fire, or other natural catastrophe – occurs on that same day, losing access to remote sensing satellites for a day can be crucial for border security and news reporting. It would be difficult to characterize that significant occurrence and thus to evaluate the damage that would negatively affect the rescue operations. Space essential infrastructures are subject to distinctly different hazards than other sectors' crucial technologies, necessitating a different management approach and thinking style. For example, according to Kelso (2007), there were 2,864 operational satellites in all Earth orbits as of January 22, 2007. Two thirds of all payloads in low-Earth orbit, or 1,899 payloads, are at risk of being hit by debris from ASAT tests.

13.4.2 Possible Correlations Between Fragmentation Events and Smart Cities

The analysis of ASAT tests suggests that the fragmentation of objects in orbit could have impacted many critical infrastructures, including related services in smart cities. Satellites disintegrate as they re-enter the atmosphere, but some of the debris may be heat-resistant and continue to fall to Earth, increasing the likelihood of destruction. Unfortunately, because the density of Earth's atmosphere is continually changing, it is complicated to anticipate exactly where debris will impact.

Each year during the previous ten years, around a hundred satellites and rocket bodies with a combined mass of about 150 tons have re-entered Earth's atmosphere. Even though the exact mass is unclear, the re-entries of the two CZ-5B core stages in 2020 and 2021 were the largest uncontrolled re-entries since Salyut 7 in 1991 and will be the heaviest until 2025.

13.4.3 A System of Systems Approach to Security System Architectures

At both the discursive and operational levels in cities and outer space, techniques have been used to attempt to control and manage security. The former indicates the politicization of the threat, which makes the issue at hand "visible" and threatens to make it easier to dispatch funding and access operational resources to solve it. The latter implies setting boundaries so that the identified threat can be contained and addressed. The modeling of the outer space events described in this research has demonstrated that vulnerabilities in outer space could trickle down to almost all critical sectors of smart cities. As the examples show, how various data flows are observed, tracked, separated, and addressed demonstrates that the concept of containment is taking more subtle forms of manifestation in practical terms. To borrow an idea from environmental criminology, containment of threats is less about designing fences and gates and more about finding the proper algorithm that sorts and comprises the malign elements while allowing the "good" flows to pass.

As shown by the scenarios examined in this chapter, neither individual nation-states nor local authorities fully comprehend the effects of a significant interruption of space services. Control rooms in smart cities and in ground stations do not communicate with each other. Identifying which space infrastructure needs to increase its level of resilience, conducting a thorough analysis of security-related critical dependencies of our urban-specific societies and economies to particular space assets, and evaluating the level of redundancies already in place are some steps we could take to reduce our vulnerability to shortages and disruptions of critical space-based services.

A "security-by-design" strategy would encourage taking security needs into account for crucial city- and national-level systems . Additionally, the city-level security criteria should be considered when designing new space infrastructures or updating old ones and determining the acceptable vulnerability levels of new services. For instance, a set of minimum-security standards that must be satisfied while building satellites and ground components would lessen their susceptibility to hostile operations, such as cyberattacks. The development of such a set of universal basic security standards would need to be closely coordinated by nation-states and municipal governments.

Built-in security systems architecture resilience should involve all value chains, from creating capabilities for identifying and reducing present threats to establishing dynamic reaction capabilities in case the risks eventuate. In this case, resilience should start with the raw materials used in various technologies and end with the construction of resilient services for security and defense.

All these ideas, nevertheless, could find fertile land when thinking of smart cities and outer space services as bound together by a "system-of-systems" epistemology. Security system architectures are to expand their meaning into a more fluid, boundless, and rapidly changing environment. Moreover, the relationship between all these elements of the system of systems creates more than the sum of its parts.

Smart cities thus either make acquisitions from various companies or, in the best-case scenario, develop their own cloud-based software solutions. This implies that metropolitan authorities are limited to acting as middlemen between ground station owners and customers. Thus, access to critical information may be impeded by this chain of command. Given how many crucial infrastructure sectors rely on this constellation of commercial entities that solely follow market norms, this is a missing link from an operational, tactical, and primarily strategic perspective that should be considered.

13.5 Concluding Remarks

While advancements in space shift the focus from a military, government-centric perspective of security, aspects of governance are also be reinvented, marking the shift toward commercial interests. Governance as a process of consensus-making among all stakeholders thus becomes a quest for finding the middle ground between strengthening national sovereignty and promoting economic benefits of increasingly fragmented commercial actors. Security discussions have become more complex and multifaceted. Using the systems-of-systems framework, these topics of interest could be analyzed and understood better. Firstly, in terms of technologies developed, at the pace of the current boom, humanity will soon have fully automated systems in place, complex on-board satellite processing capabilities, or autonomous satellite-to-satellite communications. Nevertheless, these technologies that integrate artificial intelligence and machine learning elements introduce new vulnerabilities and are based on complex algorithms that reflect how societal perspectives are formed. Therefore, it is essential to stress how language and imagination create the basis for future algorithms and decisions in this realm.

Moreover, the cyber aspects of warfare are becoming prominent. This adds to the already growing capabilities of electronic warfare and is likely to expand even more. These typologies of hybrid warfare could impact both outer space and cities. The governance of security is a systemic socio-spatial process that connects material and non-material systems, including institutions and practices, along with various logics, intentions, perceptions, and histories. The relationship between parts of these systems plays a great role in diminishing the disruptive effects of the domino effects that could have very diverse causes. The current research has aimed to disentangle and highlight a part of this process, looking not only at the governance of security but also going deeper into the process of interactions through the laws, norms, power, and language of an organized society. The research has thus tried to un-black box the intricacies of contemporary security governance to offer ideas for improvement.

As a result, this study adds to the continuing discussions about the spatialization of security procedures and advances academic research in urban and space governance studies. Urban security, as a new spatial logic of flow and connectivity, represents a process where urbanized forms of outer politics and more spatialized forms of urban governance are mutually constitutive and a domain in which gaming can play a more significant role in creating resilient cities. Furthermore, complex system governance (Katina et al. 2021; Keating and Katina 2019; Keating et al. 2014, 2022) provides a fertile ground for the concatenations among outer space, smart cities, and governance.

13.6 Exercises

1 Discuss the need for a smart city in the twenty-first-century landscape.
2 Develop an illustrating model of interdependence between urban and space systems.
3 Discuss the importance of a system-of-systems approach in dealing with risks and vulnerabilities in space systems.
4 Discuss the importance of a system-of-systems approach in dealing with risks and vulnerabilities in a smart city.
5 Discuss the possible contributions of governance to smart city and critical space infrastructures.

References

Australian Space Weather Forecasting Centre. (2022). *Power failure in Canada during 1989.* c=AU; co=Commonwealth of Australia; ou=Department of Sustainability, Environment, Water, Population and Communities; ou=Central Office; ou=Bureau of Meteorology; ou=Space Weather Services. https://www.sws.bom.gov.au/Educational/1/3/12.

Botezatu, U.E. (2022). Defensible smart cities: A system-of-systems approach for vertically integrated spaces. Dissertation, Universitatea Politehnica Bucureşti. https://upb.ro/orase-inteligente-aparabile-o-abordare-a-sistemului-de-sisteme-pentru-spatii-integrate-vertical-defensible-smart-cities-a-system-of-systems-approach-for-vertically-integrated-spaces-botezatu-ulp.

Broadband Commission for Digital Development. (2013). *The State of Broadband 2013: Universalizing Broadband.* International Telecommunication Union. https://ifap.ru/library/book539.pdf.

Calida, B.Y. and Katina, P.F. (2015). Modelling the 2008 financial economic crisis: Triggers, perspectives and implications from systems dynamics. *International Journal of System of Systems Engineering* 6(4): 273–301. https://doi.org/10.1504/IJSSE.2015.075487.

Cannon, P. (2013). *Extreme space weather: impacts on engineered systems and infrastructure.* Royal Academy of Engineering. https://www.raeng.org.uk/publications/reports/space-weather-full-report.

CENTRA Technologies. (2011). Geomagnetic storms (IFP/WKP/FGS(2011)4). Organisation for Economic Co-operation and Development. https://www.oecd.org/gov/risk/46891645.pdf.

Faria, L.D.A., Silvestre, C.A.D.M., and Correia, M.A.F. (2016). GPS-dependent systems: Vulnerabilities to electromagnetic attacks. *Journal of Aerospace Technology and Management* 8(4): Article 4. https://jatm.com.br/jatm/article/view/632.

Gebbers, R. and Adamchuk, V.I. (2010). Precision agriculture and food security. *Science*, 327(5967): 828–831. https://www.science.org/doi/10.1126/science.1183899.

Georgescu, A., Gheorghe, A.V., Piso, M.-I et al. (2019). *Critical Space Infrastructures: Risk, Resilience and Complexity*. Springer International Publishing. https://www.springer.com/us/book/9783030126032.

IFP Energies Nouvelles. (2018). Smart city: Energy challenges facing sustainable cities. IFPEN. https://www.ifpenergiesnouvelles.com/article/smart-city-energy-challenges-facing-sustainable-cities.

Ioannides, R.T., Pany, T., and Gibbons, G. (2016). Known vulnerabilities of global navigation satellite systems, status, and potential mitigation techniques. *Proceedings of the IEEE*, 104(6): 1174–1194. https://doi.org/10.1109/JPROC.2016.2535898.

Kappenman, J. (2010). *Geomagnetic Storms and Their Impacts on the U.S. Power Grid (Meta-R-319)*. Oak Ridge National Laboratory. https://irp.fas.org/eprint/geomag.pdf.

Karthikeyan, P., Katina, P.F., and Anandaraj, S.P. (2023). *Approaches to Data Analytics and Internet of Things Through Digital Twin*. IGI Global. https://doi.org/10.4018/978-1-6684-5722-1.

Katina, P.F. and Gheorghe, A.V. (2023). *Blockchain-enabled Resilience: An Integrated Approach for Disaster Supply Chain and Logistics Management* (1st ed.). CRC Press.

Katina, P.F., Pinto, C.A., Bradley, J.M. et al. (2014). Interdependency-induced risk with applications to healthcare. *International Journal of Critical Infrastructure Protection* 7(1): 12–26. https://doi.org/10.1016/j.ijcip.2014.01.005.

Katina, P.F., Pyne, J.C., Keating, C.B. et al. (2021). Complex system governance as a framework for asset management. *Sustainability* 13(15): Article 15. https://doi.org/10.3390/su13158502.

Keating, C.B. and Katina, P.F. (2019). Complex system governance: Concept, utility, and challenges. *Systems Research and Behavioral Science* 36(5): 687–705. https://onlinelibrary.wiley.com/doi/10.1002/sres.2621.

Keating, C.B., Katina, P.F., and Bradley, J.M. (2014). Complex system governance: Concept, challenges, and emerging research. *International Journal of System of Systems Engineering* 5(3): 263–288. https://www.inderscienceonline.com/doi/abs/10.1504/IJSSE.2014.065756.

Keating, C.B., Katina, P.F., Chesterman, C.W. (eds.). (2022). *Complex System Governance: Theory and Practice*. Springer International Publishing. https://link.springer.com/book/10.1007/978-3-030-93852-9.

Kelso, T.S. (2007). Analysis of the 2007 Chinese ASAT test and the impact of its debris on the space environment. In: *Proceedings of the Advanced Maui Optical and Space Surveillance Technologies Conference* (ed. S. Ryan ed.) The Maui Economic Development Board. https://celestrak.org/publications/AMOS/2007/AMOS-2007.pdf.

Krausmann, E., Felton, C., Murtagh, W. et al. (2014). *Space Weather and Financial Systems: Findings and Outlook*. European Commission Publications Office. https://publications.jrc.ec.europa.eu/repository/bitstream/JRC92297/lbna26882enn.pdf.

Lyons, J. (2012). Documenting violations of international humanitarian law from space: A critical review of geospatial analysis of satellite imagery during armed conflicts in Gaza (2009), Georgia (2008), and Sri Lanka (2009). *International Review of the Red Cross* 94(886): 739–763. https://doi.org/10.1017/S1816383112000756.

Mattern, S. (2021). *A City is Not a Computer: Other Urban Intelligences*. Princeton University Press. https://press.princeton.edu/books/paperback/9780691208053/a-city-is-not-a-computer.

National Research Council. (2008). *Severe Space Weather Events: Understanding Societal and Economic Impacts: A Workshop Report*. National Academies Press. https://doi.org/10.17226/12507.

Nichols, P.R.K., Carter, C.M., Hood, J.P. et al. (2022). *Space Systems: Emerging Technologies and Operations*. New Prairie Press. https://kstatelibraries.pressbooks.pub/spacesystems.

North American Electric Reliability Corporation. (2010). High-impact, low-frequency event risk to the North American bulk power system: a jointly-commissioned summary report of the North American Electric Reliability Corporation and the US Department of Energy's November 2009 Workshop. Department of Energy. https://www.energy.gov/ceser/articles/high-impact-low-frequency-risk-north-american-bulk-power-system-june-2010.

North American Electric Reliability Corporation. (2012). Effects of geomagnetic disturbances on the bulk power system. North American Electric Reliability Corporation. https://www.oecd.org/gov/risk/46891645.pdf.

Renn, O., Jovanovic, A., and Schröter, R. (2011). *Future Global Shocks: Social Unrest*. Organisation for Economic Co-operation and Development. https://pdf4pro.com/amp/view/oecd-ifp-project-on-future-global-shocks-cfbc9.html.

Steinberger, J. (2008). A survey of satellite communications system vulnerabilities. Thesis, Air Force Institute of Technology. https://scholar.afit.edu/etd/2729,

Van, W.J.-A. (2008). Space for peace? The use of space technology to monitor conflict trends and human security in Africa. *Conflict Trends* 2008(4): 12–17. https://journals.co.za/doi/10.10520/EJC16031.

Zell, H. (March 2, 2015). *Technological Affects of Space Weather Events*. NASA. http://www.nasa.gov/mission_pages/sunearth/science/Tech-affects.html.

14

Gamification for Resilience

A Research Agenda

14.1   Introduction

Undoubtedly, humans are living in a moment when they praise themselves with the belief of being well-informed, intelligent, wiser, and capable of making even better judgments – and yet incapable of explaining the lack of (un)resilient cities. As the twenty-first century unfolds, catastrophic and unforeseen events such as climate change, disease pandemics, economic fluctuations, and terrorist attacks are playing out on a global scale. Moreover, urban risk and vulnerability levels keep increasing due to the number of people living in the cities (Mitroliou and Kavanaugh 2015). And while there is no lack of methodological approaches (see Jackson 2000, 2003, 2019), each methodology is developed with the context of the problematic situation and the purpose of the analysis. Well, the landscape of the twenty-first century is rapidly changing and challenging those who take the lead in developing sustainable and resilient habitable cities.

These practitioners must contend with increasingly complex and interdependent critical systems. A concise summary of the new challenging world involves (Keating and Katina 2012, 2016, 2019):

- *The increasing complexity of systems and their problems:* the present and future world of the systems engineering practitioner will be marked by more highly interconnected systems, emergence in their behavior/structure/performance, higher levels of uncertainty, incomplete/shifting/fallible knowledge, and exponentially increasing information.
- *The contextual influences impacting system design, execution, and development:* every system is influenced by unique circumstances, factors, patterns, stakeholders, and conditions that enable (and constrain) the structure, behavior, and performance of a system.
- *The ambiguity in system definition, understanding, and predictability:* lack of clarity in systems and their context creates conditions where historically stable approaches and expectations are questionable for continued relevance in producing successful outcomes.
- *The holistic nature of complex systems:* in addition to technical (or technological) aspects of a system, there is an increasing need to consider the human/social, organizational/managerial, policy, political, and information aspects of systems. This results in the "joint optimization" of the technical and social subsystems that constitute the totality of our systems and is critical for complete system development.

Climate change, housing, overcrowding, poverty, sewerage problems, slums and squatter settlements, transport, trash disposal, unemployment, urban crimes, urban pollution, urban sprawl, and

Gamification for Resilience: Resilient Informed Decision-Making, First Edition.
Adrian V. Gheorghe and Polinpapilinho F. Katina.
© 2023 John Wiley & Sons, Inc. Published 2023 by John Wiley & Sons, Inc.

water issues, to name a few, are examples of the several risks and vulnerabilities facing densely populated areas around the world. The terms "resilient city" and "city resilience" have emerged in recent years as a possible response to the problems mentioned earlier (Rockefeller Foundation 2014, 2015). The present research suggests using gamification's "serious gaming," "SimCity 2013®," and a quantification platform, "ReIDMP," (i.e. Resilience Informed Decision-Making Process) to understand better and guide sustainable and resilient city development. In an attempt to classify serious games, five areas are suggested (Laamarti et al. 2014):

- **Activity:** refers to the type of activity performed by the player as required by the game – a function performed by the player as a response and/or input to the game, including physical exertion, physiological, mental, or interpersonal communication.
- **Application area:** refers to the different applications domains relevant to serious games, including education and advertisement.
- **Environment:** refers to the environment of the digital game and can be a combination of several criteria, including 2D/3D, virtual, or mixed reality.
- **Interaction style:** refers to whether the player's interaction with the game is done using traditional interfaces such as a keyboard, mouse, or Joystick or using some intelligent interfaces such as a brain interface, eye gaze, movement tracking, and tangible interfaces.
- **Modularity:** refers to the channel by which information is communicated from the computer to the human(s) participating in the game and is the sensory modalities the player experiences in the game, including visual, auditory, and haptic.

Each area has specific applications as well as advantages and disadvantages. Table 14.1 provides an overall classification of the taxonomy of serious games, as adopted and modified from Laamarti et al. (2014).

14.2 Research Synopsis

Thus far, the present authors have illustrated a need for new and innovative approaches to embedding gaming in the decision-making for developing resilient cities. In summary, the practice of resilient city development, while desirable and capable as-is, can benefit from the ideas of gamification, especially in dealing with risks and vulnerabilities in the ever-shifting landscape of

Table 14.1 A taxonomy of serious games.

Activity	Application Area	Environment	Interaction Style	Modularity
Physical exertion	Education	Social presence	Keyboard/mouse	Visual
Physiological	Well-being	Mixed reality	Movement tracking	Auditory
Mental	Training	Virtual environment	Tangible interface	Heptic
	Advertisement	2D/3D	Brain interface	Smell
	Interpersonal communication	Location awareness	Eye gaze	
	Healthcare	Mobility	Joystick	
		Online		

twenty-first-century cities. And while studies that focus on risk (i.e. rapid risk assessment) and vulnerability (vulnerability assessment) are extensive, there remains a scarcity of literature discussing how gamification could be combined with risk, and vulnerability, to make better decisions and aid in the development of resilient cities – *a gap we have addressed in the present volume.*

However, at the most fundamental level, rigorous research must establish a paradigm with which knowledge claims can be contrasted (Churchman 1968; Warfield 1976). Despite this claim, the literature suggests that there isn't one widely accepted approach to the knowledge claim (Burrell and Morgan 1979; Flood and Carson 1993). As it turns out, this is a discussion related to philosophy and undoubtedly worth exploring, given the relevance of risk and vulnerabilities in twenty-first-century cities. Additionally, if one takes the view of Burrell and Morgan (1979) and the extensions of Flood and Carson (1993), in that case, the key issues are ontology, epistemology, methodology, and nature of human beings, which are also related to knowledge claims. Ontology deals with how an observer views reality. Epistemology deals with how one obtains and communicates knowledge. Nature of man deals with how man is described concerning environment/systems. Methodology deals with attempts to investigate and acquire knowledge in the world in which we find ourselves.

14.2.1 Methodology

A methodology involves procedures for gaining knowledge about systems and structured processes involved in intervening in and changing systems (Jackson 1991). Following Burrell and Morgan (1979), methodological approaches can be categorized into two opposing extremes: *idiographic* and *nomothetic*. An **idiographic** view of a methodology supports subjectivity in the research of complex systems, as suggested by Flood and Carson (1993, p. 248):

> *the principal concern is to understand the way an individual creates, modifies, and interprets the world. The experiences are seen as unique and particular to the individual rather than general and universal. External reality is questioned. An emphasis is placed on the relativistic nature of the world to such an extent that it may be perceived as not amenable to study using the ground rules of the natural sciences. Understanding can be obtained only by acquiring firsthand knowledge of the subject under investigation.*

The opposing view of methodology is **nomothetic**. A nomothetic view of methodology supports the traditional scientific method – i.e. reductionism (Churchman, 1968, 1971). Reductionism is described as (Flood and Carson 1993, pp. 247–248):

> *analyze relationships and regularities between the elements of which the world is composed ... identification of the elements and the way relationships can be expressed. The methodological issues are concepts themselves, their measurement, and the identification of underlying themes. In essence, there is a search for universal laws that govern the reality that is being observed. Methodologies are based on systematic processes and techniques.*

There is no shortage of methodologies to intervene in and change systems. Examples include Systems Analysis, Systems Engineering, Operations Research, Complex System Governance, Critical Systems Heuristics, Interactive Planning, Organizational Cybernetics, Organizational Learning, Sociotechnical Systems, Soft Systems Methodology, Strategic Assumption Surfacing and Testing, Systems Dynamics, Systems of Systems Engineering Methodology, and Total systems

Intervention. The reader is directed elsewhere to proponents of these methodologies, classifications, descriptions, advantages, and disadvantages (Jackson 2000, 2003, 2019). Each methodology is developed and grounded in certain core conceptual foundations. Moreover, selecting a method is based on the context of a problematic situation and the purpose of analysis (Katina 2015).

In this regard, a key research question is proposed: *What is the methodological basis for gamification for the resilience of a city?* Again, while the literature that discusses risk, vulnerability, and gamification is extensive, there remains a scarcity of literature discussing how gamification could be combined with risk and vulnerability to help make better decisions in developing resilient cities. A need to address pressing issues in cities is already established. And yet, current methodologies, as suggested in the present literature, are insufficient in addressing present challenges – let alone possible future issues. Moreover, the present research lends itself toward a nomothetic approach to methodology. However, gamification for resilience research also includes aspects of idiography, as much as it embraces subjectivity in complex situations, especially when considering elements of risk and resilience perception.

14.2.2 Epistemology

An epistemological aspect of research deals with how a researcher (i.e. a system observer) begins understanding problematic situations and communicating knowledge to fellow researchers. This dimension provides the form of knowledge, how knowledge is acquired, and what is considered to be "true" or "false" (Burrell and Morgan 1979). There are two opposite extremes of epistemology: positivism and anti-positivism. A **positivistic** approach to research indicates that "knowledge is hard, real, and capable of being transmitted in a tangible form" (Flood and Carson 1993, p. 247). This stance of epistemology supports the idea that it is possible to explain and predict what happens in the social world by searching for regularities and causal relationships between its constituent elements. The growth of knowledge is essentially a cumulative process in which new insights are added to the existing stock of knowledge, and false hypotheses are eliminated (Burrell and Morgan, 1979). In the **anti-positivism** view, "knowledge is soft, more subjective, spiritual, or even transcendental – based on experience, insight, and essentially of a personal nature" (Flood and Carson 1993, p. 247).

In this regard, a key research question is proposed: *What is the epistemological basis for gamification for the resilience of a city?* Again, while the literature that discusses risk, vulnerability, and gamification is extensive, there remains a scarcity of literature discussing the epistemology of gamification for resilient city development.

However, the topics of gamification and resilience can be subjective, and, as such, the research might be rendered as anti-positivistic. Indeed, this is the case when people hold different views on whether gaming is necessary for creating a resilient city and, if they agree, what gaming approach should be taken to develop resilient cities. Moreover, the present text also contains aspects of positivism since the presented knowledge is hard and capable of being transmitted in a tangible form – another ReIDMP case could be undertaken for a different location.

14.2.3 Ontology

Ontology deals with the existence of entities and how such entities can be grouped based on similarities and differences. Moreover, ontology can also describe how "an observer views the nature of reality or how concretely the external world might be understood" (Katina et al. 2014, p. 49). Two opposite extremes of ontology are *realism* and *nominalism*. Based on Burrell and Morgan (1979) and extrapolations from Flood and Carson (1993), **realism** is captured as "external to the individual imposing itself on individual consciousness; it is a given 'out there'" (p. 247). Realism suggests that reality is objective.

On the other hand, **nominalism** describes reality as a product of individual consciousness. More significantly, nominalism ascribes to the assumption of individual cognition. Under nominalism, "the social world external to individual cognition is made up of nothing more than names, concepts and labels which are used to structure reality" (Burrell and Morgan 1979, p. 4). The utility of "concepts," "labels," and "names" is based on their convenience as tools that can make sense of and describe reality (Flood and Carson 1993).

In this regard, a key research question is proposed: *What is the ontological basis for gamification for the resilience of a city?* Again, while the literature that discusses risk, vulnerability, and gamification is extensive, there remains a scarcity of literature discussing the ontology of gamification for resilient city development.

A case can be made that realism is the approach for the present research. For example, the suggested ReIDMP model contains aspects of objectivity. However, a case can also be made for the nominalistic view of the present research, especially in the established estimations for resilience. The city's reality is conceived, simulated, developed, and interpreted based on stakeholders. However, in as much as these ideas are partially dependent on the cognition of observers (researchers), one should make the mistake of assuming that, for example, gamification for resilience is a fallacy.

14.2.4 Nature of Human Beings

The nature of human beings is the final component of research consideration. This aspect provides a stance on humans and their activities in society. It has been suggested that two opposite extremes of *determinism* and *voluntarism* can describe the nature of human beings (Burrell and Morgan 1979; Flood and Carson 1993). A **deterministic** view suggests that humans are "mechanistic, determined by situations in the external world; human beings and their experiences are products of their environment; they are conditioned by external circumstances" (Flood and Carson 1993, p. 247). The **voluntaristic** view suggests that humans are "completely autonomous and free-willed" (Burrell and Morgan 1979, p. 6) and that therefore they have a "creative role [in their environment] and [can] create their environment" (Flood and Carson 1993, p. 247).

In this regard, a key research question is proposed: *What are the human nature underpinnings for gamification for the resilience of a city?* Again, while the literature that discusses risk, vulnerability, and gamification is extensive, there remains a scarcity of literature discussing the nature of humans in gamification for resilient city development.

At this point in this research, it should be evident that the present authors took human beings as being voluntaristic. They are endowed with the ability to do something regarding the development of resilient cities. They are responsible for developing methodologies, methods, frameworks, models, and techniques that shape research and intervene in their cities. However, there is a case that humans are deterministic when dealing with resilient city development. In this case, human beings can be seen as conditioned by external circumstances and incapable of truly developing cities that can withstand any risks and threats. This view is not far-fetched given increasing and unprecedented threats created by humans (Arbesman 2016; Bostrom 2015; Diamond 1999; Harari 2017; Osterholm and Olshaker 2017) along with human incapability to control natural hazards (e.g. solar flares).

In the end, these philosophical issues underpin research and solutions that could be undertaken in gamification for the resilience of cities in the twenty-first century and beyond.

14.3   Research Agenda

In the present text, we have attempted to offer a, perhaps crude, viewpoint that could be used to address the development of resilient cities through gamification with the support of several assessments (i.e. rapid risk assessment, vulnerability assessment, integrated regional risk assessment, etc.). Moreover, the results of case applications (Norfolk and Portland) indicate the efficacy of the ReIDMP model.

Further research is suggested along the stream of practical tools and case applications. More importantly, it is only at this point (and considering philosophical underpinnings) that one might realize that there are many more questions than answers – the challenge of creating traction as a theoretically and conceptually grounded approach to improving city resilience through gamification.

Furthermore, research in gamification for city resilience is certainly not confined to a prescribed approach or privileged to any intellectual school of thought. This section provides one additional suggestion to organize development further. These developments are based on previous work on emerging knowledge (Keating 2014; Keating and Katina 2011; Keating et al. 2022). Figure 14.1 provides a framework for the holistic development of gamification for a city's resilience.

Figure 14.1 suggests a purposeful consideration and balanced development along several interrelated lines of inquiry: philosophical, theoretical, axiological, methodological, axiomatic, method, and application. Even though convincing arguments might be made for one development area having priority over another, what is absolute is that the exclusion of any of the areas will not support holistic field development:

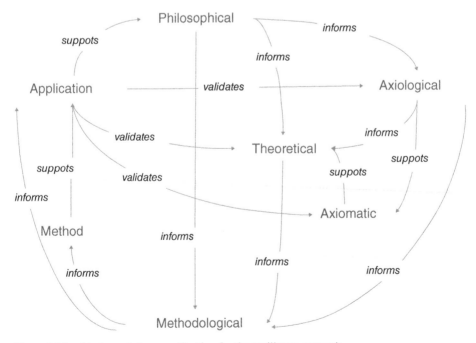

Figure 14.1   A balanced view gamification for the resilience research.

- *Philosophical*. Development is directed at establishing a theoretically consistent articulation of gamification for the resilient city. The emerging system of values and beliefs providing grounding for theoretical development is the primary contribution of this area. A strong, coherent, and articulated philosophical grounding is essential to provide a foundation upon which other field developments can be consistently based.

- *Theoretical*. Development focused on explaining gamification for the resilient city and developing explanatory models and testable conceptual frameworks. The range of theoretical developments advances the understanding of resilience through gamification. The theoretical development of gamification for resilience must be actively pursued and not left to chance.

- *Axiological*. Development that establishes the underlying value, value-judgment frameworks, and belief propositions fundamental to understanding the variety of perspectives informing gamification for the resilient city. The absence of axiological considerations for the development of gamification for resilience fails to recognize the important value foundations upon which other development areas can utilize as a foundational reference point.

- *Methodological*. Development is undertaken to establish theoretically informed frameworks that provide high-level guidance for designing, analyzing, deploying, and evolving gamified resilience. Generalizable methodologies transition from the conceptual foundations (philosophical, theoretical, and axiological) to applications that address gamification for resilience along with any emergent issues.

- *Axiomatic*. Development of the existing and emerging principles, concepts, and laws that define gamification for resilience and constitute the "taken for granted" knowledge upon which the phenomenon rests. This also includes integrating knowledge from other informing and related fields/disciplines. For b gamification for resilience, the grounding in the axioms and supporting propositions of General System Theory (Klier et al. 2022; von Bertalanffy 1968) might provide a strong starting point for further axiomatic development.

- *Method*. Development focused on generating the specific models, technologies, standards, processes, and tools for gamification for a city's resilience. This is the development of practitioners' supporting toolsets and capabilities. Based on the solid conceptual foundations provided by other field development areas, the methods should be compatible with the field's philosophical, methodological, axiomatic, and axiological predispositions. This approach encourages consistency in the development of methods.

- *Application*. This emphasizes the advancement of the practice of gamification for a city's resilience through the deployment of conceptually sound technologies and methods. Applications not rooted in the conceptual foundations of the field are not likely to be either consistent or conceptually congruent with the deeper underpinnings upon which the field rests. As such, applications void of the field's philosophical, theoretical, and axiomatic foundations are not likely to produce the intended utility for which they have been designed.

Even though cogent arguments might be made for one development area having priority over another, what is absolute is that excluding any of the areas will not support holistic field development. Moreover, in this high-level change, specific questions might be crafted based on the needs of stakeholders. For example, the academically inclined might be interested in frameworks that can be constructed (or derived) from existing methodologies (e.g. soft systems methodology and systems of systems engineering) to guide gamification for a city's resilience. On the other hand, policy-makers might be interested in the implications of, for example, voluntarism/determinism before and during gamification for a city's resilience as well as tools for governance leading to long-term sustainable city resilience. For example, simply having the ReIDMP model does not mean effective control, communication, coordination, and integration of complex and interdependent systems in a resilient city (Katina et al. 2014, 2021; Keating and Katina 2019; Keating et al. 2022). These research questions might be addressed holistically and at multiple levels involving a range of technology/technical, organizational/managerial, human/social, and political/policy issues, as well as their interrelationships.

14.4 Concluding Remarks

It is indisputable that having an innovative approach to resilient city development is necessary; however, what might be disputable is the use of gaming in the development of resilient cities. And although present researchers, through this volume, suggest that gamification for resilience is necessary and, indeed, the way forward, much research remains.

It would be "easy" to focus on the limitations of the present research, including the development of practical tools and case applications – all worthwhile endeavors. However, rigorous research is the basis for knowledge claims. In this case, a knowledge claim discussion can't escape the philosophical adventures, which tend to include issues of ontology, epistemology, methodology, and the nature of humans. This discussion is the basis for the proposed research framework for purposeful resilient city development using gamification. Several interrelated lines of inquiry are offered, including philosophical, theoretical, axiological, methodological, axiomatic, method, and application. It is via the understanding of these deep conceptual and consistent underpinnings that knowledge can be accrued. As we conclude this research, one might as well read this research with a sense of optimism regarding the "storms" that cities are facing; however, we have a feeling that the storms are just beginning.

14.5 Exercises

1 Discuss the nature methodology that can be developed to aid in evaluating and developing resilient cities.
2 Discuss the nature epistemology that can be developed to aid in evaluating and developing resilient cities.
3 Discuss the nature ontology that can be developed to aid in evaluating and developing resilient cities.
4 Discuss the nature of man that can be developed to aid in evaluating and developing resilient cities.
5 Discuss the nature axiology that can be developed to aid in evaluating and developing resilient cities.

References

Arbesman, S. (2016). *Overcomplicated: Technology at the Limits of Comprehension*. Current.

Bostrom, N. (2015). *Superintelligence*. Oxford University Press.

Burrell, G. and Morgan, G. (1979). *Sociological Paradigms and Organisational Analysis*. Ashgate Publishing.

Churchman, C.W. (1968). *Challenge to Reason*. McGraw–Hill.

Churchman, C.W. (1971). *The Design of Inquiring Systems*. Basic Books.

Diamond, J.M. (1999). *Guns, Germs, and Steel: The Fates of Human Societies* (1st ed.). W.W. Norton & Company.

Flood, R.L. and Carson, E.R. (1993). *Dealing with Complexity: An Introduction to the Theory and Application of Systems Science.* Plenum Press.

Harari, Y.N. (2017). *Homo deus: A Brief History of Tomorrow* (Illustrated ed.). Harper.

Jackson, M.C. (1991). *Systems Methodology for the Management Sciences.* Plenum Press.

Jackson, M.C. (2000). *Systems Approaches to Management.* Springer.

Jackson, M.C. (2003). *Systems Thinking: Creative Holism for Managers.* Wiley.

Jackson, M.C. (2019). *Critical Systems Thinking and the Management of Complexity* (1st ed.). Wiley.

Katina, P.F. (2015). *Systems Theory-based Construct for Identifying Metasystem Pathologies for Complex System Governance* PhD., Old Dominion University. http://search.proquest.com.proxy.lib.odu.edu/docview/1717329758/abstract/29A520C8C0A744A2PQ/2.

Katina, P.F., Keating, C.B., and Jaradat, R.M. (2014). System requirements engineering in complex situations. *Requirements Engineering* 19(1): 45–62. https://doi.org/10.1007/s00766-012-0157-0.

Katina, P.F., Pyne, J.C., Keating, C.B., and Komljenovic, D. (2021). Complex system governance as a framework for asset management. *Sustainability* 13(15). Article 15 https://doi.org/10.3390/su13158502.

Keating, C. B. (2014). Governance implications for meeting challenges in the system of systems engineering field. *2014 9th International Conference on System of Systems Engineering (SOSE),* 154–159. IEEE. https://doi.org/10.1109/SYSOSE.2014.6892480.

Keating, C.B. and Katina, P.F. (2011). Systems of systems engineering: Prospects and challenges for the emerging field. *International Journal of System of Systems Engineering* 2 (2/3): 234–256. https://doi.org/10.1504/IJSSE.2011.040556.

Keating, C.B. and Katina, P.F. (2012). Prevalence of pathologies in systems of systems. *International Journal of System of Systems Engineering* 3(3/4): 243–267. https://doi.org/10.1504/IJSSE.2012.052688.

Keating, C.B. and Katina, P.F. (2016). Complex system governance development: A first generation methodology. *International Journal of System of Systems Engineering* 7(1/2/3): 43–74. https://doi.org/10.1504/IJSSE.2016.076127.

Keating, C.B. and Katina, P.F. (2019). Complex system governance: Concept, utility, and challenges. *Systems Research and Behavioral Science* 36(5): 687–705. https://doi.org/10.1002/sres.2621.

Keating, C.B., Katina, P.F., Chesterman, C.W., and Pyne, J.C. (eds.). (2022). *Complex System Governance: Theory and Practice.* Springer International Publishing. https://link.springer.com/book/10.1007/978-3-030-93852-9.

Klier, S.D., Nawrotzki, R.J., Salas-Rodríguez, N., Harten, S., Keating, C.B., and Katina, P.F. (2022). Grounding evaluation capacity development in systems theory. *Evaluation* 28(2): 231–251. https://doi.org/10.1177/13563890221088871.

Laamarti, F., Eid, M., and El Saddik, A. (2014). An overview of serious games. *International Journal of Computer Games Technology* 2014: e358152. https://doi.org/10.1155/2014/358152.

Mitroliou, E. and Kavanaugh, L. (2015). *Resilient Cities Report 2015: Global Developments in Urban Adaptation and Resilience.* Resilient Cities. www.cakex.org/sites/default/files/documents/RC2015__Congress_Report__Final.pdf.

Osterholm, M.T.O.P. and Olshaker, M. (2017). *Deadliest Enemy: Our War against Killer Germs* (1st ed.). Little, Brown Spark.

Rockefeller Foundation. (2014). *City Resilience Framework.* Rockefeller Foundation/ARUP. https://www.rockefellerfoundation.org/wp-content/uploads/City-Resilience-Framework-2015.pdf.

Rockefeller Foundation. (2015). *City Resilience and the City Resilience Framework*. Rockefeller Foundation/ARUP. https://www.rockefellerfoundation.org/wp-content/uploads/100RC-City-Resilience-Framework.pdf.

von Bertalanffy, L. (1968). *General System Theory: Foundations, Developments, Applications*. George Braziller.

Warfield, J.N. (1976). *Societal Systems: Planning, Policy and Complexity*. Wiley-Interscience.

Glossary of Terms

A glossary, also known as a vocabulary or clavis, is an alphabetical list of terms in a particular domain of knowledge with the definitions for those terms. This section contains a glossary of the current knowledge domain terms adapted and modified from several sources (Blashki & Isaias 2013; Captain Up Academy 2022; Marczewski 2014). Generally, this glossary contains explanations of concepts relevant to a certain field of gamification, and in this sense, the terms are related to the notion of ontology. The listed terms have been used in the present text in one form or another or are closely related to the domain knowledge. We suggest using this section to refer to terms used or as reference material. Readers interested in a glossary of elements of the Agon Framework, especially those with no self-explanatory names related to complex concepts, should consult Luca Piras's (Piras 2016) website.

Activity Loop The "loop" means a set of actions for which users are motivated to return.

Cognitive Process Support Elements Gamification uses game elements guiding the player to support task resolution. It implies adapting the interaction to the user profile and communicating relevant and useful information (goal, mean, feedback, and outcome).

Engagement Engagement is an essential element of the player experience. When users are engaged, they feel motivated to succeed and continue.

Extrinsic Motivation Anything you do to obtain something, whether badges, points, money, or recognition, is extrinsic motivation. It refers to the motivation that comes from outside an individual.

Extrinsic Reward Something external, such as monetary rewards for doing something.

Fiero An Italian word used in gamification to describe a sense of great achievement or triumph over adversity – the sort that has your fist pumping in the air!

Flow A concept described by Mihaly Csikszentmihalyi. It is a place between boredom and frustration where the player's skills match the challenge level. They lose all sense of self, and time seems to go by much faster.

Game Aesthetics The beauty of the game, including the graphics, images, and fonts.

Game Dynamics These can be described in terms of our desires. Humans all have the desire to be recognized and achieve success. These are the game dynamics that take place when playing games. It also means emergent activities of the users as they interact with mechanics.

Game Elements/Components The bits taken from games include progress bars, missions, points, badges and leaderboards.

Gamification for Resilience: Resilient Informed Decision-Making, First Edition.
Adrian V. Gheorghe and Polinpapilinho F. Katina.
© 2023 John Wiley & Sons, Inc. Published 2023 by John Wiley & Sons, Inc.

Game Mechanics Constructs of rules designed for interaction with the game state, providing gameplay.

Game Thinking Game-related design methods and ideas (e.g. gamification, serious games) used to create solutions.

Gamification Applying elements of game mechanics such as badges, rewards, and points to encourage engagement with a product or service in non-game contexts. Gamification is exciting because it promises to make the hard stuff in life fun. Gamification is also related to:

- The use of game elements and game thinking in non-game contexts.
- Making more game-like experiences.
- Pervasive user-centric design.

Intrinsic Motivation Anything you do because it feels good is intrinsic motivation, even if you do not make any progress at all. For example, listening to a joke. It also means internal reasons to do something. Examples include:

- **Relatedness**: social connection to others.
- **Autonomy**: freedom/agency to act as you wish.
- **Mastery**: achieving something, such as learning a new skill.
- **Purpose**: three variations exist. A sense of direction (e.g. goals or storylines/narratives), feeling that you are involved in something with greater meaning, and altruism (e.g. selfless acts for the benefit of others).

Leaderboards Leaderboards show where players are ranked in a gamified system. They are implemented to show which players have achieved the most.

Loyalty Allegiance to something. Once users feel a sense of loyalty, they will keep returning. You have to make them feel special enough to do so. People loyal to a brand will go out of their way, ignoring value and convenience to own products from that brand.

Motivation Elements Gamification first drives motivation through the triggering of emotions. It implies using game elements that answer users' needs beyond usability (e.g. value, accomplishment, social). Second, it exploits game elements that are part of the persuasive technology tools to create engagement.

Naches A Yiddish word that means "feeling of pride at the achievement of your children." In gamification, it describes the feeling people get when people achieve something thanks to the help they have given them.

Player Journey Taken from Amy Jo Kim, the player journey consists of On-Boarding (i.e., the first steps taken in a new system, e.g. an interactive tutorial), Habit Building (i.e., the phase where a user/player is using the system and improving), and Mastery (sometimes referred to as End Game, where the user/player has mastered the system and is probably looking for the next challenge).

Player Also called the user is the target person who will be using the gamified system.

Points & Badges These are among the most visible elements of gamification. They mark achievements, encourage users to continue, and motivate them.

Sensory-Motor Modalities. Gamification uses extensive game multimodal coding (visual, audio, and haptic) for aesthetic purposes and to communicate an atmosphere, a theme, or needed information.

Serious Game A real game that is built primarily for purposes other than pure entertainment.

References

Blashki, K., & Isaias, P. (2013). Emerging research and trends in interactivity and the human-computer interface. In Https://services.igi-global.com/resolvedoi/resolve.aspx?doi=10.4018/978-1-4666-4623-0. IGI Global. https://www.igi-global.com/book/emerging-research-trends-interactivity-human/www.igi-global.com/book/emerging-research-trends-interactivity-human/77385.

Captain Up Academy. (2022). The complete gamification glossary. *Captain Up*. http://gamificacion.socialmove.cl/wp-content/uploads/2016/03/The-Complete-Gamification-Glossary.pdf.

Marczewski, A. (2014, September 19). The language of gamification – Short glossary [Updated]. Gamification & Life in General. https://www.gamified.uk/2014/09/19/language-gamification-short-glossary/amp.

Piras, L. (2016, June 24). Acceptance and gamification glossary. *Luca Piras Website*. https://pirasluca.wordpress.com/home/acceptance/glossary.

Index

Gamification for Resilience: Resilient Informed Decision-Making, First Edition.
Adrian V. Gheorghe and Polinpapilinho F. Katina.
© 2023 John Wiley & Sons, Inc. Published 2023 by John Wiley & Sons, Inc.

Printed and bound by CPI Group (UK) Ltd, Croydon, CR0 4YY

27/10/2024

14580679-0002